Pope Benedict XVI
A biography of Joseph Ratzinger

John L. Allen, Jr.

continuum

For Laura Ileene Allen
1937–1999
Et in arcadia ego ...

The Continuum International Publishing Group Ltd
The Tower Building, 11 York Road, London SE1 7NX

The Continuum International Publishing Group Inc
15 East 26 Street, New York, NY 10010

www.continuumbooks.com

ISBN 0-8264-1361-7 (paperback)

Published in 2000 as *Cardinal Ratzinger:
the Vatican's enforcer of the faith*

Printed by MPG Books, Bodmin, Cornwall, UK

Contents

Publisher's Preface

On Tuesday 19 April 2005 in the late afternoon, after one of the shortest conclaves ever, Joseph Ratzinger emerged on the balcony of St Peter's in Rome as the newly elected Pope, taking the name Benedict XVI.

Ratzinger has been the most powerful figure in the Church after Pope John Paul II for the past two decades. As Prefect of the Congregation for the Doctrine of Faith, Ratzinger's two main targets were secularism and moral relativism, and the crusade against these will continue in this new papacy. What the fight against communism was for John Paul II, the fight against rampant secularism will be for Benedict XVI. In this respect, he will be even more controversial than his predecessor. He began life under the Weimar Republic, which collapsed because it took moral relativism to extremes.

Essential to understanding this new Pope is to understand his attitude to the Magisterium and the Deposit of Faith. Ratzinger's mission is to preserve these and to propound the truth as he understands it.

John L. Allen's masterly biography throws clear light on the character of The Holy Father. A man of towering intellect and moral strength, Ratzinger is a man of paradoxes. For a man who has wielded such power in the Roman Catholic Church to initiate his papacy by declaring himself 'a simple and humble worker in the Lord's vineyard' is striking to say the least.

This book is essential reading for anyone who wishes to understand Ratzinger's background, the complexity of his character, and where he may guide and lead the Church in the coming years.

Certainly in terms of facing the challenges ahead, it could be argued that there was no one else up to the job.

Preface

*I*t may seem curious for an author to open a biography with details of his own life rather than his subject's, but I feel compelled to offer some explanation of the dynamics that led me to write this book. One might wonder why a reporter for the *National Catholic Reporter,* with its reputation as a progressive critic of the Catholic establishment, would choose to write about the chief doctrinal conservative of our time. Or, one might assume that I chose Ratzinger in order to smear him, gambling that the cardinal has enough enemies to guarantee sales of a few books. My hope here is to present my interest in Ratzinger from the inside out, so that it might appear, as it does to me, neither enigmatic nor mean-spirited but a sincere attempt at understanding.

I am a child of Vatican II. I mean that not just spiritually or ideologically, but chronologically. I was born in 1965, the year the Second Vatican Council ended, into a middle-of-the-road Catholic family and community that basically welcomed the changes the council had unleashed. As a consequence, I never memorized the Baltimore Catechism, never went to Mass in Latin, never collected indulgences or kept a balloon between me and my dance partner to leave room for the Holy Spirit. Instead, I grew up reading *Christ among Us,* watching *Jesus Christ Superstar* in my CCD class and planning my Sundays around the 11:30 A.M. folk mass.

Michael Harrington once wrote a book on poverty called *The Other America,* and his idea of two nations sharing the same geography but inhabiting separate spheres of existence stuck with me. Later I found that this concept also captured my sensation of growing up in one kind of Catholic church, then finding another ensconced in Rome when I began my work as a church affairs writer. I am the product of what I can only call "the other Catholicism."

I attended Catholic schools until I got to college and I was an altar boy for the better part of my youth. I earned both of the Catholic awards offered by the Boy Scouts (the *Ad Altare Dei* medal and the Pope Pius XII award). I remember my mom reciting the rosary with me on the few occasions when we couldn't make it to Sunday Mass, and encouraging me to pray before I went to bed. At one point in my Catholic high school, I was in a club designed for young men considering the priesthood, and later in my life, I actually spent a few months as a religious novice. In short, I had a thoroughly—even pervasively—Catholic upbringing.

But that upbringing was of the post-Vatican II sort. Hence I never worried about non-Catholics going to hell, and I took for granted that women could be around the altar and simply assumed that one day they would be priests. I was told, and believed, that one could be a good Catholic and still have doubts about certain points of church teaching such as the ban on artificial birth control. I never learned to think of priests as lifted out of the community, set apart in some mysterious sense. The value of "full, active, and conscious" participation in the Mass by laity seemed intuitively obvious. It would have struck me as fantastic had anyone suggested that just three decades later advocating any of these ideas in the public conversation of the Catholic church would stamp someone as a "radical."

I remember sitting in Mass one Sunday as our pastor and a well-known layperson modeled how the new rite of confession, now called reconciliation, was going to work, and thinking: I wonder what will change next? I took for granted that church practices and structures were fluid, that they could evolve, and that they would.

I also imbibed in my parish and in my school that being Catholic meant being concerned for justice. I remember clearly the day Father Chuck, one of the many Capuchin Franciscans who were my teachers, spoke to my freshman religion class about how Catholic doctrine had led him to oppose the war in Vietnam. I began making the connections between Jesus, the church, and social activism, and as the United States cranked up its military activities in Latin America under Reagan during my high school years, I was ready with a moral critique that led me by a short path into political activism. I still think the single best piece of writing I did for my high school newspaper was an editorial defending, on the basis of Catholic "just war" principles, college students who refused to register for the draft.

There was of course much superficiality about my early postconciliar experience. I spent more time with crayons and construction paper than with the Bible, and when my older Catholic friends occasionally break out into "Panis Angelicus" or some such hymn I feel uncatechized because I don't know the words. There was, at times, an uncritical embrace of the culture. When the young priest in the play *Mass Appeal* complains about going to Mass on the Feast of the Assumption and hearing the choir belt out "Leavin' on a Jet Plane," I shudder in recognition.

Despite the banality, I can't help feeling that the baseline of what I experienced was right: I came to believe that being Catholic means caring about the world and about other people, and it means finding God in the midst of those concerns.

As I look back now, I realize that my experience wasn't this univocal. I know there were people, even in my little hometown in western Kansas, who had vastly different visions of church, who were greatly pained by what they saw happening in my classrooms and in my parish. One of them, a Capuchin priest who administered my first communion, today has a television series on Mother Angelica's EWTN cable channel. I recently heard him tell people that they shouldn't attend a wedding of persons from different faiths because it's the same as saying to the couple, "I'm happy you're going to hell." As a child and a young man, however, I wasn't much aware of those dissenting voices. The brand of Catholicism I picked up—faithful but evolving, open to dissent, engaged with society—was what I assumed was meant by the term "mainstream."

This still describes the vast majority of the adult Catholics with whom I work, worship, and socialize. If it were up to these Catholics, the church tomorrow would probably ordain women and married men, permit birth control, and stop demanding loyalty oaths. Polls show that my friends and colleagues reflect where a solid majority of Catholics in the Western world are on those issues. Because these are the people with whom I share my life, these positions seem natural and almost inevitable to me. It was not until I began writing professionally on Catholicism in the early 1990s that I realized how many powerful figures within the church regard this brand of Catholicism as a mistake. They see it as a product of the turbulence that always follows an ecumenical council, and they are determined to bring it back under control.

Of course, I always had the sense that the pope and the Vatican were "more conservative" than most people I knew. I was unprepared, however, for the vastness of the gulf that seemed to separate the Catholicism with which I had grown up from the statements and policies flowing from Rome. The turning point for me was December, 1997, five months after I had started work at the *National Catholic Reporter,* when I was assigned to do a story about a new Vatican pronouncement on lay ministry. In technical parlance this was an "interdicasterial" document, meaning it was issued by several Vatican offices at once, and its general thrust was to reassert a sharp distinction between laity and the ordained priesthood. The authors believed that a softening of that distinction, in which priests had come to be seen as members of the community distinguished by function rather than essence, was one of the major problems facing the church. It was then I realized that I didn't understand what the church must look like to those who author such documents. I didn't understand the needs they perceive or the dangers they obviously see.

I also realized that my ignorance was interfering with my work as a reporter. I could do no more than caricature views for which I had no understanding. I needed to break through to the other side of my own perceptions, and in the end that meant wrestling with Cardinal Joseph Ratzinger. More than any other figure in contemporary Catholicism, more so even than the pope, he embodies the hostility to the "other Catholicism" I have described.

I am, by the way, assuming that the concerns expressed in that document on lay ministry, and scores of Vatican pronouncements like it, are genuine. I do not subscribe to the theory that curial officials such as Ratzinger make policy solely in order to secure their own power, though I would not deny that such considerations play their own, often unconscious, role in shaping decisions. I believe Ratzinger's theological arguments are more than ex post facto rationalizations for exercises of authority. I believe his analysis of church and world is sincere, and I wanted to understand it—and, where necessary, be challenged by it. If conversation within the church is ever to move forward, it seems to me, Catholics need to do more than impugn one another's motives. They need to understand one another's concerns and make some effort to speak the same language.

I knew the official catechetical rationale for the positions Ratzinger takes, but I needed more. I needed to understand how any religious leader in the modern world could believe that silencings and condemnations and banning books accomplish anything other than inflamed resistance and public incredulity. I needed to know how positions that seemed so obviously detrimental to women, to the intellectual life, to the cause of social justice, all of which the church cares a great deal about, could be so deeply entrenched and so vigorously defended by the best and brightest of Catholic officialdom.

In pursuit of insight, I've read almost everything Ratzinger has written, dusting off the rudimentary German I acquired in graduate school so I would not be restricted simply to those works that have found their way into English translation. I've spoken to both friends and foes of the cardinal, read most of the profiles of him published in the last twenty years, studied the official texts of the documents he's issued. I've spoken to dozens of people who studied under Ratzinger, who worked under him, who have taken positions for or against him in the public life of the church. I volunteered to fly to Rome to interview him and was turned down, but did have a chance to talk with him during a February 1999 visit to Menlo Park, California. I also met him, twice, at the fall 1999 European synod in Rome.

At the end of that road, honesty compels me to admit that there is a deep logical consistency to Ratzinger's vision (as he formulates it today; his positions on many issues inside the church have shifted from where they were at the start of his career). Moreover, Ratzinger is not the vengeful, power-obsessed old man who lurks like a bogeyman in the imaginations of many on the Catholic Left. On the occasions I have met Ratzinger, I found him charming, with a shy personal style and an active wit. I watched him, aging and obviously uncomfortable, allow his picture to be taken at a reception with wave after wave of goofy seminarians, fawning admirers, chatty academics, even Buddhists in saffron robes. Through it all, he maintained a sense of humor and a personal kindness that left a deep impression. I have spoken with dozens of people who know Ratzinger well, and to a person they speak of his calm, peaceful spirit and his remarkable ability to listen.

Bishop Peter Cullinane of Palmerston, New Zealand—certainly no right-wing crony of Ratzinger—said this to me about him during that February 1999 visit to Menlo Park:

> I regret very much that Cardinal Ratzinger gets a bad press because I think people, due to a lot of prejudices or their own theological positions, don't always give themselves the opportunity to really hear the man, to really hear what he's got to say. He is a man of tremendous faith, of great integrity, very great intellect and great dedication. I just wish people would allow themselves the opportunity to listen more carefully to what he's saying, what's behind what he's saying, where he's coming from, what theology really means to him. I think if people really did that they would find that one of the big barriers slips away.

Having listened to Ratzinger myself, I think Cullinane is right. I can say without irony, and despite the incredulity of some of my colleagues, that in the unlikely event I ever had access to Ratzinger as a confessor, I would not hesitate to open my soul to him, so convinced am I of the clarity of his insight, his integrity, and his commitment to the priesthood.

In the end, however, I also came away wishing that Joseph Ratzinger would make the same intellectual and existential effort to understand the Catholicism in which I grew up as I have made to understand the Catholicism he has spent the last twenty years defending. I am convinced that Ratzinger is penetrating and sincere; and yet I cannot wish him success in curbing the evolving, socially engaged, compassionate Catholicism that was the incubator of my faith. I believe his is a voice that needs to be respectfully heard, and respectfully challenged. I hope this book will contribute to that argument.

Two technical points need to be made here. First, Ratzinger has tried to draw a sharp distinction between his writings as a private theologian and the documents produced under his authority at the Congregation for the Doctrine of the Faith. "I would never presume to use the decisions of the congregation to impose my own theological ideas on the Christian people. . . . I see my role as that of coordinator of a large working group," he said in 1996. As I studied Ratzinger's corpus, however, it became clear that in many congregation documents over the last twenty years one can find themes and expressions that are obviously Ratzinger's. Whole passages of the 1984 instruction on liberation theology, for example, could just as easily have come from Ratzinger's personal work on eschatology. In those cases where I quote from congregation documents to illustrate Ratzinger's thinking, I do so having made a judgment that the writing in question is largely his own.

Second, a note about the spelling of Ratzinger's first name. In German, the "ph" combination is usually expressed by the simple "f," so that it's normally "Josef" rather than "Joseph." In Ratzinger's case, although some of his German works do employ the more common form, his Vatican stationary uses "Joseph" as do all of his English translations. Hence that's the convention I adopt here. Nor is Ratzinger's preference for the "ph" of recent vintage; that is how he spelled his name on his first Mass card, in German, in 1951.

This book is the fruit of my labor, and therefore all its sins, both by commission and of omission, are no one's but my own. I feel obliged, however, to acknowledge those who helped along the way. Michael Farrell, my editor at the *National Catholic Reporter*, was generous both in his critique of the book as it evolved and in the flexibility he showed in allowing me to bring the project to completion. Similarly, my colleagues Tom Roberts and Tom Fox were supportive in their feedback. Gill Donovan's expert proof-reading skills and reactions to the content were immensely helpful. Eugene Kennedy and Robert Blair Kaiser both read early drafts of the book and offered encouragement. Several of Ratzinger's former graduate students, especially Joseph Fessio, Hansjürgen Verweyen, Michael Fahey, and Charles MacDonald offered important perspectives. Franz Haselbeck of the state archives in Traunstein, Bavaria, was extremely kind in facilitating long-distance research. To those other sources and friends who for various reasons must remain nameless, a hearty thank you.

To the students of the Notre Dame High School journalism program in Sherman Oaks, California, from 1993 to 1997, a thank you for first enkindling my passion for writing and reporting. I would like to mention in a special way Song Chong, Joel Feldman, Maya Kelly, Davon Ramos, Kathy Wang, and Christina Almeida, my editors-in-chief during those years, whom I regard as colleagues and friends.

To my wife, Shannon Levitt-Allen, I give thanks for her long-suffering patience and steadfast conviction that this book would see the light of day. I offer this book to my mother, Laura Ileene Allen, who died too young on January 25, 1999. Her constant faith in me, even when undeserved and misplaced, always kept me going. I also dedicate the book to my grandparents, Raymond and Laura Frazier, whose relentless love for my mother in every moment of her life is powerful testimony to this world's capacity for good.

1

Growing Up in Hitler's Shadow

Joseph Aloysius Ratzinger was born on April 16, 1927, the youngest of three children in a lower-middle-class Bavarian household. Just a month later, Charles Lindbergh became the first person to fly solo across the Atlantic in the *Spirit of Saint Louis*. Lindbergh's path would intersect, in a remote way, with Ratzinger's again. During the 1930s, Lindbergh emerged as one of the leading American sympathizers with National Socialism. In 1941, he gave a famous speech identifying the three forces leading America into war as "the British, Roosevelt, and the Jews." Radio broadcasts of this remark played widely across Germany, no doubt including Ratzinger's hometown of Traunstein. The Nazis had ensured that radios were cheap and plentiful so their propaganda could reach every corner of the Reich.

In Rome, Pius XI was five years into his pontificate in 1927, and more concerned with increasing devotion to his new Feast of Christ the King than with the gathering war clouds in Europe. Germany was in the late stages of the Weimar Republic, menaced by the threat of a Bolshevik worker's uprising as well as by various conservative and nationalistic factions. Hitler was the leader of one of those factions, the National Socialists, despite the fact that he was not a German citizen. He renounced his Austrian citizenship in 1925 and was not granted German citizenship until 1932, on the eve of his run for president. At about the time Ratzinger was born, Hitler recruited a new publicist to his team named Joseph Göbbels.

In rural southern Bavaria, April 16, 1927, was one of those snowy, bitterly cold days the region sometimes gets in the spring. Bavarians are a tough lot, in part because by butting up against the Alps, they get some of the worst weather in middle Europe. It did not help that Ratzinger entered the world at 4:15 A.M., in the icy chill of the early morning. His older brother and sister were not allowed to come to his baptism for fear of getting sick.

Perhaps it was fate that Ratzinger was born on Holy Saturday, and his parents were named Joseph and Mary. Like another child of another Joseph and Mary, Ratzinger grew up to become a sign of contradiction, a scandal to some and a sort of savior to others. Ratzinger reports in his 1998 autobiography that because he was born on Holy Saturday, he was baptized with the newly blessed Easter water in the small parish church in the village of Marktl am Inn. It is difficult not to read some kind of sacred meaning into the scene, and Ratzinger has not resisted, seeing it as a symbol of the human condition in its "not quite" relation to Easter and the resurrection.

Now seventy-three, Ratzinger's childhood memories are the ones most closely tied to his understanding of who he is and what he believes. Listening to him and reading him today, it is striking that Ratzinger rarely makes reference to his mid-twenties through mid-forties, the years as a professional theologian during which he achieved wide fame. When Ratzinger wants to strike an autobiographical chord, he always looks back to his early days in one of four small Bavarian towns. Those memories are of intimate moments shared with his family; of the rock-solid Catholic ethos of Bavaria, expressed in the liturgy and the simple faith of the people; of his own intellectual awakening, fueled by classical languages and literature; and, finally, of the political and social upheavals of the day, most dramatically, the rise and fall of Hitler's Third Reich.

Memory, however, is selective. When people reach back across their lifetimes, memory becomes a redactor, editing images so they cohere with the person's current understanding of self. People reshape, reinterpret, and distort their pasts in light of their present interests and priorities. To fully understand Ratzinger, therefore, it is necessary to round out his picture, to recover some of the elements of his early days that his own published recollections and remarks have omitted.

Of special interest is the most famous member of the Ratzinger family prior to Joseph, his great-uncle Georg Ratzinger (not to be confused with Joseph's brother of the same name). This elder Ratzinger was a rebel inside the church and out, and those who know Joseph Ratzinger today sometimes wish he had a bit more of his famous relative in him. As we will see, Georg Ratzinger had a dark side as well.

The question of Ratzinger and the Third Reich also merits special attention. Neither Ratzinger nor any member of his family was a National Socialist. Ratzinger has said several times that his father's criticism of the Nazis was responsible for the four moves the family made during Ratzinger's first ten years. Such opposition by itself is unremarkable; many German Catholics complained about the party's encroachment on the church. Neither the elder Ratzinger nor either of the two sons took part in any kind of resistance. Although Ratzinger today calls such resistance "impossible," there were in fact several models in his immediate orbit, including members of the Communist Party, Jehovah's Witnesses, and fellow Catholics.

More important is the question of what conclusions Ratzinger draws from the war. Having seen fascism in action, Ratzinger today believes that the best antidote to political totalitarianism is ecclesial totalitarianism. In other words, he believes the Catholic church serves the cause of human freedom by restricting freedom in its internal life, thereby remaining clear about what it teaches and believes. It is a position he defends ably, but it is strikingly different from the conclusions of many of Ratzinger's German theological peers who also lived through the Nazi era.

If his childhood under the Nazis was one stream of influence on the young Ratzinger, the other was his intellectual awakening in the seminary and graduate school. Ratzinger's mental reservoir was filled with images and arguments from the various thinkers he encountered. Four such men have had great intellectual impact on Ratzinger: Augustine, Bonaventure, Guardini, and Balthasar.

A school of philosophical thought fashionable today says human identity is formed by a mental "bundle," referring to a unique set of memories arranged and recalled in idiosyncratic fashion. To understand Joseph Ratzinger, therefore, we need to understand what was in his bundle.

Bavaria

Almost as much as John Paul II is Polish, Joseph Ratzinger is Bavarian. In 1998, when he presented his new autobiography to the German-speaking world in a press conference, he did so in the Kloster Andech monastery in Upper Bavaria. Introducing Ratzinger, Abbot Odilo Lechner said in praise of the cardinal, "You have always made it clear that heaven and earth are bound together in a special way in Bavaria."

When the Roman Empire fell, Bavaria was divided into three sections: the north occupied by the Franks, the west by the Alemanni, and the south and east by the Baiuvarii, the tribe that eventually gave the territory its name. This division still exists today, as Bavaria is an amalgam of three distinct regions: Franconia in the north, Swabia in the west, and the "real Bavaria" in the south and east. Ratzinger's family comes from this "real" Bavarian stock.

The Wittelsbach kings of Bavaria were opponents of the Protestant Reformation, and during the sixteenth century Bavaria became an officially, and strictly, Catholic state. Even today one could parachute into Bavaria at random, landing at however remote or isolated a spot, and be within eyesight of a Catholic church or shrine. Jesuit Michael Fahey, a student of Ratzinger's during his days in Tübingen, says this is a critical point in understanding Ratzinger. He is spiritually and culturally Bavarian, which means he is most comfortable in an all-Catholic setting. An appreciation for diversity was not something he imbibed growing up, and a preference for homogeneity remains part of his character.

The Wittelsbachs did not always rule the area that forms Bavaria today. The archbishop of Salzburg governed a large chunk of land in Upper Bavaria, including much of the territory where Ratzinger grew up, for several centuries. It did not become part of Bavaria until the time of Napoleon. Ratzinger writes that he grew up under the spell of Salzburg, especially its most famous son, Mozart.

Bavaria opposed Prussia in the 1866 war with Austria, but the Wittelsbachs were so impressed with Bismarck's graciousness in victory that they joined his federation in time to be on the winning side in the 1870 Franco-Prussian War. Under the terms of the federation, Bavaria retained its own military, postal service, and railways. It also kept its own diplomatic service, which is how the young Eugenio Pacelli came to be named the apostolic nuncio to Bavaria in 1917, before being elected as Pius XII in 1939.

In 1918, the last Wittelsbach king was forced by the Allies to abdicate, and a socialist government under Kurt Eisner was elected. In 1919, however, a Communist uprising ended in Eisner's murder and the declaration of the Soviet Republic of Bavaria, the only such soviet government ever erected in Western Europe. This brief state was quickly and brutally suppressed by the German army. The bloody days of 1919 loomed large in the political imagination of Bavarians for many years to come; Ratzinger was born only eight years later, and the instinctive fear of Marxist-inspired violence was still fresh in the minds of his countrymen. Pacelli himself was held at gunpoint by members of the Bavarian "Red Guard," who had proclaimed the soviet republic, an experience that strengthened his own fierce anti-communism. Yet it should be noted that most of the bloodletting in Bavaria happened not under the Communist revolutionaries, but during a week of terror after they had been suppressed, during which the army executed more than 1,000 people.

As things got progressively worse, Bavaria was divided among adherents of the Catholic-backed Center Party and the National Socialists, with small but meaningful followings for the Social Democrats and the Communists. After Hitler became chancellor, Bavaria basked in the general economic recovery that washed over Germany. In the war's later stages, Bavaria was pounded by Allied bombs and suffered the hardships of occupation;

however, because Bavaria was in the American occupation zone, conditions after the war were somewhat better than elsewhere.

In the decades that followed, Bavaria's character mirrored that of the rest of Germany: socially and politically conservative and economically prosperous. Today Bavaria is known as one of the most culturally traditional and politically conservative pockets of the country. Despite its economic success, Bavaria has resisted urbanization to a remarkable degree. In the early 1990s, almost half of the population still lived in locales of less than 5,000 population. Ratzinger grew up in a series of those Bavarian hamlets, and his family has deep roots in the Bavarian soil.

Great-Uncle Georg

Before the cardinal, the most famous Ratzinger was Joseph's great uncle on his father's side, Georg, one of the towering Bavarian figures of the nineteenth century.[1] In a 1985 special anthology of Bavarian biography published in Regensburg, Georg Ratzinger made the list of the 1,000 most important Bavarian personalities of the past 1,500 years. His fame came as a journalist, an author, and a politician. Over the years, he edited a number of newspapers, including the *Wochenblattes für katholische Volk* and the *Volksfreundes*. His best-known book was *Die Volkswirthschaft in ihren sittlichen Grundlagen* (The economy in its ethical foundations), published in 1881 and brought out in a second edition in 1885. Ratzinger was twice elected to the Bavarian and the federal legislatures.

In light of who Joseph Ratzinger has become, there are three aspects of his great-uncle's life that hold most interest: his connection to Johann Ignaz von Döllinger; his "option for the poor" in his own political career; and his anti-Semitism.

Georg Ratzinger was born in Rickering, Bavaria, in 1844, the son of a farmer. He went to *gymnasium* in Passau and studied Catholic theology at the University of Munich. There he won a prize for his dissertation on the history of the church's care for the poor. During his four years at the university, 1863 to 1867, Ratzinger studied under and became the assistant of the most controversial Catholic figure of his day, Johann Ignaz von Döllinger.

Döllinger was then coming into his own as a fierce critic of Roman centralism and the movement towards papal absolutism called "ultra-montanism" (meaning "beyond the mountains," in reference to the fact that the biggest supporters of an authoritarian papacy were in France, England, and Germany, not in Italy). Italians at the time were engaged in a war against the papacy in order to unify the country. It is one of the great ironies of modern Roman life that every day at noon a cannon goes off, celebrating the Italian victory over the pope!). Döllinger's key idea was the "organic development" of church tradition, a notion he shared with England's John Henry Newman. Early in his career, Döllinger employed the idea to refute Protestantism, which he saw as an unacceptable break in historical continuity. Later, Döllinger came to believe that the greatest enemy of historical continuity in the church was the papacy itself, that its claims to absolute authority were foreign to the true Catholic understanding.

In 1863, Döllinger organized (probably with Ratzinger's help) a congress of a hundred Catholic theologians in Munich. In his opening address, Döllinger blasted scholasticism, a narrow school of theology based on a particular reading of Thomas Aquinas and regarded by Rome as the official theology of the church. He called for an assertion of scholarly independence from Vatican authority.

Around the same time Döllinger suggested the creation of a German national church headed by a metropolitan, with only a symbolic connection to the papacy. In the same vein, he called for education of German priests in universities rather than seminaries. This latter suggestion became more or less standard practice. Ironically, it was Döllinger who convinced the German bishops they should meet on a regular basis. The meetings anticipated the creation of bishops' conferences, against whose power Joseph Ratzinger would later struggle so mightily.

By 1867, in his inaugural address as the rector of the University of Munich, Döllinger went further: "The papacy is based on an audacious falsification of history," he declared. "A forgery in its very outset, it has, during the long years of its existence, had a pernicious influence on church and state alike." To no one's surprise, when Vatican I declared the pope infallible in 1870, Döllinger led the dissent. He was excommunicated in March 1871 and fired from the university. Ludwig II of Bavaria befriended Döllinger, however, and Döllinger went on to have a successful political career. Though Döllinger said that he belonged to the Old Catholics who split from Rome over the infallibility issue "by conviction," he never attended their services and refused to become their first bishop. After his excommunication, he continued attending Catholic Mass, but did not receive communion.

Georg Ratzinger, who was ordained to the priesthood in 1867, resigned as Döllinger's assistant in order to take up his first pastoral appointment in Berchtesgaden. There is no evidence that he ever publicly associated himself with the ecclesial positions of his mentor, yet there are two intriguing hints in this direction. First, Ratzinger voluntarily resigned his priesthood in 1888, in a day when laicized priests were rare. Second, politically Ratzinger gravitated away from the Center Party, which was the established Catholic party, and toward the farmers and workers parties, both of which had a definite anticlerical tone. In any event, Ratzinger assisted Döllinger during the four years, 1863 to 1867, in which his antipapal views took their sharpest form.

Politically, Georg Ratzinger was an apostle of the new Catholic social teaching, officially expressed for the first time in Leo XIII's *Rerum novarum* in 1891. The idea was to carve out a Christian alternative to both Marxism and capitalism, to develop a blueprint for a state based on Catholic social principles. Ratzinger served in the Bavarian Landtag from 1875 to 1878 and again from 1893 to 1899, and in the national Reichstag from 1877 to 1878 and 1898 to 1899. His first term in each chamber was as a member of the Patriots' Party, a Catholic party launched in 1869 to combat the effects of the *Kulturkampf* in Bavaria. Ratzinger's second term in each was served as a deputy of the new Bauernbund, or "Farmers' Party," he helped launch in 1893. In between, Ratzinger was a member of the Center Party.

Aside from the irony of a Ratzinger holding elected office as a priest (which today's Ratzinger, along with the pope, sees as a betrayal of the priest's office), there is a special measure of poetic justice in Georg Ratzinger's politics. They were to some degree in the nineteenth century what Latin American liberation theology attempted to be in the twentieth: a means of empowering the poor and translating Catholic social teaching into public policy.

In the 1860s a series of farmers' alliances were created in Bavaria to protect the interests of small and medium-sized farms against the major landowners and the financal and industrial upper classes. In the 1880s, when prolonged economic stagnation hit Germany (prompting, among other things, a wave of emigration to the United States), many of these small farmers were threatened, as were a whole range of small businesses that suddenly faced mounting debts and growing tax burdens. Many of the Catholic "little people" in Bavaria felt the Center Party was too closely tied to the nobility, the new commercial elites, and the upper levels of the church hierarchy, and had failed to look out for their interests.

In this climate the Bauernbund emerged as a political alternative to defend the interests of the rural poor, and Georg Ratzinger was among its leaders. The creation of the Bauernbund was, to use a later vocabulary, Ratzinger's own "preferential option for the poor." He was willing to stand against church authority, which identified itself with the Center Party. Ratzinger stood on the floor of the Bavarian and federal legislatures time and again and thundered against the excesses of capitalism.

In terms of policies the Bauernbund stood for a mix of populist protectionism and progressive social measures, such as child labor laws and minimum wages. The Bauernbund's chief goal was a system of social supports that would insulate poor farmers and small traders from the "boom and bust" cycles. They also supported nationalization of the school system and the abolition of Bavaria's upper house of parliament, which the nobles and the church dominated. In all these questions, Ratzinger's Lower Bavarian faction of the Bauernbund was consistently the most radical, alienating more moderate members from Franconia and Swabia. Ratzinger himself died in 1899, but the Bauernbund lived on, becoming for Bavarian peasants what the Communists and Social Democrats were to the urban masses in the cities: the party of protest. In 1912, the Bauernbund joined forces with the Social Democrats and the liberals in a grand coalition and, in that sense, helped create the political basis for Bavaria's soviet revolution.

There is a darker side to Georg Ratzinger in his attitudes toward Jews. Uriel Tal, in his study *Christians and Jews in Germany,* identifies Ratzinger as one of the leading figures in shaping anti-Jewish sentiment in Catholic circles in nineteenth-century Germany.[2] Because of Bismarck's *Kulturkampf,* Tal notes, there was a strong Catholic reaction against modern secular culture. Bismarck had attempted to wipe out Catholicism as a threat to the stability of the Prussian state, suppressing religious orders, taking over Catholic schools, and withdrawing public funding for Catholic institutions. He invoked the principles of Enlightenment and secular liberality, and Jews came to be seen as the carriers of this ideology. The Catholic bishop of Mainz, W. E. Freiherr von Ketteler, expressed this idea in 1872: "The principal representative of the allegedly liberal Germanism is Judaism." In addition to this religious motive for anti-Judaism, Ratzinger's populist economic instincts led him to blame banking and financial elites, and to him that meant especially the Jews, for the suffering of his rural Bavarian constituents.

These two influences led Ratzinger to adopt extremely anti-Jewish attitudes. In *Volkswirthscaft,* for example, he suggests that the traditional German values of discipline, modesty, family integrity, and Christian faith were being undermined by the financial power of Jews. Jews, as Ratzinger came to see them, betrayed the ethical principles of monotheism from the very beginning. They were a cunning people who moved from one culture to another and from one economic region to another, impoverishing, corrupting, and undermining. They were now at work ruining the German economy and German civilization.

Ratzinger expressed these ideas subtly in works published under his own name, more crudely in works written under pseudonyms. These latter included *Jüdisches Erwerbsleben: Skizzen aus dem sozial Leben der Gegenwart* (The Jewish life of acquisition: Sketches from the social life of the present), published in 1892 and again in 1893 and 1894) and *Das Judentum in Bayern: Skizzen aus der Vergangenheit und Vorschläge für die Zukunft* (Judaism in Bavaria: Sketches from the past and proposals for the future), published in 1897.

Joseph Ratzinger's only published comment on his great-uncle, as far as one can tell, came in a 1996 interview with German journalist Peter Seewald, which later became the book *Salt of the Earth*. It is worth reproducing here in full:

> *Question:* There was a Georg Ratzinger who played a certain role in Bavarian history?
> *Ratzinger:* He was a great-uncle of mine, my father's uncle. He was a priest and had a doctorate in theology. As a representative of the state and national assemblies, he was really a champion of the rights of the peasants and the simple people in general. He fought—I've read this in the minutes of the state parliament—against child labor, which at that time was still considered a scandalous, impudent position to take. He was obviously a tough man. His achievements and his political standing also made everyone proud of him.

Ratzinger has every right to admire his great-uncle, whose political and literary works were impressive. One hears, too, an echo of Joseph Ratzinger's description of his own defense of "simple believers" against theologians who would rob them of their faith, an instance perhaps in which he sees himself continuing his illustrious ancestor's work. Yet Ratzinger cannot be ignorant of his uncle's anti-Judaism, and along with expressing legitimate family pride, it seems reasonable to expect some comment on views that obviously played their own unintended role in creating the conditions in which the Holocaust was possible. There is no basis for suspecting that Joseph Ratzinger harbors any of his great-uncle's sentiments about the Jews—indeed, his public record is full of denunciations of anti-Semitism—but Jews might be saddened at his silence here nevertheless.

The Four Hometowns

Ratzinger's childhood was spent inside the triangle of land bordered on the west by the Inn River, on the east by the Salzach, and the south by the Alps. The Inn and the Salzach come together in the north. This triangle is about 40 miles across and 40 miles long, so it encompasses a total territory of approximately 160 miles, with no real urban center. It consists of a number of small—some extremely small—villages and towns. This area was governed by Salzburg for much of its history.

In the Ratzinger family, there were two older children, Maria (born 1921) and Georg (1924). Their father, Joseph, was a rural police officer and police supervisor, or *Gendarmerie-Kommissar*. The mother, Maria, was a skilled cook who usually worked in small hotels, what today would be thought of as "bed and breakfast" establishments. Maria and Joseph were married in 1920. Joseph died in 1959 at the age of eighty-two; Maria died in 1963 at seventy-nine. Looking back in 1998, Ratzinger said his father gave him his "critical mind," whereas his mother imparted a "warm-hearted religious sense." Yet his father was certainly not unreligious. Ratzinger says his father went to church three times on Sundays, once at the 6:00 A.M. mass, then to the main liturgy at 9:00 A.M., and then again to a devotional service in the afternoon.

Ratzinger's older brother Georg, also a priest, has had a highly distinguished career, serving for thirty years (1964 to 1994) as the *Domkapellmeister*, or conductor, of the *Domspatzen* in Regensburg. It is the famed "sparrows choir," a mixed group of men and boys. Under Ratzinger, the choir issued several successful recordings, toured the world, and in 1965, had the honor of performing at the closing session of Vatican II. He was made a monsignor in 1968, and eventually raised to the rank of apostolic pronotary, the highest grade of monsignor. He holds the Bavarian Order of Merit.

Maria, the sister, supported the family financially while Georg and Joseph were in the seminary. She then made a career out of being Joseph's secretary and housekeeper. Fahey believes that Maria, now deceased, exercised tremendous influence on Ratzinger; whenever the cardinal speaks of how the "simple faithful" may be scandalized by some theological innovation, Fahey says that probably reflects Maria's reaction.

It is an often-overlooked fact of Ratzinger's life that his formative years coincided almost precisely with the lifespan of the Third Reich. Hitler first came to power in 1933 when Ratzinger was six, and the war ended in May 1945 when Ratzinger was eighteen. Though the Ratzinger family opposed National Socialism, there was a deeper context to the Nazi rise to power in Germany: a recovery of the values of community and authority, a nostalgia for the past, an appreciation for faith and sacrifice, which most Germans felt had been squandered under the liberalism of the Weimar Republic. This wave of traditionalism carried Hitler to power, but it also produced yearning and hope within the church, only recently rejected as outmoded. It was in some ways a romantic, optimistic time for German Catholicism, and that is the context in which Joseph Ratzinger's religious imagination took shape.

Marktl am Inn

Ratzinger opens his 1997 memoir, *Milestones*, with the remark that it is not easy to say what his hometown really is. His family moved four times before he was ten years old, leaving him with a sense of belonging to the region far more than to a particular town. As will be developed below, the place with the best claim to being Ratzinger's childhood home is Traunstein, because that is where he spent the critical years of ten to sixteen. The place where it all started, however, was Marktl am Inn, a village on the western edge of his Upper Bavarian triangle.

The family lived in a large, if unspectacular, white, three-story wood home. Today the house bears a plaque designating it as the birthplace of Ratzinger, "Archbishop of Munich-Freising." It has not, as of this writing, been updated. Marktl is a town of 2,750 inhabitants residing in approximately 1,000 households, population figures that have held relatively steady since Ratzinger's childhood. As a civil servant working in a supervisor's capacity, the elder Ratzinger had a steady income, which automatically distinguished him from the farmers, whose fortunes fluctuated with every rain and snowstorm. The elder Ratzinger was thus a few steps up on the social ladder, though his status did not rival that of the mayor or the leaders of the various councils that most Bavarian villages still possess.

Life in Bavarian villages such as Marktl was, by American standards, remarkably regulated: One could not hunt in the forests or fish in the streams owned by the village without permission; one could not slaughter one's own livestock without registering the deed; one could not plant new crops without authorization; one could not do even minor work on one's own house without sanction from the village authorities. The system ensured stability and kept the peace among neighbors. Of course, it also ensured a steady stream of work for the rural gendarmes. Such regimentation helps explain why most Germans after 1933 did not feel themselves to be living in a totalitarian state, as the level of government intrusion in their lives was not much different from the time before Hitler came to power.

Though Ratzinger was too young to remember much of Marktl (the family left when he was only two), as an adult looking back, he knows these were difficult times for the family and for the nation amid the dying gasps of the Weimar Republic. He writes in *Milestones*, "Unemployment was rife; war reparations weighed heavily on the German economy; battles among the political parties set people against one another; endless illnesses visited the family."

Tittmoning

In 1929, the Ratzingers moved to Tittmoning, located across the triangle on the Salzach River; the city's bridge actually constitues the border with Austria. Ratzinger says that Tittmoning "remains my childhood's land of dreams." Slightly larger than Marktl, Tittmoning today has a population of 5,697.

The dominant feature of church life in Tittmoning is the *Stift,* a residence for secular priests living together in community similar to members of a religious order. The *Stift* was the creation of Bartholomew Holzhauser, a Catholic mystic who also recorded a series of apocalyptic visions during the Thirty Years War. The *Stift* looms like a small castle on a hill above the town. Also on a hill overlooking the Salzach is the Ponlach Chapel, a baroque-era shrine that Ratzinger remembers with great tenderness. It is the days as a child in Tittmoning that seem to evoke the warmest memories for Ratzinger. He writes of happy days spent in the field, looking for items for the family nativity set, and of pious outings to the Ponlach Chapel. He describes visiting an eldery lady in Tittmoning at Christmas, whose nativity set covered virtually her entire living room, and being struck by the simple power of her faith.

Tittmoning, like most of Germany, was deeply traumatized by the Second World War. In 1940, the army used the *Stift* as a residence for its officers. Beginning in the early 1930s, a prison facility in Tittmoning was used for interrogations and detention of political enemies. Conditions were not as harsh here as in the concentration camps—the closest of which was at Dachau, about seven miles outside of Munich—but nevertheless thousands of inmates died in these sorts of environments. The Ratzingers moved away in 1932, but the family returned to Tittmoning for visits during the 1930s, and undoubtedly Joseph knew that the facility existed and had at least some inkling of what was going on there.

The Tittmoning prison housed one of the Reich's most unusual inmates, Josef Johan Cosmo Nassy (1904–1976), a Surinam-born American of both mulatto and Jewish ancestry—in other words, a Black American Jew. Nassy had immigrated to the United States at the age of fifteen, was educated as a sound engineer, and obtained a U.S. passport. He moved to Belgium and got married, and it was in Brussels that the Nazis arrested him in 1942, apparently because he was American but not knowing that he was of Jewish descent. He was not Jewish himself, but that didn't matter to Nazi racial theorists. In Tittmoning Nassy was forced to do kitchen and hygiene work by the Nazi guards, but was apparently not mistreated in any other way. He was liberated along with the rest of the prisoners by the American army in 1945.

Nassy, both in a previous camp in Belgium and in Tittmoning, did a series of more than 100 paintings and drawings that are today considered among the masterpieces of the Second World War. They depict the bleakness of camp life, the guard towers and barbed wire that circumscribed the lives of the inmates. Despite the relatively mild conditions in the camp, the faces of black men and Jews in Nassy's work show hardship, pain, and often hopelessness. The images present a side of life in Tittmoning in the late 1930s and 1940s that Ratzinger has never discussed. In 1989, an exhibition of Nassy's work was staged at Yad Vashem, the Israeli Holocaust memorial.

Aschau-am-Inn

Ratzinger has said that his father's criticisms of the Nazis forced another re-location, this time in 1932 to the even smaller village of Aschau-am-Inn at the foot of the Alps (to be more precise, the foot of the Kampenwand, 1,669 meters high) and seven miles from the largest lake in Bavaria, the Chiemsee. The Ratzingers were assigned lovely housing on the second story of an old country home that had been built by a farmer and rented to the police. As the police supervisor, Ratzinger was entitled to the upper floor; his lieuten-ant lived on the lower floor, where the offices were also located. There was a meadow outside and a carp pond, in which the young Joseph Ratzinger once almost drowned while playing.

Aschau is said to be one of the most beautiful small villages anywhere in the world, with stunning views of the Alps and the Priental, or Prien Val-ley. A nearby village was the home of "Müllner Peter," one of the more fa-mous Bavarian painters. Officially, the village describes itself as a health re-sort and winter sports location. There's also a fair bit of church history here, starting with the Hohenaschau Castle, which looks down into the valley, and which dates from the twelfth century. Its *Schloßkapelle,* or Castle Chapel, is a terrific example of baroque piety, as are the two magnificent towers of the local baroque-era church.

It was in Aschau that Ratzinger says he first fell in love with the Catholic Mass. He writes of how the windows of the church would be cov-ered with dark curtains during Holy Week, so that when the pastor sang out "Christ is Risen!" during the Easter celebration the curtains would fall and the entire church would be suddenly flooded with light. "This was the most impressive portrayal of the Lord's Resurrection that I can conceive of," Ratzinger wrote. It was at this time that Ratzinger first received a *Schott,* or missal, for the Mass, with the Latin and German texts printed side by side so that people could understand what was going on. This was actually an innovation, as the notion of "active participation" by the faithful in the Mass was associated with the progressive liturgical movement just then be-ginning to gather steam in the church. Ratzinger dates his passion for the lit-urgy to this period.

Traunstein

In 1937, at the age of sixty, Ratzinger's father qualified for his civil service pension and retired. The family moved again, this time on March 6, 1937, into a house on the outskirts of the city of Traunstein, by far the largest place Ratzinger lived in as a young man and the place where he would pass through the crucial ages of ten to sixteen. Because of Traunstein's size, Rat-zinger was also exposed much more closely to the political and military turbulence of Hitler's Reich. Hitler had actually lived in Traunstein from 1918 to 1920, first as a guard at a POW camp and later as a member of the army reserve.

Traunstein is the name of both a city, comprising then about 11,000 inhabitants, and of the Landkreis around it (the German equivalent of an American county). The Landkreis encompasses a number of small villages, all of which orbited the city. In 1936, there were 55 such communities in the Landkreis, with a total population of 60,344 spread over 13,711 households.[3] Children from the villages would go into the city for school, their parents for shopping and gossip. The Ratzingers in 1937 moved into an old farmhouse the father had purchased in 1933, anticipating his retirement. It sat on the outskirts of Traunstein in a little village called Hufschlag. It was surrounded by meadows, forests, wells and mountains, and for the young Ratzinger children it was a dream home.

For two years Ratzinger made the daily walk to school in the center of the city, a trip that took him about a half-hour. The *gymnasium* offered a classical curriculum emphasizing Greek and Latin. Ratzinger noted that two headmasters from his school were removed because they did not support the Nazis, and local historian Gerd Evers confirms that two teachers, Carnier and Parzinger, were taken into custody for thirteen days, while the director of the school was shipped off to Munich. Ratzinger believes the classics fostered an independent spirit: "In retrospect it seems to me that an education in Greek and Latin antiquity created a mental attitude that resisted seduction by a totalitarian ideology," he wrote. He says that his music teacher had the students revise a Nazi song book, crossing out phrases such as *Juda den Tod* (death to Judah) with *Wende die Not* (dispel our plight). Not long after, Ratzinger says the Nazis began an educational "reform" designed to get rid of the classical emphasis in the *gymnasia*.

It was also in Traunstein that both young Ratzinger men fell under the spell of Mozart, the native son of Salzburg just across the Salzach River. Of Mozart, Ratzinger said in 1996, "His music is by no means just entertainment; it contains the whole tragedy of human existence." The cardinal said in the 1980s that he tries to get in fifteen minutes a day at the piano, playing Mozart and Beethoven. Brahms, he said, is too difficult.

In 1939, Ratzinger entered the minor seminary in Traunstein, the first step in his ecclesiastical career. His older brother Georg had gone in earlier, and Joseph knew some of his classmates. The seminary required him to live at school, a distasteful experience because he was compelled to spend two hours every day on the playing field. Ratzinger, who was no good at sports and was smaller and weaker than most of the older boys, said he got tired of being a drag on his team day after day.

In 1942, after Hitler's invasion of Russia, the course of the war began to turn against the Germans. Eventually the seminary was needed as a military hospital, and all the seminarians were sent home. Georg was drafted into the army, while Joseph returned to the *gymnasium*, where he says he discovered great literature, especially Göthe and Schiller, but he was also depressed by the death toll of soldiers published daily in the papers, among them older friends from school. Here he passed the time until 1943 when he was pressed into service.

In 1941, membership in the Hitler Youth was made compulsory, and Ratzinger's brother Georg joined. Later Joseph too was registered as a member, though after he left the seminary he did not go to any meetings. Back in the Traunstein *gymnasium*, Ratzinger said that an understanding mathematics teacher let him keep his tuition reduction despite the fact that he did not have a Hitler Youth certificate. Thus Ratzinger was only briefly a member of the Hitler Youth and not an enthusiastic one.

The way Ratzinger describes his Traunstein experience today, it sounds as if most of the political chaos and the war was "out there," while he was reading great literature, playing Mozart, joining his family on trips to Salzburg, and poring over Latin conjugations. To the extent the war intruded, it was in the form of his father's denunciations of the Nazis, or newspaper notices that friends and classmates had died in some faraway place. The truth, however, is that the horrors of the Reich were right there in Traunstein, staring Ratzinger in the face, just outside the door of the *gymnasium* or across the seminary playing field. Local historian Gerd Evers captures the scene this way, quoting a report in the *Indianapolis Star* written by a correspondent shortly after the American army occupied Traunstein: "This was once a calm, small city of the picturesque Voralberg at the foot of the Bavarian Alps. The war and its consequences transformed it into an over-populated lunatic asylum of hopeless inhabitants."

The clearest expression of this lunacy was the Nazi campaign against the Jews. After the Nazi rise to power in 1933, a sign hung over the entrance to the Traunstein *Stadtplatz*, the central square in the city, reading: "Do not buy from the Jew. He sells you, farmers, out of house and home." On the night of November 9, 1938, *Kristallnacht*, brownshirt members and other Nazis attacked the homes of Traunstein's few Jewish citizens, smashing in their windows and threatening them with death or deportation to one of the camps if they did not leave the city.

The best-known Jewish family in Traunstein, the Holzers, left the next day for Munich. The father, Willi, was a real estate agent. His wife and five children lived with him at Kernstraße 9 by a grocery store. They had hoped the urban environment of Munich would offer protection, but the Holzers were arrested and sent to Dachau in 1941. Only one daughter, Clara, survived. Another Traunstein Jew, Rosa Moosbauer, was arrested after *Kristallnacht* and told to prepare herself for transport to the camps. She drowned herself instead. Her marriage had been dissolved after adoption of the 1935 Nüremberg laws. The houses of both the Holzers and Moosbauer were seized by the Traunstein *Landratsamt,* or regional council, and auctioned off, with proceeds to the Nazi state. Other Jews in Traunstein, including the Railia, Jonas, and Model families, fled Germany.

A few Traunstein citizens tried to ameliorate the attacks on the Jews. A farm family named Gasteiger sheltered a Jew from Berlin named Valerie Wolffenstein and her sister for two weeks. A Munich professor named Franz Herda arranged to shelter a Jew named Albertine Gimpel with a friend in Traunstein; Gimpel eventually survived the war. Herda was an art professor who emigrated to the United States, where Albert Einstein allowed him to paint his portrait in gratitude for his help to Jews. As Evers notes, this sort of defiance "was restricted to a small minority." On November 12, 1938, the regional party leader declared Traunstein *Judenfrei,* meaning "free of Jews."

Like Tittmoning, Traunstein also had a prison for political criminals. Acclaimed German writer Luise Rinser (who would later become the secret, if celibate, lover of Karl Rahner) was held there from 1943 to 1945. She had been wrenched away from her two young children after a friend denounced her on charges of "high treason" for reasons that still remain mysterious. Rinser published her diary of her days in the Traunstein women's prison years later; in English, the book is called *A Woman's Prison Journal.*

Rinser was forced to work as an office cleaner, in a bakery, and in a factory. Although there was no immediate threat of death, Rinser spent two years in a starved, filthy, verminous, and continually ill state. In her diary, Rinser records with remarkable detail her impressions of the other prisoners she encountered. There was the wife of an SS officer, denounced by her husband so he could enjoy an affair. There was a young girl whose experiences in Auschwitz had driven her insane.

Out of 11,500 inhabitants recorded in the city of Traunstein in 1939, by 1945 some 523 were dead and another 73 missing. One hundred of these people died in the Allied bombing during the month of April 1945. Even in the closing days of the war, its brutality still reached down into Traunstein. As the Soviet army advanced from the east, the Nazis had evacuated the concentration camps and were driving their prisoners on forced marches into the interior of Germany. Inmates too weak to keep up would be shot and abandoned along the way; at various times, thirty-six prisoners died in the Traunstein vicinity this way.

On May 2, the SS drove a final column of prisoners into Hufschlag, the village where Ratzinger's family lived. The guards, knowing the American army could arrive in the area any time, decided to implement Himmler's order that no prisoners should fall into the hands of the enemy. The sixty-two inmates were led to the edge of the forest on May 3, where the SS opened fire. Only a twenty-five-year-old Pole named Leo Neumann survived, by falling to the ground when the first shots rang out and playing dead. Some children from a nearby farm discovered the bodies.

Though Ratzinger has offered many details from the war years about army service, about schooling, and so on, it is striking that he leaves out any mention of these upheavals. In a city of fewer than 12,000 people, even allowing for the chaos and confusion, Ratzinger must have known what was happening. Even if Ratzinger was not aware of them at the time, he certainly knew the history by 1997 when he wrote his memoir. One gets the impression that the Third Reich has meaning for Ratzinger today primarily as an object lesson about church and culture, and only the details consistent with that argument have passed through the filter of his memory.

Resistance in Traunstein

Ratzinger's family, shaped by its Bavarian heritage expressed in the strong convictions of his father, opposed National Socialism. Ratzinger says that his father stood in the Catholic and French-leaning political tradition in Bavaria, as opposed to the pan-Germanic faction that welcomed the Nazis. This opposition, however, never translated into active resistance. Ratzinger said of his father's attitude in Aschau, "He made no public opposition; that wouldn't have been possible even in the village."

In fact, as Ratzinger must know, resistance *was* possible. In Traunstein there were examples of it, among people known to Ratzinger and his family. Such resistance was risky, and a few Traunsteiners paid the ultimate price for it. There is no shame in being unwilling to risk one's life; but equally, the urge to self-preservation is not the same thing as impossibility.[4]

Broadly speaking, opposition to the National Socialists after 1933 took three forms: active resistance, passive resistance, and "internal immigration." The first refers to acts such as spreading anti-Nazi propaganda, establishing ties with anti-Nazi forces outside the country, and sabotage; the second was a refusal to cooperate with the regime in key ways, such as loyalty oaths or military service; and the third is internal dissent without overt demonstrations, often taking the form of a very apolitical stance coupled with immersion in art, literature, science, or religion. Most Germans who disapproved of the Nazis chose the third option.

In Traunstein, as in the rest of Germany, many of the leading examples of active resistance were among members of the Communist party. Traunstein had an active Communist movement since the First World War. Records for the Communist party in Traunstein in 1932 show 170 members, and the party got 859 votes, or 16.9 percent of the total, in the 1932 Reichstag election—one of the highest percentages in the area, and a close third to the Nazis. (The Bavarian People's Party, the local version of the Catholic Center party, placed first as it did in every election.) Even if many of those who were openly Communist in 1932 had been driven into silence by 1937, their sympathies were unchanged. In his later discussions of the 1968 student uprisings in Europe, Ratzinger made it sound as if this were his first real encounter with Marxism "on the ground," that before he had known Marxism only as an intellectual system. But he must have known Communists in Traunstein as a boy. Indeed, because his parents also disliked the Nazis, they would have taken a special interest in the fate of their neighbor Communists.

The Communists, along with the Social Democrats, were Hitler's first victims. Party members were rounded up and shipped to camps for "re-education" shortly after Hitler came to power. In Traunstein, the first mass arrest of Communists took place on March 3, 1933, with party members sent to Dachau. Most were later released but kept under close observation and frequently harassed or arrested. Hans Reider, for example, was a resident of Traunstein and a Communist since 1927, and he was detained repeatedly. Once, for taking part in a demonstration against unemployment, he was sent to Dachau for several months.

Initially the basis for arresting Communists was ideological: by definition, Communism as an expression of international workers' solidarity stood in opposition to nationalism, which was one cornerstone of Hitler's program. As time went on, however, the Communists were arrested because they developed into the core of ongoing resistance. A small group of Communists in Traunstein played leading roles in this network, keeping lines of communication open with sympathizers in Czechoslovakia in order to pass on reports about the reality of the National Socialist system. Key Communists and opposition leaders in Ratzinger's community included Hans Braxenthaler, J. Hofmann, and L. Lohner. They published subversive brochures and collected money for anti-Nazi causes.

In early 1937, the same time that the Ratzinger family moved into the house outside Traunstein that the father had purchased several years earlier, Braxenthaler was forced to flee to Prague to escape arrest. He later returned to a secret hideout on Hochberg, a mountain just outside Traunstein, where he continued to produce anti-Nazi literature. Facing the constant threat of capture by the Gestapo, Braxenthaler killed himself on August 7, 1937. The monthly report of the Nazi supervisor for the area said matter-of-factly that Braxenthaler "withdrew himself from arrest" through his suicide.[5] He left behind a wife and two daughters. Seven of the remaining eight members of the party were arrested at the same time and sent to the camps. In light of Ratzinger's later conclusions about the intrinsic connection between Catholicism and resistance to the Nazis, it is interesting that the most spectacular acts of resistance in his own hometown were committed by Communists.

A second example of active resistance is indirectly connected to Traunstein. In the spring of 1942, a group of students at the University of Munich began distributing a series of subversive brochures exposing rumors of German war crimes, such as the slaughter of 300,000 Jews in Poland. Calling themselves the "White Rose," the students asked why Germans remained apathetic in the face of such atrocities, and explicitly said that Germany's salvation could only come through an Allied military victory.

One of the key figures in the White Rose was Christoph Probt, who had grown up in Rupholding, another village near Traunstein. His father had remarried with a Jewish woman after Christoph was born, and the Nüremberg laws and other oppressive Nazi measures caused him such stress that he killed himself in 1936. In Munich, Probt met the leaders of the White Rose, including Hans and Sophie Scholl, and philosophy professor Kurt Huber, who was their intellectual leader. In all, the group distributed six leaflets, typing hundreds of copies of each on different typewriters and leaving bundles of leaflets in phone booths and outside lecture halls. On February 18, 1943, Hans and Sophie Scholl left stacks of the latest brochure on university stairwells. They believed Gestapo agents were closing in on them, so they dumped their remaining leaflets inside the university courtyard and were quickly detained. Probt was arrested shortly thereafter when another White Rose member was found with a draft of a new brochure by Probt in his pocket. Hans and Sophie Scholl and Probt were tried, convicted, and executed all on the same day, on February 22, 1943. They were tried by a *Volksgerichtshof,* a special Nazi court that operated outside the normal judicial system.

In the few hours between the death sentence and the execution, Probt asked to be baptized a Catholic. As he walked to the guillotine, Hans Scholl shouted, "Long live freedom!" Probt said to his friends, "We shall see each other again in a few minutes." Eventually eighty people were arrested in connection to the White Rose. Three others, including Huber, were executed. The final insult came when Huber's widow received a bill of 600 marks from the Nazi regime for "wear of the guillotine." Despite Nazi attempts to suppress news of what had happened, Probt and the others quickly became heroes, especially as the war turned against the Germans after their defeat at Stalingrad. In Traunstein, Probt's name became synonymous with youthful idealism.

In terms of passive resistance, one of the most remarkable examples inside the Third Reich was offered by Jehovah's Witnesses. Members refused to take part in elections, to exchange the Nazi "Heil Hitler" greeting, to take the loyalty oath to Hitler required of soldiers and civil servants and recited in school classrooms, to work in the defense industry, or to be inducted into the military. On the basis of this last point alone, they were subject to the death penalty. Of the 20,000 Jehovah's Witnesses in Germany, some 300-plus were actually executed by the Nazis, and many of the rest were in camps when the war ended.

There were approximately forty Jehovah's Witnesses in Traunstein, the church having taken root there after the First World War. Several were hauled before the local courts. Sebastian Schürf was an ex-Catholic who had converted to the Jehovah's Witnesses in 1932 because he disapproved of the Catholic church's accommodating stance during the First World War. Schürf was arrested four times: once in 1937, twice in 1939, and for the last time in 1943. After his fourth arrest, he was sent to a camp and stayed there until liberation in 1945. His wife, Josefa, had also been arrested in 1943 and released. Six weeks before the end of the war, she was taken into custody again. She watched as a Polish slave laborer accused of molesting a German girl in a barn was summarily hanged. Josefa, however, was set free.

Valentin Haßlberger offers an example of what could happen to Jehovah's Witnesses who refused to fight. A father of four children, Haßlberger was arrested once for resisting military induction and served nine months. He was released to change his mind, and when he declined, he was arrested again and sent to Landsberg Prison. There he was put to work with fertilizers and poisonous chemicals, and given no chance to wash his skin at the end of each day's labor. By January 1945, he was so sick that prison officials expelled him, and he eventually made his way back to Traunstein. On May 4, 1945, the very day of the Nazi surrender and thus the end of the Third Reich, Haßlberger died.

Traunstein also had two examples of passive resistance from more "establishment" figures. Rupert Berger was the local leader of the Bavarian People's Party (the Volkspartei, an offshoot of the Center Party, though it shared some of the nationalist tendencies of the Nazis). He was also a leading figure in the party's self-defense group called the Bayernwacht. The Nazis viewed the group as a potential base of opposition and threatened Berger. He fled March 9, 1933, but was arrested and sent to Dachau, where he was severely beaten. Upon release, he and his family were ordered out of Traunstein. He returned in 1945 and went on to be elected mayor in 1946, the first of several terms in office. In this case we can be absolutely certain Ratzinger knew of Berger's story, because the Ratzinger brothers and Berger's son, also named Rupert, were ordained to the priesthood together in Munich on the same day: June 29, 1951.

Finally, Traunstein's pastor, Father Josef Stelzle, was a vocal critic of the National Socialists. On the Feast of the Epiphany in 1934, he preached a sermon that led to his arrest. He said,

> Christ was born for all and died for all, white, yellow, and black. Today there are movements who do not want this to be true, who want a falsified Aryan Christ. These populist movements preach a so-called positive Christianity, a sham Christianity, a German Christianity which gives the overlords credibility, and which brings disease over the people. Beware these false prophets! Ask yourself whether they mean the real Christ, the child of Jews, who was born in Bethlehem. . . .

The words of the sermon are preserved in the police report ordering his arrest.

After a few days Stelzle was released with orders to leave Traunstein, but he returned within the year. The Nazis tried to pressure the church to move him, but without success, and Evers says he was a continual "thorn in the flesh" for the regime. In October 1935, he preached a sermon for the youth in the parish in which he told them their priorities should be church first, family second, and the state third. Despite his confrontational stance, Stelzle survived the war. He died in 1947.

Ratzinger's hometown thus offered ample evidence that resistance, if costly, was not impossible. It also suggests that heroism and fidelity were not restricted to Catholicism, a point that will become important below.

Ratzinger at War

Ratzinger's military service began in 1943, when he and his entire seminary class (which had been temporarily disbanded) were drafted into the antiaircraft corps. They were assigned to Ludwigsfield, north of Munich, where their job was to protect a plant for the Bavarian Motor Works. This particular plant made motors for airplanes. Ratzinger's group was later transferred to Innsbruck, Austria, and then to a point southwest of Munich near Lake Ammer. During this time, Ratzinger's group was not only doing its military duty but also took a reduced load of academic coursework.

Ratzinger reports in *Milestones* that the group was attacked by the Allies in early 1943, with one dead and many wounded. Ratzinger told *Time* magazine in 1993 that because of a badly infected finger during this time he never learned to fire a gun, and his own weapon was never loaded, so he did not take part in the combat. In the same *Time* interview, Ratzinger said that he had witnessed slave laborers from the Dachau concentration camp while he was on duty at the BMW plant.[6]

On September 10, 1944, Ratzinger was released from the antiaircraft unit, and by the time he returned to Traunstein, his draft notice for regular military service was on the table. On September 20, 1944, Ratzinger joined his unit, which was assigned to a camp in a spot where the borders of Austria, Czechoslovakia, and Hungary meet, approximately 200 miles away from Traunstein. Here Ratzinger says his unit fell under the command of former members of the Austrian Legion. He calls them "fanatical ideologues who tyrannized us without respite."

Despite its name, the Austrian Legion had its roots in Bavaria. It was formed in the early 1930s by a group of Nazi partisans who fled Austria and dreamed of marching back into Vienna in triumph, a dream that Hitler realized for them when he occupied the country in 1938. Over time, and with the influx of a large number of like-minded Bavarians, the Austrian Legion grew to a fighting force of 15,000 men divided into three commando groups. Throughout the 1930s they engaged in a series of cross-border raids designed to destabilize Austria and prepare it for a Nazi takeover.

Ratzinger says that his Austrian Legion commanders had done time in prison under former Austrian Chancellor Engelbert Dolfuß, whose short-lived rule from 1932 to 1934 was a fascinating blend of Catholic social teaching and fascism. Dolfuß was trying to apply the doctrine of the corporate state outlined by Pius XI in 1931's *Quadragesimo anno,* which called for replacing class antagonisms with cooperative units in society based on guild and profession. Politically, Dolfuß took his cue from Mussolini and ruled by absolute decree. Because Dolfuß saw Austria as a cradle of Catholic civilization, he was a fierce opponent of Hitler and the Nazis, and he had imprisoned scores of Nazi demagogues and street fighters.

After Hungary fell to the Russians, Ratzinger says his unit was put to work putting up tank traps. Ratzinger told *Time* that during this assignment he saw Hungarian Jews being shipped to their deaths. Hungary's Jews were the last in Eastern Europe to be rounded up by the Nazis, as the puppet government there defended them for most of the war. In 1944 the deportations began, and within a few months virtually the entire Jewish population of the country was wiped out, with the exception of some 20,000 Hungarian Jews saved by Swedish diplomat Raoul Wallenberg, who issued false Swedish passports and thus allowed them to escape. (Wallenberg died under mysterious circumstances after the Soviet occupation of Hungary.) Nearly half a million Hungarian Jews were deported to the camps, mostly to Auschwitz, by the Nazis in less than two months, an urgency that testifies to the mania of their captors. All told, Holocaust historians say, some 620,000 Hungarian Jews were murdered.

As the bottom fell out of the German war effort, Ratzinger and his fellow conscriptees were given their civilian clothes and put on a train for home. He was eventually drafted for military service again but was assigned to the barracks at Traunstein. Here Ratzinger and the others were forced to march through the city singing war songs, probably to convince the locals things were still under control. In late April Ratzinger decided to desert and swung around the edge of town to avoid sentries under orders to shoot deserters. Two soldiers saw him, but they let him go. When the Americans arrived in the spring of 1945, they chose the Ratzinger house as a headquarters. Joseph was identified as a solider and sent off to a prisoner of war camp near Ulm. Rumors persisted in the camp that the Germans were to be conscripted by the Americans for a war against the Soviets, but nothing came of it. Ratzinger was released on June 19, 1945, and hitchhiked a ride home with a dairy trucker. His brother Georg found his way back from Italy a short time later, and the Ratzinger brothers enrolled in the seminary in the fall.

Lessons from the Third Reich

What lessons has Ratzinger drawn from the horrors of the Third Reich, to which he was such an intimate witness? In what ways do these traumatic days shape his thinking?

Most fundamentally, Ratzinger understands the twelve years of the Third Reich as a trial by fire for the Catholic church, in which the church was triumphantly vindicated. He believes that Catholicism presented the only real challenge to the authority of National Socialism inside Germany. He concludes that Catholicism's main contribution to the cause of human dignity lies in maintaining its own inner strength and discipline, because only a unified church clear on its core convictions can stand up to the pressure of a totalitarian state.

In forming this assessment, Ratzinger has been influenced by two factors. First is the example of his parents, especially his father, who criticized the Nazis strenuously. "My father was one who with unfailing clairvoyance saw that a victory of Hitler's would not be a victory for Germany but rather a victory of the Antichrist that would surely usher in apocalyptic times for all believers, and not only for them," Ratzinger writes in *Milestones*. It was his father's Bavarian patriotism, and even more his Catholic faith, that Ratzinger believes allowed him to see so clearly what a monstrosity National Socialism was.

This equation of Catholicism with resistance to the Nazis was solidified for Ratzinger by the numerous priests and religious in Germany who opposed the Third Reich and paid the ultimate price. At Dachau, for example, more than 1,000 of the dead were Catholic priests; so many priests were interned at Dachau that they had their own barracks, the Priesterblock. One estimate is that 12,000 religious were victims of persecution and harassment by the Nazis, representing about 36 percent of the diocesan clergy of the time. There is no question that Catholic opposition to National Socialism was widespread and often heroic. Of course the clearest and most immediate example for Ratzinger was Traunstein's own pastor, Josef Stelzle.

Ratzinger's view is set out in *Milestones*, where he characterizes the spirit of German Catholics immediately after the war:

> No one doubted that the church was the locus of all our hopes. Despite many human failings, the church was the alternative to the destructive ideology of the brown rulers; in the inferno that had swallowed up the powerful, she had stood firm with a force coming to her from eternity. It had been demonstrated: The gates of hell will not overpower her. From our own experience we now knew what was meant by "the gates of hell," and we could also see with our own eyes that the house built on rock had stood firm.

Ratzinger here is expressing no more than the consensus among most German Catholics after the war. There was a tremendous spirit of triumphalism in the German Catholic community, a sense that they had fought the Nazis and won.

This conviction was expressed by Pope Pius XII, so strong a Germanophile that he was known in the Vatican as *il papa tedesco* ("the German pope"), who sent a message to German Catholics in June 1945. The pope said: "No one could accuse the church of failing clearly to point out the true character of the National Socialist movement and the danger it represented to Christian culture." Taking their cue from Pius XII, the German bishops in November 1948, in their first postwar pastoral message, praised the clergy for resisting the Nazis, thanked Catholic parents for defending Catholic schools, and stressed their own resistance to Nazi encroachment. In a 1946 address to the bishops of England, Cardinal Josef Frings of Cologne put the matter with stark simplicity: "We German Catholics were not National Socialists."

Ratzinger does not pretend that this spirit of Catholic resistance was universal. He acknowledged in a 1998 interview with the German magazine *Focus* that, "in Catholicism at the time there were many shades of opinion, many judgments and hopes that one could control Hitler, above all in academic circles." He has blamed the German bishops' conference for issuing statements that were too mild. Yet as Ratzinger sees it, the dominant Catholic ethos during the Reich was one of opposition; he once called Catholicism "a citadel of truth and righteousness against the realm of atheism and defeat."

There is much to support this view. In Catholic villages all over Germany, the Nazis had limited success in convincing people to embrace the new liturgies and doctrines of the Third Reich. Voting records through the 1920s and 1930s show that the Nazis consistently drew most of their votes from Protestant areas, in part because Catholic voters remained stubbornly loyal to their own party, the Center, and its satellites such as the Bavarian People's Party. Ratzinger proudly pointed this out in *The Ratzinger Report*: "It is well known that in the decisive elections in 1933 Hitler had no majorities in the Catholic states."

The Nazi leadership saw the Catholic church as one of its most important internal foes. In Catholic localities, Nazi Party members were often forbidden to take part in Catholic processions on the grounds that such events were an implied form of political protest. In a 1993 study of life during the Third Reich in a German Catholic village, authors Walter Rinderle and Bernard Norling report that the only violence during the twelve years of Hitler's rule occurred when a Nazi yelled "Heil Hitler" during the act of consecration at Mass, at which point several parishioners dragged him out of the church and beat him until the police arrived. Such was the tension between church and state in many small Catholic enclaves.[7]

During the 1930s, Nazi officials confiscated monastic properties, initiated criminal action against priests, suppressed Catholic youth organizations, prohibited clergy from teaching religion in the public schools, shut down Catholic newspapers and publishing houses, and removed nuns from the nursing profession. One bitterly resisted measure was the attempt to wrest control of schooling away from the church and place it in the hands of the Reich; another was an order in 1941 that schools in Catholic areas must take the crucifixes off their walls. All these measures were part of the Nazi program of *Gleichsaltung*, or "coordination," which meant that social institutions should reflect the ideology of the state. In this effort, Catholics were seen as the main obstacle. In turn, Catholics saw National Socialism as a new form of Bismarck's *Kulturkampf*.

In August 1932, the German bishops banned membership in the Nazi Party:

> It is the unanimous conclusion of the Catholic clergy and of those genuinely concerned to further the interests of the church in the public sphere that if the party were to gain the monopoly of power in Germany, which it is so hotly pursuing, the prospects for the church interests of the Catholics would be gloomy indeed.

Although this ban was lifted in 1933, several Catholic prelates continued to be outspoken opponents of the regime. Cardinal Michael von Faulhaber of Munich, for example, preached a series of sermons in Advent 1933 defending the Old Testament against Nazi anti-Semitic readings, advanced especially by chief Nazi theorist Alfred Rosenberg. "God always punishes the tormentors of His Chosen People, the Jews," Faulhaber warned. In 1938, during *Kristallnacht,* Faulhaber loaned a truck to the chief rabbi of Munich so he could salvage religious articles from his synagogue.

Faulhaber was also a contributor to *Mit brennender Sorge* (With burning concern), the 1937 encyclical from Pius XI that denounced Nazi attacks upon the church. It remains the only papal encyclical ever written in German. One of its more stirring passages reads,

> The culmination of revelation in the gospel of Jesus Christ is final, is binding forever. This revelation has no room for addenda made by human hand, still less for an ersatz or substitute religion based on arbitrary revelations, which some contemporary advocates wish to derive from the so-called myth of blood and race.

The bishop of Münster, Clements August Count von Galen, was even more sharply critical of National Socialism. In 1941, he preached a series of sermons condemning Nazi policies on euthanasia, forced sterilization, Gestapo terror, and concentration camps. According to one survivor of the White Rose movement, secretly distributed copies of Galen's sermons helped to galvanize resistance. His remarks were so defiant that a Nazi Party official, Walter Tiessler, actually proposed in a letter to Martin Bormann that they hang the bishop. He told Bormann he had discussed this issue with Joseph Göbbels, who said only Hitler could order such an action. Galen survived, but Tiessler's proposal demonstrates the risk some outspoken Catholic leaders took.

Individual Catholics, both laity and clergy, often risked death for their rejection of National Socialism. In 1999 the German bishops' conference published *Martyrologium Germanicum,* a list of twentieth-century German martyrs, including some 300 Catholics who died for their faith at Nazi hands. In presenting the publication, Cardinal Joachim Meisner of Cologne said, "The Catholic church does not have to be ashamed of its role during the course of this century."

These are the memories that German Catholics of Ratzinger's generation carry with them, which allow them to conclude that their church stood firm. This conclusion becomes even more understandable when placed in the context of what happened within Germany's other great confession, the Evangelical (Protestant) church, where complicity with the Nazis was actually institutionalized in the form of the Glaubensbewegung Deutsche Christen, the German Christians Movement.[8]

The movement began in 1933 as an explicit attempt to unite Christianity with devotion to Hitler as the savior of the German *Volk*. These Protestant Christians adopted an officially pro-Nazi stance, even adding hymns to Hitler to their worship manuals. They reorganized Protestantism within Germany, from a decentralized confederation to a more unified structure under the command of a *Reichsbishop*, an instance of the *Führerprinzip*. The aim was to build a Christian community based not on baptism but on race, on the *Volk*. The movement claimed more than half a million members all through the 1930s, and it split German Protestantism in half. Nor can it be assumed these were merely opportunists or careerists, because under the Nazis the smart career move was to jettison religious belief altogether. These were genuinely committed Christians and equally committed Nazis who believed they could find a biblical basis for the Nazi faith in "blood and soil."

The fact that no such schism occurred inside Catholicism reinforced the impression that it was the Roman church that stood firm, despite the courage of the so-called "Confessing church," which opposed the Nazis, and despite the acts of individual heroism of Protestant thinkers such as Dietrich Bonhoeffer. Indeed, in 1934 a Lutheran pastor, Dr. Karl Thieme, led a group of his coreligionists who appealed to Pius XI to accept them into the church on the grounds that in Nazi Germany the gospel could only be preached through Roman Catholicism.

All of this suggests that Ratzinger's view of what happened under the Reich, shared as it is by most German Catholics of his era, is a rational one. It is also, however, based on a selective reading of the historical evidence. The truth is that during the Third Reich, Catholicism was every bit as much a fellowship of sinners as it was a communion of saints.

First, Hitler came to power on the back of Catholic support. Catholic leaders never supported the Weimar experiment with democracy, which they saw as a legacy of the Enlightenment and the *Kulturkampf*. The "Enabling Act," which was the legal instrument giving Hitler the power to rule by decree, passed by the Reichstag on March 24, 1933, was able to squeak through only after it was endorsed by Monsignor Ludwig Kaas, the leader of the Center Party. Kaas acted in coordination with the German bishops. Four days later, on March 28, the German bishops rescinded their ban on Nazi party membership. On April 1, Cardinal Adolf Bertram of Breslau addressed German Catholics in a letter, warning them "to reject as a matter of principle all illegal or subversive activities." To most Catholics it looked like the church wanted a modus vivendi with Hitler.

The same impression was created a few weeks later when Hitler held a plebiscite to endorse his decision to pull Germany out of the League of Nations, which received the endorsement of the Catholic press and of several Catholic bishops. When Hitler and the church came to terms for a concordat, or treaty, later in 1933, it cemented the impression that Hitler was a man the church "could do business with." A famous Nazi election poster of the era shows Hitler with the smiling papal nuncio, who says on the day the concordat was signed: "For a long time I have not understood you. For a long time, however, this has bothered me. Today I understand you."

Many ordinary Catholics objected to attacks on their church, but there was simply no opposition to Nazism *tout ensemble*. The two issues that provoked opposition among Catholics were the abolition of confessional schools in 1937, which triggered protests in many parishes, and the crucifix removal order in 1941. Resistance to the latter was so strong the order was quickly revoked; in Traunstein, more than 2,000 Catholics showed up for a demonstration. But there was no systemic Catholic opposition to the government as such, nothing like the action of the Dutch Catholic bishops who in May 1943 forbade Catholic policemen from cooperating in hunting down Jews, even if it cost them their jobs.

Germans had no history of political democracy and no bill of rights. Looking across the Salzach to Austria, Germans saw the example of Chancellor Dolfuß, a Catholic totalitarian. There was no sense that Hitler was unusual or that fascism as he practiced it was a perversion. Moreover, with public works such as water pumps and autobahns under construction, the economy restored, and widespread political tranquility, most Germans during the 1930s were satisfied with Hitler's rule. A *New York Times* correspondent in the mid-1930s reported that it was a riddle why Hitler bothered rigging elections, because a free and fair vote would probably have given him about eighty-percent support. In the midst of this general contentment, the Catholic church offered no programmatic or ideological reason to oppose Hitler. It drew the line at the preservation of its own institutions and doctrines but did not challenge the consensus that Hitler was doing a good job for the country, his views on Jews, gypsies, Communists, and political opponents notwithstanding.

In fact, there were key points at which Nazi and Catholic attitudes intersected and created a basis for mutual support. Both groups hated the Weimar Republic. The Nazis opposed Weimar because it was allegedly too Jewish and led by the "November Criminals" who sold out the country after the First World War; Catholics objected to it because it smacked of liberalism, sexual degeneracy, and an irreligious spirit. Cardinal Faulhaber, for example, gave a speech in May 1933 in which he expressed thanks for the *Volksgemeinschaft,* or spirit of community, which Hitler had fostered, and rejected "liberal individualism." Moreover, Catholics shared with Nazis an instinctive fear of the Bolsheviks. This was especially true in Bavaria, where memory of the 1919 Soviet uprising was still fresh. In Traunstein, for example, the Catholic trade associations decided to participate in the official workers' celebrations sponsored by the Nazis, because they no longer "honored class struggle as previous socialist May Days." In other words, the May Day celebrations were acceptable now that they had Nazi, rather than Communist, overtones.

Finally, there was a form of anti-Jewish sentiment that was openly accepted among Catholics, based in part on the theological argument that the Jews sinned by rejecting Christ and in part on the historical fact that many Jews had played leading roles in the *Kulturkampf*. As early as 1925, a Franciscan priest named Erhard Schuland wrote a book called *Katholizismus und Vaterland* (Catholicism and fatherland) that called on Germans to fight "the destructive influence of the Jews in religion, morality, literature and art, and political and social life." Schuland expressed what was very much the consensus in German Catholicism of the day, that anti-Judaism was not only permissible but necessary, but that it should be expressed with "moral means."

At the official level, too, the example of the bishops was mixed. Archbishop Konrad Gröber of Freiburg was known as the "Brown Bishop" because he was such an enthusiastic supporter of the Nazis. In 1933, he became a "sponsoring member" of the SS. After the war, however, he claimed to have been such an opponent of the Nazis that they had planned to crucify him on the door of the Freiburg Cathedral. Bishop Wilhlem Berning of Osnabrück sat with the Deutsche Christen Reichsbishop in the Prussian State Council from 1933 to 1945, a clear signal of support for the Nazi regime. Cardinal Bertram also had some affinity for the Nazis. In 1933, for example, he refused to intervene on behalf of Jewish merchants who were the targets of Nazi boycotts, saying that they were a group "which has no very close bond with the church." Bishop Buchberger of Regensburg called Nazi racism directed at Jews "justified self-defense" in the face of "overly powerful Jewish capital." Bishop Hilfrich of Limburg said that the true Christian religion "made its way not from the Jews but in spite of them."

Even Faulhaber, so courageous in other ways, was not consistent. In November 1939, he celebrated a special solemn Mass in Munich to celebrate Hitler's escape from an assassination plot. Moreover, Faulhaber's defense of the Jews was ambiguous. In his Advent sermons he said the church has "no objection to the endeavor to keep the national characteristics of the people as far as possible pure and unadulterated, and to foster their national spirit by emphasis upon the common ties of blood which unite them." He said that the Jews could not claim credit for the wisdom of the Old Testament: "People of Israel, this did not grow in your own garden of your own planting. This condemnation of usurious land-grabbing, this war versus the oppression of the farmer by debt, this prohibition of usury, is not the product of your spirit." Later, when a Swiss newspaper carried an article about Faulhaber's sermon defending the Jews, the cardinal had his secretary write to correct a possible misimpression. The cardinal intended his sermons as a defense of the Old Testament children of Israel, he wrote, and did not intend to take a position with respect to the Jewish question of today.

This lack of firm episcopal leadership allowed the church to become an adjunct of the Nazi regime in key respects. After April 7, 1933, civil servants in Germany were required to prove that they were not Jews. Because births had been registered by the state only since 1874, the church was called upon to provide many records. The Catholic church cooperated right up to the end of the war. Likewise, after the 1935 Nüremberg laws that forbade marriage between Aryans and non-Aryans, most Catholic priests did not perform such ceremonies, even though the number of Jewish conversions to Catholicism was accelerating because of the persecution.

That the bishops were not unblemished during the war was driven home for Germans in a special way in 1969, when it was disclosed that an auxiliary bishop of Munich, Matthias Defregger, while a captain in the army in 1943, had enforced an order to execute seventeen Italian civilian hostages. Though Defregger had told his ecclesiastical superiors about the deed immediately after the war, they suppressed it until *Der Spiegel* magazine broke the story. After this revelation, it became more difficult for many Germans to accept the "Catholicism as victor" theory.

Also relevant here is the experience of de-Nazification. Allied commanders initially relied on the clergy in Catholic areas to recommend untainted civilians for leadership roles in a new civilian government. The bishops realized that if they excluded all former Nazis, whatever government was created would be dominated by Social Democrats and Communists. Finding this unacceptable, they ignored directives and declared many ex-Nazis "clean." Faulhaber actually had forms, which came to be known as *Persilscheine,* roughly "whitewash papers," printed for this purpose. The Allies, especially the Americans, stopped soliciting church input. A Rhineland politician by the name of Leo Schwering wrote in his diary in 1945, "They [the priests] recommend persons who are politically questionable but in whom they have confidence because they are good Catholics. Surrounded by the black cassock and its recommendation, they smuggle themselves in." In this light, Ratzinger's appraisal seems one-sided and even distorted in its emphasis on the moral courage of the church, at the expense of an honest reckoning with its failures.

Perhaps as important for understanding Ratzinger today is to ask how his understanding of the church's experience under the Nazis influences his policies as prefect of the doctrinal congregation. Ratzinger laid out his views in a lecture entitled "The Spiritual Basis and Ecclesial Identity of Theology," delivered at St. Michael's College in Toronto in 1986.[9] He opens by mentioning Heinrich Schlier, who in 1935 was one of the leading figures in the Confessing church, the branch of German Lutheranism that rejected the Deutsche Christen movement and the Nazis. Schlier came to see, Ratzinger says, "that theology either exists in the church and from the church, or it does not exist at all."

After a review of how the Deutsche Christen movement compromised itself, Ratzinger comments at length about the relationship between theology and the teaching authority of the church:

> This situation made it evident that the liberty of theology consists in its bond to the church and that any other freedom is a betrayal both of itself and of the object entrusted to it. . . . This insight imposed itself then with burning intensity, although it was by no means acknowledged as obvious by the majority of theologians. It became the boundary line between liberal accommodation, which, in fact, quickly turned from liberality into a willingness to serve totalitarianism, and the decision for the Confessing church, which was simultaneously a decision for a theology bound to the Creed, and, therefore, to the teaching church. Today, in our outwardly peaceful times, it is not possible immediately to make out the contours in such stark relief. It is true that, on the whole, Catholic theologians would not challenge at the level of principles the magisterium's right to exist. . . . Nevertheless the intrinsically necessary and positive value of the magisterium has also lost its self-evident character in the general consciousness of today's Catholic theology. . . . It is impossible to remain indefinitely in such a state of inner cleavage. If the church and her authority constitute a factor alien to scientific scholarship, then both theology and the church are in equal danger. In fact, a church without theology impoverishes and blinds, while a churchless theology melts away into caprice.

Ratzinger is saying that a theology that distances itself from church authority makes itself a plaything of other forces. In the case of Nazi Germany, this was the National Socialist state. Theology either serves the church, or it serves the political and cultural consensus of the moment. It is in this sense that Ratzinger called the Catholic church "a bastion against totalitarian derangement" in *The Ratzinger Report*.

Given the history of the Deutsche Christen movement, and given the way Ratzinger remembers the role of the Catholic church in the Third

Reich, his argument is logical. It is not, however, historically sound. Some German theologians who had been the most vocal in asserting the need for a theology close to the church and critical of liberal science also endorsed Hitler, such as the Protestant Friedrich Gogarten. As Robert P. Ericksen has shown in his impressive 1985 study *Theologians under Hitler*, factors such as personal background and environment go much further in explaining the stance individual theologians took toward Hitler than do their intellectual positions. Karl Barth, for example, was Swiss, and hence less impressed by the appeal of pan-German nationalism; Dietrich Bonhoeffer had an English family tie, and had lived in both London and New York, and thus he had a more cosmopolitan outlook than the most enthusiastic apostles of the *Volk*.[10]

Ratzinger's reading of the war omits what many people would consider its main lesson, namely, the dangers of blind obedience. Millions of Germans like the Ratzingers, who passed Nazi prisons on their way to school and work, who watched Jews driven out of their communities, who knew that political opponents of the Nazis such as Hans Braxenthaler died for their resistance, nevertheless did little to stop what was happening. In this regard, Ratzinger is no more culpable than any other decent German citizen. The point is that many Germans failed to question, to dissent, and where necessary to fight back.

Bernard Häring, a Redemptorist priest and moral theologian, offers an interesting comparison. Born in Bottingen, Germany, in 1912, he was fifteen years older than Ratzinger. As a young priest he had hoped to be sent to a Redemptorist mission in Brazil, but ended up at the University of Tübingen at the outbreak of the Second World War pursuing a doctorate in moral theology. Under the Nazis the German army did not have chaplains, so many German priests volunteered for noncombat duty in order to offer pastoral care to the soldiers. For this purpose Häring entered the medical corps and ended up on the eastern front in Russia. In early 1943, Field Marshall Friedrich von Paulus ordered the German Sixth Army, which included Häring's outfit, to surrender to the Russians. Most of the soldiers in Häring's battalion wanted instead to try to make it back to Germany, fearing death at the hands of the Russians. They asked Häring to lead them. He did so, caring along the way for the sick and the frostbitten; his story was later told in novel form by Italian author Guilio Bedeschi in *Il Peso dello Zaino* (The weight of the knapsack).

After the group made it back, Häring rejoined his unit, but he was not celebrated as a hero. Instead he was tried as a deserter and sentenced to a "death battalion." The army would assign soldiers convicted of capital offenses to impossible situations, expecting few to survive. Häring escaped and joined another regiment that knew nothing of his status. He was with them in Poland when the Russians captured the regiment. In an incredible coincidence, they were in a village in Poland where he had served during the earlier German advance. The villagers remembered Häring so fondly they persuaded the Russians to hand him over to them, and then they smuggled him back to freedom.

These experiences shaped the later direction of Häring's thought. As a moral theologian, he argued for a morality based not upon rules and limits but on the responsible exercise of human freedom. This approach was rooted in his perceptions of the war. In his autobiography, Häring wrote, "Unfortunately, I also experienced the most absurd obedience by Christians toward a criminal regime. And that too radically affected my thinking and acting as a moral theologian. After the war I returned to moral theology with the firm decision to teach it so that its core concepts would not be obedience but responsibility, the courage to be responsible."

Häring and Ratzinger, in other words, arrived at nearly opposite conclusions from their experiences of the Third Reich: Ratzinger stresses the importance of obedience, Häring its dangers. Häring also derived pastoral consequences from his wartime experiences. During a press conference at Vatican II, he was asked about ecumenism. He said:

When I was in Russia, when the village people learned I was a priest, they would come to me to baptize their children and celebrate the liturgy. I baptized the children. I celebrated the liturgy. I didn't ask if they were going to raise their children as Roman Catholics. I knew they weren't. I didn't ask if they accepted papal supremacy before we joined in the eucharistic liturgy. . . . Or if we were going into battle, I would call the men together. "This may be anyone's turn," I would say. "Are you ready to meet your creator? I will absolve all who are sorry for their sins. I will give the Eucharist to those who wish it." I didn't ask if they were Catholics or Lutherans or anything.

Perhaps what separates the two men is that Häring is most concerned with what the Nazi experience has to teach *individuals,* about conscience and the need to exercise independent judgment. Ratzinger is most concerned with lessons of the Third Reich for the *church,* especially its need for firm commitment to core doctrinal principles. The difference is understandable, as Häring is an ethicist and Ratzinger a systematic theologian. What Roman Catholicism has yet to resolve is what happens when these two impulses conflict—when conscience and obedience stand in tension.

Graduate Studies in Munich

Ratzinger left behind the war in 1945 and quickly finished his days at the minor seminary. He entered the Herzogliches Gregorianum, the theological institute associated with the University of Munich, on September 1, 1947. It was not the regular diocesan seminary, but it offered a rigorous course of study for clergy wanting to pursue a career in academic theology. Owing to the devastation of the war, the institute had taken up temporary quarters in an old royal hunting lodge called Fürstenried just south of the city, which had been purchased by the archdiocese as a retreat center. Though the cramped quarters and inadequate library resources were annoying, Ratzinger would later look back on Fürstenried, especially its elaborate garden, fondly, describing it as the place where all his early life decisions took shape.

The Nazis had closed down the Munich institute in 1938 because Cardinal Faulhaber had refused to appoint a professor known to be a Nazi sympathizer. Thus the faculty had to be rebuilt, with most members drawn from institutions in what had been eastern Germany. Those institutions had been closed after the Poles occupied the territory east of the Oder and Neisse rivers and expelled all the Germans.

Ratzinger says the star of the new faculty was Friedrich Wilhelm Maier, one of the biblical scholars responsible for pioneering the "two source" theory to explain the composition of the synoptic gospels of Matthew, Mark, and Luke. According to the theory, Mark wrote first, sometime before the destruction of Jerusalem in A. D. 70, and Matthew and Luke both drew on Mark. In addition, Matthew and Luke shared another source, a collection of the sayings of Jesus known in biblical circles as "Q," short for the German word Quelle, or "source." Though the two-source theory is a commonplace of scholarship today, at the time it struck many as a dangerous innovation. Maier was harassed by the Vatican. Under the impact of Pius X's antimodernist drive in the 1910s, he had been kicked out of academia, only able to get a job teaching again in the late 1920s. Ratzinger says the treatment produced in Maier "a certain bitterness towards Rome," yet adds that Maier was a man of "deep faith" who took care with the formation of young men entrusted to him. It is a motif in Ratzinger's thought we will see recur. He experiences an injustice at the hands of church authorities, directed either at himself or others, and expresses regret for the bitterness and hurt it caused. He avoids, however, any structural conclusions about the proper use of such authority.

Ratzinger received his doctorate in theology from the University of Munich in July 1953. Although he writes fondly of all the professors under whom he studied, it is also clear from his work that none of these men exercised a primary influence on Ratzinger. Instead, Ratzinger's intellectual journey was shaped by what he was reading, both the ancient fathers of the church and more recent theological work. In that massive body of literature, there are four figures, two belonging to earlier periods of church history and two older contemporaries, who had great impact. To understand Ratzinger, we need to situate him with respect to these four men.

Augustine

Ratzinger's first important work was a study of Augustine, written as part of his doctoral program in Munich in the early 1950s. He received his doctorate in theology in 1953. The title of the completed work was *Volk und Haus Gottes in Augustins Lehre von der Kirche* (People and house of God in Augustine's doctrine of the church). Ratzinger has time and again testified to his fascination with Augustine. In 1969, he wrote, "I have developed my theology in a dialogue with Augustine, though naturally I have tried to conduct this dialogue as a man of today." As recently as 1996, Ratzinger referred to himself as a "decided Augustinian." Ratzinger has also said that if he were trapped on a deserted island, the two books he would want would be the Bible and the *Confessions.*

That Ratzinger gravitated to Augustine rather than St. Thomas Aquinas, the Dominican theologian and Angelic Doctor of the church, was itself a minor act of rebellion. In 1879, Leo XIII had issued *Aeterni patris,* an encyclical that enshrined Aquinas as the official philosopher of the Catholic church. So-called "neoscholastics," or those theologians who followed a rigid adaptation of Aquinas's thought first worked out in the sixteenth century, used Leo's document as a club to suggest anyone who departed from their point of view was flirting with heresy. In that sense, Ratzinger's preference for Augustine was a bit daring, though very much in keeping with the intellectual ferment of the pre-Vatican II era.

Ratzinger's love for Augustine is part of his fascination with the "Fathers of the Church," a group of approximately 100 apologists, spiritual writers, and theologians who lived during the first eight centuries. After the Council of Trent ended in 1563, most Catholic seminarians and theologians no longer studied the Fathers, because Trent seemed to be the definitive and eternal expression of Catholicism, rendering anything that had gone before superfluous. But in the first decades of the twentieth century, as the desire for change began to build in the church, there was a cry for a "return to the sources," meaning both Scripture and the Fathers. The movement usually goes by the French word *ressourcement.* It had enormous impact in the liturgy, as students of the ancient Mass discovered that active participation by the laity, using the vernacular language, and Communion in the hand actually had deeper roots than the more mysterious and solemn Latin Mass that Trent had formalized. The idea became to reform the church by recapturing aspects of its tradition that had been lost or suppressed, and Ratzinger was one of its proponents.

Like Ratzinger himself, Augustine's career as a theologian was interrupted by his nomination as a bishop, and for the rest of his career his thought was formed on an ad hoc basis by the practical need to fight various heresies. In his doctoral essay, Ratzinger wrote that Augustine's ideas were worked out in "polemic against error." Augustine's theological masterpiece was *City of God,* a twenty-two-volume opus written in response to the Fall of Rome in 410. He asserted the superiority of the church to any human society and closely identified the visible institutional church with the "city of God." The city of God is a stranger here on earth, Augustine believed, and it must be in the world but not of the world. As Dominican Aidan Nichols noted in 1988, this idea of Christian estrangement from the world is "perhaps the most insistent refrain in Ratzinger's criticism of the Catholic church's modern self-reform."

Like Augustine, Thomas Aquinas drew a distinction between nature and the supernatural. For Aquinas, however, the distinction was a warrant for optimism about human freedom. He believed that the human mind is able to fathom nature without direct divine illumination, opening up a whole realm of thought and action that is not specifically "religious." Augustine takes a more dim view of the human intellect unaided by divine grace. In *Volk und Haus Gottes,* Ratzinger writes approvingly of the shift in Augustine that led to his conversion: the realization that the wisdom he had sought in the classical authors (e.g., Cicero) was false and that true wisdom came only in Christ. The end result of Augustine's position is greater skepticism about the world and a more defensive position with respect to solutions based on "natural law." That skepticism about nature unaided by grace has carried through in Ratzinger. American moral theologian Charles Curran once said his biggest problem with Ratzinger was that Curran was more of a Thomist.

In *Salt of the Earth,* Raztinger quotes a homily given by Augustine in which he tells the story of a son who wakes his father from sleeping sickness. The father becomes angry because he wants to sleep, but the son says "I can't let you." The church also must not let its members sleep, Ratzinger says. The church must "raise her index finger and become irksome." It is a good summary of what Ratzinger took away from his master.

Bonaventure

Bonaventure's aspiration was to think and write full time as a professor at the University of Paris, but he became drawn into the controversies swirling inside the early Franciscan movement. In 1257 Bonaventure was elected minister general of the order. In 1273 he was appointed bishop of Albano, Italy, and became a cardinal. He died while taking part in the Council of Lyons in 1274, arguing for the reunion of the Eastern Orthodox churches with Rome.

By the early twentieth century Bonaventure caught the fancy of Catholic thinkers who wanted to do more than repeat the neoscholastic party line. Bonaventure was himself a "scholastic," as he wrote at the same time as Thomas, but he took a very different approach. Thus by studying him theologians could prove that the tradition had more diversity than neoscholasticism realized. Ratzinger's teachers were for these reasons much interested in Bonaventure, and under their influence he devoted his *Habilitationschrift,* the book-length contribution to original research that German doctoral students are required to complete, to Bonaventure's theology of history (*Die Geschichtstheologie des heiligen Bonaventura,* or "Salvation history of St. Bonaventure").

Ratzinger found that salvation history was a central concern for Bonaventure, shaped largely by controversy within the Franciscans over the writings of Joachim of Fiore, a twelfth-century mystic and prophet. Joachim had divided history into three epochs: an *ordo conjugatorum,* an age of the Father in which humanity lived under the Law, covering the period of the Old Testament dispensation; an *ordo clericorum,* an age of the Son in which priests dispense God's grace, referring to the period inaugurated by the New Testament; and finally an *ordo monachorum,* an age of the Spirit in which all Christians will live directly in grace and freedom without the need for clerical intermediaries. Joachim predicted this age would begin in the middle of the thirteenth century and would be launched by new religious orders that would usher in the age of the Spirit. Many in the nascent Franciscan movement believed that they were doing just this, and that ecclesiastical authorities who resisted them were resisting the work of the Holy Spirit. Radical Franciscans came to the brink of schism, even proposing that a collection of Joachim's works be recognized as a third book of Scripture.

As Ratzinger saw it, Bonaventure rejected much of what Joachim had to say, but did allow for the possibility that Francis might have triggered some kind of new stage in human affairs. Ratzinger approves Bonaventure's doubts about Joachim but goes even further, insisting that Catholic doctrine allows only for one "new age," the Second Coming of Christ. Ratzinger wrote of the danger in Bonaventure's tolerance of Joachim: "For, in a certain sense, a new, second 'end' is set up next to Christ. Even though Christ is the center, the one who supports and bears all things, still he is no longer simply that *telos* in whom all things flow together and in whom the world is ended and overcome."

Aidan Nichols, in his study of Ratzinger's theology, draws the obvious conclusion: "Before the name 'liberation theology' was ever heard of, Ratzinger had arrived at a judgment about this uncanny thirteenth-century anticipation of liberationist eschatology." Ratzinger had Joachim of Fiore in the back of his mind in the course of his decade-long crusade against liberation theology. He accused liberation theologians of trying to build the kingdom on earth, of minimizing the institutional church, of replacing spirituality with politics. These were the very tendencies that, in different language, Bonaventure had warned of in Joachim.

Romano Guardini

Those who know Ratzinger say Guardini is his favorite modern theologian. In tribute to Guardini, Ratzinger gave a keynote speech at a Munich celebration in 1985 commemorating the 100th anniversary of Guardini's birth, and in 1992 he authored an introduction to a new edition of one of Guardini's seminal works, *The Lord*.[11] Born in Verona, Italy, Guardini moved with his family to Mainz, Germany, in 1886 when he was just one year old. As a college undergraduate he tried his hand at chemistry and economics and failed at both. In 1905 he underwent what he would later call a profound religious conversion. He described the event in terms strongly reminiscent of Augustine's *Confessions,* and indeed Augustine along with Plato and Bonaventure were the formative intellectual influences on Guardini as they were for Ratzinger.

Guardini was ordained a priest in 1910, became a German citizen in 1911 because otherwise he would be ineligible for most jobs teaching theology (then as now salaried by the state), and went on to complete his dissertation on the doctrine of salvation in the thought of St. Bonaventure. Like Ratzinger, Guardini had an early taste of how church authority could sting. His seminary rector was fired because of his alleged "modernist" sympathies, an action Guardini would later refer to as one of "the frequent sins of orthodoxy."

From 1915 to 1939, Guardini wrote the works that would make him one of the most famous theologians of his era: *On the Spirit of the Liturgy, The Opposites,* and *The Lord.* He also became the national leader of a Catholic youth movement in Germany known as Quickborn, and the spiritual leader of its retreat center at Burg Rothenfels, where he was a liturgical innovator. Well before Vatican II authorized it, Guardini had turned his altar around and said key parts of the Mass in German. His leadership of the youth movement brought trouble with the Nazis, because they did not want competition with the Hitler Youth. In 1939 he lost his professorship in Berlin, and the Nazis seized Burg Rothenfels and disbanded Quickborn. In 1941 the Reich prohibited Guardini from giving public lectures, though he never openly opposed the regime. After the war Guardini continued to teach and publish, ending his career with more than a hundred articles and seventy books to his credit. In 1965 Paul VI offered to make him a cardinal as a form of tribute; Guardini declined. When he retired from the University of Munich in 1963, his chair was taken over by the Jesuit theologian Karl Rahner.

By writing critical essays on artists such as Fyodor Dostoyevsky and Rainer Maria Rilke, Guardini helped open the church to modern culture. By pushing the boundaries of liturgical reform, Guardini helped bring a movement that had been largely concentrated in Benedictine monasteries out into Catholic parishes and into the mainstream of Catholic thinking. He encouraged greater Catholic appreciation of the Bible among the laity. In all of these ways, Guardini helped blaze the trail that Vatican II would follow. Guardini contributed to the council in another important way, by helping to articulate the image of the church as the "mystical body of Christ." For Guardini this expressed the notion that all the members of the body, clergy and lay alike, should be active in the life of the church. Guardini saw the "mystical body" model navigating between two extremes: the neoscholastic definition of the church in purely institutional terms, and the liberal Protestant congregationalist understanding of the church as a social contract.

Ratzinger regards Guardini's thinking on the liturgy as one of his most important contributions. In his 1992 introduction to a reissue of *The Lord,* Ratzinger says that by focusing on the liturgy as the arena in which believers meet the living Christ, Guardini pointed a way out of the radical skepticism that had gripped liberal Christianity under the influence of scientific biblical criticism.

Guardini's blind spot, according to most observers, was history. He never accounted for historical development, whether in the Bible or in the formulation of doctrine. His use of Scripture was uncritical in ways that scholars today would find almost painful; as biographer Robert Krieg pointed out in 1997, Guardini treated the infancy narratives as if they were newspaper reports. Similarly, Guardini's thinking could not easily account for the historical unfolding of church teaching, as changing times and new discoveries create new possibilities for expressing the same truth with greater clarity.

Guardini was also mute on the social gospel. He was politically conservative, taking part in fierce right-wing Catholic criticism of the Weimar Republic. Guardini witnessed the brief socialist republic established in Bavaria in 1919, which was crushed by the army, and regarded it as proof of the instability of democracy. He was also largely silent on ecumenism, an omission all the more striking because it was one of the important currents in European, especially German, theology before the Vatican II.

Like Ratzinger, Guardini argued that only the Catholic church could give the concept "God" objective meaning. "If a person means only God, then he can say 'God' and mean only himself. There must be an objective reference. . . . There is however only one: the Catholic church in its authority and certainty." Although Guardini is a more supple thinker than this equation suggests, his statement, and many like it from Ratzinger, lends itself to a kind of slippery slope in which the ideas of "God" and "church" gradually coalesce until they become indistinguishable.

Hans Urs von Balthasar

Born in Lucerne, Switzerland, in 1905, Balthasar died on June 26, 1988, two days before John Paul II was to make him a member of the College of Cardinals, as he had earlier done with their mutual friend, French Catholic theologian Henri de Lubac (who shared with John Paul and Balthasar a disillusionment with what happened after Vatican II).[12] Ratzinger and Balthasar knew one another well, and collaborated on several projects. In 1971 the two wrote a book together, *Two Say Why: Why I Am Still a Christian*. Balthasar's masterpiece is his trilogy, consisting of *Herrlichkeit* (his work on aesthetics), *Theodramatik* (primarily on Christology), and the uncompleted *Theologik* (about God's "logic," leading into meditations on the Trinity). Under Ratzinger's patronage, Christoph Schönborn, now the cardinal of Vienna, and two other priests started a residence ten years ago in Rome for young men discerning a vocation to the priesthood. The name is the "Casa Balthasar." The young men are steeped in Balthasar, de Lubac, and Adrienne von Speyr, a visionary and lifelong collaborator with Balthasar. Ratzinger sometimes spends an evening there and always attends the board meeting in February.

Balthasar studied at Zurich, Vienna, and Berlin before completing a doctorate degree in German literature in 1929. That same year he entered the Jesuit order. He never acquired a doctorate in theology, though he studied under both Guardini and de Lubac. He spent four years, 1933 to 1937, working with de Lubac in Lyons. Balthasar is the only great Catholic theologian of the twentieth century who never taught theology. For that reason, his work is *sui generis* with respect to the usual categeories of theological concern. Balthasar thought and wrote across a stunningly broad field of concerns, from early church fathers to modern French literature, from aesthetics to Christology to the role and function of authority in the church.

The real twist in Balthasar's life came in 1940, when he met Speyr, a medical doctor and the wife of a professor at Basle. Speyr was a Protestant at the time, but under Balthasar's influence she decided to convert to Catholicism and he received her into the faith. Speyr claimed to be a mystic with a special mission for the church, and Balthasar was convinced. Over the next twenty-seven years, until Speyr's death in 1967, the two collaborated closely. They founded a community, the Johannesgemeinschaft (Community of John), designed to allow people to live the traditional vows of poverty, chastity, and obedience in the midst of the secular world, and also founded a publishing house, the Johannesverlag. Balthasar's attachment to Speyr was so profound that in 1950 he left the Jesuits in order to continue his work with her. He was eventually incardinated into the Swiss diocese of Chur. Balthasar believed that Speyr ranks with St. John of the Cross as one of the church's great mystics, visionaries who were granted insight into the "dark night" of souls separated from God.

During the years leading up to the council, Balthasar's fascination with the church fathers, his rediscovery of the Bible, his desire to restore Christology as the center of the faith, all helped create the climate that made Vatican II possible. His 1952 essay, "The Razing of the Bastions," was considered one of the defining moments in solidifying a consensus that Catholic theology needed a new direction. Balthsar became progressively more embittered after the council, in ways that both preceded and reinforced Ratzinger's own thinking. In 1979, for example, when the pope took away Hans Küng's license to be a Catholic theologian, Balthsar wrote approvingly, "John Paul II is safeguarding nothing less than the fundamental substance of Catholic faith. No one can deny this was urgent after years of dogmatic, moral and liturgical permissiveness. . . . Perhaps it is inevitable that the pope should give the impression of Hercules cleaning out the Augean stables." As Peter Hebblethwaite once put it, comparing your theological opponents to the contents of the Augean stables marks a "new low in theological controversy."

Yet Balthasar was more than a polemicist. One way to understand Balthasar is to compare him to fellow Jesuit Karl Rahner. Both men agreed the "two-story" model of nature and grace shared by previous generations of Catholic theologians, which saw grace as something "added on" by God to nature, was insufficient. Rahner's answer was "transcendental theology," arguing that God is the driving force inside all nature and inside each human person at a depth level (the "supernatural existential"). Balthasar went another direction, arguing for an "analogy of being" in which the human person shares a common ground of being with God but remains more distant, more corrupted by sin, than Rahner's thought allows.

As the years went by, the gulf between Rahner and Balthasar widened. In 1996, Balthasar published an attack on Rahner in which he accused him of negating the necessity of the crucifixion by imparting too much divinity to the human person. The debate was highly technical, but at bottom some very simple questions were involved: How good is humanity? How optimistic ought we to be about people and what they can create? Rahner, and with him the majority of post-Vatican II theologians, opted for a relatively optimistic and world-embracing stance; Balthasar, de Lubac, Ratzinger, and others took a more bleak view, suggesting that without fidelity to revelation, humanity is fated to error. The "analogies of being," however, still allowed too much closeness between God and man for the great Protestant theologian Karl Barth, who called the idea "the invention of the anti-Christ."

Balthasar said more than once that he was after a "kneeling theology," one rooted in contemplation and the spiritual life. He understood Jesus primarily through the Gospel of John, so it's very much the postresurrection Christ, not the earthly Jesus, who interested him. In fact, one of his major criticisms of liberation theology was that it put too much stress on the historical Jesus of scholarly reconstructions and not on the Christ of Catholic faith. Balthasar noted that St. Paul didn't feel the need to say anything at all about the historical Jesus outside the facts of his death and resurrection, and Balthasar predicted that the scholarly search for a "definitive stratum" in the life of the historical Jesus will end in the dissolution of Christian faith. He cautions against becoming a "Jesus-ian" instead of a Christian. He ended his book *Kennt uns Jesus, Kennen Wir Ihn?* (Jesus knows us, can we know him?) by thundering, *"Aut Christus aut nihil!"* (Either Christ or nothing!)

Students of Balthasar say the impact of Speyr appears above all in his meditation on Holy Saturday, when, according to the Apostles' Creed, Jesus "descended into hell" after his death on the cross. In Catholic thought, the point of doing so had always been understood as freeing the heroes of the Old Testament, such as Abraham and Moses, who could not have been saved earlier because they had not known of Christ. Balthasar, however, seized upon this article of the creed to argue that the descent into hell was the final act of abandonment of Jesus by the Father, that Jesus was actually damned and suffered in hell alongside the others who had said a final "no" to God. Balthasar expressed the hope that because of this act of solidarity by Jesus with the damned, hell would prove to be empty. Balthasar always said that his favorite church father was Origen, who had himself believed in the doctrine of *apokatastasis,* or universal salvation. It was a daring, provocative argument, noted both for its theological insight as well as the beauty of the language with which Balthasar unpacks it.

It is also an area of Balthasar's thought that some have labeled "unorthodox." We know Ratzinger disagrees with Balthasar on this point. In a conversation in Rome after his appointment as prefect, he told Michael Waldstein, who today runs a theological institute in Austria, that Balthasar was influenced too much in this area by Speyr. She was a convert from Protestantism, Ratzinger said, and hence carried the imprint of John Calvin on her thinking. Some observers might suggest that it is proof of Ratzinger's generosity of spirit and of his tolerance for other views that he could still shower praise on Balthasar despite this disagreement. Yet others might legitimately ask: If Balthasar could hold a differing position on such fundamental articles of the faith as hell, salvation, and the meaning of Christ's passion, and still be celebrated as a fully Catholic theologian, why cannot figures such as Edward Schillebeeckx, Hans Küng, and Charles Curran get the same treatment?

Ordination

Ratzinger was ordained to the priesthood in the Freising Cathedral by Cardinal Michael Faulhaber on June 29, 1951, along with his brother Georg and their friend and classmate Rupert Berger. It was the feast day of SS. Peter and Paul, a traditional day for priestly ordinations. The two Ratzinger brothers then offered their first masses on July 8 in their village of Hufschlag outside Traunstein.[13]

In Bavaria, any priest's *Primiz,* or first mass, is a cause for rejoicing, but a *Doppelprimiz* was a huge social event and an occasion of tremendous pride for the Ratzinger parents. Over 1,000 people from all over the Landkreis poured into the village on Saturday in advance of the Sunday liturgies. Lights were blazing all over the village to point the way to the Ratzinger home. That evening a local choir and the Catholic Youth of Traunstein sang and performed in the summer starlight for the pilgrims who had gathered for the festivities. Cannons were fired in honor of the new priests. Father Els from Traunstein also gave a talk to the crowd, urging the priests to lead their people to an always greater appreciation of the joy of Christianity.

By 7:00 A.M. on Sunday, St. Oswald's Church in Hufschlag was overflowing. The brothers, along with Berger, processed through the decorated streets toward the church. Clergy from neighboring churches joined other dignitaries in forming the procession, holding blazing candles and crucifixes and banners. The Ratzinger brothers then offered their first masses, Joseph first and then Georg (routine concelebration had not yet been approved), while the choir, under the direction of Dr. Hugger, sang a composition by Haydn.

Ratzinger delivered his first sermon, a reflection on the five-fold task that Faulhaber had entrusted to him: to offer sacrifice, to bless, to preside, to preach, and to baptize. He urged the faithful to contemplate the Holy Eucharist during the Mass, then thanked the crowd and asked for their help in carrying the grace and duty of his calling correctly. The three new priests joined in a prayer of blessing. When it was over, the choir and faithful joined in singing a booming Te Deum. Later everyone assembled in a local gathering spot, the Sailerkeller, where the new priests delivered after-dinner speeches.

The key mementos from that day were the first mass cards for each brother, which were reproduced in the local newspaper. Both Joseph and Georg had selected a Scripture verse for their cards. Joseph's was a line from Paul's Second Letter to the Corinthians (1:21): "We aim not to lord over your faith, but to serve your joy."

2

An Erstwhile Liberal

No cardinal of the Roman curia has ever enjoyed Joseph Ratzinger's global celebrity status. Ratzinger has sold thousands of books in dozens of languages and has been profiled by virtually every major newspaper or magazine in a corner of the world with a Catholic population. Anytime Ratzinger shows up to speak, he draws an overflow crowd, usually including a coterie of protesters. On his home turf in Europe, his fame has transcended the borders of church life; he's a bona fide public figure, with a cultural profile something like William F. Buckley, Jr.'s in the United States. His pronouncements on cultural issues, such as his 1986 malediction about pop music being a "vehicle of antireligion," make the front page of European papers.

In a 1998 poll in Germany's *Bunte* magazine, Ratzinger came in at number 30 in a contest to name the "200 most important Germans." He was the top Catholic official, and the second-highest religious figure of any sort, despite the fact that he has not lived in Germany since 1981. He finished ahead of tennis star Steffi Graf (#47) and Theo Weigel, then the head of Germany's powerful central bank (#49). To be sure, Ratzinger's fame has been eclipsed by that of his boss, John Paul II, probably the most commanding media figure of the late twentieth century. If Ratzinger worked for a sleepier pope, his own celebrity would stand out in greater relief. Still, by curial standards, Ratzinger is a phenomenon, a highly public figure in an institution that craves secrecy.

There's only one curial figure from the television era who could compete with Ratzinger in terms of star power: Cardinal Alfredo Ottaviani, the archconservative Roman prelate who held Ratzinger's job during Vatican II. Ottaviani, an intimidating man with enormous jowls and an aquiline nose, was the best thing going for the press corps that covered the council. Anytime a reporter needed a quote from somebody opposed to the liberals' agenda, Ottaviani was ready to supply one, and many of his colorful remarks have passed into legend.

During a particularly stormy council session, Ottaviani heard one too many bishops speak about "collegiality," the idea that all the bishops collectively govern the church alongside the pope. If that were true, it would mean that the pope's power was not absolute; and hence those who spoke in the pope's name, especially Ottaviani, would have less authority. Ottaviani wasn't buying it. In one of the most famous speeches in church history, he said the Bible offers only one example of the apostles acting collegially: in the Garden of Gethsemane, when Jesus is arrested. The collegial act? "They all fled."

Today quips like these bounce around the halls of the Vatican about Ratzinger, too. It is the nature of the job. Yet there is a special irony about Ratzinger being the butt of the same kind of jokes that dogged Ottaviani. At Vatican II, Ratzinger was one of the theological young Turks leading the charge against the status quo Ottaviani embodied. Ratzinger was an aggressive, deeply intelligent young thinker, dissatisfied with many of the answers offered by the church's official authorities. He was among the behind-the-scenes plotters who ensured that the council foiled Ottaviani on virtually every issue.

Ratzinger was present for all four sessions of Vatican II as the chief theological advisor to Cardinal Joseph Frings of Cologne, Germany. Frings repeatedly squared off against Ottaviani over the direction the council ought to take. It was Frings who, in one of the most dramatic moments of the entire four years of Vatican II, proclaimed that Ottaviani's office was a "source of scandal" to the world. Protestant observer Robert MacAfee Brown, who was in the council hall on the day Frings spoke—November 8, 1963—said his criticism of Ottaviani had "blown the dome off of St. Peter's."[1]

Given Ratzinger's image today as a strong conservative and Roman enforcer, it is easy to forget how central he was to Vatican II. Theologians played a uniquely important role during the council, drafting documents and organizing coalitions and preparing their bishops for floor debates, and Ratzinger was the very heart of all this activity. So influential were German theologians and bishops, in fact, that the best early history of the council was titled simply *The Rhine Flows into the Tiber*.[2] In the opinion of virtually anyone who has ever studied Vatican II, Ratzinger was among the theologians who had the greatest impact.

Because of this history, his fiercest critics have invested Ratzinger with something of a *Star Wars*–esque mythical quality. How does one move from Ratzinger, the progressive firebrand, to Ratzinger the chief inquisitor? Every time Ratzinger censures a thinker, bans a book, condemns a line of thought, or otherwise involves himself in trying to redirect some of the currents that flowed from the council, people wonder if this can be the same person. In the imagination of some liberal critics, Ratzinger's life story would make a script worthy of George Lucas: the young Jedi Knight who went over to the Dark Side of the Force.

Whatever one makes of it, the claim that Ratzinger "switched sides" does appear to be fairly well grounded. On a number of issues Ratzinger has executed an about-face in his views from the time of the council, all of them concerning central questions of theology and church life. The liberal Swiss theologian Hans Küng, in light of such reversals, once suggested that Ratzinger had sold his soul for power. Küng, a friend and colleague of Ratzinger who got him his job at the University of Tübingen, said acidly back in the early 1970s, "To be a cardinal in Germany these days you have to start early." Whether or not he accurately read Ratzinger's intentions, Küng was right about where Ratzinger was headed.

Why Does It Matter?

Middle-of-the-road Catholic theologians and historians often react to the charge that Ratzinger has defected from his Vatican II liberalism as interesting but irrelevant. People are entitled to change their minds, they say, and we would not want a doctrinal chief who is so rigid that he (or she) could never evolve. The fact that Ratzinger has been willing to modify or abandon earlier positions may be a sign of intellectual vitality. Others would reject the premise altogether, arguing that there has been an underlying continuity in Ratzinger's thought that is more important than any evolution on specific issues. There is wisdom in both views. Nevertheless, there are three reasons that the question of whether Ratzinger has abandoned his earlier convictions is deeply important in the context of Catholicism at the start of the twenty-first century.

Historical

Perhaps the most bitterly contested issue in the Catholic church today is the question of who has a better claim to the legacy of Vatican II: reformers who seek a servant church more tolerant of internal diversity, or restorationists who want the church to accent its traditional guarantee of unity in strong papal control. The question is, which instinct better expresses what Vatican II intended? Or, from a "strict constructionist" point of view, which better expresses the legislative intent of the council fathers? If it is true that Ratzinger has abandoned his earlier beliefs, that his "take" on the council today may be better explained by biographical factors rather than by the historical evidence, then it is an important finding for the progressive side of this argument. Whoever controls how Vatican II is remembered to a very great extent controls the direction of the church. Ratzinger's testimony is essential to deciding what the council intended, and any assessment of his testimony would be incomplete without asking how and why it has shifted over the years.

Moreover, Ratzinger himself has entered the historical debate. In a 1993 interview with *Time* magazine, he asserted, "I see no change in my theological positions over the years." It is, therefore, a fair exercise to test that claim against the facts.

Political

The problem with political arguments in contemporary Catholicism is that too often the disagreeing parties simply talk past one another, having very little intellectual common ground upon which to base the discussion. Progressive Catholics are steeped in the writings of Rosemary Ruether, Matthew Fox, or Karl Rahner, but they are largely ignorant of Dietrich and Alice von Hildebrand, or Hans Urs von Balthasar, or Matthias Scheeben, or any of the other thinkers and writers who make up the intellectual constellation of conservative Catholics. Neither side is willing to spend the intellectual effort to deeply understand the concerns that drive their opponents, the arguments that have led them to the conclusions they hold, the alternatives they have considered and rejected.

Each side often suspects the other of being cavalier in its convictions and insufficiently grounded in the authentic depth of the Catholic tradition. By understanding which roads Ratzinger has taken, and exactly where his own thinking veered away from the course so many others followed after Vatican II, progressives might be better able to articulate the case for change outside the sycophantic circle of the already convinced. Likewise, conservatives might grasp why they are often accused of having subverted the council.

Ecclesiological

Marx said that intellectual systems are determined by economic or social situations. He was an absolutist, but that fact is not essential to grasp his basic insight that ideas are often influenced by external factors such as status and privilege. If it is true that Ratzinger's theological beliefs have been reframed as his role in the church has changed, it suggests that church authorities are not exempt from the normal forces that shape the decisions a particular person will make. It suggests that church authorities may need to adopt a more humble stance before their own conclusions, realizing their thinking may reflect the imprint of influences that have little to do with the gospel. Of course, this is putting the point baldly; those who know Ratzinger say he strives to be open to more than one school of thought, and to impose only the church's judgment rather than his own. However, the point is that his instincts about what the church's judgment should be have changed over the years, and that development may have been motivated by factors alongside neutral theological judgment.

Two Careers

In the thirty years from his ordination in 1951 to his appointment to head the Congregation for the Doctrine of the Faith in 1981, Joseph Ratzinger achieved enormous success in two distinct careers in the Catholic church, first as a theologian and then as a cardinal. In both, Ratzinger rose swiftly. He moved through a succession of German universities in a short time, generally moving on to bigger and better appointments. He started out at Freising, then moved to the University of Bonn in 1959. There he befriended Frings, and was named his *peritus,* or theological expert, at Vatican II. In 1963 he moved to the University of Münster, and in 1966 he arrived at the university whose very name is evocative of Germany's leading position in the world of academic theology: Tübingen. Ironically, the man who secured Ratzinger's appointment was Hans Küng, who later would become one of Ratzinger's fiercest critics. In 1998, in an interview with me, he compared the Congregation for the Doctrine of the Faith under Ratzinger to the Soviet KGB.[3]

In 1968, Ratzinger watched a wave of student uprisings wash across Europe, and they were especially strong at Tübingen. Marxism seemed poised to replace Christianity as the unifying system of meaning in Europe, and even Ratzinger's own students were chanting "accursed be Jesus!" as a revolutionary motto. The experience shocked him and helped to stimulate his more conservative stance.

In 1969, Ratzinger moved back to Bavaria to take a teaching position at the new university in Regensburg. He eventually became dean and vice president. He also became a theological advisor to the German bishops, as well as a member of the new International Theological Commission created after Vatican II. During these decades, Ratzinger earned a reputation as an intelligent, diligent scholar, and his fame in theological circles as a central figure at Vatican II helped his ascent.

In 1977 Ratzinger was named archbishop of Munich-Freising. Though Ratzinger wrote in 1997 that the appointment was a surprise and that he wanted to decline, a trusted friend insisted he accept, and the papal nuncio demanded that he sign a handwritten pledge on hotel stationary agreeing to take the job. His subsequent rise up the ladder was swift. Paul VI made Ratzinger a cardinal in 1978. In 1979, Ratzinger played a key behind-the-scenes role among the German bishops in support of John Paul II's decision to strip Küng of his right to call himself a Catholic theologian, an act that cemented the rift between the two men. In 1980 Ratzinger was named by John Paul to serve as the *relator*, or chair, of the special Synod on the Laity, where he earned high marks as a good listener and astute thinker. The new pope first asked Ratzinger to head the Congregation for Catholic Education shortly after his election, an invitation Ratzinger declined because he felt he could not leave his post in Munich so soon. In 1981, however, he accepted the pope's offer to take over as prefect of the Congregation for the Doctrine of the Faith. Ever since John Paul has steadily invested more and more authority in Ratzinger's office.[4]

To understand how remarkable Ratzinger's rise has been, it is important to recall that for most of church history, a career as a theologian has not been the preferred path to a cardinal's red hat. Ambitious young clerics typically will go to Rome for seminary, where it is important to make contacts early on as well as to achieve a reputation as "safe" in terms of doctrine and personal habits. The new priest will put in a year or two in a parish, then move to a job in the bishop's office, then if he is lucky, return to Rome to work in a congregation (the secretariat of state or the doctrinal office are the plums), and eventually win a bishop's miter. The system is set up to ensure the promotion of predictable, institutional men. In the American bishops' conference, it is easy to spot those prelates who followed this path: William Levada in San Francisco, for example, or Justin Rigali in St. Louis. They are conservative, deeply loyal to Rome often at the expense of their own bishops' conference, and yet possessed of an urbanity that makes them gracious and charming. In this context, a career-minded young cleric would be ill advised to pursue serious work in theology. Being a professional academic holds too many risks, demands too often that one say daring things.

This traditional distance between theologians and their fast-track confreres was, if anything, even more pronounced among members of Ratzinger's generation, because so many thinkers had suffered at the hands of church authorities after Pius XII's *Humani generis* in 1950 only to be rehabilitated at Vatican II. Yves Congar, John Courtney Murray, Henri de Lubac . . . the list seemed to extend indefinitely.

Most previous heads of the doctrinal office in Rome have not been well-regarded professional theologians. The argument has always been that "when Peter intervenes, he does so as the fisherman"; in other words, that the pope's charism of protecting the deposit of faith does not depend on specialized theological knowledge. In fact, a former staff member of the doctrinal congregation once told me that the church needs pastoral control over its theologians in the same way that the state has civilian control over the military. Before Ratzinger, this had become a sore point for many Catholic theologians, who felt they were being disciplined by people in the curia who were actually incapable of understanding their work. When Ratzinger was selected for the top doctrinal job, many theologians applauded, hoping that despite his rightward drift Ratzinger could be expected to have sympathy for the guild. Instead, Ratzinger has if anything felt more free to criticize theologians, because he has the credentials to offer a critique "from the inside."

For most Catholic theologians, creative tension between authority and the church's intellectual class is natural. When someone moves from exploring the boundaries to enforcing them, as Ratzinger has, it naturally arouses suspicion. This has made exchanges between Ratzinger and some theologians more pointed, often more bitter, as these theologians know it is not that Ratzinger does not understand them. He understands full well, yet insists their work is unacceptable. This turns the dispute into something more than a natural tug-of-war between competing interests in the church: a sense of betrayal, of someone who "ought to know better," enters into things. Ratzinger himself must feel it acutely, as he knows the dynamics of the professional Catholic theological community very well. It is similar to what happens when a reporter becomes an editor, or a teacher becomes an administrator. The questions arise: Did he sell out? Did he earn his success by betraying his earlier convictions?

Ultimately, that is a psychological question beyond a biographer's power to answer. What is clear is that Ratzinger's positions on several issues have evolved over the course of his career, and that evolution made him attractive to church authorities. Those who know Ratzinger best believe that he would today be articulating the views expressed in his Vatican work even if he were still at Regensburg. It may well be true that Ratzinger's changes of heart were not fueled by ambition; even so, there is no doubt as to the conclusion someone who *is* ambitious would draw from Ratzinger's success.

Vatican II

When Vatican II opened in 1962, Joseph Ratzinger was thirty-five years old. He had been a theologian on his own right for less than a decade. To understand how this young and still obscure professor from Germany was able to play a critically important role in the pivotal Catholic event of the twentieth century, one has only to recall the ancient wisdom: It's not *what* you know, it's *who* you know. In Ratzinger's case, he knew Herbert Luthe, an old seminary friend who by this time had become the personal secretary to Cardinal

Joseph Frings of Cologne. Luthe is today the bishop of the German diocese of Essen. When Ratzinger moved to the University of Bonn in 1959, he moved into the Cologne archdiocese, and Luthe arranged a meeting with Frings. He and Ratzinger hit it off, and whenever Frings needed theological advice, he turned to his new friend and protege.

Cardinal Josef Frings

Frings was a legend in European church circles. He was an accomplished Scripture scholar, a graduate of the Pontifical Biblical Institute in Rome. That fact alone sensitized him to the potential excesses of the Holy Office, as he knew how badly Scripture scholars had been harassed in the middle years of the century. Ottaviani and his circle worried that the historical-critical method, which revealed the various strata and competing ideologies contained within the Bible, threatened to call the whole concept of revelation into question. During the council Frings and Ratzinger would defend modern Scripture studies with vigor.[5] Frings was an amateur mountain climber, but by the time the council opened he was seventy-six and in declining health. He was nearly blind, which meant that he had to rely on others to read all the preparatory documents, proposals, memoranda, and other papers floating about before and during the council. In that regard, he came to depend on Ratzinger and Luthe even more than most bishops leaned on their *periti*. Despite his infirmities, his speeches in the council hall were clear, precise, and direct, and when he spoke he usually had people's attention.

Frings was positioned to be one of the most influential voices in the council even before it began. For one thing, he was well known in the Third World as chair of the German bishops' conference; its international aid agencies, Misereor and Adveniat, distributed vast amounts of aid to impoverished countries, made possible through Germany's generous *Kirchensteuer,* or "church tax." Thus the bishops in Brazil, in India, in Nigeria all knew him and had reason to feel grateful. Because the archdiocese of Cologne is one of the most wealthy in Europe, he had similar patronage powers with his continental peers.

Moreover, Frings had a reputation as an ecclesial moderate, especially in comparison to his colleague in Munich, Cardinal Julius Döpfner, who was seen as a progressive. Thus when Frings spoke for reform, his words carried additional weight. That he emerged as a leader of the "progressive" wing was evidence for many observers that the bulk of the council stood behind the progressive position.[6] Finally, he was also rumored to have good connections with the pope, John XXIII. On the way home from the 1958 conclave that elected Pope John, Frings told Luthe that there might be a council, and word got around. When it came true, Frings's reputation as an insider was set in cement.

Heading into Vatican II, there was a flurry of behind-the-scenes work to get things organized. A short list of bishops with the most sway quickly emerged: Suenens of Belgium, Alfrink of the Netherlands, König of Austria, Helder Cámara of Brazil, Maximos IV the Melkite patriarch, and Frings, and Döpfner. As bishops began to organize themselves heading into the council, Frings was at the center of it all.

Ratzinger's Recollections

In trying to reconstruct Ratzinger's role at the council, one has several sources. First there are his own contemporaneous accounts, presented in the commentaries he wrote after each session.[7] We also have the commentaries he contributed to the famous Vorgrimler series on the documents of Vatican II (*Commentary on the Documents of Vatican II*, published by Crossroad in five volumes, 1967–1969), as well as accounts of his views and activities from observers and historians of the council. One can also draw general conclusions about Ratzinger's positions from analyzing the speeches and documents of Frings, who relied heavily on Ratzinger to prepare these materials. Lastly, we have Ratzinger's later recollections, presented in interviews and his 1997 memoirs, *Milestones*, which covers his life up to 1977.

How reliable are those later memories? Consider a test case: Ratzinger's attitude toward the draft documents sent out by the curia before the council opened. It was clear that the preparatory commissions that had prepared these documents, staffed with curial officials, wanted their drafts to be rubber-stamped by the council. Frings and other progressive leaders did not want it to happen this way. In *Milestones*, Ratzinger says Frings sent him the drafts the curia had prepared, and although he found individual things to haggle about, "I found no grounds for a radical rejection of what was being proposed, such as many demanded later on in the council and actually managed to put through."

Based on all the other evidence, this is not true. Frings was one of the ringleaders in the campaign to reject the curial drafts. In May 1961, he and Döpfner wrote to the pope to suggest the council be delayed because the quality of the preparatory work was so poor. In a meeting of fellow bishops, he called the curial drafts "completely unsuitable" and "so inadequate." It is hard to imagine that Frings would have taken such a strong stand if his trusted theological advisor had been telling him otherwise.

On the very first working day of the council, October 13, 1962, the curial plan was for conciliar commissions to be elected. All the members of the preparatory commissions were to be selected, so they would be able to speed the curial drafts through the council. The plan rested on the assumption that if more than 2,000 bishops had to vote on the first day, they would be too disorganized and unfamiliar with one another to mount much resistance. Frings, however, along with Cardinal Liénart from Lille, proposed a delay "so that the candidates could first become better known." Despite a ban on cheering in the hall, the bishops roared their approval. It was the first test of strength, and Frings won. There is no indication in any of this that Ratzinger disapproved.

Still, we do not have to speculate about what Ratzinger thought. According to the second volume of the massive *History of Vatican II,* edited by Guiseppe Alberigo and Joseph A. Komonchak, Ratzinger along with Yves Congar, Hans Küng, and Karl Rahner asserted that the drafts had to be rejected. Ratzinger is said to have held the opinion that they were "incapable of speaking to the church." Moreover, if Ratzinger truly felt the curial drafts were acceptable, it is hard to understand why he spent much of 1962 reworking the schema on the church along with Rahner, then spoke to several meetings of bishops outlining why the new proposal was superior to the curial draft.

In his own 1963 commentary on the first session, Ratzinger proclaims that the decision to reject the curial drafts and go back to work was a "great, surprising, and genuinely positive result." He calls the delay of the election of commission members engineered by Frings a sign that the council was resolved "to act independently and not to degrade itself into a rubber stamp of the preparatory commissions." This is how Ratzinger described what was at stake:

> There was a certain discomforting feeling that the whole enterprise might come to nothing more than a mere rubber-stamping of decisions already made, thus impeding rather than fostering the renewal needed in the Catholic church. . . . The council would have disappointed and discouraged all those who had placed their hopes in it; it would have paralyzed all their healthy dynamism and swept aside once again the many questions people of our era had put to the church.

This obvious disjunction between what Ratzinger remembered in 1997 and what he wrote in 1966 suggests that we will do better in general to follow his statements from the time. His later memories are of more value in documenting how his attitude has shifted over time than in establishing what his role was in the event itself.

Ratzinger at the Council

During the four sessions of the council, held in the fall of each year from 1962 through 1965, Frings, Ratzinger, and Luthe lived in the Anima, the German-speaking residence for priests and seminarians in Rome. In his 1998 book, *Im Sprung Gehemmt* (The failed leap), Vienna auxiliary bishop Helmut Krätzl talks about those days when he was a young seminarian at the Anima watching Frings and Ratzinger help to shape the council. He describes Ratzinger as a titan in the eyes of the seminarians, and a man who "inserted himself energetically for a renewed vision of the church."[8]

Krätzl's memoir stresses how central Ratzinger was to everything that happened. Though Ratzinger's official role was as an advisor to Frings, he was not simply a behind-the-scenes man in the sense that others at the council did not know who he was or what he was doing. Although Ratzinger could not speak on the council floor, he was a public figure in every other way. He gave lectures on council topics at various spots in Rome and in Germany, he organized briefing sessions for council fathers, and he published a well-known series of council commentaries.

At Vatican II, the *periti* were supposed to answer only the questions asked of them by the bishops, were to do so objectively and without projecting their own conclusions, and were not to organize support for certain points of view or to give interviews or publish their personal opinions. Despite repeated public proclamations of these rules, however, *periti* honored them more in the breach than in the observance. Most observers believe that Vatican II would never have taken the course it did had it not been for the theological convictions and political savvy of its *periti*—and, of course, the openness of the bishops who listened to them.

As early as October 10, 1962, before the first day of business, Ratzinger emerged as a key resource for the German-speaking bishops. On that day all the bishops of Germany, Austria, and Luxembourg assembled in the Anima to discuss strategy. Ratzinger gave the main talk, going over the plans for a new draft document on revelation. Ratzinger was thus essential in forming the first impressions of the German-speaking bishops—who represented undoubtedly the single most influential block in the council—and his influence grew steadily.

After the decision on October 13 to wait to elect commission members, behind-the-scenes activity got underway to circumvent the curial drafts. Ratzinger and Rahner worked on a draft schema on revelation, which was in place by October 25. On that date, Frings hosted a meeting for cardinals Alfrink, Suenens, Liénart, Döpfner, Siri, and Montini (the future Paul VI). Ratzinger was asked to present the draft, which played to good reviews, though Montini felt it was best to work as much as possible with the existing documents. By all accounts Ratzinger was impressive; later Montini, as pope, would make Ratzinger archbishop of Munich and raise him to the status of cardinal.

After the council decided to delay the schema on revelation, Ratzinger and his colleagues were able to reshape it to bring it into substantial agreement with the principles outlined in the original Rahner-Ratzinger draft. After difficult negotiations and a series of compromises, it was finally approved during the last session, on November 18, 1965. *Dei verbum* (On the word of God) is the Vatican II document over which Ratzinger exercised the greatest personal influence.

In the mind of Ratzinger, the most important document of Vatican II is the Dogmatic Constitution on the Church, *Lumen gentium.* It capped the decades-long effort to restore a doctrine of the church based on Scripture and the Fathers, and it attempted to restore a balance between pope and bishops that many felt had been lost after the declaration of papal infallibility at Vatican I. That council intended to issue a declaration about bishops, but had been interrupted by the Franco-Prussian War. Many insiders felt that the purpose of Vatican II was to complete the unfinished business of Vatican I. In the general report from the council, which was published on July 2, 1964, following the second session, Ratzinger is credited with helping to shape articles 22 and 23 from chapter 3 of *Lumen gentium*, which were the crucial passages on collegiality and the role of the bishops. He also wrote the commentary on this section of *Lumen gentium* for the Vorgrimler commentaries immediately after the council.

During the third session of the council, in the fall of 1964, Ratzinger was asked to serve on an editorial committee that redrafted the decree on missionary activity. This work, which also involved the famous French theologian Yves Congar, extended into the fourth session. Frings rose on the council floor to support the document.

All in all, Ratzinger made anyone's short list of the most important theologians at Vatican II. In 1969, Karl Lehmann of Germany, the future bishop of Mainz and chair of the German bishops' conference, wrote in an essay on Karl Rahner that Rahner, Congar, Ratzinger, Küng, and the Dutch Dominican Edward Schillebeeckx "broke through the schemata that had been prepared as finished products into an open country of greater theological freedom." It is interesting to note that of the names on Lehmann's list, two—Küng and Schillebeeckx—were investigated by the Holy Office in the years after the council, with Küng eventually losing his license to teach as a Catholic theologian.

How Ratzinger Changed

The debate over Ratzinger and Vatican II usually operates at a fairly abstract level. Liberals invoke the catchphrase, *aggiornamento,* associated with the council, using it to mean a spirit of change, modernity, and open-mindedness, and then accuse Ratzinger of having abandoned this "spirit." Quite naturally, Ratzinger insists that what matters about Vatican II are the documents themselves, not some amorphous "spirit" allegedly contained within them. On the other hand, defenders of Ratzinger often draw a distinction between two schools of thought at the council: *aggiornamento* and *ressourcement*, the latter being a "return to the sources" impulse that found its primary expression in the liturgical movement, in the recovery of the church fathers, and in a new appreciation for Scripture. Both schools agreed on the need to break out of the church's neoscholastic rut in the 1950s, but the *aggiornamento* people wanted to "modernize" the church and bring her into dialogue with the culture, whereas the *ressourcement* circle wanted to recover elements of tradition that had been lost. One impulse looked forward and the other primarily back. To put all this into political terms, *aggiornamento* was a liberal impulse, *ressourcement* more conservative. Ratzinger's apologists say that he was a *ressourcement* man all along, and thus has not really changed.[9]

Like the "spirit of Vatican II" argument, the *aggiornamento-ressourcement* distinction, valid so far as it goes, does not really help us answer the question of whether Ratzinger changed, because *ressourcement* is itself a broad idea from which one can draw multiple conclusions. In fact, many of the figures in Catholicism today one thinks of as the most "liberal," such as Richard McBrien and Charles Curran, argue that their positions are actually more "traditional," more grounded in the sources, than their right-wing detractors. So the question is, what conclusions did Ratzinger's reading of *ressourcement* lead him to at the time, and how do they square with what he is saying today?

On six issues, discussed in turn below, one can see a clear difference between the positions taken by Ratzinger at the council and those adopted by him today. In some cases the shift is a matter of outright contradiction; in others, it is a more subtle matter of shifts in emphasis. But Ratzinger today has clearly lost the ardor he once felt for Vatican II, a point driven home by a 1985 comment to Associated Press writer Richard Ostling: "Not all valid councils have proven, when tested by the facts of history, to have been useful."

Collegiality

The theory of collegiality holds that the bishops are jointly the successors of the original Twelve Apostles who followed Jesus, and thus they form a "college." As such, they together enjoy supreme authority for the church. This authority does not exceed the pope's, but neither is it subsumed into the pope's. The pope "together with the college" was the conciliar formula. Many details were left vague, but the idea was that the bishops ought to have a voice in governing the church, not just at the level of their individual dioceses but in terms of shaping universal policies. No voice spoke more consistently or emphatically on this theme than Frings, and one is entitled to assume he did so with the assistance and support of his *peritus*: at least Ratzinger never registered a dissenting note in any of his commentaries or contemporary recollections. During the preparatory meetings leading up the council, Frings objected to what the draft document on the church said about bishops. It asserted that although the office of bishop comes from Christ, the particular authority of the bishops comes from the pope. Frings said he worried that the bishops would be "decapitated" and insisted on strong language on their independent authority.

During floor debate, the curial forces insisted that the idea of collegiality had no basis in ancient texts. Frings rose during the second session and demolished the argument. First, he noted that the practice of bishops exercising joint authority is clear from the earliest stages of the church, from the "council of Jerusalem" recorded in the Book of Acts, through all the councils in the first centuries that defined key doctrines. Moreover, Frings said that if a doctrine cannot be taught by the church simply because it does not appear in the ancient texts, then the church should never have proclaimed Mary's assumption or papal infallibility. All truths of the faith, he said, are not equally clear from the beginning. It was a telling argument, and given Ratzinger's strong background in patristics, it undoubtedly reflects his influence.

Once again, we do not have to guess at Ratzinger's attitude. Ratzinger himself commented on the doctrine of collegiality several times. In his report on the first session, he wrote that he looked forward to a time of "fruitful tension" between the periphery and the center given the new doctrine on the role of the bishops. He said that strain between Rome and the bishops is inevitable, but it will be a healthy form of exercise for the entire Body of Christ. In an essay on the "prefatory note" decreed for *Lumen gentium* by Paul VI, Ratzinger noted that Vatican I was actually considering condemning the idea of collegiality, because some Protestants had seized the term to argue that a church could not be both collegial and hierarchical. Ratzinger sniffed that this was still the opinion of some "Roman theologians." It was not the last time he would use that phrase with contempt. But the Roman theologians are wrong, Ratzinger wrote, because the council was using the term "college" in its patristic sense, which allowed for the possibility of greater and lesser members.

In the same commentary, Ratzinger says that one of *Lumen gentium*'s greatest advances is to treat the church not simply as a legal institution but as a sacrament, a living sign of God. The idea has implications for collegiality, he said. "Insofar as the idea of law is isolated from or associated with the sacramental idea, law in the church will be a thoroughly centralized affair or an intrinsically collegiate one." In other words, the more the church is a sacrament, the more collegial it will be. In perhaps the most remarkable line in view of his later career, Ratzinger notes that, legally speaking, the pope is perhaps not obligated to consult the bishops or the faithful before ruling on an issue, but there is a moral obligation to do so. "Now among the claims which his very office makes upon the pope we must undoubtedly reckon a moral obligation to hear the voice of the church universal," he wrote.[10] The drift of Ratzinger's thinking at the council is clear. The church was too centralized, too controlled from Rome, and there was a need, both practical and theological, to shift power back to the bishops.

In his 1963 commentary on the first session of the council, Ratzinger notes how unbalanced the "vertical" and "horizontal" lines of authority had become in the church. There were strong vertical ties linking bishops to the pope, but "hardly any horizontal ties among the bishops themselves." He saw the emergence of a "horizontal Catholicity" as one of the most important achievements of the council, one in which "the curia found a force to reckon with and a real partner in discussion." He saw the interaction among bishops in the council as a form of collegiality in action:

> What the bishops said and did was far more than an expression of a particular theological school. It was rather the expression of another school which they had all attended, the school of their very office, the school of communion with their faithful and with the world in which they lived.

Ironically, Ratzinger's major concern in 1965 with Vatican II's treatment of collegiality was that it might turn bishops into "little popes" and increase clericalism, rather than following the road to its end and discovering beyond the collegiality of bishops "the brotherhood of the whole church." In other words, his fear was that the development of collegiality would not go far enough.

Compare that conviction to how Ratzinger looked back at the exercise of collegiality at Vatican II in *Milestones* in 1997: "More and more the council appeared to be like a great church parliament that could change everything according to its own desires. Very clearly resentment was growing against Rome and against the curia, which appeared to be the real enemy of everything that was new and progressive." Ratzinger seems to be suggesting that the bishops were motivated less by a sober consideration of the best interests of the church than they were in settling scores with the curia. Thus the idea of collegiality, which had struck Ratzinger as a legitimate theological concern in 1964, was by 1997 simply a matter of power politics.

Ratzinger's later view of collegiality is expressed most fully in a series of lectures on ecclesiology presented to the bishops of Brazil in 1990. Ratzinger analyzes what it means for the bishops to be successors of the apostles. Because the original apostles moved around, Ratzinger argues that being a bishop means being oriented to the universal church even before the local church; that one is a bishop of the Catholic church before one is the bishop of Boise or Bratislava. He says that only the pope is the descendant of a particular apostle, Peter. Every other bishop takes his place as a descendant of the apostolic college, so there is an essential "we-ness" to the episcopacy. How is this "we-ness" manifested? Ratzinger says it is in solidarity with other bishops of the region, and in submission to the primacy of the bishop of Rome. The practical conclusion is that bishops must not assert independence from Rome.

Ratzinger then makes one other point. He says the catholicity of the church is not just geographic but diachronic, meaning that it extends through time. "A majority that formed at some juncture against the faith of the church at all times would be no majority: the true majority in the church reaches diachronically across the ages, and only when one listens to this plenary majority does one remain in the apostolic 'we.'" His point? A bishop who takes his cure primarily from the people rather than from the papacy has ceased to be a bishop.

This shift in Ratzinger's thinking is clear in the policies he has pursued as prefect, many of which have attacked precisely the "horizontal Catholicity" Ratzinger had hailed at the time of the council. A case in point is offered by the six-year struggle over the new American lectionary, the collection of Scripture readings for use at the Mass, that unfolded during the 1990s. At their 1991 meeting, the U.S. bishops overwhelmingly approved a new translation of the lectionary that used so-called "inclusive language," meaning nonsexist terms such as "person" instead of "man." The translation was prepared with the assistance of the best Catholic Bible scholars, linguists, and theologians in the country. One might assume that American bishops could be relied upon to determine which English-language translation of the Bible is best suited for use in their country. In fact, however, the curia first accepted and then rejected the American translation, and over time it emerged that Ratzinger was the driving force behind the latter decision. He faulted the translation for serious doctrinal errors, especially the use of "person" instead of "man" in the Psalms, which he argued made it more difficult to read them as anticipations of Christ. After years of negotiations, with the bishops arguing for more understanding and the Vatican refusing to budge, Ratzinger convened an eleven-member working group in Rome, and it made the changes to the lectionary he wanted. It was an extraordinary procedure on many levels. Among other things, at least three members of the group were not native English speakers, and only one had a graduate degree in Scripture.

Ratzinger the prefect had undercut collegiality in precisely the area he himself noted it first took shape in the thinking of the council: governance of the liturgy. In his 1963 commentary on the first session of Vatican II, he wrote:

> The formulation of liturgical laws for their own regions is now, within limits, the responsibility of the various conferences of bishops. And this is not by delegation from the Holy See, but by virture of their own independent authority. . . . Perhaps one could say that this small paragraph, which for the first time assigns to the conferences of bishops their own canonical authority, has more significance for the theology of the episcopacy and for the long desired strengthening of episcopal power than anything in the *Constitution on the Church* itself. For in this case an accomplished fact is involved, and facts, as history teaches, carry more weight than pure doctrine.

In other words, the council had acknowledged the bishops as real decision-makers, not in theory but in actual fact, by leaving decisions on liturgy to the conferences. By reclaiming this authority for Rome, Ratzinger attacked episcopal collegiality at its very root.

Bishops' Conferences

The concept of a national or regional bishops' conference is a natural one: all the bishops of a country or region meet on a regular basis to compare experiences, pool resources, and where they deem it appropriate, to issue statements. The formal existence of conferences is quite recent, though as many theologians point out they are really nothing more than a new form of the ancient "particular council," at which the bishops of a given region would come together and solve problems or clarify doctrine together, as opposed to a general council in which all the bishops of the world take part. Because we know of particular councils as early as the 300s, the institution is far more ancient than either the office of cardinal (tenth century) or the Roman curia (sixteenth century). The fact that bishops' conferences had not been more common, or more powerful, in the years before Vatican II is another indication of how imbalanced the distribution of power in the church had become.

In the United States, the National Conference of Catholic Bishops in Washington, D.C., is a leading example of the growth in bishops' conferences after the council. It employs scores of full-time staff members and operates diverse ministries. By most accounts the U.S. conference really hit its stride in the 1980s, when it issued two documents: *The challenge of peace,* on nuclear war, in 1983; and *Economic justice for all* in 1986. These publications were years in the making, enjoyed strong consensus among the bishops, and generated broad social discussion even outside the boundaries of the Catholic church.

Reading the documents of Vatican II, all this seems a logical development. In his Vorgrimler commentary in 1966, Ratzinger too saw it that way: "The church is essentially plural, is a *communio,* centralization has its limits, and ecclesiastical acts at a national or provincial or diocesan level have their importance." In his commentary on the first session of Vatican II, Ratzinger wrote that he expected episcopal conferences to form intermediate bodies of a "quasi-synodal" kind between the individual bishops and the pope. It is also worth recalling the language on *Lumen gentium* in chapter 3, paragraph 23, the very paragraph Ratzinger had a hand in crafting: "The episcopal conferences at the present time are in a position to contribute in many and fruitful ways to the concrete realization of the collegiate spirit." In his 1965 commentary on the third session of the council, Ratzinger wrote that the "same reality" established by the early church in synods and patriarchates today takes the form of bishops' conferences.

The real "smoking gun" here, however, is an article Ratzinger published in the first volume of *Concilium* in 1965, which is worth quoting at length:

> Let us dwell for a moment on the bishops' conferences, for these seem to offer themselves today as the best means of concrete plurality in unity. They have their prototype in the synodal activity of the regionally different "colleges" of the ancient church. They are also a legitimate form of the collegiate structure of the church. One not infrequently hears the opinion that the bishops' conferences lack all theological basis and could therefore not act in a way that could be binding on an individual bishop. The concept of collegiality, so it is said, could be applied only to the common action of the entire episcopate. Here again we have a case where a one-sided and unhistorical systematization breaks down. . . . We would rather say that the concept of collegiality, besides the office of unity which pertains to the pope, signifies an element of variety and adaptability that basically belongs to the structures of the church, but may be actuated in many different ways. The collegiality of bishops signifies that there should be in the church (under and in the unity guaranteed by the primacy) an ordered plurality. The bishops' conferences are, then, one of the possible forms of collegiality that is here partially realized but with a view to the totality.[11]

It is important to note that these were not simply Ratzinger's private opinions, but the understanding of church authorities immediately after the council. Under Paul VI, the Vatican issued a *Directory on the pastoral ministry of bishops,* which ordered that a bishop accept "with loyal submission" the actions taken by a majority of his conference, "for they have the force of law through the church's highest authority, and he puts them into practice in his diocese although he may not previously have agreed with them or they may cause him some inconvenience."

These principles are difficult to reconcile with the document *Apostolos suos,* issued from Rome in August 1998, which asserted that bishops' conferences have no right to teach authoritatively. Thus a conference may not issue statements on doctrinal or moral issues unless it is unanimous, so that all the bishops impart their individual authority to the document, or unless it is previously approved by the Vatican. The document capped a decade-long discussion about the exact theological status of bishops' conferences, with Ratzinger as the major force demanding a more restrictive stance. He explained that *Apostolos suos* would protect individual bishops who disagree with their conferences, adding that "truth is not arrived at by majority vote."

When did Ratzinger change his mind? Peter Hebblethwaite, the late dean of Vaticanologists, reported that the first instance in which Ratzinger voiced his new reservations was in January 1983, when certain American bishops were called to Rome to face scrutiny on the second draft of their letter on war and peace. At that time, Hebblethwaite's sources told him, Ratzinger argued that a bishops' conference does not have a *mandatum docendi,* or a "mandate to teach." Such a mandate belongs only to the individual bishop as a successor to the apostles, or to the pope; there is no level in between.

In the 1984 interview that became *The Ratzinger Report,* Ratzinger offered two additional reasons for his doubts about bishops' conferences. The first had to do with the experience of Nazi Germany. Ratzinger said the statements put out about the Nazis by the German bishops' conference were too tame and bureaucratic, whereas individual bishops were more courageous. Second, Ratzinger said that the appearance of democratic decision-making in a conference is often just an illusion. He noted that of the 2,135 bishops at Vatican II, only 200 ever spoke over all four sessions. Thus the views of a small minority can often gain a falsely inflated degree of authority in such a setting.

Leaving aside the accuracy of his views about the council, what accounts for Ratzinger's change of heart? Note when the change came: his doubts surfaced only when he arrived in Rome and started facing the assertiveness of well-managed conferences with whom he disagreed. Here I think Hebblethwaite has it right when he suggests Ratzinger is using theology to serve ideological purposes:

> For it is evident that the prefect of the Congregation for the Doctrine of the Faith will find an individual bishop on his *ad limina* visit to Rome more pliable and docile than a self-confident episcopal confer-

ence on its own territory. . . . The truth of the matter is that an episcopal conference can stand up to Ratzinger. That is why he tries to cut them down to size.

As a related matter, Ratzinger has also shifted his understanding of the Synod of Bishops, created by Paul VI at the beginning of the fourth session of Vatican II. The first synod was held in 1967, and the synod on the episcopacy set for October 2001 would be the twentieth. In 1965, Ratzinger saw the synod as a means of continuing the council: "If we may say that the synod is a permanent council in miniature—its composition as well as its name justifies this—then its institution under these circumstances guarantees that the council will continue after its official end; it will from now on be part of the everyday life of the church." By 1987, however, in *Church, Ecumenism, and Politics,* Ratzinger declared flatly: "It [the synod] advises the pope; it is not a small-scale council, and it is not a collegial organ of leadership for the universal church." He argued that according to *Lumen gentium* 22, the college of bishops can act with legal force only in an ecumenical council or by all bishops dispersed around the world acting together. The college cannot "delegate" its authority, hence the synod cannot act like a council.

The Role of the Holy Office

If the Catholic church created holy days for church politics as well as for saints, November 8 would probably appear on ecclesial calendars as the "Feast of the Holy Uprising." On that day in 1963, on the floor during the second session of Vatican II, a curial official took a tongue-whipping the likes of which has never been seen in an official Catholic assembly before or since. Four hundred years of pent-up frustration exploded in a single speech by Cardinal Frings.

Frings rose to address a whispering campaign that had been making the rounds for a little over a week in Rome to the effect that a vote taken on October 30, which established that a large majority of bishops supported collegiality, was invalid because the questions were poorly worded. The council's Theological Commission, stacked with curial loyalists, was suggesting that it alone had the power to determine if collegiality passed doctrinal muster. To Frings this seemed like one more attempt from the curia to win back by intrigue what it had lost in open debate, and he had had enough.

"I am astonished that Cardinal Browne, vice president of the Theological Commission, has put this vote in doubt," Frings said, as quoted by Xavier Rynne, the pseudonymous chronicler of Vatican II whose reports appeared in the *New Yorker*. "The commission has no other function but to execute the wishes of, and obey the directives of, the council. Furthermore we must not confuse administrative roles with legislative ones."

Here came the thunderclap: "This also goes for the Holy Office, whose methods and behavior do not conform at all to the modern era, and are a cause of scandal to the world." Frings was speaking in Latin, but he was perfectly understood, and when he came to "cause of scandal" applause broke out—long, loud, sustained cheering, though such interruption was a technical violation of council rules. "No one should be judged and condemned without being heard, without knowing what he is accused of, and without having the opportunity to amend what he can reasonably be reproached with." Frings went on to add that too many bishops were working in the curia, when many of their jobs could be done by laymen. "This reform of the curia is necessary," he said. "Let us put it into effect." When he finished, Frings was greeted with another volley of applause. Protestant observer Robert MacAfee Brown later said it was "the right speech, by the right man, and at the right time" in that it perfectly captured the sense of the council fathers.

Ottaviani was due up among the morning's speakers three slots later. Shaking with anger, he brushed aside the rule that bishops were to stick to their prepared texts and responded directly to Frings. First Ottaviani said he could only conclude that Frings's criticism of the Holy Office was based in ignorance, because he did want to attribute less charitable motives. He insisted that the Holy Office always examines cases carefully, and always calls in acknowledged experts before it makes a judgment on anyone's writing. Second, Ottaviani asserted that an attack on the Holy Office is an attack on the pope himself. Finally, he dismissed the whole notion of collegiality.

The structure of the council's proceedings provided almost no opportunity for this sort of direct clash of ideas. Thus the exchange between Frings and Ottaviani became in some ways the defining moment of the entire council, and the question of the Holy Office's future became symbolic of everything else at stake. When Paul VI called Frings that afternoon to congratulate him, it seemed reform in the Holy Office had the pope's support and was all but inevitable. In fact, Paul VI did later decree a series of reforms, including the name change from "Holy Office" to "Congregation for the Doctrine of the Faith"; the pope said he wanted the new congregation to support good theological work, not primarily to condemn doubtful material.

Nowhere in his writings from the period is there even the slightest hint that Ratzinger differed with Frings about the need for reform. Indeed, his writings are filled with dismissive remarks about the "Roman theologians" and "Roman schools" who presume to represent all the versions of legitimately Catholic thought. Ratzinger later noted with approval the speech delivered by Archbishop Michele Pellegrino of Turin in the closing session of the council: "Who would dare to affirm that the rights and dignity of laypersons and priests have been religiously respected, whether by bishops or priests of over-exuberant zeal, or indeed, by cardinals of the Roman curia?" In his 1965 commentary on the third session of the council, Ratzinger complained of an "all too smoothly functioning central teaching office which prejudged every question almost before it had come up for discussion."

In his commentary on *Gaudium et spes* in the Vorgrimler commentary—in which, as we will see later, Ratzinger expressed serious reservations about certain aspects of the document—he noted that the council did not choose between competing accounts of how the doctrine of original sin should be understood. "Here, too, there was agreement that the essential content of Trent cannot be abandoned, but that theology must be left free to inquire afresh precisely what that essential content is." Such statements certainly suggest a Ratzinger who agreed with his boss that theologians need a New Deal from the Holy Office, a program of support rather than condemnation.

In his commentary on the decree on revelation, Ratzinger spells out his views on theological liberty in greater detail. In noting how the Holy Office tried to choke off debate before the council even though Catholic tradition is supposed to make room for different "schools" among theologians, Ratzinger observes,

> Something that could not be fitted into the antitheses of "Thomism," "Scotism," "Molinism," etc., was not known as a "theological school" but simply as an innovation and therefore did not come under the protection enjoyed by the differences among the "schools," the number of which, however, appeared to be settled.
>
> It was only the council that brought home the fact that the classical "schools" have today become as unimportant as the conflicts between them: it has also emerged that Catholic theology has remained alive, that new "schools" and conflicts have formed within it and that these new groups and their questions are also legitimate forms of Catholic theological work.

It is as succinct and trenchant a defense of theological liberty from a Catholic perspective as one is likely to find. It also happens to be precisely the same argument made by Leonardo Boff and the liberation theologians, or Matthew Fox and the creation spirituality movement.

In 1964, in his commentary on the second session of Vatican II, Ratzinger even suggested that the Holy Office should take lessons from secular democracies in the protection of individual rights. He said the council was open "to introduce the positive results of modern legal thinking into ecclesiastical structures. These structures had often taken shape during the age of absolutism and therefore were all too human in origin."

Perhaps the most dramatic piece of evidence demonstrating the gulf between the Ratzinger of Vatican II and Ratzinger the Vatican prefect comes in the form of a statement he agreed to sign in 1968. It originated at Nijmegen in the Netherlands, where *Concilium* was published, by many of the same *periti* and sympathetic bishops who made up the journal's first contributors and editors. The statement was eventually signed by 1,360 Catholic theologians from 53 countries, suggesting that it very much represented the consensus of the professional theological community at the time.[12] Ratzinger joined his friends and collaborators in asserting that "the freedom of theologians, and theology in the service of the church, regained by Vatican II, must not be jeopardized again." The signers—including Hans Küng, Karl Rahner, Edward Schillebeeckx, Yves Congar, J. B. Metz, and Roland Murphy—pledged their loyalty to the pope but argued that the teaching office of pope and bishops "cannot and must not supersede, hamper and impede the teaching task of theologians as scholars."

"Any form of inquisition, however subtle, not only harms the development of a sound theology, it also causes irreparable damage to the credibility of the church as a community in the modern world," the statement reads. The signers said they expect the pope and bishops to support them as theologians

> for the welfare and well-being of mankind in the church and in the world. We would like to fulfill our duty, which is to seek the truth and speak the truth, without being hampered by administrative measures and sanctions. We expect our freedom to be respected whenever we pronounce or publish, to the best of our knowledge and in conscience, our well-founded theological convictions.

The signers offered seven proposals because their "work as theologians seems again to be increasingly jeopardized at the moment." They were:

- that the Roman curia, especially the doctrinal congregation, must take into account and express in the composition of its members "the legitimate pluriformity of modern theological schools and forms of mental outlook";
- this should apply first of all to the decisionmaking organ of the doctrinal congregation, the plenary assembly of cardinals, where an age limit of seventy-five should be imposed;
- only those acknowledged as outstanding professional theologians should be consultors to the congregation, with a fixed term of office and no one appointed who is over seventy-five;
- the members of the International Theological Commission, set up to advise the congregation, must be representative of the different theological schools; the congregation must consult with the commission; and the

authority of the doctrinal congregation, and of doctrinal committees within national bishops' conferences, must be clearly circumscribed and limited;

- when the congregation feels obliged to disapprove of a theologian, this must be done in an orderly and legal fashion, with the proceedings worked out and published;
- the defendant should have certain rights, such as to have his thinking judged solely on the basis of his actual published works in the original language, to have counsel from the start of the investigation, to get all relevant documents in writing, to refer any dispute to two more professional theologians (one appointed by the defendant), to be accompanied by a professional theologian and to speak whatever language he or she chooses in the event of a personal interview, to not be bound by secrecy, and to have any eventual condemnation backed up by argument;
- that concern for truth in the church "must be carried out and fulfilled in accordance with the tenets of Christian charity."

The statement also notes that any administrative or economic measures against authors or publishers beyond what is envisioned here "are to be avoided in the present social situation, as they are as a rule useless or even harmful."

Ratzinger clearly and unambiguously associated himself with this statement, and it is perfectly consistent with what he was saying and writing at the time. We will examine the details of how the doctrinal congregation works under Ratzinger later, but suffice it to say that most of the reforms he urged in 1968 have been ignored during his twenty-year tenure. Theologians still do not have the right to counsel from the very beginning of an investigation—indeed, an investigation can be in process for years before the theologian even knows about it. The International Theological Commission is in no sense representative of the actual diversity in Catholic theology today. The congregation still attempts to bind people to secrecy about its procedures and decisions.[13]

The distance Ratzinger has covered in the years since Vatican II can perhaps be best glimpsed by comparing his decision to sign the 1968 Nijmegen Declaration with his reaction to the 1989 Cologne Declaration, signed by 163 theologians and issued after John Paul II decided to override local wishes and appoint the deeply conservative Joachim Meisner as archbishop of Cologne. The heart of the Cologne statement was a reiteration of the right of free and open discussion in the church in language strikingly reminiscent of the Nijmegen document. It decried a "new Roman centralism," and argued that "the church exists for the service of Jesus Christ. It must resist the permanent temptation to abuse its gospel of God's justice, mercy and faithfulness for its own power by making use of questionable forms of control." With respect to theologians being banned from teaching in seminaries and theological faculties, the signers rejected what they called "intolerable" interference. The Cologne Declaration was signed by many of the same people who put out the Nijmegen statement twenty years before, including Küng and Schillebeeckx.

By 1989, Ratzinger had been the prefect of the doctrinal congregation for eight years. Although some European bishops greeted the Cologne Declaration as "an invitation to dialogue," Ratzinger did not. He responded to the declaration in blistering terms, asserting that "there is no right of dissent" in the church and suggesting that the theologians who signed the declaration were engaged in a "political power ploy." Ratzinger also showed that he was willing to use raw political muscle to make his point, giving an interview on November 13, 1989, in which he argued that the theology faculties of universities in Germany might need to be cut. He said there might not be enough "qualified" people to fill the country's theology jobs. He was, in effect, hitting theologians where it hurts, warning them that their jobs could be at stake. In Germany theologians teach at state universities, but if a bishop withdraws the person's canonical license, he or she must find a position in another department or at another university.

Just a few months later, in 1990, the doctrinal congregation issued a document, *On the ecclesial vocation of the theologian,* which underscored Ratzinger's demand for submission. Though he told the press the document had been in the works before the Cologne Declaration, it was widely viewed as a response in the sense that it criticized a "crisis" of dissent and rejected many of the reforms Ratzinger had supported in 1968.

The Development of Tradition

If tradition is a once-and-for-all matter, if the practical consequences and verbal expressions of doctrines arrived at hundreds of years ago are themselves sacred, then theological work would be limited to finding new and better arguments for those formulae and consequences. This is essentially the position taken by Cardinal Alfredo Ottaviani at Vatican II; his episcopal motto was *Semper Idem,* or "always the same." If, on the other hand, doctrines are a human attempt to express the content of divine revelation, then the words and mental categories with which they are expressed are in principle open to improvement and amendment. Moreover, the practical consequences drawn from those doctrines, reflecting the assumptions and circumstances of a given historical period, are also open to change.

This latter perspective seems to better capture what Joseph Ratzinger stood for at Vatican II. His views are best set out in his contribution to the *Commentary on the Documents of Vatican II* on the decree on revelation. Ratzinger wrote that "tradition must not be understood as something given once and for all, but must be understood in terms of the categories of growth, progress, and knowledge of the faith." He said the decree "realizes that fidelity in the sphere of the spirit can be realized only through a constantly renewed appropriation." He said that Vatican II's method was to take note of what had been written at Trent and Vatican I, and then "interpret it in terms of the present, thus giving a new rendering of both its essentials and its insufficiencies." He said he entirely agreed with the great Protestant theologian Karl Barth's formulation of the method of Vatican II as "moving forward from the footsteps of those councils."

It seems ironic now that one of Ratzinger's biggest concerns in 1967 with *Dei verbum*, the decree on revelation, was that it failed to develop a set of criteria for the legitimate criticism of tradition. He worried that by its stress on "tradition," *Dei verbum* might lead the church into the belief that "whatever is, is right"; in other words, that if something is part of the tradition then it must be maintained for that reason. He wrote,

> There is, in fact, no explicit mention of the possibility of a distorting tradition and of the place of Scripture as an element within the church that is *also* critical of tradition, which means that a most important side of the problem of tradition, as shown by the history of the church—and perhaps the real crux of the *ecclesia semper reformanda*—has been overlooked.

To be sure, Ratzinger warned in his commentary about the dangers of turning the teaching office of the church over to Bible scholars and historians, suggesting that their shifting hypotheses were no basis upon which to base life decisions. But he also spoke in stirring terms about the need for the church to welcome their arguments as a legitimate way of keeping the tradition honest. In the same document, Ratzinger recognized that one of the problems in applying "tradition" is that it is not always clear where the objective content of revelation ends and the subjective biases of the one expressing that revelation begins: "The explanation, as the process of understanding, cannot be clearly separated from what is being understood," he wrote.

A longer extract from Ratzinger's article on revelation in *Commentary on the Documents of Vatican II* expands his thinking:

> The whole spiritual experience of the church, its believing, praying, and loving intercourse with the Lord and his Word, causes our understanding of the original truth to grow and in the today of faith extracts anew from the yesterday of its historical origin what was meant for all time and yet can be understood only in the changing ages and in the particular way of each. In this process of understanding, which is the concrete way in which tradition proceeds in the church, the work of

the teaching office is one component (and, because of its nature, a critical one, not a productive one), but it is not the whole.

Today Ratzinger is more concerned with arresting the development of tradition than with defending it. He has warned that the church is not a "laboratory for theologians" and that the "givens" of faith put limits to speculation, and he has stressed that submission to the magisterium is intrinsic to the identity of a Catholic theologian. The clearest contrast with his earlier views comes on the role of Scripture as a critic of tradition. In 1966, Ratzinger wanted to recover the role of Scripture as a tool for assessing church teaching and practice. By 1997, however, he warned that this tendency to wield Scripture against the church was one of the most dangerous currents to flow out of Vatican II. His change of heart was certainly informed by his long struggle against the liberation theologians, who insisted that the historical Jesus had come to heal the human person *both* body *and* soul and that, by overspiritualizing Jesus' message, the church had neglected a key component of the gospel. Ratzinger has drifted toward Balthasar's insistence on the Christ of faith versus the Jesus of history, with the result that he emphasizes the eternal over the developmental. Ratzinger has, in other words, come to embrace a position very close to the one against which he warned at the close of Vatican II.

Liturgy

There are few subjects about which Ratzinger writes today more passionately than the liturgy. In *Milestones,* Ratzinger describes in touching language how as a young man he became caught up in the drama of the Catholic Mass in all its grandeur and mystery. He said he had the feeling that in the Mass he came up against a rite that transcended mere human invention, that seemed to put him in touch with the very depths of God. "It was a riveting adventure to move by degrees into the mysterious world of the liturgy, which was being enacted before us and for us on the altar," he writes.

> It was becoming more and more clear to me that here I was encountering a reality that no one had simply thought up, a reality that no official authority or great individual had created. This mysterious fabric of texts and actions had grown from the faith of the church over the centuries. It bore the whole weight of history within itself, and yet, at the same time, it was much more than the product of human history.

Understandably, Ratzinger is anxious to protect the rite that had such a powerful impact on him. Ratzinger has never attacked the so-called "new Mass," but he has been bitterly critical of the way liturgical changes were implemented after Vatican II, especially Paul VI's decision to suppress the old Latin Mass, also called the Tridentine Mass. "The prohibition . . . introduced a breach into the history of the liturgy whose consequences could only be tragic," Ratzinger wrote in *Milestones*. "I am convinced that the crisis in the church that we are experiencing today is to a large extent due to the disintegration of the liturgy."

Ratzinger has said Latin Masses on several occasions since John Paul II authorized celebration of the older rite in 1988. In April 1998, Ratzinger celebrated the Latin Mass in Weimar, Germany, for 350 members of the Lay Association for the Classical Roman Rite in the Catholic Church. Prior to that Ratzinger was the featured speaker at a conference sponsored by Una Voce, an international activist group seeking to promote the Latin Mass. Though Ratzinger has said what he wants is a new "liturgical movement" that would build on the valid contributions from Vatican II, it is clear that the movement he anticipates would also revive a great deal of the preconciliar liturgy.

Ratzinger's preference for older liturgical practices became crystal clear in 1993, when he contributed a short preface to a book by German priest Klaus Gamber, *Turned towards the Lord*, in which Gamber argued that one of the central liturgical innovations of Vatican II—turning the altars towards the congregation, in order to include the people at Mass more actively—should be reversed. Ratzinger said he found Gamber's arguments persuasive, but for the sake of "liturgical peace," he would not act on them immediately. Eventually, however, he said the church needs a "reform of the reform." The position of the altar is in some ways symbolic of the larger question of what is really happening at Mass. Is the priest renewing Christ's sacrifice on the cross, in which case the faithful are essentially witnesses to the sacred mystery? Or are the priest and faithful together renewing Christ's Last Supper, sharing a meal and recalling his example? How integral, in other words, is the congregation to the symbolic drama? By turning the altar around, the new rite of Mass sought to help the faithful become more active participants. In Ratzinger's view, however, this change led to an overly "horizontal" view of the Mass at the expense of its "transcendent" dimension. In other words, that participants focus so much on what they are doing that they lose sight of what God is doing.

In 1998, Ratzinger also expressed the hope that the use of Latin might return to wider use in the liturgy. He called on a new generation of bishops to foster use of Latin as an antidote to the "wild creativity" of liturgy after the council that has "made the mystery of the sacred disappear." Ratzinger said that the current crop of bishops

> have had a formation and education according to which the ancient liturgy is a closed case, a quagmire which risks damage to unity, above all in contrast to the council. We must make it possible to form a new

generation of prelates which realizes that the ancient liturgy does not have to represent an attack on the council, but a realization of the council. The ancient liturgy is not obscurantism, is not a ferocious traditionalism . . . but it is really the desire to be with divinity.[14]

However defensible the views expressed in such comments, this is not the Joseph Ratzinger of Vatican II. Far from a critic of liturgical innovations such as use of the vernacular language, turning altars around, and emphasizing the active participation of the faithful, Ratzinger at the time of the council was a strong proponent of each of these ideas.

In his commentary on the third session of the council, for example, Ratzinger referred to the Latin Mass celebrated in the church of his youth as "archaeological." It presented "a picture so encrusted that the original image could hardly be seen." It was "a closed book to the faithful," Ratzinger wrote, as it had been "an irrelevancy to the saints of the Catholic reformation," noting that St. John of the Cross and St. Teresa of Avila drew none of their spiritual nourishment from the Mass. Compare those words to his reverential language above about the "mysterious fabric of texts and actions had grown from the faith of the church over the centuries," and the reversal in Ratzinger's perspective emerges in clear relief.

Frustration with the Latin liturgy was a constant theme in Ratzinger's commentaries on the council. In his first report, he complained strongly about the opening liturgy in 1962, which showed "no trace of the liturgical movement" and especially offered no "active participation of the faithful." He said the closing liturgy was much better, especially because the responses were sung in common, symbolizing the active participation he felt had been missing from the first Mass. On the use of Latin, Ratzinger quoted Maximos IV, the Melkite patriarch, approvingly in his commentary from the first session: "Language is for men, not angels."

Ratzinger went on to argue that language is an incarnation of the spirit, which, because it is human spirit, "can only think by speaking, and, in and from speech, lives." Ratzinger also attacked the use of Latin in the church's seminaries, saying that it played a significant role in the "sterility" of Catholic theology in those places. He called the use of Latin there a "forced union with a language that is no longer the vehicle of movement for the human spirit." It should be noted that this was an especially daring statement for Ratzinger to make in light of John XXIII's 1962 document *Veterum sapientia,* which had mandated the strict use of Latin in clerical education. Ratzinger was, in fact, directly contradicting the conclusions of the Holy Father. Ratzinger applauded the celebration of an Eastern-rite liturgy at the first session of the council as a correction to "Latin exclusivity." In his commentary on the second session, Ratzinger applauded Paul VI for ending his programmatic speech for the council by speaking in Greek and

Russian, thus "stepping out of the space of Latinity into the universality of the church of all nations."

On the subject of turning the altar around, there is no direct literary evidence of what Ratzinger thought at the time of the council. But it is fair to conclude that Ratzinger was at least aware of the fact that his favorite theologian, Romano Guardini, had pioneered the use of a turned-around altar in the Masses he celebrated for German youth at Burg Rothenfels. Nowhere does Ratzinger register any dismay at this innovation; on the contrary, he lavishes praise on Guardini for "rediscovering" the ancient sense of the liturgy and making it come to life.

As for active participation, here's what Ratzinger wrote in 1958 in *Die christliche Brüderlichkeit*. The book was his first real exposition of his own theological views:

> The recognition that *ekklesia* (church) and *adelphotes* (brotherhood) are the same thing, that the church that fulfills herself in the celebration of the Eucharist is essentially a community of brothers, compels us to celebrate the Eucharist as a rite of brotherhood in responsory dialogue—and not to have a lonely hierarchy facing a group of laymen each one of whom is shut off in his own missal or devotional book. The Eucharist must again become visibly the sacrament of brotherhood in order to be able to achieve its visible, community-creating power.

Ratzinger concedes in *Milestones* that his views on liturgy have evolved over the years. "I was not able to foresee that the negative sides of the liturgical movement would afterward reemerge with redoubled strength, almost to the point of pushing the liturgy to its own self-destruction." Fair enough. One cannot always anticipate the consequences of changes at the time they are made, and it is legitimate to voice reservations once those consequences become clear. But such reservations ought to be accompanied by honest self-disclosure. Ratzinger was not a passive bystander when the new direction of the liturgical movement was set by Vatican II; he helped put it on that course. He cannot blame anonymous "liturgical experts" who foisted their private agenda on the church. The principles that guided their work were developed in full public view and approved by the bishops at the council, with Ratzinger's support.

Ecumenism

In his speeches on the floor of the council, Frings touched upon ecumenical issues twice. When he first addressed the draft schema on the church (the document that eventually became *Lumen gentium*), he praised the document's "ecumenical tone." He said he especially appreciated the nonjuridical and nonapologetic tone toward non-Christians. He also applauded a recent statement made by Paul VI, in which the pope acknowledged that the Catholic church must share the fault for the present separation of the Christian churches. During the second session, Frings addressed the status of mixed marriages. He said that denying the validity of a mixed marriage, in which a Catholic and non-Catholic are married by someone other than a Catholic priest, is an obstacle to ecumenical progress and that the church should return to the "older discipline" of affirming such marriages.

Ratzinger addressed ecumenism himself most thoroughly in his commentary on the second session of the council, published in 1964. There Ratzinger comes across as a committed ecumenist. He laments the "new obstacles" that some bishops in the council would place in the way of relations with other Christian churches in the form of exaggerated Marian piety. He says sardonically that concern with Joseph the husband of Mary, with the rosary, with consecration to Mary, with devotion to the heart of Mary, with assigning Mary the title "Mother of the Church," and the quest for other such titles that one might bestow on Mary—all these things, he says, do not reflect well on the theological enlightenment of the bishops at the council. On the other hand, Ratzinger welcomed new language in the draft decree on ecumenism that recognized non-Catholic Christians received baptism and the other sacraments "in their own churches and ecclesial communities." It was the first time, he noted, the council had assigned any significance to separated churches as well as separated brethren. "The new text now says unmistakably and clearly, although in passing, that these Christians exist not merely as individuals but in Christian communities which are given proper Christian status and ecclesial character." Ratzinger goes on to link decentralization and ecumenism, arguing that as Catholicism rediscovers allowable diversity in the forms taken by its local churches, the various separated churches will be more disposed to find a home within this communion.

On a practical level, Ratzinger the prefect has done very little to advance ecumenism and a fair bit to retard it. In 1998, just as the Anglican and Roman Catholic churches were on the verge of signing a major theological agreement, Ratzinger issued a document claiming that the Catholic church's refusal to accept the ordinations of Anglican priests as valid was in fact an infallible teaching. At the very least, this was a remarkable case of poor timing. He forced a year's delay in the signing of a breakthrough agreement between Lutherans and Catholics on the doctrine of justification, though in the end his efforts saved the agreement. More importantly, Ratzinger the prefect now regards ecumenical reunion as a far-distant, almost eschatological aim, and certainly he no longer regards the goal of reunion as providing a basis for decentralization in the church.

Though strictly speaking "ecumenism" refers only to relations with other Christian churches ("interreligious dialogue" being the preferred term for relations with Islam, Buddhism, and so on), Ratzinger the prefect has been a fierce opponent of movement toward Catholic détente with other religions. In 1986, for example, John Paul II convened a summit of leaders of a number of the world's faith traditions in Assisi, Italy; although they did not "pray together," they "prayed at the same time," and by papal standards this was a remarkable gesture of good will. Ratzinger actually gave a newspaper interview in which he said flatly, "This cannot be the model!" It was one of the very few occasions in which Ratzinger openly and publicly criticized one of John Paul's decisions.

Before and After: A Case in Point

The evolution in Ratzinger from cautious reformer to sharp conservative can be examined close up through the lens of his views on the reception of the Eucharist by divorced and civilly remarried Catholics. The discipline of the church has traditionally been that Catholics who divorce and remarry under civil law are ineligible to receive the Sacraments until the church issues an annulment, a formal declaration that the first marriage never existed. Many Catholics struggle with the annulment process, sometimes because their former partners or church authorities refuse to cooperate and sometimes because the necessary evidence of "impediment" to marriage is difficult to obtain. Increasingly, too, some Catholics find the very idea of an annulment offensive. Rather than the fiction of finding some technical reason to claim they were never married, they prefer what they see as a more honest admission that a valid marriage has broken down.

For these reasons, many divorced and civilly remarried Catholics make a judgment in conscience that they have done all they can to make things right and, even in the absence of an annulment, come forward to receive the Eucharist. A few pastors refuse them; many quietly encourage the practice. Many church leaders have suggested that this quiet flexibility should be expanded, noting, for example, that in Eastern churches the Sacraments are understood not as rewards for good behavior but as medicine for the soul. Vatican authorities, however, have insisted that the traditional rules be upheld.

In a 1972 essay on the question, Ratzinger argued for the more flexible approach based on his reading of the church fathers, especially St. Basil, the fourth-century bishop of Caesarea:

> The demand that a second marriage must prove itself over a longer period as the source of genuine moral values, and that it must be lived in

the spirit of faith, corresponds factually to that type of indulgence that can be found in Basil's teaching. There it is stated that after a longer penance, communion can be given to a *digamus* (someone living in a second marriage), without the suspension of the second marriage; this in confidence of God's mercy who does not leave penance without an answer. Whenever in a second marriage moral obligations have arisen toward the children, toward the family and toward the woman, and no similar obligations from the first marriage exist; whenever also the giving up of the second marriage is not permissible on moral grounds, and continence does not appear as a real possibility (*magnorum est,* says Gregory II—it is beyond the ordinary strength of the parties); it seems that the granting of full communion, after a time of probation, is nothing less than just, and is fully in harmony with our ecclesiastical traditions. The concession of communion in such a case cannot depend on an act that would be either morally or factually impossible.

Ratzinger situates this conclusion in the context of church tradition:

The anathema (of the Council of Trent) against a teaching that claims that foundational structures in the church are erroneous or that they are only reformable customs remains binding with its full strength. Marriage is a sacrament; it consists of an unbreakable structure, created by a firm decision. But this should not exclude the grant of ecclesial communion to those persons who acknowledge this teaching as a principle of life but find themselves in an emergency situation of a specific kind, in which they have a particular need to be in communion with the body of the Lord.

As doctrincal prefect, Ratzinger was compelled to revisit this issue in the mid-1990s when a number of German bishops, including his former *Communio* colleagues Karl Lehmann and Walter Kaspar, called for greater flexibility in admitting remarried persons to the Sacraments, along the lines suggested in Ratzinger's essay. In response, on September 14, 1994, the Congregation for the Doctrine of the Faith issued its *Letter to the bishops of the Catholic church concerning the reception of Holy Communion by the divorced and remarried members of the faithful.*

The document amounted to a strong reassertion of the traditional discipline, rejecting many of the arguments Ratzinger himself had advanced in 1972. "Authentic understanding and genuine mercy are never separated from the truth," the document said. Civilly remarried persons "find themselves in a situation that objectively contravenes God's law. Consequently, they cannot receive Holy Communion as long as this situation persists." Moreover, the document argues, to admit these persons to the Sacraments would lead the faithful "into error and confusion regarding the church's teaching about the indissolubility of marriage." Marriage, the document insists, is a public reality that concerns more than just the partners involved, and no judgment in conscience can "prescind from the church's mediation." To do so would be, in effect, to deny that marriage is a sacrament.

"Communion with Christ the Head can never be separated from communion with his members, that is, with his church," the document concludes. For that reason, "in absolute fidelity to the will of Christ," civilly remarried persons must be excluded from the Sacraments. "It will be necessary for pastors and the community of the faithful to suffer and to love in solidarity with the persons concerned so that they may recognize in their burden the sweet yoke and the light burden of Jesus."

The letter raises a host of complicated theological issues that are still very much under discussion within the church. What it illustrates beyond question, however, is the difference between Ratzinger the conciliar theologian and Ratzinger the doctrinal prefect.

The Consistent Thread: Church and Culture

Beneath the shifts on specific issues, there is a bedrock conviction that has remained constant in Ratzinger from the council to the present: a pessimistic view about the relationship between church and culture. The key that unlocks how Ratzinger could change so dramatically since the council is the realization that events in the late 1960s and afterward increasingly drove Ratzinger's doubts about the world to the forefront of his thinking. This basic Augustinian outlook is mediated for Ratzinger through the impact of Luther on German theology, with his heavy emphasis on the fallen state of the world.

When *The Ratzinger Report* appeared in 1984, it was Ratzinger's views on culture that immediately galvanized controversy. He said that Western culture is hostile to the faith in critically important ways. He even called it "hellish" to the extent that it promotes a vision of life based on pleasure. Because the popular understanding of Vatican II emphasized a détente between the church and the world, it was leading Catholicism seriously astray. As he put it,

> It is time to find again the courage of nonconformism, the capacity to oppose many of the trends of the surrounding culture, renouncing a certain euphoric post-conciliar solidarity. . . . I am convinced that the damage we have incurred in these twenty years is due, not to the "true" council, but to the unleashing *within* the Church of latent polemical and centrifugal forces; and *outside* the Church it is due to the confrontation with a cultural revolution in the West: the success of the

upper middle class, the new "tertiary bourgeoisie," with its liberal-radical ideology of individualistic, rationalistic and hedonistic stamp.

Too many theologians, Ratzinger said, have learned to take their starting point not from the church and her doctrines, but from the "signs of the times" in the world: "It becomes difficult, if not altogether impossible, to present Catholic morality as reasonable. It is too distant from what is considered to be obvious, as normal by the majority of persons, conditioned by the dominant culture with which not a few 'Catholic' moralists have aligned themselves as influential supporters." In a 1996 interview, Ratzinger returned to the same theme: "We ought to have the courage to rise up against what is regarded as 'normal' for a person at the end of the twentieth century and to rediscover faith in its simplicity," he said.

While his analysis may be a bit more severe today, these basic beliefs about the incompatibility between church and culture were well in place by the time Vatican II concluded. We see them presented most dramatically in his reactions to the council's last major accomplishment, passage of *Gaudium et spes*, the "Pastoral Constitution on the Church in the Modern World."

Although *Gaudium et spes* went through the same extensive process of comment and editorial revision as all the council documents did, it reflects a distinctively French spirit. The document was in many respects the brainchild of Cardinal Leon Suenens of Belgium, and bears strong traces of the thinking of Jean Daniélou and Yves Congar. Indirectly it is evocative of Teilhard de Chardin, the French Jesuit philosopher and paleontologist who argued that evolution was the unfolding of God's transcendence over time. The "Frenchness" of the document came through above all in its optimistic tone and its readiness to read the "signs of the times" for hints of God's design. *Gaudium et spes* was also the only council document to be composed and distributed in a vernacular language—French—and then translated into Latin.

The text's predominantly French flavor left Ratzinger cold. Indeed, when Frings spoke on *Gaudium et spes*, he was surprisingly negative, articulating many of the concerns that also troubled Ratzinger. He argued that the meaning of the image of the church as the "People of God" in the document was ambiguous (almost certainly picking that up from Ratzinger's doctoral work on "People of God" in Augustine). Frings also insisted that what *Gaudium et spes* meant by "the world" was inexact. He said the "whole scope" of the document was at fault, and that the problems could not be fixed with a word or a sentence. That position did not prevail, but it is a reliable indicator of where Ratzinger stood.

Ratzinger's own views on *Gaudium et spes* are presented in detail in his article for the *Commentary on the Documents of Vatican II*. It is the one place where the Ratzinger of the council seems a familiar figure, a thinker in basic continuity with the later direction of his career. No single text reveals better the core theological convictions that have stayed with Ratzinger.

On the document's use of "People of God" as a metaphor for the church, for example, Ratzinger writes:

> This way of speaking of the church involves no small danger of sinking once more into a purely sociological and even ideological view of the church through ignoring the essential insights of the Constitution on the Liturgy and the Constitution on the Church and by over-simplifying, externalizing and making a catchword of a term which can only keep its meaning if it is used in a genuinely theological context.

Ratzinger said that it seemed to many people, "especially theologians from German-speaking countries, that there was not a radical enough rejection of a doctrine of man divided into philosophy and theology." This too reflects Ratzinger's earlier preference for Augustine over Aquinas. Because the human intellect is incapable of grasping truth without divine illumination, then "philosophy," in the sense of a human effort to understand nature without reference to faith, is futile.

Ratzinger identified himself with those critics of *Gaudium et spes* who argued that the document brought into question the very purpose of revelation. "The text as it stood itself prompted the question why exactly the reasonable and perfectly free human being described in the first articles was suddenly burdened with the story of Christ. The latter might well appear to be a rather unintelligible addition to a picture that was already quite clear in itself," he wrote. Ratzinger disassociated himself from the document's language on the human being as the image of God, arguing that strictly speaking the human person is the image of God only through Christ and thus it refers more to a future promise than an essential endowment.

Ratzinger disliked the "French" tone of *Gaudium et spes:*

> The basically optimistic atmosphere, which was given to the council by this affirmation of the present, must have combined in the authors of the draft with a view of the world rather akin to that of Teilhard de Chardin, though endeavors were made to keep specifically Teilhardian ideas out of the conciliar text. Finally, there was the fact that the strong stress, deriving from Luther, on the theme of sin, was alien to the mainly French authors of the schema, whose theological presuppositions were quite different. Their thought probably sprang from a theological attitude which was Thomistic in tendency and also influenced by the Greek fathers.

Ratzinger goes on to quote Teilhard's famous quip to his critics: "You are all hypnotized by evil," suggesting that it captures something of the spirit of *Gaudium et spes*. He also suggests that the christology in *Gaudium et spes* leans too heavily on the Incarnation and Easter, not enough on the Passion.

In the same commentary, Ratzinger accuses the document of falling "into downright Pelagian terminology." (Pelagius was an early Christian theologian, later declared heretic, who believed that one's salvation was not preordained or a matter of pure divine grace, but that it could be "earned" through good works and right living.) He also suggests that the text left itself open to serious misinterpretation. "One cannot escape the impression," Ratzinger wrote, that "the theologically quite justifiable will to optimism which dominates the whole text has been misinterpreted and has led to anodyne formulas which it need not necessarily have given rise to at all."

In Ratzinger's own 1966 commentary on the fourth session of the council, published as *Die letze Sitzungsperiode des Konzils,* Ratzinger is even more caustic about *Gaudium et spes*. Its authors, he wrote, had

> unfortunately dragged beyond the protecting walls of the theology faculty building just those affirmations which theology shares anyhow with any spiritual-ethical picture of man whatsoever. Whereas what is proper to theology, discourse about Christ and his work, was left behind in a conceptual deep-freeze, and so allowed to appear, in contrast with the understandable part, even more unintelligible and antiquated.

In a mid-1970s retrospective on Vatican II, Ratzinger objects to the tendency to assume that *Gaudium et spes* is the council's crowning achievement, and, hence, the basis for interpreting everything else it said. Instead, Ratzinger asks if it might not be more suitable to regard it as a provisional attempt to apply the vision of faith found in the three dogmatic constitutions on liturgy, the church, and divine revelation to a specific historical situation. For anyone looking for a clue as to what kind of prelate Joseph Ratzinger would be, here it was.[15]

What Happened?

Ratzinger today argues that he is faithful to the letter of the sixteen documents of Vatican II, while rejecting the liberalizing spirit many claim to have derived from them, but there is more to it than that. Documents as long, complex, and so obviously the product of compromise as those of Vatican II open themselves to many different readings. It won't do, then, simply to assert that one is "faithful to the documents"; there is also the question of

Ratzinger's outlook, his instincts, and how they help shape what the documents mean to him.

At the close of Vatican II, Ratzinger seemed to hold two instincts about the council in tension within himself: (1) a strong sense of the need for structural reform in the church, leading to greater tolerance for diversity and different schools of thought; and (2) a trepidation that the council's overly optimistic embrace of "the world" left it somewhat blind to the reality of sin. In the years after the council, the pessimistic undertone of Ratzinger's comments on *Gaudium et spes* became the leitmotif for his understanding of the council. He came to read *Lumen gentium* not as a charter for progressive reform, as he had at the time it was adopted, but rather as a stabilizing antidote to the ecclesial "avalanche" unleashed by *Gaudium et spes*. So, the question is, what happened? Certainly no one can look inside Ratzinger's soul and read the answer, but it is fair to suggest that at least four factors played a part.

The 1968 Uprisings

The year 1968 was a tumultuous one. In the United States, students occupied buildings at Columbia University while protestors and police slugged it out in the streets of Chicago; in Prague the brief flowering of resistance to the Communists ended in the rattling of tanks through the city streets; and in Western Europe a wave of leftist-inspired student uprisings swept across the continent.

As all this chaos was unfolding, Ratzinger was teaching at Tübingen. The 1967 celebration of the 150th anniversary of the creation of the Catholic theological faculty at Tübingen was a high-water mark of sorts for Ratzinger in the postconciliar period. He says that almost immediately afterward, Marxism became the dominant intellectual system at Tübingen and made the adherents of other points of view feel like "petty bourgeois." What really shocked Ratzinger, however, was that the theology faculties of Tübingen became the "real ideological center" of the movement toward Marxism. Ratzinger wrote in 1997,

> The blasphemous manner in which the cross now came to be despised as a sign of sadomasochism, the hypocrisy with which some still passed themselves off as believers when this was useful, in order not to jeopardize the instruments that were to serve their own private ends: All of this could and should not be made to look harmless or regarded as just another academic quarrel.

In *Salt of the Earth,* Ratzinger added to his impressions of that time. "There was an instrumentalization by ideologies that were tyrannical, brutal, and cruel. That experience made it clear to me that the abuse of the faith had to be resisted precisely if one wanted to uphold the will of the council," he said.

One event in particular stuck with him as symbolic of the excesses of the period. The Protestant Students Union distributed a flyer on campus that asked the provocative question: "So what is Jesus' cross but the expression of a sado-masochistic glorification of pain?" The flyer also asserted that, "The New Testament is a document of inhumanity, a large-scale deception of the masses." Ratzinger said that he and another professor pleaded with the students to withdraw the flyer, but to no avail. His Protestant colleague had urged the students, "The cry of 'Cursed be Jesus' must never again be heard in our midst!" but they were unmoved.

During the turbulence at Tübingen, Ratzinger had an ugly personal encounter with either students or graduate staff, depending on how one reconstructs the events. This will be explored in more depth in the next chapter, but it undoubtedly added to his apprehension about the forces being unleashed in the culture. Ratzinger suggests that he learned from the experience that the kind of liberalizing he had supported within the church at Vatican II was leading to chaos because any sense of what is distinctively Christian about the church had been lost: all anyone seemed to care about from the council was *Gaudium et spes* and the "signs of the times." In order to be faithful to the whole council, Ratzinger felt he had to take a more conservative course. "Anyone who wanted to remain a progressive in this context had to give up his integrity," he said.

The chronology also supports this conclusion. In late 1968 Ratzinger was still progressive enough to sign the Nijmegen statement demanding sweeping reforms in the Holy Office, designed to allow far greater scope to free theological inquiry. In 1969, however, he moved from Tübingen to Regensburg—a new university had just been opened in that Bavarian city, which gave Ratzinger a chance to literally "start over"—and things began to look different.

In a 1971 lecture at the Bavarian Catholic Academy in Munich, Ratzinger took up the topic of "Why I Am Still in the Church." He asked his audience: "How is it possible that in the very moment in which the council seemed to have harvested the mature crop of the awakening of the previous decades, instead of these fulfilling riches it produced a frightening emptiness? How could it happen, that this disintegration resulted from such a promising beginning?" Ratzinger went on to argue that council enthusiasts had lost their perception of the "whole church" in their passion for reforms; they had lost sight of the state for their city, lost sight of the forest for the trees.

The year 1971 marked in a sense the "coming out" of the more conservative Joseph Ratzinger. In that same year, he began to serve as an advisor to the German bishops in their decade-long investigation of Hans Küng. By 1972, Ratzinger had enlisted with Balthasar, de Lubac, and the other defectors from the progressive circle of the council in launching *Communio,* their competitor journal to *Concilium.* From that point forward, Ratzinger's trajectory was set for the rest of his career.

Perceptions of Decline

There is little debate that the years since Vatican II have been hard ones for the Catholic church in many parts of the world, at least as measured by the traditional indicators: Mass attendance, vocations to the priesthood, vocations to the religious life, and adherence to church teaching. Many worried Catholics naturally link these declines to Vatican II, simply because most of them set in shortly after the council closed. This perception that Vatican II "hurt the church" has also played a role in Ratzinger's defection from the progressive camp.

In the twenty years from the close of Vatican II to the 1985 Synod of Bishops, the number of Roman Catholic priests in the world declined by 28,000, the number of nuns by 114,000. Trends in America generally reflect the global situation. In 1950 there were 28 million Catholics and 147,000 sisters, or one sister for every 190 Catholics. Projections for the year 2000 call for 62 million Catholics and approximately 80,000 sisters, one sister for every 750 Catholics. The peak year for women religious in the United States was 1965, with 179,954 sisters. As for priests, the American Catholic church had 59,000 in 1975 and a total of 48,000 as of 1999, to serve a Catholic population that, swelled by Hispanic immigration, has grown by twelve times. At this writing, the number of parishes without a resident priest is at 2,393, up from 549 in 1965, and as the average age of priests creeps steadily higher, that number is all but certain to grow, unless bishops decide to close or consolidate enough parishes to keep the ratio constant. There were hints in the late 1990s that the numbers of new recruits to the priesthood may be edging up, but nowhere near the level necessary to replenish those who will be retiring in the coming years.

The numbers are similar for members of the church's religious orders, such as the Jesuits, Dominicans, and Franciscans. A joke making the rounds in the 1980s has it that a Jesuit house somewhere in Europe had a sign over the door: "Will the last one to leave the order please remember to turn out the lights?" This kind of gallows humor does little to reassure someone like Ratzinger. In 1984, in fact, he argued that the decline has been most severe within the orders most in the avant-garde of church reform efforts: "It has often been the traditionally most 'educated,' the intellectually best equipped orders that have undergone the gravest crises," Ratzinger said.

Mass attendance, too, has taken a hit. Polls showed that a whopping seventy-eight percent of Catholics at least claimed to attend Mass weekly in 1958. By the late 1990s the number was hovering around thirty-five percent, and most pollsters believe that Mass attendance is overreported; the real number is probably about twenty-five percent. That is considerably higher than in Europe, where in some countries the rate dips into the single digits, and it is higher than the total for America's mainline Protestants, but it is still a dramatic falloff. In Latin America, weekly Mass attendance is said to go as low as ten percent in areas suffering a severe shortage of priests.

Ratzinger sarcastically suggested in 1996 that measured against the steep decline among Catholics who actually practice their faith, the priest shortage may not be as bad as it seems. "Looked at relative to the number of children and the number of those who are believing churchgoers, the number of priestly vocations has probably not decreased at all," he said.

Polls also suggest a lessened enthusiasm among many Catholics for their faith. In 1952 eighty-three percent of Catholics said religion was "very important" in their lives; by 1998 only fifty-four percent would say so. Likewise, polls show a solid majority of Catholics, at least in developed nations, reject papal teaching across a wide range of issues: birth control, married priests, women's ordination, and homosexuality.

All in all, it is enough to make any serious Catholic wince. Of course, there are many different ways to interpret this data. American sociologist and novelist Father Andrew Greeley argues that many of these declines set in, not after Vatican II, but after Paul VI's encyclical *Humanae vitae* in 1968, which reaffirmed the papal ban on birth control and bitterly disappointed many Catholics hoping for change. In fact, Greeley says the hemorrhaging would have been much worse if not for the optimism and new life generated from the council.

Others argue that the drop in priests and sisters has been offset by growth in lay responsibility for the church. There are currently 30,000 professional lay ministers in the American Catholic church, with another 20,000 in training, performing tasks that were exclusively clerical just a generation ago, from teaching catechism to signing checks. Moreover, there are millions of laypeople helping to run the church without drawing a paycheck. They are eucharistic ministers, or members of parish councils, or volunteer catechists. All this new life is exactly what the council intended, many would argue, and it, rather than the painful losses in religious vocations, is where our focus ought to be.

Anyone whose job it is to worry about the institutional health of Catholicism might be irresponsible not to perceive a crisis these days; but whether the crisis lies in the way Vatican II was received by the church, as

Ratzinger now seems to think, or whether the real problem lies in the continuing gap between Vatican II's promise and the day-to-day ecclesial reality, is another matter.

The Pathology of Faith

An obvious point often overlooked in considering Ratzinger is the nature of his job. In the same way that doctors see health risks everywhere, lawyers see possible torts, and police officers see criminal activity, Ratzinger senses heresy lurking around every corner in part because it is what he is paid to do. Someone once expressed this by saying that the function of the Holy Office is to deal with the "pathology of faith," that is, the Catholic faith at its most distorted. Ratzinger will hear about the vast majority of Catholic parishes in the world only if there is a problem, will read the publications of most Catholic theologians only to probe their weakest or most confused points, will examine the files of most priests only when they have done or said something dubious. When this is all you see, you might justifiably conclude that this is all there is. As the saying goes, if all you have is a hammer, sooner or later everything looks like a nail.

One must add that the vast majority of Ratzinger's mail is from aggrieved Catholics with a complaint. Simply by process of self-selection, those Catholics most likely to write to the Vatican are conservative, so Ratzinger gets a picture of local churches that tilts to the right. Nor do we have to speculate that right-wing Catholics try to influence Ratzinger through the mail. An unusually public and well-documented example occurred in Australia in 1999, sparked by a controversy over the so-called Third Rite of confession, in which the priest offers absolution to a group rather than one-on-one. Though the rite is supposed to be reserved for cases of "grave necessity," it has come into widespread use in Australia since Vatican II. Many people felt it better captured the social dimension of sin and forgiveness. On a practical level, many pastors reported that people liked it and showed up for church to experience it, especially during Advent and Lent, when Catholics are traditionally urged to make a confession.

The Third Rite did not sit well, however, with a group called the Australian Catholics Advocacy Centre, led by a lawyer from Sydney named Paul Brazier. Many Australians claim that Brazier represents the sentiments of only a minuscule percentage of the total Catholic population of the country. However, he was able to mobilize a small group of observers to fan out into parishes during Lent in 1999 and fill out detailed five-page "witness observation forms" about exactly what was going on during penance services. If they collected evidence of any abuses, the witnesses would then swear out formal legal affidavits. Brazier collected all this evidence, compiled it into dossiers, and mailed it to Rome. Though he will not say exactly where it went, it seems clear that Ratzinger got copies, as did Cardinal Jorge Medina Estévez, who runs the Congregation for the Sacraments.

The effort paid off when just a few weeks after the dossiers started arriving on Roman desks, the Vatican issued a document reiterating the ban on the Third Rite and warning of "just penalties" for priests who celebrate it. In Australia, this was treated as a major coup for Brazier and his Advocacy Centre. Even the cardinal of Sydney, Edward Clancy, had to admit that it played out as a "victory" for Brazier. Clancy complained that Rome had listened to a handful of right-wing malcontents rather than the country's own bishops—an obvious sore point for prelates everywhere.[16]

The point is that this is the kind of mail Ratzinger gets every day. One begins to understand how Ratzinger can be so convinced that left-wing dissent is on the loose throughout the Catholic world. This factor does not account for Ratzinger's drift to the right before he came to Rome, but it does help explain why those instincts have hardened into firm convictions during his twenty years in power.

Power

As Ratzinger took on an increasingly conservative stance, he was rewarded with greater access to power and privilege, culminating in his 1997 appointment as archbishop of Munich. Ratzinger's altered stance was certainly in line with where the political winds in the German bishops' conference were blowing during the 1970s, as the staunchly conservative cardinal Joseph Höffner of Cologne eclipsed the moderate but aging cardinal Julius Döpfner of Munich. It is also indisputable that after Ratzinger's appointment to Rome, his revised positions on collegiality, on the theological status of bishops' conferences, on the role of the doctrinal congregation, and on development in the tradition all bolstered his career.

Every power structure has an ideology, and those who are charged with maintaining the system are selected because their experiences and outlook conform to that ideology. It is not that Ratzinger consciously modified his views in order to gain power or increase it. There is no indication that in 1970, for example, he could foresee that within eight years he would be a cardinal of the church. But no one is fully conscious of all the motives and forces that shape his decisions, and certainly Ratzinger—like anyone inside the Catholic hierarchy—is not innocent of the attitudes that are more likely to advance one's career. This is not to accuse him of insincerity, but rather to observe that the system offered him incentives to move farther and faster down the path he chose.

One more word about Ratzinger and Vatican II. We have seen how by the end of the council, Ratzinger's discomfort with some of its underlying premises was growing, a trend apparent above all in his commentary on *Gaudium et spes*. No one in 1965 could have forseen where that discomfort would take him. But in *The Rhine Flows into the Tiber*, Father Ralph M. Wiltgen's superb history of Vatican II, the book's penultimate page contains a line that comes close to foreshadowing later events. Wiltgen writes:

> Father Ratzinger, the personal theologian of Cardinal Frings and former student of Father Rahner, had seemed to give an almost unquestioning support to the views of his former teacher during the council. But as it was drawing to a close, he admitted that he disagreed on various points, and said he would begin to assert himself more after the council was over.[17]

More prescient words have rarely been written.

3

All Roads Lead to Rome

As Vatican II closed on December 8, 1965, two Roman artists were putting the finishing touches on a work of *aggiornamento* of their own. Ettore De Concilis and Rosso Falciano had been commissioned to design the interior of a new Roman church dedicated to St. Francis of Assisi. In the spirit of the "signs of the times," the duo adorned the new church with images of John XXIII, Fidel Castro, Soviet premier Alexey Kosygin, Mao Tsetung, Bertrand Russell, Giorgio La Pira, Italian Communist party leader Palmiro Togliatti, Sophia Loren, and Jacqueline Kennedy. It was a thoroughly—indeed, it must be said in hindsight, excessively—ecumenical Communion of Saints. Such was the spirit of the age.

This kind of high 1960s scene may sound quaint now, like the soundtrack of *Hair*, evoking distant memories of a silly, naive, yet exuberant moment in cultural history. But for many church leaders, the syncretism on display inside that new Roman church was more alarming than exhilarating. It seemed possible to many in the years after the council that the distinctiveness of Catholicism was threatening to evaporate, that the avant garde in the church was doing little more than sprinkling holy water on mid-1960s radicalism. Through Pope John's open window, it seemed to some, the baby was being tossed out with the bathwater.

In retrospect, it is easy to see how figures such as Joseph Ratzinger might have drawn that conclusion. In theological circles, the late 1960s was the era of the "death of God" theology, championed by figures such as Paul van Buren, who argued that a transcendent God did not make sense in modern culture. Christianity should re-present itself, van Buren concluded, as an ethical code based on the historical man, Jesus of Nazareth, and not on a supernatural "Christ." It was perhaps never a majority view among serious theologians, but one would not know that from all the newspaper and television coverage such views got. Harvard theologian Harvey Cox, in 1965's *The Secular City,* argued to great critical applause that organized religion was heading for extinction. Modern culture itself, Cox said, had taken over its function as the bearer of humanity's deepest hopes and dreams.

In the Catholic church, the spirit of *aggiornamento* seemed to endorse the idea that God is at least as likely to be found "out there" in politics, the arts, and modern life as "in here," in the church. A church that had previously styled itself as a fortress suddenly became a sieve; everything from the culture seemed to get through. British theologian Adrian Hastings summed up the mood in 1991 when he wrote of Ratzinger, "His road back to traditionalism could appear the only way to escape a theological disintegration which threatened not just Vatican I, but Chalcedon and Nicaea as well."

The seriousness of the threat became vividly clear in those fevered days of the summer of 1968, when blood flowed in European streets and on campuses. Ratzinger's previously tidy and self-contained academic universe in Tübingen was not spared the tumult of the times, and in these days he came face-to-face with what he could later describe only as "terror."

Peals of dissent reverberated through the church like thunder after Paul VI's encyclical *Humanae vitae* was issued on July 25, 1968. The timing of *Humanae vitae* ensured that the general antiestablishment feeling sweeping across the West would bring the Catholic church squarely in its sights. To millions of Catholics who saw the ban on birth control as a residue of medieval antisexual prejudice, Paul's refusal to change the teaching seemed to legitimize a radical skepticism about every claim to truth or authority made by church authorities.

Ratzinger left Vatican II teetering between optimism about a revitalization of the church's inner life and pessimism about the church's relationship with the world, and it seems clear which way the cultural winds were nudging him. Rooted in an Augustinian/Bonaventuran outlook, Ratzinger has always stressed the critical distance that must separate the church from the culture. In the 1950s, when ghetto Catholicism seemed safely insulated from the more dangerous currents of modern life, this was chiefly an academic conviction. But during the late 1960s, amid all the chaos inside and outside the church, as Ratzinger watched the "opening to the world" emerge as seemingly the only thing Catholics understood of the council, his internal alarms became louder and more insistent, and his tone increasingly pessimistic.

In 1964, Ratzinger had agreed to serve on the board of a new theological journal called *Concilium,* launched as a forum for continuing theological reflection in the line of those who had led the reform forces at Vatican II. In 1972, however, Ratzinger, Henri de Lubac, Hans Urs von Balthasar, Walter Kasper, and Karl Lehmann formalized their disillusionment by launching *Communio,* a rival journal. Some of these theologians are today viewed as the intellectual architects of the Catholic "restoration," the effort to restore elements of church life and teaching they felt had been squandered in the immediate postconciliar rush to modernity. *Communio* became the chief forum for Ratzinger to share his theological ideas with the world. (Lehmann and Kasper, in a curious progression, seemed to drift back toward the center as bishops of German dioceses; in 1994, both joined in a call to allow remarried divorcees to return to the Sacraments, a plea which was rejected by Ratzinger.)

It is a telling indicator of the way the wind has blown in the church under John Paul II that the members of the *Communio* circle have been rewarded: Ratzinger is prefect of the doctrinal congregation, Lehmann became a bishop in 1983 and Kasper in 1989, and De Lubac and Balthasar were both made cardinals. Balthasar died a few days before he was to receive the red hat. The *Concilium* stalwarts—Rahner, Schillebeeckx, Küng, Metz—have received no similar honors.

This was all very different from the Joseph Ratzinger who wrote a 1962 study calling on theologians to have the "courage to suffer" for speaking out about defects they saw in the church.

> The servility of the sycophants (branded by the genuine prophets of the Old Testament as "false prophets"), of those who shy from and shun every collision, who prize above all their calm complacency, is not true obedience. . . . What the church needs today as always are not adulators to extol the status quo, but men whose humility and obedience are not less than their passion for the truth: men who face every misunderstanding and attack as they bear witness; men who, in a word, love the church more than ease and the unruffled course of their personal destiny.

In the same piece, Ratzinger denounced the church for abandoning the century to disbelief through the creation of too many norms and also for "entrenching herself behind exterior safeguards instead of relying on the truth, which is inherent in liberty and shuns such defenses."[1]

The shift in Ratzinger's temperament was accompanied during these years by a shift in geography. In the summer of 1966, he had accepted an appointment to the Catholic theology faculty at the University of Tübingen, the "big leagues" of the German theology scene and among the leading centers for Christian theology worldwide. After 1968, however, Ratzinger wearied of fighting what he considered a lonely battle against Marxism, and decided to help launch a new Bavarian university in Regensburg. It was at

Regensburg that Ratzinger began educating a generation of students who would go on to play leading restorationist roles in their own national churches; for instance, Jesuit Joseph Fessio in the United States, Father Vincent Twoomey in Ireland, and Dominican Christoph Schönborn in Austria, now the cardinal of Vienna. It is instructive to compare these later graduate students of Ratzinger with his earlier disciples, some of whom have gone on to become critics of their former mentor. That divergence more than anything else underscores the chasm between the conciliar and the postconciliar Ratzinger.

It was during these critical years, the late 1960s through 1977, that Ratzinger reached the peak of his career as a theologian. His most important work therefore took shape in the context of growing alarm about the condition of the church. Much of it now seems defensive rather than creative, and it is one reason most of his colleagues believe Ratzinger will be of greater interest 100 years from now to church historians than to theologians. He will be studied for insight into his times, not for his ideas.

The end of Ratzinger's career as a full-time theologian and professor can be dated to 1976, when news came that Cardinal Döpfner of Munich had died. Ratzinger's road to Rome did not take long to complete; ordained Döpfner's successor in March 1977, Ratzinger was a cardinal by June, and by the end of the next year had participated in two papal conclaves. In Munich, he used his new authority to discipline two old colleagues, whom he felt were pulling the church into dangerous waters: Johann Baptist Metz and Hans Küng. Within four years, he was John Paul II's *eminence gris* as the chief doctrinal authority of the Catholic church.

Ratzinger the Theologian

In more than forty years of academic life, Ratzinger has authored or coauthored forty books in addition to countless journal articles, contributions to *Festschriften,* and prefaces to the works of fellow scholars. His peak period of 1965 to 1977 is bracketed by two major books: the first his most successful and the second the one he considers his best. *Einführung in das Christentum* (Introduction to Christianity) was published in Munich in 1968; Seabury brought out an English edition in 1979. The book, styled as a meditation on the Apostles' Creed, emerged out of a series of lectures in Tübingen in 1967 and thus predates the crisis of 1968, though it hints at some of the storm clouds then gathering.[2]

By the standards of academic theology, *Introduction to Christianity* was a runaway success, making it by far Ratzinger's best-known title. It is his only serious contender alongside works such as Hans Küng's *On Being a*

Christian or Bernard Häring's *The Law of Christ* as a piece of theological writing that exerted a significant influence on Catholicism in its own time. In the early 1970s, it was a must-read in seminaries and theological institutes around the world. Ratzinger styled the book as an overview of Christianity that would be accessible outside the bounds of theological specialists, though it is nevertheless a demanding read. It has been issued in editions in French, Dutch, Croatian, Portuguese, Japanese, Slovenian, Hungarian, Korean, English, Spanish, Russian, Italian, Czech, Arabic, and Polish, and it still generates healthy sales, no doubt helped by the fact that its author has gone on to such wide fame.

Reading the *Introduction* now, it seems clear that Ratzinger's doubts about the direction of the church after the council, his sense that it was ludicrous and self-destructive to stress *aggiornamento* in a world that was itself falling apart, were coming into focus as he wrote. Yet as a sort of first-fruit of the council, the book did not strike a defensive note with its audience. Instead, it was celebrated as daring, liberating, a model of the kind of searing honesty in Catholic intellectual life that Vatican II made possible. Ratzinger's book was no legalistic manual stuffed with rules and regulations; this was a meditation on faith that reached into the depths of human experience, that dared to walk naked before doubt and disbelief, in order to discover the truth of what it means to be a modern Christian. It marked, in short, a transformation in how theologians presented the Catholic faith.

The work that closes this period of Ratzinger's life, *Eschatologie: Tod und ewiges Leben* (Eschatology: Death and eternal life), 1977, is a volume in a series called *Kleine Katholische Dogmatik* brought out by a colleague of Ratzinger's in Regensburg. Ratzinger called this "my most thorough work, and the one I labored over the most strenuously." It was translated into English in 1988 by Michael Waldstein, an admirer and acquaintance of Ratzinger who today runs a theological institute in Austria under Schönborn's sponsorship. Waldstein, too, rates the volume on eschatology as Ratzinger's most important theological achievement.

In between these two books, Ratzinger published a number of works on the church. This body of writing is of interest not only because it reflects the drift of Ratzinger's thinking at the time, but because it is in his ecclesiology that we see the most direct connection between Ratzinger the theologian and Ratzinger the prefect.

Introduction to Christianity

The book is styled as an exposition of the Apostles' Creed. It opens with what is certainly Ratzinger's most memorable literary flourish, his version of an old German folktale called *Hans im Glück* (rendered in English as "Lucky Jack"). It is a parable about a young man who finds a large lump of gold. As he is walking along, he decides the lump is too heavy to carry, and so he first exchanges it for a horse, then the horse for a cow, then the cow for a goose, and finally the goose for a whetstone. Hans then tosses the whetstone into a nearby stream, on the premise that he is not giving up anything of real value and by tossing it away he gains complete freedom.

"How long his intoxication lasted," Ratzinger wrote, "how somber the moment of awakening from the illusion of his supposed liberation, is left by the story, as is well known, to the imagination of the reader." Ratzinger then draws the conclusion: "Has our theology in the last few years not taken in many ways a similar path?" Ratzinger uses the story to declare his purpose in the book: To meet the challenge of Christian belief head on, without watering it down or making it seem more "reasonable."

A rumor long surrounded this famous opening page, to wit, that the *Hans im Glück* of Ratzinger's story was actually Hans Küng. Ratzinger, however, denied this rumor in 1996: "It has absolutely nothing to do with Hans Küng, I have to say that quite decidedly. An attack on him was the furthest thing from my mind." Ratzinger also said that the story was written before the events of 1968, though in retrospect, "it was perfectly suited to describe the situation at the time."

Over the next few pages Ratzinger reflects on an image from the Danish philosopher Søren Kierkegaard, who once described the situation facing the Christian preacher as akin to someone dressed up as a circus clown trying to tell a village about a fire. The more the clown protests that the fire is getting closer, the more the villagers roar with laughter, taking it all as part of the act. When they finally see for themselves that the clown was serious, it is too late: the fire consumes them all.

The Christian situation today is actually far more problematic than even Kierkegaard anticipated, Ratzinger says, because for the Christian it is not a simple matter of stepping out of this clown costume and putting on modern dress. Indeed, this is precisely what Rudolf Bultmann's program of demythologization tried to do—to strip Christianity of its "mythical" elements and focus on its existential call to authenticity. In another way, Ratzinger says, it is what *aggiornamento* tries to do, to make Christianity more palatable by taking off its edge and making it more "modern." Yet both these "convulsive efforts" fail, Ratzinger says, because Christianity at its heart is a "scandal," and it cannot be resolved by hiding its paradoxes or dissolving its doctrine into the mentality of the broader culture.

Ratzinger knows people are not led to God primarily through intellectual curiosity but through a burning need in their hearts. Loneliness and emotional impoverishment lead people to hunger for something more, and even happiness points beyond itself by posing the question of its source. The incompleteness of every human relationship, Ratzinger says, leads humanity to seek an eternal and absolute "Thou." Ratzinger then deals in cursory fashion with the notion of the created world leading humanity to God; the Thomistic notion of nature as a kind of revelation is largely alien to him.

Ratzinger offers a powerful meditation on doubt and belief, suggesting that doubt is not simply the burden of the believer. The nonbeliever is haunted by the question: But what if it is true? The hunger of modern Western people for the absolute cannot be easily satisfied, because our modes of thought make truth elusive. Under the impact of logical positivism and Marxism, Ratzinger says, the culture has reduced truth to the level of fact, and especially humanity's capacity to reshape social and political existence. Ratzinger asserts that this modern philosophical dynamic can be seen as a movement from the influence of Gianbattista Vico, who saw truth as the facts of the present, to Karl Marx, for whom truth is transformation of the facts of the future. To keep up with the times, Marxist-inspired theologians thus present faith as a system of rhetoric that supports political action. In this category Ratzinger includes the "theology of hope" of Jürgen Moltmann and the "theology of the world" of Johann Baptist Metz, the first of many subtle jabs in the book directed at various theological currents.

Ratzinger says that "belief" in the Christian sense of the term has nothing to do with action-oriented epistemology. "The act of believing does not belong to the relationship 'know-make' which is typical of the intellectual context of 'makability' thinking." The fundamental thing for Christianity is not doing but being, and it is here that Ratzinger most clearly reveals his roots in Platonism. Indeed, Ratzinger says it was no accident that the Christian gospel first entered the world under the aegis of Greek philosophy, with its orientation toward eternal truth. He finds confirmation of this in the Acts of the Apostles and its sense of what the Germans call *Heilsgeschichte*, or "salvation history." It is the idea that God directs history toward his saving purpose. Ratzinger means that God planned for early Christianity to emerge in an intellectual milieu more interested in being than in making. "Only then did belief become understanding," Ratzinger says.

Polytheism, Ratzinger says, leads to the concept of "tribal gods" and hence posits the welfare of the state as the will of god; atheism, on the other hand, denies the existence of a moral absolute set above the collective. Monotheism, Ratzinger says, "precisely because it has itself no political aims, [is] a program of decisive political importance, and through the relativization to which it relegates all political communities in comparison with the unity of the God who embraces them all, it forms the only definitive protection against the power of the collective and at the same time implies the complete abolition of any idea of exclusiveness in humanity as a whole."

Ratzinger demands that the full impact of a profession of belief in Jesus Christ be clear: Christians are claiming that all history, the entire cos-

mos, culminates and finds redemption in the vicissitudes of one human being. It makes one wonder, Ratzinger says, "especially when we compare it
with the religiosity of Asia, whether it would not have been much simpler
to believe in the Mysterious Eternal, entrusting ourselves to it in longing
thought . . . than to give oneself up to the positivity of belief in one single
figure and to set the salvation of man and the world on the pin-point, so to
speak, of this one chance moment in history." Ratzinger, as prefect, returns
to this theme of Eastern religious belief being "less demanding" than
Christianity.

Ratzinger cites Adolf von Harnack and Rudolf Bultmann as the two
cornerstones of modern Christology. The former said that only the historical
Jesus matters, the humble preacher of love and compassion; for the latter,
only Christ matters, the revelation of God's call to authenticity. Ratzinger
says neither of these alternatives will do. Professing allegiance to a "historical Jesus" invites chaos. Historical hypotheses come and go with every
dawn, and that is no foundation upon which to build a life. But if we are to
confess the Christ, surely that confession must have some content. The life
of Jesus must hold some significance; otherwise how can we be sure "this is
the Christ"? Ratzinger's solution lies in accepting the creed. Here we find a
"life of Christ" that is more than exegesis and historical argumentation, it is
the faith of the community that first offered Christ to the world. It "had en-
dured for centuries and by its very nature had no other aim but that of understanding—understanding who and what this Jesus really was." Ratzinger remarks that too many modern Christians have been enchanted by the
"cheerful romanticism of progress." Instead, Ratzinger says, looking at the
crucified one tells us what sort of "openness" to the world Christians
should expect and embrace—the openness of sacrifice.

Ratzinger seems to conclude that efforts at reform are usually a waste
of time. "Those who really believe do not attribute too much importance to
the reorganization of church structures. They live on what the church is."
For a man who just three years before helped Cardinal Frings demand reform in the Holy Office, this is a puzzling statement. It is likewise difficult
to reconcile this line with Ratzinger's deep admiration for Romano
Guardini, for example, and his passion for liturgical reform. Guardini was
not a man who "lived on what the church is" in any narrow, things-the-
way-they-are sense.

Ratzinger may mean, however, that the Christian vision must penetrate beneath questions of structures and systems of authority, to grasp the
Spirit who dwells deep in the church's bosom. From this point of view, it
would not be that questions of reform lack validity, but they do not concern
the church in its essence. Ratzinger hints at this when he says, "Only the one
who has experienced how, regardless of changes in her ministries and forms,

the church raises persons up, and gives them a home and a hope, a home that is hope—the path to eternal life—only such a one who has experienced this knows what the church is, both in days gone by and now."

Yet Ratzinger in other passages seems hostile to the very idea of reform. He asserts that much criticism of the church is "hidden pride" and "rancorous bitterness" and "thoughtless jargon." He says that this leads to a reduction of the church to a political entity, a society to "organize, reform, and govern." Yet just as quickly he can switch gears, calling the church "pneumatical and charismatic" rather than "hierarchical." He says the primacy of the bishop of Rome is not among the primary elements of the church, and likewise that an episcopal structure is not necessary; it is merely a means to an end. The central spiritual reality of the church, he says, must be "representation" of God, not the quest for power. Ratzinger knows how much the church has lost sight of this ideal over the years, quoting William of Auvergne: "Bride is she no more, but a monster of frightful ugliness and ferocity." God's holiness, Ratzinger says, is not "aristocratic," but rather it "mixes with the dirt of the world so as to overcome it."

This line of thought leads Ratzinger to one of the most remarkable passages in his entire corpus: "For many people today the church has become the main obstacle to belief. They can no longer see in it anything but the human struggle for power, the petty spectacle of those who, with their claim to administer official Christianity, seem to stand most in the way of the true spirit of Christianity."

In these lines, one senses the old Joseph Ratzinger grappling with the new, the worried defender of the faith circling warily around the dynamic reformer of the council. It was the latter Ratzinger who loomed largest in the pages of the *Einführung* for those who read it in the late 1960s. With his passion, his personalism, his determination to face reality not through the categories of neoscholastic thought but squarely as it presented itself, Ratzinger seemed to be opening doors for Catholic theology. The breakthrough, in other words, was not so much *what* Ratzinger said—which, though artfully expressed, was not revolutionary—but rather *how* he said it. At the same time, the new Ratzinger was clearly emerging, a man more concerned with shutting doors than opening them.

Ecclesiology

As Ratzinger became increasingly anxious about the postconciliar world, his thoughts gravitated to the church. He came to ponder what the church is and how believers ought to relate to it. This theme holds special importance for understanding Ratzinger's later attitudes and conduct.

In 1968, in an article in the Irish journal *Furrow,* Ratzinger took the liberals' side in the controversy over the new Dutch catechism. Ratzinger is not uncritical; he questions the catechism's presentation of christology, of redemption, and of the Eucharist. Yet he also praises the deep religious feeling it exudes. While acknowledging the Vatican's right to voice reservations, Ratzinger also condemns the secrecy in which the curial forces have operated: "At the same time we must deplore the fact that Rome inspired such strict secrecy on the cardinal's commission and the commission on theologians, thereby preventing not only the spread of reliable information but also the furtherance of constructive debate." Ratzinger's intervention is all the more ironic because, as prefect, he rejected the French catechism, widely regarded as just as radical as the Dutch text he defended in 1968. He also condemned *Christ among Us*, an acclaimed adult catechism that had come into use in the United States; and in a sense he helped render every national catechism irrelevant by imposing a new universal catechism in 1992.

Yet his defense of theological freedom was already in the late 1960s being mixed in Ratzinger's public statements with a call for more vigilance on the part of church authorities. In *Principles for Teaching Theology,* Ratzinger condemns church leaders for "having become dogs without a bark who out of cowardice in face of the liberal public stood by fecklessly as faith was bit by bit traded off for the mess of potage, of the recognition of modernity."[3]

In 1968 Ratzinger authored an article entitled "The Significance of the Fathers in the Elaboration of Belief." He asserts that the church fathers are the voice of a still-undivided church, that they represent the core of what Catholicism is: episcopal, sacramental, and liturgical, according to the norms of the first four ecumenical councils. Ratzinger knows the debates that raged among the Fathers, but in his mind these disputes were contained within the scope of core understandings. This conviction perhaps accounts for Ratzinger's ambivalence about the limits of open theological discussion in the late 1960s.

Ratzinger's ecclesiology took on an increasingly defensive tone. In 1970, Ratzinger and his friend Hans Meier put out a volume called *Democracy in the Church*. We will encounter Meier later in this chapter, as the Bavarian minister of education who colluded with Ratzinger in a decision to deny a university appointment to their old friend and colleague Johann Baptist Metz. In the book, Ratzinger seeks to challenge theologians who see the very idea of an institutional church as a kind of manipulation. He asserts that even in Karl Rahner, the idea of "democracy" in the church is really a buzzword for belief in this-worldly salvation, a notion that if the right program of reform is carried out, the kingdom can be built here and now—a notion foreign to traditional Catholic understanding. Ratzinger also strikes a note that will become more common in his later work, accusing advocates of democracy in the church of posing as populists but in reality refusing to accept the simple faith of the great mass of believers. "Those circles which talk especially loud about democratization of the church," Ratzinger wrote, "manifest the least respect for the faith shared by the community."

Ratzinger's most important ecclesiological work during this period was *Das neue Volk Gottes,* which appeared in 1969. In the Counter-Reformation era, he says, the emphasis was on the visible, external church; in the period after the First World War, Catholics needed a deeper spirituality and accented the invisible church. This latter stance, however, led to a "disdain" for external structures. Ratzinger quotes Augustine as a corrective: "Inasmuch as anyone loves Christ's church, to that degree he possesses the Holy Spirit." Ratzinger's synthesis is a "communion ecclesiology," arguing that the church is a mystical communion of local communities, not in the sense of a political federation, but rather a sacramental bond. It is both visible and spiritual, exterior and interior. The communion unites God and man, visible and invisible dimensions of the church, hierarchy and flock, local and universal churches. As prefect, Ratzinger would insist that fostering communion ecclesiology was the chief aim of Vatican II.

Like most big ideas, communion ecclesiology is interpreted in different ways. For progressives, calling the church a communion means it is not a monarchy or a corporation. Instead of orders being handed down from on high, decisions should reflect the sense of the community. For conservatives, calling the church a communion means it is not a democracy. Instead of determining policy by votes and pressure politics, the church operates on the basis of trust and submission to authority. Dissent has logic in a state formed by social contract, but not in a communion, where parties and factions are out of place. One measure of the shift in Ratzinger is that his earlier writings lean toward the first way of understanding the concept, his later work toward the second.

An important point for Ratzinger is that those horizontal bonds are "diachronic," meaning they include not just the members of the church alive today but all those who have ever been part of the communion of saints. It is in this sense that Ratzinger says that one cannot ascertain the *sensus fidelium,* or "sense of the faithful," merely by taking into view what a majority of Catholics thinks today. One must consider what the testimony of the church has been throughout the ages. A sacramental understanding of the church also puts a premium on the center, the papacy, as the "sign" of communion, Ratzinger writes. It is the papacy that both symbolizes and effects the bonds that tie Catholics together.

In *Das neue Volk Gottes* Ratzinger returns to his mentor St. Bonaventure, in part to warn against taking this exalted view of the papacy to an extreme. Bonaventure's own view of the role of the pope was forged in the controversies of the thirteenth century, when the mendicant orders had come under fierce attack from many "traditionalists." (Franciscans and Dominicans lived and worked not in monasteries or parishes but in the world, sustained by begging—hence "mendicant.") The Franciscans looked to a strong, assertive papacy to defend them. Bonaventure thus developed a view of the papacy that today can only seem alarmingly exalted. He argued that the pope is the "criterion" or "ideal" of humanity, that the pope has the same role in the New Testament economy of salvation as the Jewish high priest had in the Old, and that the pope acts as head of the body of Christ. Ratzinger dismisses this as overblown rhetoric, suggesting the need for a "spirit of moderation and the just mean."

Ratzinger further argues that "centralism" in the church is unnecessary. Over time, he says, the Petrine idea of a universal primacy became fused with the jurisdictional functions of the Roman patriarch, but this is unnecessary. The pope can exercise primacy without directly controlling the affairs of local churches. What the idea of primacy means is that the pope offers the definitive voice on what is of the faith—after listening to the universal church. Yet the pope must do more than project what the "average believer" holds to be the faith. We must not be governed by polls. Faith has objective criteria, and these the pope must respect. "In such cases, the pope may and must not hesitate to speak against statistics, and the power of opinion with its pretense of possessing exclusive validity."

Ratzinger affirms salvation outside the church. He suggests that one is a Christian not as an insurance policy for eternal life, but rather as a "representative" of the many. Yet at the same time Christianity is a missionary force, and Ratzinger says we cannot simply serve the world, we must strive to evangelize it as well. "There is only one legitimate form of the church's openness to the world, and so it must certainly always be. That form is twofold. It is: mission as the prolongation of the Word's procession, and the simple gesture of disinterested serving love in the actualizing of the divine love, a love which streams forth even when it remains without response."

Here Ratzinger comes to the question of the church's dialogue with the world, so emphasized in *Gaudium et spes*. Ratzinger says this dialogue cannot be Platonic, a matter of igniting sparks of insight that are already inside the human person. The Christian gospel is not, in that sense, "natural." It is wholly other, it approaches humanity from the outside, and it stirs opposition precisely because it is "unnatural." Hence there are sharp limits to dialogue. Ratzinger notes that unlike the Platonic corpus, the dialogue never became a genre in Christian literature. The Christian message is first and foremost a *kerygma,* a proclamation. It is an invitation to reception, not to dialogue. Dialogue follows belief. The church, it follows, must do more than engage the world in dialogue, it must proclaim the gospel to it. It is, in that sense, a one-sided conversation.

Eschatology

Traditionally Christian theology has organized the topics of eschatology, or the doctrine of the end of the world, into the so-called "final four": heaven, hell, judgment, and resurrection. Ratzinger integrates these topics in his own presentation and condemns modern theologians who avoid them, yet in *Eschatologie: Tod und ewiges Leben* he is after something broader. His aim is to restore a correct appreciation of eschatology to Christian life. He argues that under the impact of Marx, mistaken notions of the kingdom of God threaten the integrity of the Christian message.

One volume in a series called *Kleine Katholische Dogmatik* edited by a colleague, *Eschatologie: Tod und ewiges Leben* was written chiefly at Regensburg in the late 1970s; hence it represents the most mature form of Ratzinger's thought on the subject. Ratzinger agreed to write several volumes for the series, but the tract on eschatology was the only one he finished before his appointment as archbishop.

The leitmotif of the work is the need to separate eschatology from politics, to end the confusion of the kingdom of God with a social or political arrangement that might be achieved within this order of history. He writes that as a young professor, he had sought to detach Platonic ideas, especially that of the immortality of the soul, from eschatology. By stressing the superiority of the soul over the body to such a degree, Ratzinger says, Plato seemed too detached from the world, too distant from the real political concerns of humanity. Yet as he matured, Ratzinger says, he began to see there was a real political commitment in Plato, and in those who took up his thought. In the Athens of Plato's era, Sophists believed that truth was meaningless and the only thing that mattered was the exercise of power, hence their preference for rhetoric over metaphysics. Platonists resisted that conclusion, Ratzinger says. By insisting on objective truth, Plato put limits to power and hence relativized all human regimes.

As applied to eschatology today, Ratzinger says a recovery of the Platonic/Augustinian emphasis on individual salvation is a necessary corrective to the corporate and social eschatologies. Here Ratzinger mentions liberation theology by name and also again criticizes his old Münster colleague Johann Baptist Metz. He acknowledges that these movements have offered some real "gleams of gold"; at the same time, however, he says the hope Christianity offers is evangelical, not political. "The Kingdom of God, not being itself a political concept, cannot serve as a political criterion by which to construct in direct fashion a program of political action and to criticize the political efforts of other people." When people confuse the gospel with a political message, the distinctively Christian element is lost, "leaving behind nothing but a deceptive surrogate." In simpler terms, Ratzinger says that

Christianity offers the promise of life after death, not a better life before death.

On the one hand, Ratzinger says, the modern world hides death from our sight as a "technological problem to be handled by the appropriate institution"—hospitals or nursing homes. On the other hand, in the media, we find death converted into a "thrilling spectacle, tailor-made for alleviating the general boredom of life." In both cases, Ratzinger says, we find a willful desire to avoid confronting the deep questions death poses.

As to the day of the Second Coming, Ratzinger says in essence, "only time will tell." On hell, Ratzinger says the doctrine of everlasting punishment is clearly established by Jesus and the New Testament. Still, he is influenced enough by Origen to leave open the possibility of universal reconciliation. Ratzinger says there is a purgatory, though he suggests that it may be no more than the "purging" effect of the encounter with Jesus. On the nature of the resurrected body, he says it will be neither purely physical nor purely spiritual. There will be an actual "last day," Ratzinger says, because salvation is intended for the "total organism" of humanity.

Theological Legacy

Time and again, when I asked theologians to characterize Ratzinger's contributions, they used words such as "solid," "clear," "well ordered." As one American Jesuit theologian put it, "If Joseph Ratzinger did it, you can count on it being a solid, respectable piece of work." However, most theologians also say that Ratzinger's thinking is largely derivative. His recovery of the fathers was part of the general *ressourcement* ("return to the sources") of preconciliar theology, his attention to the human situation owes to the general philosophical movement of personalism in the twentieth century, and his communion ecclesiology comes more or less directly from Guardini and von Balthasar. Significantly, no German theology professor interviewed for this book could think of a colleague outside the circles on the far right who uses Ratzinger's original theological writings in their coursework.

Among professional Catholic theologians, the consensus seems to be that the only works of Joseph Ratzinger that will still be read 100 years from now are his commentaries on Vatican II; and these because they help explicate the thinking of those who drafted the documents, not because of their originality. Yet it is also possible that Ratzinger's work may find an audience outside the professional theological community. Like Augustine, Ratzinger shaped most of his writings in the teeth of some specific controversy, and hence much of his work has a defensive and slightly polemical tone. In that light, Ratzinger may be rediscovered by future readers who share his disillusioned mood. He may become a patron saint of the disaffected, a *fons perennis* for those Catholics who worry the world is about to swallow up the faith.

Ratzinger the Teacher

Ratzinger students almost inevitably pay tribute to his prodigious memory. A former graduate assistant told me that he once asked Ratzinger how he wrote his books. Ratzinger responded that he writes the text first, then puts in the footnotes, and only then checks the source materials. In other words, he has the capacity to recall exact quotations at great length, in various languages, and in some cases from works he has not read in decades. He also is said to be able to listen to a number of people voice a wide variety of views, then recall each person's contribution and synthesize it into an overview of the discussion.

Unlike some academics, Ratzinger never allowed his scientific stance to suffocate his faith. When he spoke, he did so as a priest first and a scholar second. "After every lecture you wanted to go into a church and pray," recalled John Jay Hughes, an American Catholic priest and convert from Anglicanism who studied in Germany and knew Ratzinger as a theology professor. Hughes said that sometimes townspeople would come in to hear Ratzinger's early morning lecture on their way to work, because the lectures were so beautiful and accessible. Ratzinger, Hughes said, had the ability to express tremendous erudition in ways that nonspecialists could comprehend.

One way to measure a university professor's impact is to look at the paths taken by his or her graduate students in their later careers. This is especially the case with German professors. The relationship between a *Doktorvater* and his *Studentenkreis* is almost a sacral one, with strong cultish elements; notions of fidelity run deep, as do charges of heresy when one deserts the fold. When the *Doktorvater* moves to another university, members of the *Studentenkreis* often move with him. Their loyalty is to the professor, not the campus.

Until recently, Ratzinger held a regular annual retreat for his former doctoral students, usually in September and most often in the Alps straddling Italy and Germany. Talks would be given, and Ratzinger would offer a synthetic summary at the end. Those who have participated say he is good at taking criticism, and his summaries are always fair. The participants would then break open some cases of wine and talk into the late hours. In the mid-1990s, however, Ratzinger's demanding schedule and his declining health combined to make these get-togethers less frequent.

The remarkable fact in Ratzinger's case is that he built up two distinct *Studentenkreise,* one dating from his early years in Bonn, Münster, and Tübingen, and another from his later years at Regensburg. On most issues, the latter group is theologically at odds with the former. Even more clearly than his theological changes of heart outlined in chapter 2, this division underlines the gap between Ratzinger before and after the council. At Bonn and Münster from 1959 to 1966, he trained theologians who were reform-minded and interested in expanding the boundaries of theological inquiry; after 1969 Ratzinger at Regensburg trained theologians who emphasize orthodoxy, submission, and patrolling the borders between church and world.

This before-and-after dynamic can best be illustrated with respect to five Ratzinger protégés: Hansjürgen Verweyen, Werner Böckenförde, Vincent Twomey, Joseph Fessio, and Christoph Schönborn.

Hansjürgen Verweyen

Verweyen is a systematic theologian who teaches at the University of Freiburg. He spent six years in the United States at the University of Notre Dame in the early 1970s. This appointment was actually due to Ratzinger, who was asked to recommend a couple of graduate students who were "from his breed" for positions in the theology department. After returning to Germany, Verweyen taught at the University of Essen before moving to Freiburg.

Verweyen's best-known work is *Ontologische Voraussetzungen des Glaubenaktes* (Ontological presuppositions for the act of faith), prepared under Ratzinger's supervision. In it, Verweyen advances a fairly daring thesis that the "Easter faith" of the followers of Jesus—their belief that he is divine as well as human—actually pre-dated the Easter event. The Resurrection did not reveal that Jesus was God; it confirmed an understanding that was already present in principle. In so arguing, Verweyen wants to refocus attention on the life of the historical Jesus, which was slipping out of view in the christology of thinkers like von Balthasar. Verweyen's argument holds that it was the things Jesus did and the stances he took that revealed his divinity first, well before the miraculous "fireworks" later. In the later clash between the liberation theologians and Ratzinger, it would be the liberationists who took up Verweyen's line of thought, though not explicit so, against his former master.

Verweyen said that he did not draw on Ratzinger much in writing the book, especially because Ratzinger himself was not terribly interested in the precise questions he was pursuing. "Ratzinger's style was to assign topics that he wasn't familiar with, so he could learn from his students," Verweyen said. Though Verweyen speaks fondly of his time with Ratzinger, he also feels the need to be extremely careful given his mentor's station in the church. He would consent to an interview only on the condition that nothing be published from it without his express written consent. "It's important when you're talking about Ratzinger," he explained.

Verweyen began his graduate career under Ratzinger at Bonn, then followed him to Münster, and finally to Tübingen, where he finished under Ratzinger in 1967. Verweyen has fond memories of Ratzinger in the classroom: "He was an excellent teacher," he recalled, "both academically and didactically. Always well prepared. Already at Bonn you could print virtually everything as it came from his mouth." Verweyen says Ratzinger's courses at Bonn and Münster were always full. "We students were very proud of him, because he was the most famous *peritus* at the Second Vatican Council," Verweyen said. He said that affection for Ratzinger began to cool among the students in 1967, just as Verweyen left for Notre Dame.

Verweyen finished his doctorate as Ratzinger was beginning to reframe his understanding of the council in light of the dangers he saw taking shape. Verweyen believes that Ratzinger's moderately progressive position at the council lost its constituency in the years afterward, as the culture, inside and outside the church, moved toward the left. People like Ratzinger and von Balthasar thought they had nowhere to go but into the traditionalist camp. Verweyen assigns some of the blame for this to Ratzinger himself. "He never went into the media like Küng and Metz did, never cared enough to try to develop an audience for his point of view and thereby hold things together," Verweyen said.

Though Verweyen emphasizes that he and Ratzinger remain on good terms, he has not tried to hide his deep disagreements with the course Ratzinger has taken. In 1994, Verweyen published a commentary on the new *Catechism of the Catholic Church*. In *Der Weltkatechismus: Therapie oder Symptom einer kranken Kirche?* (The universal catechism: Therapy or symptom of a sick church?), he quotes documents of Vatican II and even Ratzinger's own work against passages in the catechism, attempting to show that it is not a neutral presentation of the Catholic tradition but rather, in certain places, a deliberate reshaping of that tradition to serve the political and ecclesial ends of the present papacy.[4]

Despite this break with Ratzinger, when Verweyen recently turned sixty, he received a friendly letter from the cardinal congratulating him and telling him essentially to "keep up the good work." Verweyen stressed that he and his wife Ingrid, who also studied under Ratzinger in Bonn, remain grateful for his kindness. At the same time, Verweyen recognizes that personal graciousness is not the same thing as good government: "There seems to be an almost unanimous consensus among German theologians at the university level that the way many or even the majority of German bishops have been treated in (and by) Rome during the past decade differs sharply from the collegiality pronounced at Vatican II." In this regard, Verweyen says, Ratzinger is clearly striking different notes today than when Verweyen was his student.

Werner Böckenförde

Werner Böckenförde comes from a distinguished German family. His brother, Ernst-Wolfgang, is one of the country's most accomplished jurists and, at one time, was an advisor to the German bishops on their controversial program of abortion counseling. Werner, now seventy-one, is an emeritus professor of canon law and the legal relationship between church and state at the University of Frankfurt am Main. He is also a senior priest at the cathedral in the diocese of Limburg.

Like Verweyen, Böckenförde studied under Ratzinger in the early days, at Bonn and Münster. For a time he worked as Ratzinger's graduate assistant. Also like Verweyen, Böckenförde watched his former mentor move considerably to the right of his own position as the years went by. Because Böckenförde eventually settled on canon law as his discipline, he did not frequently have occasion to wade into controversial theological waters. His instincts could hardly be described as radical, or even distinguishably "progressive." Yet Böckenförde exceeds even Verweyen in his caution in speaking about Ratzinger. Contacted for an interview, he would say only his days with Ratzinger were "a long, long time ago."

Some indication of Böckenförde's attitude toward the Ratzinger years at the Vatican can be glimpsed, however, from a speech he delivered in October 1998 at an assembly in Würzburg sponsored by the German branch of the Wir Sind Kirche (We are church) movement, an international Catholic reform movement that has been denounced by Ratzinger. In the talk, Böckenförde addressed the "situation of the Catholic church today from a canon law point of view." The Wir Sind Kirche leadership was so impressed with the talk that they have given it a wide circulation.[5]

Böckenförde declared at the outset that he intends to face reality in the church as it is codified in canon law, not through the dreamy talk of the "spirit of the council" offered by some utopians. He knows what people mean when they invoke this "spirit"; describing his own immediate impressions of the council, he said, "Finally a reaction to the ultra-montanism of the last century, to the anti-modernism at the beginning of this century, and to the similarly oppressive narrowness of the fifties. The texts of the council and many of their commentaries depicted a friendlier image of the church. One felt the reins were loosened. Laypeople developed more self-confidence and stood straighter."

Yet in the 1983 *Code of Canon Law,* Böckenförde said, this is not the church one finds. "The ecclesial legislator—and this according to the church's constitution is finally the pope alone—this legislator showed himself determined, not only to stop all questioning of the hierarchical structure of the church, but in addition to fortify this structure even more." The upshot, Böckenförde said, is that in terms of canon law John Paul II decided that "no incisive consequences should come out of the council."

Listing a number of examples, from new loyalty oaths to new penalties for disobedience, Böckenförde said, "The desire for freedom and responsibility was met by the demand for obedience, simply because of formal authority rather than insight." Later Böckenförde argued that the new *Code of Canon Law* sets the understanding of freedom in the church spawned by the council on its head. "In summary, the formula says: Christian freedom finds its fulfillment in obedience." He asserted that this approach has produced a "clear dwindling of ecclesial authority."

Addressing several specific instances of new demands for obedience issued over the preceding decade, Böckenförde picked up on a February 1997 set of guidelines for confessors issued by the Pontifical Council for the Family. This document asserts that the prohibition on birth control is "definitive and unchangeable." Noting that after *Humanae vitae* in 1968 the Vatican pointedly did not declare its teaching infallible, Böckenförde says the 1997 document has upped the doctrinal ante. "Hopefully enough bishops who disagree with this addendum will make themselves known," Böckenförde said. Otherwise the pope can draw the conclusion this is the "constant teaching" of the church because no one objected to it. On the subject of a 1997 document on lay ministry, Böckenförde said he found "bothersome" its claims that the employment of lay ministers "leads to a dwindling of candidates for the priesthood" as well as the statement that bishops do not have to accept a priest's resignation just because he is seventy-five.

Böckenförde then asked: "What can we do in the face of such a closed system? What remains for the faithful who do not want to resign or flee into constant opposition, but want to bring movement into the church?" He offered several strategies, ranging from not personalizing structural disputes to demanding that bishops use the legal tools at their disposal to guarantee greater involvement in decisionmaking by laity and junior clergy. He rejects direct appeals to Rome, which he terms "donquixoteries." He calls for bishops to assert themselves against Roman control (too often they are "led by the nose by some bureaucrats of the Roman curia") and to carry the voices of their people. In this regard, he references Ratzinger: "Cardinal Ratzinger answered the question whether the Vatican planned to ask the people of God regarding faith issues in the book *Salt of the Earth*. He states that his premise is that the bishops are well informed about what men and women really believe and that they will share this information. Bishops can [therefore] be asked how they collect information about the *sensus fidelium* of the faithful, entrusted into their care, and how and if they inform Rome about this." In closing, Böckenförde expresses the hope that "believers will awaken the apostle in the bishop."

All this has a familiar ring, sounding very much like the Joseph Ratzinger of 1963 and 1964, who sharply rebuked the Roman curia and demanded greater authority for local bishops. In that sense, Böckenförde stands in continuity with his old professor. The change in Ratzinger's outlook can be effectively gauged by grasping just how much distance, theological and political, separates him from Böckenförde's positions today.

Vincent Twomey

Father Vincent Twomey is a member of the Society of the Divine Word. In his fierce orthodoxy, he exemplifies Ratzinger's second *Studentenkreis,* which formed around him at Regensburg in the 1970s. Twomey finished his doctoral dissertation in 1978, the year after Ratzinger was made archbishop of Munich, and then spent a little more than two years as a lecturer at a seminary in Papua New Guinea. He is now a member of the faculty at St. Patrick's College in Maynooth in Ireland, the national seminary and the center of "establishment Catholicism." He is also a spokesperson for Archbishop Desmond Connell of Dublin, the head of the Irish church.

Twomey's thesis prepared under Ratzinger was entitled *Apostolikos Thronos: The Primacy of Rome as Reflected in the Church History of Eusebius and the Historico-apologetic writings of Saint Athanasius the Great.* Twomey says of Eusebius's position: "It was the specific 'office' of the Bishop of Rome to detect heresy and excommunicate the heretics, as Peter had originally detected and destroyed the errors of the founder of all heresies, Simon Magus, and to authoritatively approve the teaching of the orthodox writers, as Peter had once sanctioned the gospel of Mark for reading in the churches."

Twomey's pugnacious orthodoxy has continued in his role as a church spokesperson. He wrote to the *Irish Times* to complain about a 1994 article accusing the pope of fundamentalism:

> It is grossly unfair to claim, as you do that "debate and compromise are, by definition, inappropriate in the pope's context," unless you assume that dialogue can only take place among those who lack conviction or deny the existence of objective truth in matters of religion and morality. It is indeed possible to mistake the radical nature of the church's teaching for "fundamentalism" when one's own radical teaching is being challenged, as is the case with the whole movement of secularization. The pope has attacked some of the fundamental assumptions of modern civilization, but this is not the same as "funda-

mentalism." The simplistic answers which this modern mentality offers to such complex human problems as marital difficulty (introduce divorce), AIDS (use condoms), or the so-called over-population problem (dispense contraceptives, promote abortion) as well as the fanaticism with which they are pursued, might more appropriately be termed a type of secular "fundamentalism"—should one insist on using the term.

In 1995, during the height of the Irish debate over a referendum to legalize divorce, Twomey challenged the argument that Vatican II pulled the church back from "imposing" its morality on others. "In a world that chooses to ignore what is objectively right and wrong, i.e., what is God's will for all people, the church's moral teaching thus takes on a prophetic character. One may object to this view of morality but one cannot do so on the authority of the Second Vatican Council," Twomey wrote. He also struck an Augustinian note in response to an argument that Catholics should try to find common ground with their fellow citizens on the basis of universal natural law principles. "To posit such a separation between being a citizen and being Catholic, whereby the latter is confined to the private sphere hermetically sealed off from the public sphere of law, is contrary to both classical philosophy and the universal or catholic tradition," Twomey wrote.

Finally, in a May 1999 letter, Twomey addresses himself to the question of women's ordination. "Any attempt, even by a validly ordained bishop, to ordain a woman would be utterly null and void. That has been the mind of the church for the past 2,000 years, as was recently re-affirmed by Pope John Paul II. . . . For Catholics, it is the mind of the church that, in the final analysis, interprets the mind of Christ. Today Scripture scholars might think otherwise. Tomorrow they may change their mind."

In his ridicule of the shifting hypotheses of Scripture scholars, in his rejection of a strong distinction between nature and grace, and in his "closed door" approach to the women's question, Twomey is very much in line with today's Joseph Ratzinger. He represents the kind of impact that Ratzinger's second wave of disciples are having on the church.

Joseph Fessio

Jesuit Joseph Fessio is, by any standard, a remarkable man. He is multilingual and a genuine intellectual, yet he possesses the down-to-earth bonhomie of a country politician. He is the ultimate papal maximalist and never pulls a punch in a public debate, yet on a personal level he is one of the most approachable people in the public life of the American Catholic church. Few men are more charming to talk with or more immediately helpful. Fessio is orthodoxy's ultimate champion, yet he befriended a gay Catholic liberal journalist, Bill Kenkellen, in San Francisco in the 1980s, and stayed with him as he slowly died of AIDS. When Kenkellen needed a priest to administer the last rites, it was Fessio he called. Fessio is widely perceived as a major player in the church, a man with access in the corridors of power in Rome, yet he actually lives in his own office at the Ignatius Institute. With a futon couch that becomes a bed and a prie-dieu, Fessio says he has everything he needs.

Fessio founded the Ignatius Institute in San Francisco in 1976 to promote a more traditional core liberal arts curriculum in American Catholic universities. Fessio got a look at modern intellectual currents in Northern Europe and did not like what he saw; these "deconstructionist and feminist" institutions had become "centers of dissent and opposition to Rome." His efforts to reshape the Jesuit-run University of San Francisco in a more traditionalist direction, however, largely failed. He was fired as head of the institute in 1987. Fessio also founded and still runs the Ignatius Press, which has as its mission to restock American bookshelves with "authentically" Catholic literature. This means that while Ignatius will not offer works by Charles Curran or Richard McBrien, they do publish plenty of titles by Hans Urs von Balthasar and Joseph Ratzinger. In fact, Ignatius holds a contract to publish English translations of most of Ratzinger's works.

Fessio started out as a Jesuit in the late 1960s, and although he had the full hippie regalia—long hair, a beard, sandals, a cross hanging on a leather thong around his neck—he is careful to say that he "never wavered from the orthodox faith." His provincial sent him to Europe for study in theology, and in Lyons, France, Fessio met Henri de Lubac, Ratzinger's friend and fellow *Communio* partisan. De Lubac suggested that Fessio write his dissertation on von Balthasar and suggested Ratzinger as mentor and Regensburg as the obvious locale. Fessio arrived in the fall of 1972. Fessio wrote his dissertation on the aesthetics of von Balthasar and was back in San Francisco by 1974.

It is difficult to find many American Catholic controversies in the last twenty years in which Fessio has not been involved. As a member of the three-person executive committee for Adoremus, a conservative liturgical watchdog group, Fessio helped put together a statement in 1997 that branded a pastoral letter by Cardinal Roger Mahony of Los Angeles as tantamount to heresy. In 1994, when Rome vetoed a Bible translation that had been approved by the American Catholic bishops, many suspected Fessio was involved. The translation used so-called "inclusive" language, such as "people" instead of "man." Fessio said at the time that the drive for inclusive language comes from "a certain elite class, the knowledge class and certain bishops influenced by their staffs. This is not a grassroots, popular movement." On the church's position that it cannot ordain women, Fessio says flatly, "This is not a decision. This is a statement of reality." He also maintains there are no examples of change in "authentic Catholic teaching," even when it comes to matters such as usury and religious liberty.

Fessio sits alongside Ratzinger on the board of an institution in Rome called the Casa Balthasar, a residence for young men considering a vocation to the priesthood. It is designed to introduce prospective priests to the Catholic intellectual tradition as mediated through De Lubac, Balthasar, and Adrienne von Speyer. The board meets every February, at which time Fessio usually pays a visit to Ratzinger's office. Fessio says of Ratzinger that he has a lively, if subtle, sense of humor. Once he explained that he was incorporating his institute separate from both the university and the archdiocese. "Ah," Ratzinger responded, "because of this double independence you can remain orthodox." Yet Fessio also says that claims he has a pipeline to Ratzinger are exaggerated. To those who believe Ratzinger is a harsh oppressor, Fessio says simply that Ratzinger has done no more than draw clear boundary lines where Catholicism begins and ends, and insists that those who teach in her name respect the boundaries. "How long would someone working for GM who was actually selling Fords last?" Fessio asks rhetorically.[6]

Christoph Schönborn

Few members of the Roman Catholic hierarchy enjoy a more distinguished ecclesial pedigree than does Christoph Schönborn. A member of the ancient Austrian noble family of Schönborn-Buchheim-Wolfstahl, the current cardinal of Vienna is but one of two cardinals and nineteen archbishops, bishops, priests, and religious sisters his family has produced. He is not even the first Schönborn to be the primate of the Austrian church; that honor fell to his great-great uncle, Cardinal Franz Graf Schönborn, who led the Austrian episcopacy under the old Austro-Hungarian empire from his position as the archbishop of Prague. (He had previously been the bishop of Budweis—hence he was, believe it or not, a "Budweiser.")

Perhaps owing to this background, Christoph Schönborn is not a street fighter in the way that Twomey and Fessio are. He has an Old World sense of dignity that prevents him from descending too far into the verbal trenches. Yet in his own way he too has carried on Ratzinger's Regensburg legacy, helping to push the church in a more orthodox direction. At Regensburg, Schönborn completed his doctoral work on St. Sophronius of Jerusalem (560–638), a church father most famous for his *Synodical Letter* that defended the doctrine of Christ's two natures, human and divine. Schönborn then moved on to become a professor of theology at the Dominican University of Fribourg in Switzerland. In time, he was appointed a member of the International Theological Commission. In 1987, Ratzinger named Schönborn the general editor of the new universal *Catechism of the Catholic Church*. Schönborn is the man most responsible for the contents of that document, which several astute observers of church affairs—including American Jesuit Tom Reese—believe will be the single most lasting accomplishment of John Paul II's papacy. Like Ratzinger, Schönborn's path to the episcopacy followed the "road less traveled" of professional theological work rather than a career track in ecclesial diplomacy.

When the widely beloved cardinal Franz König of Vienna retired in 1985, most Austrians believed the obvious choice to replace him was auxiliary bishop Helmut Krätzl. Instead, however, John Paul imposed an obscure Benedictine named Hans Hermann Gröer, in what many Austrians took as an attempt to rein in their "liberal" church. When charges emerged that Gröer, as an abbot, had sexually abused novice monks, and it seemed that the pope was determined to back Gröer blindly, Austrian Catholics exploded. Tens of thousands left the church, while a half-million signed a petition demanding sweeping reform in the church. Austria today has replaced Holland as the most contentious Catholic community in Europe.

When Gröer stepped aside in 1995, Schönborn was named to replace him. At first he won good marks for his moderate tone and pastoral sensitivity. He joined other bishops in publicly declaring themselves convinced that Gröer was guilty, and offered an apology to Austrian Catholics. Schönborn's reputation was tarnished in later months, however, by perceived gaffes ranging from the way he fired his popular vicar general by placing a note on his doorstep, to his failure to reprimand ultraconservative bishop Kurt Krenn of Sankt Pölten, whose abrasive style has alienated the vast majority of Austrians. More generally, many Austrians say they have been disappointed by Schönborn's resistance to the reforms in the church called for by the Dialogue for Austria, a special national assembly of Catholics that convened in Salzburg in October 1998.

In a book that came out just before the assembly met, Schönborn derided the demands of Wir Sind Kirche, the main Austrian reform group—for women's ordination, tolerance of birth control, married priests, less rigid sexual ethics, and more local control in the church—as a "Protestant" agenda. After the dialogue, he gave a speech in Frankfurt dismissing the leadership of Wir Sind Kirche as the dying embers of the 1968 generation and their "hermeneutic of suspicion."[7]

During the early 1990s, Schönborn served as chancellor of the Medo Institute in Holland, a conservative center of theological studies launched in 1990 as a counterweight to established Catholic theology programs in Northern European universities. After opposition in Holland forced the institute to relocate in 1994, Schönborn welcomed it to Austria under the name of the "International Theological Institute for Studies on Marriage and the Family." It operates out of a renovated Carthusian monastery in Gaming, Austria, with Schönborn designated by John Paul II as its "grand chancellor." The institute receives some funding from the U.S. bishops' conference. Schönborn has contacts on the Catholic right in the United States, especially at the Franciscan University of Steubenville, Ohio, known for its strongly traditionalist stance on church matters. Steubenville operates an Austrian branch campus out of the same Gaming site as the International Theological Institute. In April 1997, Schönborn traveled to the United States to receive an honorary doctorate from Steubenville for his work on the catechism.

Schönborn is an enthusiastic backer of the "new movements" in the church, such as the Legionaries of Christ, Focolare, and the Neocatechumenate. A key adviser to Schönborn, Therese Henesberger, is a Neocatechumenate member. In 1997, Schönborn authored an article for *L'Osservatore Romano* defending the new movements against charges that they amount to "sects within the church."

Schönborn has been frequently mentioned as a possible successor to Ratzinger, so much so that in 1998, at a press conference, Ratzinger cautioned that Schönborn's appointment as a cardinal member of the congregation should not be interpreted as the naming of a "crown prince." Yet Schönborn does represent in a certain sense Ratzinger's legacy. He is the most accomplished and most influential member of his second *Studentenkreis,* and given his youth—now just fifty-four—Schönborn is likely to be a force in the church for years to come. He is, therefore, ideally positioned to roll back the influence of men like Verweyen and Böckenförde—to ensure the triumph of the Ratzinger of Regensburg over the Ratzinger of Bonn.[8]

Ratzinger in the Annus Mirabilis of 1968

Joseph Ratzinger arrived at Tübingen in 1966, still enthusiastic about the promise of Vatican II and ready to take his place alongside the other budding superstars of German theology, especially Hans Küng on the Catholic side and Jürgen Moltmann on the Evangelical. Küng was serving as dean of the Catholic theology faculty when the chair in dogmatics came open, and he took the unusual step of not forming a *terna,* or list of three possibilities, to fill the position. He made Ratzinger his only suggestion, after phoning him in Münster to be sure he would accept. The faculty consented.

Küng and Ratzinger by all accounts got on very well during the Tübingen years. They had a standing dinner engagement every Thursday night to discuss a journal they edited together, making Küng the only colleague with whom Ratzinger socialized on a regular basis. They were a study in contrasts, Küng zooming around town in his Alfa-Romeo while Ratzinger peddled his bicycle wearing his professor's beret; but they seemed to connect.

Küng's increasingly progressive theological instincts, however, did not sit well with Ratzinger. By 1969, when Ratzinger departed Tübingen for Regensburg, the essentials of his more pessimistic, conservative outlook were in place. As was suggested in chapter 2, the events of 1968 had a strong bearing on this shift, and thus to understand Ratzinger's development it is important to take a deeper look at those fateful few months.

Several larger forces left the "baby boom" generation in Germany especially disposed to social protest in the late 1960s.[9] First was the legacy of National Socialism. In the drive for reconstruction after the war, uncomfortable questions about who did what under the Nazis were largely shunted aside. Two decades later, however, children of university age began to ask their parents what they did under Hitler. Often they found the answers unsatisfactory. This indictment was crystallized in 1968, when Nazi hunter Beate Klarsfeld slapped West German Chancellor Kurt Georg Kiesinger across the face in a public protest of Kiesinger's Nazi past. Kiesinger had been a go-between during the war for Joseph Göbbels, Hitler's propaganda chief, and army head Joachim von Ribbentrop.

In addition, in Germany as in the United States, the boomer generation was enormous, adding millions of adolescents and young adults to the national population. The educational system was unequipped to handle the surge. The student-teacher ratio in German universities in the late 1960s was three times as high as in the United States, and four times as high as in England. At the same time, German youth were demanding that the universities become less exclusive. As late as 1968, only seven percent of German youth qualified for a university-level education, and only three percent actually enrolled. Thus at the same time that the numbers of the traditionally college-bound were growing, there was also pressure to expand the student pool. Under the strain, university services broke down in many places, creating a general mood of frustration. The student-teacher relationship was also a contentious issue. Student activists described the relationship in Germany as resembling that of a feudal lord to his serfs; there was an almost unbridgeable gap between the lordly professor and the lowly students. This, too, sparked outrage in a generation already disposed to question the integrity of its elders.

The question of violence hung in the air during these days of protest, though the student leadership in Germany never embraced it. In fact, most of the actual violence that occurred was instigated by the police. Nevertheless, the theory and language of violent revolution was tossed around a great deal among the students and their leftist sympathizers, enough to seriously alarm a large cross-section of Germans who lived only a few miles from an actual Communist state. As bombing and terrorist actions accelerated, this climate of alarm deepened.

Although the nerve center of the student movement in Germany was the Free University in Berlin, it gripped Tübingen as well. In a 1996 essay in the *Sudddeutsche Zeitung*, a 1960s student radical named Klaus Podak reflected on the spirit at Tübingen in the days after a student named Benno Ohnesorg was shot in Berlin during a protest over a visit by the Shah of Iran, triggering a massive wave of uprisings on campuses across the country: "The revolution was approaching. Its wild, hot air reached Tübingen like a breeze. Our cheeks turned red. Our hearts beat faster. Our eyes shone. Our bodies trembled. We were excited, day and night." At around the same time, another radical named Günther Maschke became editor of a student magazine in Tübingen and turned it into a leading organ of the protest movement.

Tübingen became the intellectual Mecca of the radicals, however, mostly because Ernst Bloch was there. Widely seen as the father of the 1968 student movement, Bloch's Marxist analysis of Christianity and social change provided much of the intellectual architecture for the radicals, and he personally offered support for their protests. At one point, radicals spray-painted "Ernst Bloch University" over the Tübingen sign on the campus's old assembly hall. In *Milestones,* Ratzinger testily acknowledges Bloch's influence, saying in passing that Bloch "made Heidegger contemptible for being petty bourgeois."

Bloch was echoed by Moltmann, who developed the idea of Christian support for social revolution in his "theology of hope" (Moltmann's language reflects the influence of Bloch's masterwork, *Principle of Hope*). The Tübingen New Testament exegete Ernst Käsemann likewise lent his support to students who charged that the church had too often participated in the capitalist exploitation of the poor, and traditional theology frequently served the purpose of propping up the system. Käsemann, though no radical, had a keen sense of political responsibility; his daughter Elisabeth had been murdered on account of her political activity by the military junta in Argentina.

For Ratzinger, all this was simply too much. Frustrated that the theology faculties were emerging as the ideological center of the protest movement, Ratzinger joined forces with two Protestant colleagues, Ulrich Wickert and Wolfgang Beyerhaus, to "bear witness to our common faith in the living God and in Christ, the incarnate word," which the three men believed was under threat. Ratzinger found himself in conflict with many of his colleagues. "I did not want to be always forced into the contra position," he said, and thus he abandoned Tübingen, a height that most theologians can only dream of attaining, after only three years.

Ratzinger left Tübingen for a regional institution that had none of its tradition. Regensburg was a brand new creation of the Bavarian state. It was as if a senior editor at the *New York Times* left at the height of his career to start up a small regional newspaper in Albany. Such a decision cannot simply be explained by differing intellectual outlooks, which are, after all, the lifeblood of a great university.

It has long been rumored that one factor in Ratzinger's decision to exit Tübingen was increasing personal hostility directed at him by students. Yet he says in *Milestones,* "I never had difficulties with students. On the contrary, I was able to continue speaking to a lecture hall full of attentive listeners." He has specifically denied a rumor that his microphone was once snatched away from him by a hostile group of students, though the incident was reported in the German press.

Although Ratzinger did continue to be a popular teacher, he experienced strident opposition from some students and junior colleagues. It expressed itself in disturbances in Ratzinger's classes. Küng says Ratzinger, like several other popular professors, including himself, had been targeted for sit-ins by leftist students. "They came in and occupied the pulpits," Küng said. "Even for a strong personality like me this was unpleasant," Küng said. "For someone timid like Ratzinger, it was horrifying." Küng said that he cancelled his own lectures at the end of the semester in 1968 because he was tired of having them "invaded," and he said he and Ratzinger exchanged complaints about the experience. Küng said he also heard rumors during this time that Ratzinger's graduate students were unhappy with him, but he was "not very much interested in the details."

In *Salt of the Earth,* Ratzinger said his problems were not with students but with the "non-professorial staff." These would have been the so-called "academic middle structure," assistants to professors—equivalent to adjunct professors in the United States. On German university campuses, these were among the most aggrieved sectors, as they spent some of their most potentially productive years writing book reviews and running errands for professors. Their ordeal ended only when, and if, they too were admitted to the guild. Joined sometimes by graduate students, they often formed a second avant garde of campus unrest.

Ratzinger was also deeply disturbed by events at the student parish in Tübingen, where a group of radicals claimed the right to express a "political mandate" for the parish. These students wanted to appoint the chaplain themselves and to lead the parish into political activism. The debate deeply polarized the Catholic students at Tübingen. Ratzinger expressed his worries about the situation to his students, especially on the question of the bishop's right to appoint chaplains. It was another awakening experience for Ratzinger, an object lesson in the dangers of a politicized faith.

Ratzinger later said the Tübingen experience showed him "an instrumentalization by ideologies that were tyrannical, brutal, and cruel. That experience made it clear to me that the abuse of the faith had to be resisted precisely if one wanted to uphold the will of the council. . . . I did see how real tyranny was exercised, even in brutal forms . . . anyone who wanted to remain a progressive in this context had to give up his integrity." According to observers who were at Tübingen in the late 1960s, several of Ratzinger's graduate students, including some who had followed him from Bonn and Münster, became puzzled and frustrated at his new stance. Some deserted him to study under Küng or Metz.

The other revolution of 1968, which also left its imprint on Ratzinger, was a specifically Catholic one: the widespread global outrage at Paul VI's *Humanae vitae,* issued July 29, 1968. Many biographers of Paul believe that the anger generated by *Humanae vitae,* which reiterated the church's ban on birth control despite a widespread expectation that it would change, so shocked the pope that it explains why he never issued another encyclical during the final ten years of his reign. More than a thousand theologians from all over the world announced their dissent from the teaching, saying it contributed to "making war and poverty inevitable." They called it "immoral." Polls showed the overwhelming majority of Catholics felt the pope was "out of touch."

In Germany, some of the edge seemed to be taken off the reaction when the country's bishops, meeting in Königstein in August 1968, declared that couples who use contraception "must for themselves determine whether in conscience—free of subjective presumption—they can answer for their decision." If they felt they could do so, then use of birth control would not necessarily be a sin. The bishops noted the pope had not declared his teaching a dogma. The Austrian bishops put out a similar statement, called the *Maria Troster declaration,* as did more than twenty other bishops' conferences.

Yet at the September Katholikentag, a national Catholic gathering, in Essen, the controversy erupted anew. An Action Committee of Critical Catholics had come together to organize dissent from *Humanae vitae.* They expected a gesture of support from Cardinal Julius Döpfner, the liberal hero of Vatican II and the man who had chaired the pope's birth control commission, which recommended a change in teaching. At first Döpfner seemed prepared to offer support to the committee, but then he "switched," according to German theologian Uta Ranke-Heinemann, who was present at the event. "He started talking about how we must send a message of support to the pope, saying what courage he had shown and how correct he was. I was stunned." She said that Döpfner's attitude sealed the breach between many German Catholics and church authorities.[10]

The events of 1968, former Ratzinger student Wolfgang Beinert told *Time* in 1993, "had an extraordinarily strong impact" on Ratzinger. He had been "very open, fundamentally ready to let in new things. But suddenly he saw these new ideas were connected to violence and a destruction of the order of what came before. He was simply no longer able to bear it."

The Gustav Siewerth Akademie

Another way of measuring Ratzinger's growing conservatism during the 1970s is by looking at the company he kept. Each summer from 1970 to 1979, Ratzinger gave a course in dogmatic exegesis at an institution called the Gustav Siewerth Akademie, located in Germany's Black Forest. He taught the course with Heinrich Schlier, a Protestant exegete who had converted to Catholicism in part because of his disillusionment with the Evangelical church's response to National Socialism. Schlier was teaching at Bonn during most of these years, and was close to Ratzinger.[11]

Both men knew Gustav Siewerth, a German Catholic philosopher and author who taught at Aachen and Freiburg before his death in 1963. Siewerth had used Thomism to refute the German form of existentialism, especially as it was put forth by Heidegger. A few years after his death, a devotee of Siewerth by the name of Baroness Alma von Stockhausen decided to open a *Hochschule* in his honor, in the Black Forest where he had lived. (A *Hochschule* is equivalent to a small regional college in the United States.) The facility was called the Gustav Siewerth Haus, and it was a communal living environment and a study center before it was officially chartered as a school in 1971. A graduate student of Ratzinger's named Richard Lehmann-Dronke helped with the project.

In *Milestones*, Ratzinger describes his interest in the Siewerth Akademie as an attempt to imitiate Romano Guardini's work with Catholic youth in the prewar years at Burg Rothenfels. However, this was not a retreat with the local youth group. The Siewerth Akademie attracted a special kind of young person, someone looking for a deeply traditional experience of the faith coupled with a very skeptical, in some cases almost apocalyptic, stance toward the world, especially the progressive political and social currents pulsing through Europe in the late 1960s and 1970s.

Frau von Stockhausen was an avowed anti-Marxist, and one of her first projects was to invite a group of student radicals from what was called the "Extra-Parliamentary Opposition" in Freiburg, where she taught, to spend time with her at the Siewerth Haus. She was apparently persuasive; after a couple of months her guests were ready to admit that Marx was wrong, and two months later the leader of the group was baptized into the Catholic faith. Considering that Stockhausen said she had faced death threats from the radicals, it was quite a remarkable result.

In its early days there was a strong undertone of millenarian speculation at the Siewerth Haus, fueled especially by the Marian prophecies at Garabandal. From 1961 to 1965, four children in Garabandal, Spain, claimed to experience a series of visions of the Virgin Mary in which she spoke of a great miracle to come, followed by a warning, and then by a "Great Chastisement" if humanity did not repent. The Garabandal prophecies have subsequently formed the hardest edge of an apocalyptic Marian subculture within Roman Catholicism. One Ratzinger graduate student who visited the house during the late 1960s said the people there "lived like a quasi-religious order" and developed a fascination with these Marian end-time scenarios. "One summer they asked me what I was doing over vacation, and I said I was going home," he said. "They said something very strange is going to happen this summer, and maybe I shouldn't come back. It was all tied into Garabandal." Another Ratzinger graduate student said it was rumored while he was at Tübingen that both Ratzinger and von Balthasar took seriously the notion that the world might be ending soon, and that preparations should be made—apparently a reflection of the climate of end-time speculation at the Siewerth House.

Even apart from speculation surrounding the Chastisement, the Black Forest site fosters an exceptionally conservative version of Catholicism. Indicative of Stockhausen's views is a 1996 interview with a German magazine, in which she said her greatest source of sorrow was the way "feminism [is] revolutionizing the family, state, and church." In 1992 Stockhausen cowrote an article that amounted to an attack on Karl Rahner, calling his work "the teutonic mistake." Rahner himself was a "son of Hegel" and "nephew of Luther," and his theology was "not only boring but in the end superfluous . . . it could easily be adopted by the Freemasons."

In 1990, Otto von Hapsburg spoke at an opening ceremony at the Akademie; he demanded that the construction of the new Europe after the fall of the Berlin Wall be based on Christian principles, and said that the students of the Siewerth Akademie could play leading roles in this process. Hapsburg, a member of the European parliament from Germany, is the direct heir to the old Austro-Hungarian throne and a deep conservative in religious matters. The Mass for that opening ceremony was celebrated by Austrian bishop Kurt Krenn, one of the farthest-right prelates anywhere in the world and a former colleague of Ratzinger at Regensburg. Krenn preached on the "indivisibility of the truth." Another faculty member at the Akademie, listed as an "extraordinary professor," is Leo Scheffczyk, a

120

deep conservative and Opus Dei sympathizer who publicly regretted John Paul II's failure to declare the teaching on womens' ordination infallible. Scheffczyk coined the phrase that when Rome intervenes on doctrinal matters, it does so not under the guise of theological debate but "as the fisherman."

Stockhausen receives no money from either the church or the state, relying on private benefactors and tuition. With approximately thirty students from various points in Europe, the Gustav Siewerth Akademie is currently the smallest *Hochschule* in Germany. It exercises an outsize influence on the Catholic church in the country, however, because of Stockhausen's connections and her ability to attract sympathetic faculty such as Scheffczyk and the well-known television personality Gudio Knopp as a professor of journalism. Stockhausen and the Gustav Siewerth Akademie are representative of the new, harder edge to Ratzinger's views which emerged in the Regensburg years.

Ratzinger the Cardinal

On July 24, 1976, Cardinal Julius Döpfner of Munich died. Ratzinger later said that he suspected nothing unusual when the apostolic nuncio asked to visit him in Regensburg not long after. Shortly into the conversation, the nuncio handed Ratzinger a letter with his appointment as Döpfner's successor. Ratzinger says he went to his friend and mentor, Johann Auer, who advised him to accept the appointment. Afterward he went back to the nuncio and wrote his acceptance on the stationery of the Regensburg hotel where the nuncio was staying. The former cardinal of Milan, Giovanni Batista Montini, had predicted that one could expect great things from two people who came to the world's attention during Vatican II: Hans Küng and Joseph Ratzinger. As Paul VI, Montini had just moved his own prophecy toward realization.

As archbishop, Ratzinger is said to have had rocky relations with the priests in his archdiocese. Some of that tension can be glimpsed in a statement a group of Munich priests issued in response to 1984's *The Ratzinger Report,* three years after their shepherd left for Rome: "Those who, like Ratzinger, exalt themselves in such a triumphalistic manner above everything . . . exclude themselves as dialogue partners," the priests said. Nevertheless, Ratzinger's ascent in the hierarchy was swift. Named archbishop in March and consecrated on May 28, by June 27 Ratzinger was in Rome receiving his cardinal's red hat. Ratzinger stayed in Munich less than four years, but during this time he showed clearly, through his relationships with three key men, the kind of doctrinal prefect he was likely to make.

Karol Wojtyla

Ratzinger and the cardinal of Kraków, Karol Wojtyla, first met one another at the conclave in 1978 following the death of Paul VI, though they had been exchanging books since 1974, according to papal biographer George Weigel. Wojtyla at least knew of Ratzinger since the mid-1960s. When Ratzinger's *Introduction to Christianity* came out in 1968, Cardinal Stefan Wyszynski banned it in the Warsaw archdiocese but Wojtyla permitted it in Kraków. Both men had been at Vatican II. Wojtyla found in Ratzinger the same deep orthodoxy he possessed, coupled with the sort of first-rate modern theological training that Poland's isolation denied his countrymen. For central Europeans, Germany is seen as the intellectual pacesetter of the region, and Wojtyla certainly would have been impressed with Ratzinger's eminence in German theological circles.

When Paul VI died in 1978, Ratzinger was actually on several short lists of candidates to succeed him, in both the conclaves that elected Albino Luciani in August and Karol Wojtyla in October. There was not much to distinguish Ratzinger and Wojtyla as potential *papabile*. Both were young (Wojtyla fifty-eight and Ratzinger fifty-one) and intelligent conservatives, and neither was Italian. Ratzinger, however, already carried too much baggage as a theologian who had so publicly changed his mind about Vatican II. Wojtyla was much less well known, a minor figure at Vatican II who lived in a closed-off society under the Communists in Poland.

Two journalists, Tad Szulc and Peter Hebblethwaite, report that Ratzinger played a role in the conclave that elected Wojtyla. Both agree that on Sunday, October 15, the first day of the conclave, several ballots proved inconclusive. In these early stages, there had been a few scattered votes for Wojtyla. Szulc reports that Cardinal Franz König of Vienna and others began canvassing for Wojtyla on Sunday evening, and by Monday morning appeared to have the votes to elect him. The first ballot, however, did not produce the required two-thirds majority. At this stage, Szulc says, Cardinal John Krol of Philadelphia (a Pole) brought the other American cardinals on board for Wojtyla, and Ratzinger delivered the other German votes.[12]

Hebblethwaite believes Ratzinger was a much more active campaigner for Wojtyla. He points out that Ratzinger delivered one of the sermons during the *Novemdiales,* or nine days of mourning specified in the preconclave procedures. In this sermon, he warned his brother cardinals that there would be pressure on them to elect someone in favor of a further "opening to the left," the "historic compromise" with the Communists that had been a key element of Pope Paul VI's realpolitik. Ratzinger urged the cardinals to resist this temptation. In a preconclave interview in the *Frankfurter Allgemeine Zeitung,* Ratzinger said that John Paul I had been critical of liberation theology, and this should be continued in his successor. (John Paul I had dispatched Ratzinger as a papal legate to a Marian congress in Ecuador in September 1978, where Ratzinger cautioned against Marxist ideologies and the theology of liberation.) Ratzinger warned of "pressure from the forces of the left." Based on this evidence, Hebblethwaite says Ratzinger was active on Wojtyla's behalf in the conclave on Sunday evening, assisting König in arguing that Wojtyla was a logical choice because he spoke good Italian and could help unite East with West.

The new pope wasted little time in signaling his interest in Ratzinger. Shortly after his election, he said to Ratzinger, "We'll have to have you in Rome." He offered Ratzinger the position of prefect of the Congregation for Catholic Education, but Ratzinger demurred, saying it was too soon to leave Munich.[13]

In 1980, at the Synod for the Family, Wojtyla named Ratzinger the *relator*. In that capacity, Ratzinger chaired the sessions of the synod, managed its inner workings, and synthesized the various speeches into a report for the pontiff. The topic, "the family," was expected to be contentious because it touched on birth control: the first time the bishops of the world had a chance to formally voice their feelings about *Humanae vitae* to the pope. By most accounts, Ratzinger hit the right notes. He upheld the magisterial position on every issue: in his keynote address, for example, he lamented that "traditional forms of family life are in contrast with the technical civilization of the Western world." He attacked chemical means of contraception, calling them "in contrast with the natural order of things." He likewise defended virginity before marriage and heterosexual monogamy. "There can be no marriage unless it is indissoluble between one man and one woman," he said. Yet in his role as synthesizer, Ratzinger showed his professorial ability to grasp and articulate differing points of view. "There are fathers who have insisted that the usual formulas not be repeated, as if doctrine had been made once and for all," he said. Others believe "the church must not be overwhelmed by current opinions, as if it were a sociological doctrine, but must prophetically preach the medicine of the gospel to the ills of the world."

Praise for Ratzinger's handling of the synod, however, was not universal. At one point, Ratzinger asked a group of experts to draft a set of propositions intended to form the basis for the synod's final report. The drafting was based on the bishops' first round of small group meetings, and Ratzinger wanted the bishops to discuss this draft in the second set of meetings. The bishops chosen to represent the small groups, however, rejected Ratzinger's draft, insisting that the propositions must arise from the delegates themselves in the small groups. Ratzinger was forced to back down.[14]

As the cardinal of Munich, Ratzinger involved himself in the Solidarity movement in Poland. When the pope flew to Poland in June 1979 to celebrate Mass at Nowy Targ, Ratzinger was at his side along with, among others, Cardinal Krol of Philadelphia. In 1981, when the Polish Communists imposed martial law, Ratzinger joined a protest rally in Munich along with Franz Josef Strauss, the leader of the Bavarian wing of the conservative Christian Democrats. About 1,500 people participated.

One of the few rocky moments in the relationship between Ratzinger and John Paul came in November of 1980, when the pope traveled to Bavaria. Prior to the trip, Ratzinger took pains to ask his flock to be on its best behavior. At a press conference a few days beforehand, he said the world might "form or alter its image of Germany" in light of the pope's visit. Thus Ratzinger asked Bavaria to show itself as "noble, friendly to guests, joyful and generous." He also asked Catholics who harbored criticisms of the church not to spoil the joy of the papal visit and not to play up to the media during communal experiences of prayer and Eucharist.

A sign of dangers ahead came in the form of a statement of "critical expectations" for the visit issued by the Katholische Jugend Münchens (Catholic Youth of Munich). Among other things, the signers expressed their hope that John Paul would come ready to engage in a full discussion of the Petrine office—in retrospect, a prescription for frustration.

The pope's plane arrived in Munich on the day of his visit at 8:20 A.M., and he proceeded to the Thereisienwiese for an open-air mass despite the bitterly cold November weather. During the mass, plans called for two elected representatives of the Bundes der Deutschen Katholischen Jugend (Union of German Catholic Youth) to deliver talks welcoming the Holy Father. Though the talks were supposed to have been screened in advance, there was apparently some confusion between the priest assigned to do the editing and Ratzinger's office. Just before the mass began, an aide to Ratzinger demanded that seventeen lines be cut from a talk to be given by a twenty-nine-year-old social worker named Barbara Engl. It was too late at that stage, because the full text of her talk had already been handed out in the newsroom. Engl later insisted she had not been told about the deletion before she spoke.

She delivered her speech, titled "The Impression of Many Young People," as planned. In it, she told the pope that "the church in the Federal Republic fearfully holds the line at the status quo," that it "reacts to questions of relationships, of sexuality . . . too often with prohibitions," and that young people are interested in "the stronger participation of women in church offices." Observers said the pope sat stiffly during the talk, praying a rosary, and did not respond when it was over. It was, in some ways, a replay of the scene from October 1979 when American Mercy sister Teresa Kane publicly asked the pope to open all ministries of the church to women.

In the storm of media interest that followed, church authorities hastened to distance themselves from Engl. A spokesperson for Ratzinger said that evening that Engl "has tricked us." Five days later Bishop Paul Cordes, a German who by then was working in Rome at the Pontifical Council for the Laity, criticized Engl strongly in a long interview with the *Katholischen Nachrichtenagentur*. Five more days later, Ratzinger said Engl's remarks had been neither "tactful nor appropriate." Despite her insistence that she had faithfully complied with all of Ratzinger's instructions, six months after the event Ratzinger declined to meet with Engl or the other speaker, Franz Peteranderl, to discuss what had happened.[15]

Despite this glitch, John Paul approached Ratzinger in 1981 about taking over at the Congregation for the Doctrine of the Faith for Croatian cardinal Franjo Seper. The appointment, according to papal spokesperson Joacquín Navarro-Valls, was a "very personal choice" by the pope. A former colleague of Ratzinger's put it this way: "This Polish pope decided to rely very much on a well-known German theologian to interpret modern thought for him. This selection came at the very time, however, that Ratzinger had actually withdrawn from modern thought."

Johann Baptist Metz

Both Ratzinger and Metz arrived in Münster in 1963. In fact, it was Ratzinger's recommendation that secured Metz's chair in fundamental theology. Metz would remain there until 1993, while Ratzinger was gone within six years to Tübingen. During those six years, however, the two men became friends, worked together during Vatican II, and stayed in contact thereafter. Like Ratzinger, Metz (born one year later, in 1928) was an American prisoner at the end of the Second World War. The memory of the Third Reich always loomed large for Metz; he urged Christians "never to forget the perspective of Auschwitz." However, Ratzinger later said that as he watched Metz work out his ideas on "political theology," the belief that Christianity necessarily implies a political commitment on behalf of social justice, he became increasingly nervous: "I saw a conflict emerging that could go very deep indeed."

Though some of Metz's ideas were taken up by the student protesters in 1968, he remained on the periphery of that time, always critical of the tendencies toward violence and the dissolution of Christianity into a revolutionary ethos. Metz was considered a leading figure on the German theological scene. When the German bishops needed someone to prepare the final document of their mid-1970s synod, they unanimously chose Metz. He also served as a consultor to the Vatican Secretariat for Dialogue with Non-Believers.

None of these mainstream credentials seemed to matter, however, when Metz came up for an appointment to the University of Munich in 1979. The university senate had unanimously recommended Metz as their top choice on a list of three names to replace the retiring professor Heinrich Fries. Under the terms of the 1924 Bavarian concordat with the Holy See worked out by Eugenio Pacelli, later Pius XII, the archbishop of Munich has the right to direct the Bavarian education minister to select one of the other candidates on the list if he does not find the top choice acceptable. Ratzinger exercised this right and told his old friend and colleague, Hans Meier, at that time the education minister, to appoint Heinrich Döring instead. Though Ratzinger defended his decision as based on "appropriate pedagogical considerations," the move generated swift and vocal criticism from across the Catholic spectrum in Germany.

The strongest protest came from another of Ratzinger's old friends and colleagues, Karl Rahner, who published a letter to the cardinal in German newspapers. It was startling in its ferocity:

You had no reason for rejecting Metz. You yourself had previously offered him an identical position at the University of Würzburg. What grounds do you have to justify your reversal now? Is the real reason Metz's political theology? This violation of a century-old tradition in the manner of appointing professors makes a farce out of your responsibility to protect academic freedom in the university.

Is Metz unorthodox or immoral? If so, why has no accusation been made against him all these years? I can only presuppose that the reason is your personal opposition to Metz's political theology. I myself do not agree on all points with Metz, but there is absolutely nothing to justify excluding him from a teaching position.

Cardinal Ratzinger, could your real reason be that Metz has influenced the development of Latin America's liberation theology, which you criticize? Twenty-five years ago the Holy Office in Rome forbade me to write anything further on the subject of concelebration. That was a senseless, unscientific manipulation by church bureaucrats. I judge your action against Metz to be of the same category.

I am not under the illusion my protest will change anything. For many years as theology professor, I have taught that the church is a sinful church and in many instances it errs in its teaching and decisions. That is true yesterday, today and tomorrow. Moreover, it is also tragically true that very seldom does any church leader ever admit truthfully that he has made a mistake. And in such cases there is no practical court of appeal in the church to correct the situation.

The average Christian often has the bitter impression that his faith-inspired loyalty to the church is abused. And yet, he knows that he is powerless before the law. In society in such a case one can legitimately revolt against such misused power. But not so for the believing

Christian. We can truly say that sensitivity to basic human rights must still develop within the church.

It is not sufficient under these conditions to say that those who are suffering should spiritually identify themselves with the suffering Christ. One must protest the injustice and misuse of power. Cardinal Ratzinger, do you understand now why I am protesting?

Metz himself said little in 1979, though in 1989 he was one of 300-plus European theologians to sign the famous "Cologne Declaration" demanding greater academic freedom and more local control in the selection of bishops.[16]

Rahner died in 1984 without a gesture of reconciliation with Ratzinger. The cardinal and Metz, however, seemed to bury the hatchet at a 1998 symposium in Ahaus, Germany, in honor of Metz's seventieth birthday. During the one-day event, both Ratzinger and Metz gave speeches on one of Metz's favorite themes, apocalyptic imagery in the Bible and its importance for Christian theology. The two men later engaged in a half-hour dialogue. Other presenters included Moltmann and Jewish scholar Eveline Goodman-Thau. Ratzinger said during the symposium that he had come to "show respect" for Metz. News accounts called the exchanges between the two men "cordial" and "conciliatory." During their dialogue, Ratzinger agreed with Metz that "the suffering of others must be the central standard of action, not only for Christians, but also in secular politics and society." Metz in turn picked up a favorite theme of both Ratzinger and John Paul, arguing that an apocalyptic understanding of the preciousness of time should be asserted against "an intoxicating relativism."

"I am not 100 percent sure myself, but many of my colleagues had the impression that this [Ratzinger's appearance] was a gesture of reconciliation toward the theological community," Metz said in a telephone interview with me for the *National Catholic Reporter (NCR)*. Hans Küng, however, derided Metz for appearing with Ratzinger without making the case for internal church reform. "It is astonishing" and "a deep scandal" that Metz "would offer the Grand Inquisitor a forum," Küng wrote in an open letter published before the Ahaus symposium.

"He is the chief authority of the Inquisitorial office. It's like having a general conversation about human rights with the head of the KGB," Küng said in an *NCR* interview with me at the time. "This is practically a capitulation to the Roman system, a kind of making peace with Ratzinger, when the real task of political theology should be to identify itself with the suffering people in our church. They are abusing talk about God to avoid dealing with problems in the church."

It was all a bit much for Metz. "Sometimes Küng conducts himself like a second magisterium. To tell you the truth, one is enough, at least for me,"

Metz told me. He said he was "very hurt, very disappointed, very angry" about Küng's comments. Küng was unrepentant: "This event was simply a very nice occasion to show Ratzinger as a smiling Inquisitor who can talk about highly theological subjects in a serene manner," he said. "He thought everybody would be impressed."

Hans Küng

Which brings us to Hans Küng. There is no figure anywhere in the world more closely associated with Vatican II, both its promise and its perils, than the seventy-two-year-old Swiss theologian. His book *The Council, Reform and Reunion,* was widely perceived as the unofficial template for Vatican II. "Never again would an individual theologian have such influence," wrote Peter Hebblethwaite. In the years since, Küng has become the public face of liberal Catholicism, advocating reform inside the church and ecumenical progress outside.

Born in Lucerne, Switzerland, in 1928, Küng went to Rome when he was twenty to study at the Papal Gregorian University. He was actually conservative as a young seminarian. When Pope Pius XII declared the doctrine of Mary's bodily assumption into heaven, for example, Küng was a loud supporter, decrying the "pride" and "hypercriticism" of German theology professors who objected to it. In that sense, Küng's intellectual path is the mirror-image of Ratzinger's, moving from right to left; their friendship at Vatican II may be explained by the fact that they met one another in the middle. In 1955, Küng's study of the doctrine of justification in Karl Barth became a sensation. He argued that Barth's understanding is Catholic in its essentials. It was this work that in all probability prompted the Holy Office to open its file on Küng. In another irony, Küng had been encouraged to expand his dissertation on Barth into a book by fellow Swiss theologian Hans Urs von Balthasar.

Küng was first contacted by the Vatican in April 1967 to answer charges against his book *Die Kirche* (The church), which focused especially on his understanding of papal authority. On May 30, 1968, Küng wrote a letter to Archbishop Paolo Philippe, who was then secretary of the congregation. In that letter, Küng made several requests: (1) for access to his file ("I hardly need to mention that in all civilized states of the West even criminals are guaranteed complete access to the dossiers that pertain to them"); (2) that any earlier decision made without his involvement be set aside; (3) for a written list of the perceived problems with his book; (4) for the names of the experts who investigated his book; (5) for permission to speak in German during any formal meetings; and (6) that his expenses to travel to Rome be covered (otherwise, he said, they could hold the meeting in Tübingen; "my house would be at your disposal"). Carbon copies of that letter went to

Bishop Joseph Leiprecht of the diocese of Rottenberg, in which Tübingen is located, and to Ratzinger, who was then dean of the theological faculty. Ratzinger was thus involved, at least in a tangential way, with the Küng case from its very beginning.

In July 1970, Küng's real bombshell exploded over the Catholic world. His book *Infallible? An Inquiry* seemed to challenge the 1870 declaration of papal infallibility at Vatican I, questioning both its theological soundness and its disastrous implications for ecumenism. It must be said that Küng's was hardly the only voice raising such criticisms. Dutch bishop Francis Simons of Indore, India, for example, wrote a book called *Infallibility and the Evidence* in 1968, charging that if infallibility is valid, the New Testament should support it, but it does not.

Shortly after Küng's book appeared, the German bishops' conference began an investigation. In January 1971, Küng appeared before a hearing of the doctrinal commission of the conference, consisting of bishops Volk and Wetter (who would later replace Ratzinger in Munich), and their theological advisors, Ratzinger and Heinrich Schlier. On February 8, 1971, the bishops' conference issued a statement denouncing Küng's book. The Italian bishops likewise condemned the book on February 21.

Ratzinger contributed to a 1971 volume edited by Karl Rahner that contained essays critical of Küng's book. Both Ratzinger and Rahner expressed strong reservations about the argument in *Infallible?*; Küng complained that he had not been invited by Rahner to contribute an essay in his own defense. The rupture between Küng and Rahner was not yet complete as of 1972, however, when Küng held a graduate seminar on the infallibility issue at Tübingen and invited Fries, Lehmann, Rahner, and Ratzinger; he actually covered their expenses to come. Küng had also invited Cardinal Seper to send a representative, but he declined. In a September 22, 1973, letter to Seper, Küng characterized the seminar as a healthy, good discussion.

What many people believe to be Küng's masterpiece, *On Being a Christian,* appeared in 1974. In many quarters the book was instantly hailed as a classic, but reaction within the circles of Catholic academic theology was mixed. In 1976, a volume of essays in response to the book was published in Germany, containing contributions from Ratzinger, Rahner, von Balthasar, Lehmann, and Kasper, among others. Ratzinger was unusually acrimonious. *On Being a Christian,* he wrote, expressed an "option for a label which in reality is an empty formula"; it moved theology "out of life and death seriousness and into the questionable interests of the literary"; in it Christian faith is "handed over to corruption at its very foundation"; the church disappears "literally into the saying of nothing"; it contains "an undisguised arrogance"; its theology is "rootless and ultimately nonbinding"; Küng was "going it alone, alone with oneself and modern reasonableness";

the book expressed "a school certitude, a party certitude, not a certitude for which one can live and die, a certitude for comfortable times in which the ultimate is not demanded"; its theology "lands ultimately in the abstruse," and "leads nowhere." Küng objected bitterly to Ratzinger's analysis in a May 22, 1976, article in the *Frankfurter Allgemeine,* writing that it contained "numberless misrepresentations, insinuations, condemnations." Overall, Küng referred to the volume of essays as "an outright shot in the back." Among friends, Küng has suggested that Ratzinger was jealous that his early fame and popularity with the students could not keep pace with Küng's.

The German bishops initiated an investigation in response to *On Being a Christian.* In 1977, Küng appeared before a panel in Stuttgart to discuss the bishops' concerns about the book and his other work. The minutes from this meeting were later published as the "Stuttgart Colloquium." Döpfner had proposed the meeting just before he died. In his letter to Küng, Döpfner said he wished to have Ratzinger and Lehmann with him as his advisors. Küng objected to Ratzinger, arguing that his essays about *Infallible?* and *On Being a Christian* lacked objectivity. Ratzinger was dropped. In the Stuttgart session, Küng explained why he didn't want Ratzinger there: "I have not wished the absence of Herr Ratzinger here because I do not wish to speak to him, but because I had at least imagined (which has been confirmed here) that there might enter into this colloquium a fundamental sharpness and emotionality which would not be wished by me." Küng said during the session that he had once discussed a point of christology with Ratzinger, "when one could still speak with him," which suggests that the two were not, in fact, on speaking terms in 1977. Yet there was still a grudging respect. As Küng said of Ratzinger, "he is too smart and knowledgeable not to know that all these matters are very difficult issues."[17]

In the meantime, Ratzinger had been consecrated archbishop of Munich, and he became involved in the internal discussions within the bishops' conference about the Küng affair. Several letters moved back and forth between Ratzinger, Küng, and Cardinal Josef Höffner of Cologne, Küng's chief critic among the bishops during much of the 1970s. In 1978, the bishops thought they had won an informal understanding from Küng that he would not provoke any new debate over infallibility. When Küng wrote an introduction to August Bernhard Hasler's book on the subject in 1979, they felt he had violated this understanding. Matters got worse in September of 1979, when Küng wrote a highly critical analysis of the pope's first year in office that was picked up by major newspapers all over the world.

The first hint of a disciplinary measure came in an October 16, 1979, radio interview given by Ratzinger, in which he was strongly critical of Küng's article about the pope. In early November, the German cardinals

Volk, Höffner, and Ratzinger were in Rome for a meeting with the pope. In an interview afterward with the German Catholic news agency, Ratzinger used the term *missio canonica* for the first time in connection to the case, saying that Küng cannot teach Catholic theology and hold the positions he does. The *missio canonica* is the license that a Catholic theologian must hold in order to teach at a pontifically recognized institution.

A friendly letter from Ratzinger reached Küng on November 16, giving Küng hope that he might still be spared the worst—but it was not to be. On December 18, 1979, the German bishops held a press conference announcing a declaration from the Congregation for the Doctrine of the Faith that Küng was no longer qualified to be a Catholic theologian. The language was virtually identical to that Ratzinger had employed in his interview, leading Küng to believe that Ratzinger knew about the decision in advance. Later in December, a meeting in Rome involving Küng's bishop, the three German cardinals, Seper, Cardinal Agostino Casaroli, and John Paul II confirmed the decision. Moser then wrote to Küng and formally withdrew the *missio canonica*.

In a sermon on December 31, 1979, Ratzinger defended the action against Küng in terms that would become familiar over the next two decades: "The Christian believer is a simple person: bishops should protect the faith of these little people against the power of intellectuals." Though it would be another two years before Ratzinger took up his Vatican post, Küng and Metz were, in a sense, his first two cases. Already his chief concerns were clear: attempts to emphasize the social and political dimension of Christianity, or to challenge Roman authority, were not to be tolerated. There would be no hesitation, no muddled half-moves, when the time came to act, and there would be no reversals when the inevitable outcry of protest rolled in.

John Paul knew, in other words, what he was getting when he called Ratzinger to Rome. The rest of the church would soon find out.

4

Authentic Liberation

*I*n July 1985, a remarkable gathering of theological firepower took place at the Monastery of the Sacred Heart in Petrópolis, Brazil, outside Rio de Janiero. The Franciscan priest and theologian Leonardo Boff, who had been silenced indefinitely one month earlier by Ratzinger's Congregation for the Doctrine of the Faith, was there, joined by his brother Clodovis. The Uruguyan Jesuit Juan Luis Segundo was present, along with the Peruvian Gustavo Gutiérrez, the man who coined the term "liberation theology," and a host of others. It was a "who's who" of the liberation theology movement in Latin America. The ostensible purpose of the session was to discuss progress on a multivolume collection of works on liberation theology, but the subtext was clearly to show support for Boff.

Also present at Sacred Heart was Harvard theologian Harvey Cox, a liberation theology sympathizer who would later write a book, *The Silencing of Leonardo Boff,* about the clash between Rome and the Latin Americans. According to Cox, Boff told the group he had been assured by his Franciscan superiors in Brazil that the official silence did not extend to informal exchanges with friends and colleagues, so he felt free to converse about his experiences in Rome, especially the interrogation at the doctrinal congregation. He told the group he had come to feel there was something wrong, something un-Christian, about a concentration of ecclesial power that acknowledges no constraints and answers to no one but itself. Yet, Boff said, he was determined to stay with the church, not to trigger the Latin American schism that Rome obviously feared from the liberation theology movement.

Boff spoke of how touched he had been by the support from the Brazilian bishops. According to Cox, Boff said that one Brazilian bishop had even asked him to do a careful study of all of Ratzinger's writings, especially his just-published interview with Italian journalist Vittori Messori that became *The Ratzinger Report,* and then draw up an indictment charging Ratzinger with heresy. Cox did not say what the basis for the charge would have been, but presumably it would have resembled the argument made by Segundo in his book *Theology and the Church: A Response to Cardinal Ratzinger and a Warning to the Whole Church,* which appeared in 1985. Segundo concluded that Ratzinger had overturned Vatican II's teaching that God's will can be glimpsed in social and political movements that aim at human liberation.

Boff refused the bishop's offer, saying that he would not wish to subject anyone, Ratzinger included, to the kind of ordeal he had been through. Nevertheless, the fact that a Catholic bishop could seriously envision pressing charges of heresy against the church's top doctrinal officer—even if it was more a political gambit than a sober theological judgment—illustrates the passionate nature of the fight over liberation theology that Ratzinger enkindled.

Fundamentally, the liberation theologians aimed to dissolve the alliance of church, state, and military that had dominated Latin America for centuries. Taking their cue from the historical Jesus as champion of the marginalized, the liberationists argued that the church must exercise a "preferential option for the poor." In practice, this meant supporting leftist political movements, some of which were avowedly Marxist and a few of which advocated violence in the cause of building a just society. Inside the church, the liberationists practiced a form of class struggle by casting their lot with the so-called "base communities" (small groups of poor people who met to read the Bible and discuss social issues) as opposed to the institutional church and its hierarchy. For two reasons, then—its embrace of leftist radicalism and its tense relationship with hierarchical control—liberation theology made the Vatican nervous.

Ratzinger believes his greatest success as the church's top doctrinal authority has been with liberation theology. When journalist Peter Seewald asked Ratzinger to identify his most important accomplishments in 1996, it was his first point. "Today there is wide recognition that our instructions [against liberation theology] were necessary and went in the right direction," he said.

It is also in the struggle with liberation theology Ratzinger has exercised his greatest social impact. In the context of the cold war, any threat to the existing order in Latin America was viewed with alarm in Washington, D.C., as the 1982 "Santa Fe document" prepared by key Reagan advisors illustrates. In this report, liberation theology is treated as an example of the broader Soviet/Marxist attempt to corrupt the "soft underbelly" of the Western hemisphere. The document recommends taking action to combat the influence of liberation theology. In doing so, the United States and its allies in Latin America had limited capabilities. They were forced to rely on police pressure and military brutality, blunt instruments that typically alienated more people than they persuaded. Ratzinger, however, was able to confront this Catholic revolution from within, to deploy the resources of the church itself to deprive the liberation theologians of both credibility and institutional support. Thus the whole of Latin American society, not just the internal life of the church, is different today because of Joseph Ratzinger.

Ratzinger was not soley responsible for this result. Broad social and cultural shifts presented the liberationists with a crisis. During the 1960s and 1970s, Latin America struggled with two kinds of oppression: political and economic. Liberation theology tried to hold them together, arguing that genuine political reform could only result from just economic systems. But as the dictators fell in the 1980s and were replaced by democratic governments, the political urgency of liberation theology abated; at the same time, the collapse of socialism in Europe made its economic analysis suspect. The situation of "the poor" was also changing, as tens of millions of former peasants became city dwellers. The threat facing the poor today, as Brazilian liberation theologian Hugo Assmann has written, is no longer oppression but exclusion. Liberation theology has yet to articulate a compelling response to this new reality.

Likewise, Ratzinger could never have succeeded if he did not enjoy the support of substantial conservative elements in Latin American Catholicism. Indeed, in many instances the zeal of the local opponents of liberation theology ran ahead of Rome's. Conventional wisdom in Latin American holds that it was right-wing bishops and activists—Cardinal Eugênio Sales in Rio de Janeiro, Cardinal Alfonso López Trujillo in Colombia, Bishop Boaventura Kloppenburg in Brazil—who really triggered the condemnations. Yet even the backing of these powerful local churchmen would not have been enough to stop liberation theology if the movement had succeeded in capturing the grassroots. But the pastoral dimension of liberation theology, especially the famous base communities, at its peak touched no more than five percent of the total Catholic population. Moreover, not every Latin American in a base community supported or even understood the project of the liberation theologians. José Comblin, himself a leading liberationist, confessed frankly in 1998 that in vilifying the First World, liberation theology simply misread the attitudes of most Latin Americans.[1] Thus a variety of forces—strong local opposition, changing political and economic realities, and an ideological stance that alienated many Latin Americans at the grassroots—combined to stymie the progress of liberation theology.

None of that, however, makes Ratzinger's role any less significant. As the social reality in Latin America was shifting, the liberationists should have been engaged in creative thinking; instead their time was largely consumed by defending themselves from Ratzinger's inquests or engaging in self-censorship to ward off a new round of scrutiny. Moreover, even if some Latin American Catholics shared Ratzinger's passion for eradicating liberation theology, that passion would have been ineffectual without Ratzinger to endorse it and act on it. Ultimately he alone had both the power and the conviction to stop the movement in its tracks.

The fight against liberation theology is at the heart of Ratzinger's legacy because it so clearly arose from his own views and instincts, as opposed to those of the pope he serves. Poland's Solidarity movement gave John Paul an instinctive sympathy for priests and laity confronting their governments and demanding social justice. By 1980 more than 800 priests and nuns had been martyred in Latin America, and certainly the pope was profoundly moved by their witness. On the other hand, the example of the Communist-backed Pax movement in Poland allowed John Paul to believe that priests and laity voicing that demand *inside the church* were subversive forces. Demands for internal reform in Poland, he believed, had been manufactured by Communist infiltrators in order to weaken the Catholic church, and thus he was persuaded when Ratzinger and local conservatives told him the same thing was happening in Latin America.

Ratzinger muzzled liberation theology at the very time that global capitalism was coming to dominate Latin America. By the late 1990s, more than a decade of rampant "neoliberalism," as the ideology of free trade and small government is known in Latin America, had generated impressive economic growth benefiting relatively few, thus making inequities much more savage and contributing to what some observers are calling "social apartheid." One can only speculate, but Latin America today might look different if, instead of silencing and harassing the liberation theologians, the Vatican had given them full support, had appointed bishops ready to back their cry for justice, if Vatican officials had joined the people in the base communities and on the picket lines. Instead, in spite of the efforts of individual bishops and theologians, the Catholic church in Latin America has played nothing like this transformative role. That fact is in no small measure due to Joseph Ratzinger.

What Is Liberation Theology?

Liberation theology has distant historical roots in the fifteenth and sixteenth centuries and the emergence of Christian humanism, and, more proximately, in Vatican II and *Gaudium et spes.* Properly speaking, however, liberation theology stems from the 1968 assembly of the Latin American bishops in Medellín, Colombia. That session endorsed a "preferential option for the poor" on behalf of the Catholic church in Latin America. The movement took its name from Gustavo Gutiérrez's 1971 book *A Theology of Liberation*. Gutiérrez himself served as a theological advisor at Medellín.

Today it is common to speak of "liberation theologies," and to acknowledge a wide range of impulses that draw inspiration from the Latin American experiment. In his 1995 book *Liberation Theologies,* Jesuit writer and theologian Alfred Hennelly distinguishes nine varieties: Latin American, North American Feminist, Black, Hispanic, African, Asian, First World, Ecotheology, and even a liberation theology of world religions. All share an emphasis on the this-worldly consequences of Christianity, but they also differ in important ways. The focus in this chapter, however, is on the Latin American form that emerged in the 1970s and 1980s, because that is the form attacked with such vigor by Ratzinger.

Four ideas have traditionally been central to this form of liberation theology.

1. The preferential option for the poor. As noted above, this phrase comes from the 1968 Medellín document. Even earlier, Vatican II's *Gaudium et spes* had urged that Christian solidarity with humanity include "especially the poor." For the liberation theologians, this is not an empty piety. It means that the church must align itself with the poor as they struggle for change against elements in society that would preserve the status quo. This insistence has led to charges that liberation theology advocates class stuggle. The liberationists, however, say that they did not invent the division of society into a wealthy elite and an impoverished majority. The church itself helped create this social order in Latin America: Catholic missionaries served as evangelizers for the European conquerers, and church leaders sided with the local elites for 400 years. The church, in short, has never been neutral. The point, say the liberationists, is not to involve the church in class struggle, which is a given of the Latin American situation. Their goal is to shift its loyalties.

2. Institutional violence. This concept too comes out of the Medellín document. Liberationists see a "hidden violence" in social arrangements that create hunger and poverty. Thus when critics accused theologians in the 1980s of advocating revolutionary violence, a charge that was largely a fabrication, they often responded: "But the church has always tolerated violence." They meant that by endorsing the status quo, church leaders were acquiescing in a system that did violence to millions of people. In such a context, charges of "fomenting violence" against those seeking change seemed disingenuous.

3. Structural sin. Liberation theologians aim to expand the traditional Catholic understanding of sin, which tends to be individualistic: sin as a

particular person's transgression, such as lying or stealing. The liberation theologians argued that there is also a social dimension of sin that is more than the sum of individual wrongful acts. Examples frequently cited include neocolonialism and the feudal nature of the relationship between the Latin American oligarchy and the peasants. By extension, the redemption from sin won by Christ must be more than the redemption of individual souls. It must also redeem, transform, the social realities of human life. Liberation theologians acknowledge, in concert with all Christian theologians, that the full measure of redemption must await the Second Coming, but they also insist that redemption, as St. Paul said, is in some sense already present. It is the responsibility of Christians to work to extend that redemption in space and time, and hence the effort to undo social sin is a constitutive part of what it means to be a Christian.

4. Orthopraxis. This term was coined by the liberation theologians as a counterpoint to the church's traditional insistence on "orthodoxy," meaning "correct belief." Liberation theologians argue that what is most fundamental is "correct action"; that is, effort leading to human liberation. Most liberation theologians say the accent on orthopraxis is a matter of balance, not of choosing between belief and action. They wanted to remedy a centuries-long Christian inclination to overemphasize belief at the expense of action. This distinction, however, lies at the heart of much of Ratzinger's critique. He argues that doctrine must come first, that one is incapable of determining which actions are the right ones without prior beliefs. By denying the priority of belief, Ratzinger argued, liberation theologians relativize Christian doctrine.

Liberation theology places a premium on social analysis. To remedy injustice, one must first understand the social mechanisms that produce it. In this analysis many liberation theologians were drawn to Marxism. Concepts such as surplus value, the distinction between the wages paid to laborers and the market value of their work, loom large in their writing. Critics found this alarming, insisting that one cannot distinguish between Marxist "science" and its ideological underpinnings of atheism, materialism, and totalitarianism.

Finally, liberationists stress the pastoral dimension of their work. In Latin America, liberation theology came to be identified with the "base communities," tens of thousands of small groups of Christians, usually ten to thirty people, who come together for Scripture study and reflection leading to action. These groups sometimes meet under the guidance of a priest, though most often they are lay-led. In the 1970s and 1980s, liberation theologians identified the base communities as major change agents in Latin American society, the place where the poor came together to take charge of their own destiny. How widespread the base community phenomenon was at its peak is difficult to say; in the 1980s, influential Brazilian liberationist Carlos Alberto Libanio Christo (better known as Frei Betto, a Dominican brother) asserted there were between 80,000 and 100,000 base communities in the country with upwards of two million participants. John Burdick, who wrote about the base communities in *Looking for God in Brazil,* refers to this as the commonly accepted number. On the other hand, one researcher who actually tried to count the communities in the early 1990s said he was able to identify only 1,000 in the São Paolo archdiocese, where one-tenth of the national population lives and an area where base communities had been heavily encouraged by Cardinal Evaristo Arns. Thus he estimated the total number was unlikely to exceed 10,000, a number that would suggest perhaps 200,000 total members.[2]

Whatever the sociological reality, the base communities were, and are, a touchstone of the movement. Many liberation theologians joined base communities or made it a point to spend time with them; in progressive Latin American dioceses, contact with the base communities became an integral element of priestly formation. The base communities also were at the root of much of the Vatican alarm about liberation theology. Because they existed independent of clerical oversight, they seemed to represent a model of "church from below"; and indeed they were sometimes presented this way by some of their more enthusiastic advocates. In their essence, however, there is nothing adversarial about the base communities, a point that mainstream liberation theologians would repeat throughout the controversies of the 1980s.

Ratzinger's Baggage

It was the historical misfortune of the liberation theologians to encounter in Joseph Ratzinger someone predisposed to be a formidable opponent. Ratzinger's baggage was both personal and professional, and as the fight wore on, it became increasingly difficult to separate the two.

German Roots

It is an article of faith among German Catholic theologians, even those sympathetic to liberation theology, that the movement has its origins in Germany. Ratzinger once jokingly suggested that Boff's problem was that he had "read too much German theology." In a March 1984 article about liberation theology, Ratzinger referred to it as "not a home-grown product but a European export." This conviction is rooted in two facts. One is that liberation theologians frequently cite German thinkers, especially Johann Baptist Metz of Munich and Jürgen Moltmann of Tübingen. Because Metz and

Moltmann were doing their most important work in the 1960s, there is a tendency to assume *post hoc ergo propter hoc:* because the liberation theologians came after them, they must have been influenced by them.

Metz pioneered "political theology," arguing that Vatican II meant that Christians must read the "signs of the times" in social and political movements and align themselves with those seeking to better the human condition. Moltmann, a Lutheran theologian, likewise aimed to recover a more radical earlier stratum of the Christian tradition buried under centuries of social respectability. He argued that belief in the crucified Jesus frees Christians from submission to "false idols," especially the social status quo. It is Jesus who offers genuine hope for social transformation; hence he called his theory a "theology of hope."

Metz and the liberation theologians did have a mutual influence. In the 1970s Metz wrote essays about the base communities, and in 1980 he composed an encomium to Ernesto Cardenal, the Nicaraguan priest who was minister of culture for the Sandinistas, on the occasion of his traveling to Germany to accept a book prize. One of Moltmann's most recent essays argues that because the effect of international capitalism in the 1990s has been to globalize the flow of capital, goods, and services, liberation theology must become globalized as well. In this context he argues for an alliance among Third World liberation theologians and the European architects of political theology.

The second point that supports the notion of the German origins of liberation theology is the fact that some of the liberation theologians themselves studied in Germany. Leonardo Boff spent 1965 to 1970 studying at the University of Munich under Karl Rahner. When Boff completed his doctoral dissertation, *The Church as Sacrament in the Horizon of World Experience,* Rahner suggested that he show it to a colleague, who liked the work and helped him find a publisher. That colleague was Joseph Ratzinger. The Jesuit Jon Sobrino likewise studied in Germany and was ordained to the priesthood in Frankfurt. Gutiérrez did a turn in Europe, studying in Louvain, Lyons, and Rome. Segundo held degrees from Louvain and from the University of Paris. Actually, if the critics of liberation theology want to blame anyone in Europe, a better candidate would be the French pioneers of *nouvelle theologie,* whose worker-priest movement offers a historical antecedent for the liberationist approach, and whose incarnational approach is more congenial to it than the skepticism about "the world" that haunts much German theology. Gutiérrez continues to have many admirers in Europe. In 1998 he received an honorary doctorate from the University of Freiburg, his sixteenth honorary doctorate; in 1993, President François Mitterand inducted Gutiérrez into the French Legion of Honor.

For the liberation theologians, however, the perception that they are doing no more than tracing out the consequences of German ideas is deeply frustrating. They insist that the origins of their movement lie in the experience of poverty in the Third World. Indeed, most Latin American liberationists take it as a point of pride that although political theology in Europe is an "academic" matter, in the Third World liberation theology is a popular phenomenon closely tied to pastoral work. Many liberationists have chided Metz and Moltmann for writing endless prolegomena to action without ever doing anything. The liberationists are, of course, aware of the important figures in Catholic theology, and they may even recognize certain sympathies, but this is a far cry from asserting that liberation theology is derivative from European thought.

Ratzinger, however, is a firm believer in the German origins theory. When he came into office at the Congregation for the Doctrine of the Faith, he did not feel a need to educate himself about the presuppositions or experiential basis of the movement. He felt he knew its history, its assumptions, perhaps even better than figures such as Sobrino and Gutiérrez, because he knew its progenitors. Most importantly, Ratzinger had already made up his mind about these politically engaged theologies. At the level of theory, he believes they relativize Christian doctrine; as a practical matter, they lead to various forms of revolutionary terrorism. On both levels, they are a danger to the faith.

Marxism

"When they talk about Marxism in the Vatican, they see a chain of images stretching to the Gulag in Sibera," Boff once remarked. There is little doubt that Boff is right about the temblors Marxism sets off inside Ratzinger. From stories about the horrors of the 1919 Soviet revolution in Bavaria, to the 1968 student radicals and the Baader-Meinhoff gang, to repression inside East Germany, Ratzinger associates Marxism with terrorism and violence. The southern border of Karl Marx Stadt, the heart of the German Democratic Republic, was not far from Ratzinger's home in Bavaria, and he knew the sort of thing of which a Marxist state was capable.

Medellín, the gathering of Latin American bishops that gave its blessing to liberation theology, took place in 1968. For Ratzinger, Medellín must seem like another ripple effect of the great wave of leftist radicalism that gripped the world in that year. The liberationists dispute this. Gutiérrez insisted in a 1998 interview with a German newspaper that "the context was entirely different," asserting that the roots of Medellín were in pastoral reflection on poverty. This seems slightly disingenuous, as poverty and pastors had both been around in Latin America long before 1968. Yet even if the temper of the times helped get liberation theology started, Gutiérrez is right that one cannot reduce the meaning of the movement to one factor in its origins.

As events unfolded in Latin America, they offered just enough confirmation of Ratzinger's fears to make his sweeping rejection of liberation theology as a front for Marxist revolution credible. A handful of priests took up arms and joined guerilla movements. Some of them were killed and celebrated as heroes, such as Father Camilo Torres, a friend of Gustavo Gutiérrez who joined Peru's Shining Path. Torres said at the time, "I feel that the revolutionary struggle is a Christian and priestly struggle. . . . I have given myself over to the revolution out of love for neighbor." For a whole generation of Latin Americans, the debate over Torres helped shape their notion of what it meant to be Catholic. In the same spirit, three priests served as ministers in the Sandinista government in Nicaragua and defended the excesses of that regime in the name of liberation.

Bishops such as Brazil's Ivo Lorscheiter repeatedly stressed that Catholics sympathetic to liberation theology "do not favor violent methods or christologies that advocate certain ideologies like Marxism." Those assurances rang hollow for Ratzinger, especially when Lorscheiter would go on, as he usually did, to insist that class struggle be accepted as part of the reality of the Latin American situation. Ratzinger recoiled from such phenomena as "Eucharistic strikes," in which pastors associated with liberation theology would deny the Sacrament to the boss or "headman" of a given area unless he met the demands of peasants or workers. He also detected the equivocation of leading figures such as Boff, who on the one hand denounced state socialism in 1985 as "authoritarian" but at the same time spoke in obviously dishonest terms about Castro's Cuba: "There are no slums in Cuba."

Ratzinger's insistence on linking liberation theology with state terror in Eastern Europe is reflected in the most widely quoted paragraph from his 1984 instruction on liberation theology:

> The overthrow by means of revolutionary violence of structures which generate violence is not ipso facto the beginning of a just regime. A major fact of our times ought to evoke the reflection of all those who would sincerely work for the true liberation of their brothers: Millions of our own contemporaries legitimately yearn to recover those basic freedoms of which they were deprived by totalitarian and atheistic regimes which came to power by violent and revolutionary means, precisely in the name of the liberation of the people. This shame of our time cannot be ignored: While claiming to bring them freedom, these regimes keep whole nations in conditions of servitude which are unworthy of mankind. Those who, perhaps inadvertently, make them-

selves accomplices of similar enslavements betray the very poor they mean to help.

Here one grasps why the struggle between Ratzinger and the liberationists was so intense: both sides believed they were dealing not with academic points of theoretical interest, but with life and death issues of slavery and oppression. The liberation theologians wanted the church to help free the Latin American poor, bound by the chains of poverty and hunger; Ratzinger was mesmerized by the Eastern European poor, held captive in Soviet-backed police states.

Ratzinger's Circle

Friends and like-minded thinkers through the 1970s were developing some of the concepts Ratzinger would later employ in his criticism of liberation theology. Two figures illustrate the point: Hans urs von Balthasar and Boaventura Kloppenburg.

Throughout the 1970s, Balthasar, Ratzinger's collaborator and mentor, kept up a steady drumbeat of criticism. Balthasar levels three basic charges against liberation theology.

1. It is regional and national in spirit, Balthasar says; in fact it takes pride in being exclusively so. He notes that many liberation theologians have spoken of the "impossibility" of transplanting their ideas into other social contexts. Yet any genuinely Catholic theology must be universal: "It is the characteristic of sects and heresies to define themselves and begin to spread starting from a given national sphere," Balthasar asserts.
2. Genuine Catholic theology never breaks with the unity of the church. It may have a special charism, but it exercises it within the unity of the one body. Balthasar does not explicitly say so, but his suggestion is that the liberationists have ruptured this communion.
3. Catholic theology must recognize that God "delivers his own hermeneutic." We do not need alien intellectual systems such as Marxism to understand revelation, because revelation itself contains the key to understanding. "Whether they are of a more personal or a more social nature, schemas for the interpretation of human existence as a whole often stand in the service of a non-Christian or an anti-Christian ideology, and they are, therefore, to be tested with double care for their 'neutrality' and possible usefulness for the Christian explanation of the world," Balthasar wrote.

Balthasar warns against attempts to politicize Christianity:

Whenever a form of Christianity which considers itself enlightened forgets that Christ's cross and resurrection have wholly fulfilled the

Old Testament's "utopian" promise ("God with us"), the result is . . . a drifting into a Judaizing mentality that now reads the New Testament through the filter of a master-slave ideology and which, consequently, takes into its own control the business of mankind's total politico-religious liberation, entirely contrary to the Old Testament's original understanding of Israel.

Balthasar insists on an exclusively personal understanding of sin: "Societal situations can be unjust, but in themselves they cannot be sinful. Only those persons can be sinful who are responsible for the existence of such situations and who continue to tolerate them even though they could abolish or ameliorate them."

Finally, Balthasar delivers this judgment: "The church must by preference side with the poor; its best members have always done so. But this option cannot compromise the universality of the church's offer of salvation to all, in such a way that it becomes a political party. It cannot, therefore, celebrate its Eucharist only with those who are materially poor, or limit its Catholic unity to the 'party' of the poor, or extend its unity to all only after a victorious 'class-struggle.'" Because Balthasar and Ratzinger both sat on the International Theological Commission in the 1970s and helped to shape its 1977 statement "Human Development and Christian Salvation," one can assume that Ratzinger shared at least part of Balthasar's critique.

Boaventura Kloppenburg is important because as a member of the Brazilian hierarchy he enjoyed a certain privilege as an "on the spot" observer. Born in Molbergen, Germany, in 1919, Kloppenburg was a Franciscan. As an auxiliary bishop in Rio de Janiero, he was one of Boff's earliest and most bitter opponents. He was later made the bishop of Novo Hamburgo, where he became a leader of the conservative wing of the Brazilian church. Kloppenburg and Ratzinger were both *peritii* at Vatican II, moved in progressive circles, and later moved to the right. Both served on the International Theological Commission in the 1970s.

The drift of Kloppenburg's thinking on liberation theology can be gleaned from a monograph he wrote in 1974 called *Temptations for the Theology of Liberation.*[3] Ironically, Kloppenburg begins by associating liberation theology with Rudolf Bultmann, whose program of "demythologizing" asserted that the historical Jesus was of no importance to Christianity because all that matters is the "Christ of faith." Kloppenburg says that liberation theology shares this view in its insistence that the gospel speaks to the here and now. This argument, at least, did not sit well with Ratzinger; he would later accuse the liberation theologians of doing exactly the opposite, putting too much emphasis on the historical Jesus.

Kloppenburg's reasoning, however, connected with Ratzinger's on other points. Kloppenburg suggests that liberation theology is too eager to align itself with secular liberation movements. "If our efforts at adaptation end by giving us a complete 'understanding' or doing away with the 'harshness of the Word,' we need no further proof that we have departed from the way of the Lord," he writes. He cautions against a neglect of interior and personal spirituality in this new emphasis on social transformation, and accuses some liberationists of a "contempt for the ontological dimensions of theology." He warns against Marxism and says, "A kingdom of God that would claim to be fully real on earth before Christ comes again would be only a snare and a delusion." He says that in the Christian understanding, redemption and sanctification are fundamentally personal, but they have a "social and even cosmic phase."

Still, Kloppenburg probably did not influence Ratzinger in any direct sense. In fact, if there is a line of influence it is equally likely to run in the opposite direction. The point is that in the 1970s, in the ecclesial company Ratzinger kept—theologians associated with the journal *Communio* and the mounting reaction against the post-Vatican II period in the church—there was a growing criticism of liberation theology. This theological climate helped set the stage for Ratzinger's offensive. His effort to break liberation theology was not a course of action he settled upon after taking office; it was something he came into the office ready to accomplish.

The Theological Critique

At the heart of Ratzinger's critique are two theological motifs, which recur in his writing on other subjects.

Truth

Because the liberationists argued that theological understanding should follow political commitment, Ratzinger believed they were saying that praxis is the standard for judging the rightness of doctrine. In other words, one decides which Christian teachings are "true" on the basis of how well they support political efforts for social justice. As early as 1968 in his *Introduction to Christianity,* Ratzinger was resisting the "tyranny of the factum," the tendency to reduce truth to what one *does* rather than what reality *is*. This mistake leads some to present Christianity as a tool for changing the world and to "transpose belief itself to this place." In other words, all doctrine is suspect unless it is useful for social change.

Ratzinger was not simply projecting this understanding onto the liberationists; some did hold this position. Juan Luis Segundo's famous line from *Theology for Artisans of a New Humanity* was, "The only truth is the truth that is efficacious for liberation." Segundo Galilea published an article in *Concilium* in June 1974 in which he argued that Moses provides a better model for the politically committed believer than Jesus does, because Moses integrated the idea of political and religious salvation whereas Jesus rejected the "Zealot solution." This certainly had the look of using praxis as a benchmark for doctrine, and it is hard to imagine a more radical application of it than to dethrone Jesus as the center of the faith. Whether this is what Galilea had in mind is irrelevant; the article could easily give this impression. Similarly, the Brazilian Hugo Assmann wrote in 1976, "The Bible! It doesn't exist. The only Bible is the sociological Bible of what I see happening here and now."[4]

Mainstream liberationists insist that there is no necessary connection between liberation theology and relativism. Ratzinger, however, could find plenty of confirmation for his fears in the corpus of liberationist writings. It was clear where his analysis would lead. The point is expressed in the 1984 instruction:

A radical politicization of faith's affirmations and of the theological judgments follows inevitably from this new conception. The question no longer has to do with simply drawing attention to the consequences and political implications of the truths of faith, which are respected beforehand for their transcendent value. In this new system every affirmation of faith or of theology is subordinated to a political criterion which in turn depends on the class struggle, the driving force of history.

The key term here is "transcendent," which is theological jargon for supernatural. By denying objective truth, Ratzinger believes, the liberationists are denying transcendence; and in so doing, they are denying God, or at least making the question of God a moot point.

The accusation that the liberationists lacked respect for truth was especially offensive to them as they were jailed, beaten, and killed precisely because they told the truth by exposing the brutality of the regimes that governed their countries. It was a stark, simple choice: speak out and you could die; keep silent and you could live. Segundo wrote of how the truth was a sacred thing for the liberationists, precisely because it was so often a matter of life and death. Again, therefore, each side saw something fundamental at stake. Ratzinger saw the faith for which countless martyrs throughout the centuries had died being revised to score political points, whereas the liberationists saw the causes for which they were being martyred ignored or obstructed by the Vatican. To them, Rome seemed afraid to draw the consequences of its own creed. The clash between these two perspectives was perhaps the most significant, both ecclesiastically and politically, in twentieth-century Catholicism.

Eschatology

Ratzinger's fundamental complaint about liberation theology is that it embodies a mistaken notion of eschatology. The liberationists, Ratzinger believes, are looking for the kingdom of God on this earth and in this order of history. This sort of utopianism is not merely wrong, Ratzinger says, it is dangerous. Whenever a social or political movement makes absolutist claims about what it can deliver, fascism is not far down the road. It is the lesson of Nazi Germany, Ratzinger argues, and it is the lesson of Soviet Russia. Thus the goal of Christianity must be to strip politics out of eschatology. As he put it in his 1987 book *Church, Ecumenism and Politics,* "Where there is no dualism, there is totalitarianism."

Ratzinger knows that most liberationists would not recognize themselves in this description. He knows they place the full realization of the kingdom in the next world. He knows this because each of the major figures in the movement—Boff, Gutiérrez, Sobrino—at different times has been compelled to write extensive "clarifications" for him, and each has addressed this point. For Ratzinger, however, their insistence that they do not *in fact* posit immanent salvation misses the point. Their system leads necessarily in this direction, so it is deconstruction of the system that is required, not merely ad hoc abandonment of it at a critical juncture.

For Ratzinger, this temptation to collapse eschatology into innerwordly social expectations is a perennial one for Christianity. As outlined in chapter 1, Ratzinger's postdoctoral work was on Bonaventure, especially his struggle with the "spiritual Franciscans." This group had anticipated a third age of the Holy Spirit inside history, based on evangelical poverty and triggered by Francis himself. In this age, the poor would be exalted and the rich cast down. Because people would be guided directly by the Holy Spirit, the institutional structures of the church would be less important. Ratzinger had therefore already found a template for how he would understand his struggle with the liberationists.

In Ratzinger's judgment, the consequences of liberation theology's warped eschatology show up in at least four ways.

1. Defections from Catholicism. By promising the poor a reign of justice that never comes, Ratzinger believes, liberation theology actually estranged them from Catholicism and led many of them to seek a transcendental faith somewhere else. In *Salt of the Earth,* he said, "For the very poor, the prospect of a better world that liberation theology held out to them was too far away. As a result they remained interested in a religion of the present, in a religion that would reach into their lives." Ratzinger has linked this neglect of the here-and-now to defections to Protestantism. The "Protestantization" of Latin America has long been a source of anxiety for

Catholic authorities, and although the numbers have sometimes been exaggerated, the trend is real. Most observers estimate twelve to thirteen percent of Latin Americans are now Protestant, a vast increase from the estimated one percent in 1930 and four percent in 1960. This defection has been a staple of right-wing criticism of liberation theology, accusing the progressives of politicizing the faith and driving people away, especially into the rapidly expanding evangelical and Pentecostal movements. The argument is bolstered by pointing to examples such as the southern Mexican state of Chiapas, where Bishop Samuel Ruiz has been called a "red bishop" for his support of uprisings among peasants and indigenous people. The rate of conversion to Protestantism for Mexico as a whole over the 1990s was ten percent, but in Chiapas it was approximately thirty percent.[5]

Many experts believe liberation theology cannot be blamed for the defections in Latin America. If this were so in Brazil, notes Comblin, there would be more losses from the São Paolo archdiocese, a hotbed of liberation theology, than from Rio de Janeiro, where it never had much support; in fact, the reverse is the case. Nevertheless, it is clear that Ratzinger sees a connection.

2. Terror. If you allow yourself to believe that a perfect society can be the work of human hands, Ratzinger believes, those hands will end up stained with blood. He expressed this idea in *The Ratzinger Report*: "The 'absolute good' (and this means the building of a just socialistic society) becomes the moral norm that justifies everything else, including—if necessary—violence, homicide, mendacity. . . . And what looks like 'liberation' turns into its opposite and shows its diabolic visage in deeds." Ratzinger even invokes Islamic militant groups such as Hezbollah as a case in point, arguing that they have converted Islam into a form of liberation theology seeking salvation from Israel.

3. Dissent. Ratzinger has long believed that, inspired by liberation theology, Catholics will perceive a form of "class struggle" between those who hold ecclesial power and those excluded from it, and will thus demand "liberation" from oppressive church structures. In attempting to refashion the church into an instrument of revolution, Ratzinger says, liberation theology forgets that its form and structure are "givens" that come from revelation rather than a social contract. Ironically, this relativism actually serves the ends of totalitarian regimes. "She [the church] is a basis for freedom precisely because her form is one of communion, which also includes a common binding commitment. Therefore, when I stand up to a dictatorship, I do so not just in my own name as a private individual, but in virtue of an inner strength that transcends my own self and my subjectivity," Ratzinger has said.

4. Collapse into the culture. Ultimately, what is at stake for Ratzinger is his Augustinian understanding of the distinction between church and culture, mediated through a heavy Lutheran emphasis on sin and the fallenness of the world. "It is time to find again the courage of nonconformism, the capacity to oppose many of the trends of the surrounding culture, renouncing a certain euphoric post-conciliar solidarity," he said in *The Ratzinger Report*. "Today more than ever the Christian must be aware that he belongs to a minority and that he is in opposition to everything that appears good, obvious, logical to the 'spirit of the world,' as the New Testament calls it." To the extent that liberation theology vests its hopes in secular political progress rather than the liberation only Christ can bring, Ratzinger says, it loses sight of the cross.

The Liberation Theology Campaign

Ratzinger's warnings of the dangers posed by liberation theology actually predate his arrival at the Vatican, and the Vatican's growing alarm about the populist thrust of the Latin American church likewise predates Ratzinger. Thus when Ratzinger arrived, liberation theology and Rome had already been circling one another, warily, and it only remained for head-on conflict to begin.

The 1970s

The Congregation for the Doctrine of the Faith first opened a file on Leonardo Boff in 1975, and the file on Jon Sobrino dates from 1980. Given the warnings being raised by the International Theological Commission in the 1970s, it was inevitable that the leading liberation theologians would come under review. At the same time, liberationist energies were building. At their Thirty-Second General Congregation in 1974, the Jesuits adopted a statement that read: "The promotion of justice is an absolute requirement." The diminutive Basque leader of the Jesuits, Pedro Arrupe, an immensely popular figure then in his fourth elected term, remarked on the decision: "If you live out this decree, then we will have martyrs." The scores of Jesuits harassed, beaten, and killed over the ensuing two decades would bitterly make Arrupe's point.

A 1977 document of the International Theological Commission, "Human Development and Christian Salvation," offered a surprisingly balanced treatment of liberation theology given that both Ratzinger and Kloppenburg were members of the body that drafted it. Karl Lehman, now the bishop of Mainz, was chair of the subcommittee that produced the document. It warned that no one should criticize theologies of liberation "if he or she is not listening at the same time to the cries of the poor and seeking more acceptable ways to respond." The document did not reject the idea of structural sin. Sin, it said, is in the first instance personal, "but it is unquestionable that by the power of sin injury and injustice can penetrate social and political institutions." The document recognized that the church cannot avoid political commitments, and it acknowledged that the basic unity between human development and the salvation won by Christ "cannot be overturned, for it is at reality's core."[6]

Nevertheless, the document also set out a number of reservations about liberation theology that Ratzinger and other critics would develop in coming years. The supernatural character of Christian redemption must not be confused with secular history; the church must not collapse into the world; Christian advocacy of social and political reform must not lead to violence; divinizing politics leads to dictatorship; Marxism must not be "baptized"; Christians must not endorse class struggle; full liberation comes only in the next world. The doctrinal congregation's 1984 instruction on liberation theology, as we will see below, can be read as an elaboration of these points.

The formal debut of Ratzinger as a critic of liberation theology came in 1978, when Pope John Paul I made Ratzinger, then the cardinal of Munich, his legate to a national Marian congress in Guayquil, Ecuador. The purpose of his trip was to deliver a warning about Marxism and social revolution (suggesting, among other things, that those who imagine that a longer John Paul I papacy would have spared the church the crusade against liberation theology and other progressive causes are probably mistaken). Ratzinger began his address by telling the Latin Americans how important what happens in their church is, because the majority of Catholics in the world are now in the Americas. "This means that the center of the world church will shift to America," he said. (In usual European fashion, Ratzinger treats North and South America as one continent.)

"It would be a terrible misfortune," Ratzinger said in this September 1978 address, if America "sold out its soul," bewitched by European economic and technological achievements, and gave itself over to a "culture of having." This culture, Ratzinger warned, is most likely to present itself in the guise of Marxism. He said that both of the "great rationalisms" of the age—Western-positivist and Eastern-Marxist—have led the world into a deep crisis. "This shows the disastrous path of an entirely rationalistic culture," Ratzinger said. The emphasis on material acquisition and distribution shared by both systems "has not solved the great North/South problems in the last twenty-five years," he said. As an alternative, Ratzinger proposed that the Latin Americans foster their own "culture of intuition and heart," which he said also exists in a different form in Africa.[7]

After John Paul I died, Ratzinger gave an interview to Munich's *Süddeutsche Zeitung* about both his Ecuador trip and the election of a new pope. Published on October 6, 1978, the interview marks his first direct public criticism of liberation theology. Speaking of the church in Latin America, Ratzinger said, "It is necessary to relieve not just economic but above all social needs." He argued that an "overhasty introduction of the industrial age" in the culture has led to "uprooting, a breakdown of the family structure, a fatherless society, a proletarization of academic life and deep divisions among the people." He said that rejection of a "pushy Americanism," by which he meant the capitalist ideology of the United States, plus the reality of social injustice created the basis for Marxist ideologies.

"Where evangelization is neglected and social aid is robbed of its Christian basis, where the much-discussed theology of liberation is blended with Marxist presuppositions, the door is opened to ideological means of struggle," he said. Ratzinger suggested that the gains being made by Jehovah's Witnesses and Mormons in the region testified to the failure of Marxism and revolution to meet the spiritual needs of the people. With respect to the papal election, Ratzinger said that despite criticism of John Paul I by "leftist forces in Italy," his negative judgment on liberation theology should be maintained under a new pope.

The critical event of 1979 as far as liberation theology was concerned was the Sandinista Revolution in Nicaragua. The uprising enjoyed the support of most base communities and the progressive elements in the Nicaraguan Catholic church. Three priests served as cabinet ministers, and one as the country's ambassador to the Organization of American States. More than anything else, this confirmed Ratzinger's belief that liberation theology's perspective on class struggle could be viewed only down the barrel of a gun.

In early 1979, in one of his first voyages as pope, John Paul II traveled to the Dominican Republic and Mexico. In Mexico he spoke to the CELAM (a federation of the Catholic bishops' conferences of Latin America) conference in Puebla, near the border with Guatemala. The second CELAM meeting in Medellín in 1968 had produced a stirring endorsement of liberation theology. Conservative members of the hierarchy, especially Cardinal Alfonso López Trujillo of Colombia, wanted a condemnation this time. The pope's remarks in Puebla seemed to lean in the direction of the conservatives. He warned priests that "you are not social or political leaders or officials of a temporal power," and told the Catholics of Latin America to adhere to a "Christian idea of liberation," not an "ideological" one. In the end, the "Puebla Declaration" that resulted was a compromise. It repeated that the church favored an "option for the poor," but the idea was hemmed in with cautions about revolution. Most liberation theologians greeted the document as a vindication, and began referring to "Medellín and Puebla" as if they constituted a single line of thought. In historical perspective, however, Puebla is actually more like a point on a downward slope, the beginning of a turn in the Latin American hierarchy's official attitude toward liberation theology. Later in 1979, John Paul said he supported the idea of a theology of liberation, but that it should not be tied exclusively to Latin America or to the sociologically poor. He quoted Balthasar to the effect that a Catholic theology must have a "universal radius."

1980

Two events in 1980 hinted at the direction the anti-liberation theology campaign would take. Sometime around March 20, three Vatican officials—cardinals Silvio Oddi of the Congregation for Clergy, Franjo Seper of the Congregation for the Doctrine of the Faith, and Sebastiano Baggio of the Congregation for Bishops—decided to recommend that the pope reassign Archbishop Oscar Romero of El Salvador. They felt his constant criticism of the government and his "option for the poor" was threatening to fatally divide the church in that country. Romero was assassinated on March 24, before the decision could be carried out. The decision to move Romero was a signal that Rome did not look favorably on the political direction of the Latin American church.[8]

In January 1979, just before the Puebla meeting, Romero had excommunicated the president of El Salvador for his failure to stop the killing of priests and laity. This sort of prophetic gesture from the once-conservative Romero had gotten him into trouble with Rome before; he noted in his diary in August 1979 that he was being accused of being a "Marxist" and a "subversive." In the spring of 1979, the Holy See asked Georgetown University in Washington, D.C., to cancel plans to award an honorary degree to Romero. The Jesuit president of Georgetown, Timothy Healy, refused and traveled to San Salvador to bestow the degree.

Over the next several years, Rome would transfer, replace, or hobble a number of progressive bishops, with the clear aim of diminishing the progressive energies in the Latin American church. Romero said in his diary the real problem was that he, like many priests, strove to be faithful to Vatican II "translated for Latin America by Medellín and Puebla." To this day, Vatican authorities have refused to acknowledge Romero as a martyr or to make him a saint. For a pope who has canonized almost three-quarters as many saints as all his predecessors combined, it is a remarkable, and telling, omission.

Later in 1980, John Paul went on his first pastoral visit to Brazil, the largest Catholic country in the world and home to the most emphatic episcopal supporters of liberation theology. His host for much of the trip was Cardinal Evaristo Arns of São Paolo, a hero to Brazilian Catholics as the man most identified with resistance to military rule. (The military had seized power in Brazil in 1964 and held it until permitting civilian elections in 1985.) Earlier in the year Arns had clashed with Vatican officials over his desire to host a conference on "Theology in the Third World" in São Paolo. Rome asked him to refrain, and when he went ahead, letters went out from the Vatican to bishops in countries where theologians had received invitations, instructing them to stop their theologians from attending. Papal nuncios followed up the letters with visits to the bishops. Thus when John Paul arrived in Brazil, Arns had reason to be wary. Nevertheless, Arns stood his ground. At one point during the trip, military officials offered to fly the pope to his next stop, saving him a bumpy overland ride in church vehicles. As the pontiff and his entourage headed off to get on the chopper, Arns pulled him aside and said, gently but firmly: "If you go with the army, you go alone." John Paul turned around and went with Arns. It was a signal of things to come: in Brazil liberation theology had powerful defenders, who had both the will and the intellectual wherewithal to put up a fight. Ratzinger understood that if he was going to crack the movement, the battle would have to take place primarily on Brazilian soil.

1981

In 1981, John Paul II brushed aside the Jesuits' constitution to impose his own leadership on the order and delayed their next general congregation for two years until he felt he could safely permit a new election. The actions were a clear rejection of the leadership of Pedro Arrupe and of the progressive direction of the Jesuits, especially their embrace of liberation theology. The pope accused the Jesuits of meddling in politics, of becoming secularized, and, especially in Latin America, of replacing traditional priestly formation with involvement in a "popular church" made up of base communities. John Paul argued that because of the Jesuits' disproportionate influence on the church, he had to make an example of them; one Jesuit official said the pope told him, "If you do it, these other orders will feel they can do it, too."

When Arrupe was hobbled by a stroke in 1981, the pope placed Father Paolo Dezza, an eighty-year-old Italian Jesuit (and later a cardinal) in charge, along with Father Giuseppe Pittau, the Jesuit provincial in Japan. The pope did not permit the Jesuits to gather in a General Congregation until September 1983, when they elected Father Peter-Hans Kolvenbach, a highly respected Dutch scholar and Middle East specialist, as general. Arrupe thus became the first Jesuit superior ever to relinquish leadership prior to death. In 1985, speaking to an assembly of Jesuits, John Paul still struck an admonishing tone: "You must watch attentively lest the faithful become disoriented by doubtful teachings, by publications or speeches that are in open conflict with the faith and morals of the church." Arrupe died in 1991, after spending almost a decade in the infirmary at the Jesuit headquarters in Rome.

1982

The stream of anti-liberation theology sentiment from the right wing of the Latin American church accelerated in 1982, exemplified by an article Kloppenburg published in *Communio* about Boff. Kloppenburg's hostility was at least partly personal; in the days when Kloppenburg was still enthusiastic about Vatican II, he had groomed Boff, a fellow Franciscan, to be his successor in the theology chair at the Franciscan university in Petrópolis. As the two men drifted apart in the late 1970s, Kloppenburg became embittered and turned into one of liberation theology's most ferocious antagonists. Boff returned the sentiment. In a 1989 interview with a doctoral student at Kent State University, Ohio, that was later published in the *National Catholic Reporter,* Boff boasted that if Kloppenburg, whom he described as the "leader of the reactionary conservative bishops," held a reception to launch a new book, he would be lucky if three friends showed up to buy copies. Boff, on the other hand, said he could sell out 300 copies of a book at one sitting. "Who then mobilizes more people?" he asked rhetorically.

In his *Communio* article, Kloppenburg singled out Boff's 1981 book *Church: Charism and Power* for special criticism. (The book was actually a collection of essays written over the period 1972 to 1981.) Kloppenburg charged that Boff wanted "a church without an institution, without power, without hierarchy, without dogmas and canon law." While most observers believe this was a distortion of Boff's positions, Boff did have some harsh words for institutional Catholicism in the book. It has become "absolutized in such a way that it tends to substitute itself for Jesus Christ, or to understand itself as his equal. . . . Tensions were, and are, frequently suffocated through a repression that often violates the basic human rights that are respected even by officially atheistic societies."

The administration of U.S. President Ronald Reagan took notice of liberation theology in 1982, in a document called "A New Inter-American Policy for the Eighties," popularly known as the "Santa Fe document" for the city in which Reagan's team of advisors worked on it. Roger Fontaine, later Reagan's Central America advisor on the National Security Council, and Lewis Tambs, ambassador to Costa Rica until he was forced to resign in the Iran-Contra scandal, were on the team. The document asserted that liberation theology was responsible for Catholic criticism of "productive capitalism" in Latin America, and suggested that it should be American policy to assist Protestant groups in "weakening" progressive Catholicism. There is no evidence that John Paul ever made a secret alliance with Reagan, as Carl Bernstein and Marco Politi once alleged, but clearly Reagan smiled upon Ratzinger's efforts to subdue liberation theology.[9]

1983

In February of 1983, Ratzinger sent a letter to the Peruvian bishops, asking them to investigate Gustavo Gutiérrez. Ratzinger listed several alleged flaws in Gutiérrez's writings: (1) a Marxist view of history; (2) a selective reading of the Bible that overemphasizes the poor; (3) treating the Holy Spirit as a source of revelation separate from the church's tradition and teaching office; (4) a class-ridden theology; (5) an emphasis on building the kingdom through class struggle, a process which also involves changing the structures of the church; (6) making the church into a partisan group, an idea "which puts in jeopardy the hierarchy and its legitimacy"; (7) a neglect of the beatitudes; and (8) a Marxist perversion of the gospel. "There are grounds for being deeply worried" about the theology Gutiérrez advocates, Ratzinger concluded.

As long as Cardinal Juan Landázuri, a progressive who had relied on Gutiérrez as his advisor at Medellín, remained in Lima, Gutiérrez could count on some protection, but he decided not to await the inevitable. Gutiérrez asked Ratzinger if he could come to Rome to meet with him. Ratzinger agreed, and in March Gutiérrez made the trip. He came back discouraged, saying Ratzinger had been pleasant, but the fight over liberation theology was "far from over." In June 1983, Gutiérrez submitted a sixty-page defense of his work to the bishops. At their plenary sessions in August and again in January, they were deadlocked over how to proceed.

In 1983 the pope went on a pastoral visit to Central America, including a stop in Nicaragua. He did not like what he saw. At an outdoor mass, John Paul looked out at banners reading, "Thank God and the Revolution," and warned his listeners against "ideological compromises and temporal solutions." As the people chanted "Peace," the pope shot back, "Silence! The church is the first to promote peace." The most famous image of the 1983 trip came on the pope's arrival in Managua, when Father Ernesto Cardenal, one of three priests serving in the Sandinista cabinet, attempted to greet him in the receiving line. Determined not to give the dissidents a "photo op," the pope withdrew his hand and waved his finger at Cardenal, saying, "First straighten out your situation with the church." Though Cardenal later dismissed the gesture as "meaningless," the straightening would eventually be imposed upon him.

That would occur a year later in December 1984, when the Vatican announced that Cardenal's brother, Fernando, the Sandinista minister of education, had been dismissed from the Jesuits. Ernesto Cardenal and another priest, Edgar Parrales, the ambassador to the Organization of American States, were involuntarily deprived of their status as priests. Ironically, Parrales had been petitioning on his own to be relieved of his vows for more than a year. At the same time, the Maryknoll order acted on Vatican instructions to expel Father Miguel D'Escoto, then serving as the Sandinista foreign minister. The head of the order, Father William Boteler, said he disagreed with the decision but had no choice. D'Escoto's impact continues to be felt in the United States through Orbis Books, which he helped publisher Philip Scharper launch in 1970 to give Third World authors access to American audiences.

On October 18–19, 1983, U.S. Senator Jeremiah Denton (R-Ala.), who chaired the Senate Security and Terrorism Subcommittee, held hearings on liberation theology. The star witness was a conservative priest, Father Enrique Rueda, who described liberation theology as part of the Soviet attempt to conquer the "soft underbelly" of the United States in Latin America. Denton expressed the hope that policymakers would take the threat seriously.

1984

1984 is the *annus mirabilis* of the liberation theology movement, the year when the struggle between the Vatican and the liberationists burst into public view. It began on March 14, with an essay by Ratzinger published in the Italian journal *30 Giorni,* which is associated with the conservative Communion and Liberation movement. In effect, Ratzinger suggested, liberation theology confronts the church with a new type of heresy that does not play by the rules. The movement "does not fit into accepted categories of heresy because it accepts all the existing language but gives it new meaning." In other words, the liberationists do not deny core doctrines such as redemption or grace outright, but they apply entirely different content to those words, so their heresy is both more subtle and more systematic. The essay amounted to Ratzinger's formal declaration of war, because now his assessment was clear—liberation theology is not just dangerous or unorthodox, it is heretical.

Ratzinger said that liberation theology relies on Marxism, and interprets Christianity as a political program of class struggle for the emancipation of the poor. It drains the categories of the faith—sin, grace, redemption—of their traditional content and pumps them up with new, sociopolitical meaning. He warned that in liberationist thinking, the "people of God" is opposed to the "hierarchy," thus setting up a class struggle inside the church. The church's magisterial teachings take the part of the rich and the dominators, and are opposed to the poor. Though the movement is mostly associated with Latin America, Ratzinger warned that there are variants of it in India, Sri Lanka, the Philippines, Taiwan, and Africa. He named Assman, Gutiérrez, and Sobrino as examples of dangerous thinkers.

The essay was apparently written as an address for a meeting of the doctrinal congregation. The circumstances under which it came to be published in *30 Giorni* remain murky. U.S. theologian Virgilio Elizondo, quoting Gutiérrez, told a wire service that Ratzinger had explained to Gutiérrez that the essay was a rough draft that had been stolen out of his desk and that it did not represent his full thinking. There was never any retraction, however, and there is nothing in the subsequent record to suggest Ratzinger does not identify himself with its ideas. At a press conference designed to clear things up, Ratzinger praised liberation theology to the extent it "put in a proper light the necessary responsibility of the Christian toward the poor and the oppressed." But he added that "the church's special option for the poor . . . excludes no one."

In March 1984, a special meeting took place in Bogotá, Colombia, between members of the Congregation for the Doctrine of the Faith and representatives of CELAM. Behind the scenes, liberation theology foes hoped for an outright condemnation, but they were frustrated by the refusal of several bishops to go along. In the end, a statement was issued that offered lukewarm praise of liberation theology but rejected Marxist analysis. One newspaper quoted a Latin American archbishop as complaining about the Vatican, "They cannot accept that anything new or inventive could come out of the Third World." Hans Küng published an account of the Bogotá meeting immediately afterward in which he reported a rift between Ratzinger and the progressive wing of the CELAM membership. Darío Castrillón Hoyos (then secretary general of CELAM and at this writing prefect of the Vatican's Congregation for Clergy) told Küng, however, in a letter that was later published in the CELAM bulletin that the bishops of Latin America were "in complete accord" with Ratzinger's views on liberation theology.

In January, the bishops of Peru voted thirty-one to fifteen in favor of some kind of criticism of Gutiérrez, but they were unable to agree upon a text. The tables turned in March when Cardinal Landázuri of Lima received a letter from Karl Rahner. The letter, dated March 16, was written exactly two weeks before Rahner died at 80. In it, Rahner issued a stirring endorsement of Gutiérrez: "I am convinced of the orthodoxy of the theological work of Gustavo Gutiérrez," Rahner wrote. "The theology of liberation that he represents is entirely orthodox. A condemnation of Gustavo Gutiérrez would have, it is my full conviction, very negative consequences for the climate that is the condition in which a theology that is at the service of evangelization may endure. Today there are diverse schools and it has always been thus. . . . It would be deplorable if this legitimate pluralism were to be restricted by administrative means." Landázuri shared the letter with other Peruvian bishops, and it had a powerful effect on heading off the momentum for a censure.[10]

On May 15, Ratzinger sent a six-page letter to Leonardo Boff asking for clarifications of his views, especially as they concerned the challenge to hierarchical authority from the "church of the people." He accused Boff of a "pitiless, radical assault" on the institutional church. At the same time, Archbishop Eugênio Sales of Rio de Janeiro withdrew the *missio canonica* from Boff's brother Clodovis and from a colleague, Father Antonio Moser. Sales accused the two men of using Marxist analysis. His action drew a formal protest from the Brazilian bishops' conference, whose members noted that Moser served on its doctrinal commission. Sales was unmoved.

The hostility of conservative Latin American hierarchs such as Sales, López Trujillo, and Koppenburg to liberation theology led some observers over the years to conclude that the Vatican's role in the crackdown has been exaggerated, that the worst enemies were home-grown. Yet throughout the 1980s, these local opponents represented a minority inside their bishops' conferences. Their hope was in Rome, and that meant Ratzinger.

Sales had long been funneling complaints to the Vatican about Arns in São Paolo, especially his program of priestly formation, which Sales alleged was tantamount to a school for revolutionaries. In the summer of 1984, Ratzinger named Cardinal Joseph Höffner of Cologne as his representative for the job of "inspecting" the formation programs in São Paolo. Höffner had been Küng's main antagonist in the German bishops' conference and an outspoken opponent of democratic socialism as "unacceptably Marxist." Höffner was dispatched without the Brazilian bishops' conference being informed, although Ratzinger had earlier promised the Brazilians that no investigation would be undertaken without their consent.[11]

Arns had divided his seminarians among eleven small formation houses, each with seven or eight young men. They were involved with base communities and also held jobs while studying so they could support their families. At a news conference in Brazil, Höffner told the media he was impressed with what he had seen. He noted that when Arns arrived in São Paolo in 1970 there were only nine seminarians, but by the mid-1980s there were ninety-three. The program, he said, could be an example for other countries. Yet when he got back to Germany, the report he submitted to Ratzinger was largely negative. That same summer, Ratzinger gave an address at the Katholikentag in Germany. Youthful protestors disrupted the talk, unfurling a banner that read: "In spite of the Inquisition, Liberation Theology lives, Herr Ratzinger."

Ratzinger's single biggest bombshell was then dropped: the *Instruction on certain aspects of the theology of liberation*, formally dated September 3, 1984, but released in late August. It warned of "new miseries and new types of slavery" that liberation theology threatened to create. While acknowledging that Christians should be "involved in the struggle for justice," and asserting that the document "should not . . . serve as an excuse for those who maintain indifference to human misery," it insisted that by applying Marxist concepts liberation theology "subordinates theology to the class struggle." It said that liberation theology tends to misunderstand or eliminate the transcendence and gratuity of liberation in Jesus Christ, the sovereignty of grace, and the true nature of the means of salvation, especially the church and her Sacraments. Liberation theology collapses sacred history into secular history. Moreover, it fosters ecclesial anarchy: "In setting aside the authoritative interpretation of the church, denounced as classist, one is at the same time departing from tradition."

After accusing liberation theology of uncritically importing Marxist analytical tools, the instruction delivered a rhetorical knockout: "This system is a perversion of the Christian message as God entrusted it to His church." The document was personally approved by the pope.

That the instruction expressed personal concerns of Ratzinger's, and not merely a consensus among Roman theologians, can be inferred by comparing it to the 1977 statement of the International Theological Commission discussed above. All the negative warnings about liberation theology had been sharpened, especially the accusation of excessive reliance on Marxist analysis. This issue had occupied one paragraph in the International Theological Commission document; in the 10,000-word instruction, it comprised more than 4,000 words. The most important positive components of the 1977 document were missing. Nowhere did the instruction concede that the institutional church inevitably makes political commitments, or that it should employ these commitments on behalf of the poor. The 1977 document reaffirmed the teaching of *Gaudium et spes* that in God's kingdom "not only love will remain, but love's labor as well," meaning that humans start to build the kingdom in this order of existence. It also stressed the basic unity between human development and Christian salvation. The instruction, on the other hand, called most forms of liberation theology "a negation of the faith of the church."

A tidal wave of reaction followed. The Vatican secretary of state, Agostino Casaroli, said that he had not been consulted, and he regretted the instruction's "negative" tone. A positive document, he said, would have been "preferable." Rumors began to circulate that the pope was unhappy; apparently he was under the impression the document had been discussed by the doctrinal commissions of the Latin American bishops, and when he learned it had not, suggested that it be regarded as a "working paper of the doctrinal congregation." Many Vatican observers believe that behind the scenes, John Paul assigned Cardinal Roger Etchegaray, head of the Pontifical Council for Justice and Peace, to begin drafting a more positive statement. Around the world, many Catholic leaders reacted with outrage. English Dominican theologian Nicholas Lash said Ratzinger had "made up a system which does not exist." In this context, the tepid response of even the moderate American bishops is notable. James Malone of Youngstown, Ohio, called the document "lucid and helpful," and Joseph Bernardin said it would help "liberation theology develop within the tradition."

Among the liberation theologians, the typical response was that because they did not hold any of the beliefs against which the document cautioned, they had not been touched by it. They did not endorse Marxism as a political system, they did not reject Christ's grace, they too saw the Sacraments and the church as essential. Some liberation theologians were actually encouraged, concluding that if these were Ratzinger's concerns, his criticism had nothing to do with them. Their mistake was in failing to give sufficient credit to Ratzinger's systematic approach. He did not care if they *in fact* held these positions; his point was that their theological presuppositions led to such conclusions, whether individual theologians recognized it or not. "We are facing, therefore, a real system, even if some hesitate to follow the logic to its conclusion," the instruction read.

An exception was Segundo, who published a book entitled *Theology and the Church: A Response to Cardinal Ratzinger and a Warning to the Whole Church* the following year. Segundo said the liberationists could not evade Ratzinger's blow by claiming it did not apply to them, and that the document was a direct attack on their work that had to be taken seriously as such. If Ratzinger is right, Segundo said, I am wrong. Marxism, Segundo argued, was a red herring; the real difference is on ecclesiology. Segundo's thesis was that Ratzinger in effect denied the teaching of Vatican II, as expressed in *Gaudium et spes*, that God's grace and salvation are universal, and hence the church must work in partnership with other people and social forces when it discerns God's purposes.

Days after the instruction was issued, Leonardo Boff arrived in Rome for a September 7 colloquy to which he had been summoned by Ratzinger to discuss the congregation's objections to Boff's book *Church: Charism and Power*. By a stroke of historical irony, September 7 is Brazilian independence day. Back in August, Boff had written Ratzinger to suggest that the exchange take place in Brazil, but Ratzinger refused. Ratzinger had insisted that a car from the congregation pick Boff up and return him to his Franciscan residence in Rome; the goal, no doubt, was to avoid the media, as Boff's arrival at Rome's Fiumicino airport September 2 had occasioned an impromptu press conference. Monsignor Josef Clemens, Ratzinger's personal secretary, did the driving, and none of Boff's Franciscan colleagues were permitted to accompany him. When Clemens arrived, Boff jokingly asked if handcuffs would be necessary. Three members of the Brazilian hierarchy—Arns, Cardinal Alósio Lorscheider, and Bishop Ivo Lorscheiter, president of the Brazilian bishops' conference—asked to be part of the colloquy, but were refused by Raztinger. After some negotiation, they were allowed to take part in the second half of the conversation.

Edward Schillebeeckx once said that the most awkward moment in such an interrogation comes in trying to make small talk over coffee. In Boff's case, Ratzinger got the ball rolling by suggesting Boff looked good in a cassock and should wear one more often, that it was a sign of witness; Boff said it could also be a symbol of power. When the colloquy broke up with no mention of a censure, the Brazilians thought they had won; Arns even flashed a "V for victory" sign at a bank of television cameras as they left. The worst, however, was yet to come.[12]

In the same month, a special meeting of the Peruvian bishops took place in Rome. Once again, Ratzinger sought action against Gutiérrez. He wanted a condemnation on three points: the use of Marxism, an overemphasis on social sin, and a refusal to disavow violence. On this last point Gutiérrez and others quoted Paul VI's *Populorum progressio*, which refused to rule out violence as a final option against a "manifest, long-standing tyranny." Perhaps fortified by the Rahner letter, perhaps by the example of the Brazilian bishops' spirited defense of Boff, the Peruvians balked.

The meeting began with Ratzinger suggesting that he serve as chairman; Landázari replied, however, that it would not be an official meeting of the bishops' conference unless he chaired it. At the end, the bishops issued no censure of Gutiérrez. Their concluding document, eventually issued on November 26, expressed appreciation for the "spiritual deepening" that liberation theology had fostered, acknowledged the reality of social sin, treated the class struggle as a fact, and demanded greater distributive justice. It even spoke proudly of liberation theology as a movement "born on our soil." Ratzinger had apparently gambled that by working through the Peruvian bishops rather than confronting Gutiérrez directly, he might get what he wanted without backlash against Rome. In this instance, the strategy backfired.

Things changed in 1989, with the appointment of Jesuit Augusto Vargas Alzamora to succeed Landázari in Lima. Vargas Alzamora, who has ties to Opus Dei, has taken a harder line against Gutiérrez. This transition demonstrates that as long as the selection of bishops is reserved exclusively to Vatican officials, there is no defeat they cannot eventually reverse.

160

On a swing through Latin America in late 1984, John Paul made reference to liberation theology at each of the stops. In Venezuela, Ecuador, and Trinidad, the pope warned crowds against alcohol, drugs, violence, idleness, prostitution, and casual sex. He admonished governments to use their national wealth to improve life for the poor, and he praised the bishops of CELAM for their preferential option for the poor. Yet he also echoed Ratzinger's argument that this option was not for a "class," and that it was open to everyone. He demanded that bishops "remove from the flock the errors that threaten it."

In October 1984, Ratzinger sent a letter to El Salvadoran Jesuit Jon Sobrino, obliging him to send the doctrinal congregation a lengthy clarification of his own views on liberation and redemption. Sobrino, a theologian on the faculty at the Jesuit-run University of Central America, had been an advisor to Romero, helping him to draft many of his pastoral letters. Sobrino quickly got an endorsement from Jesuit Juan Alfaro at the Gregorian University in Rome, who called Sobrino a "very orthodox theologian."

1985

López Trujillo and his circle called a 1985 meeting outside Santiago, Chile. If the bishops' conferences of Latin America could not be relied upon to condemn liberation theology, this ad-hoc group of conservative prelates at least was determined to be heard. They produced the *Andes statement,* which denounced liberation theology as a Marxist perversion of the faith. They said that liberation theology advocates a conflict between the "popular church" and the "hierarchical church." The session drew extended coverage on Pinochet-controlled state television, and the Chilean military invoked the document in defense of their subsequent arrest of Father Renato Hevia, editor of a progressive journal called *Mensaje.* The Andes group met again in Lima in January of 1986, this time joined by Darío Castrillón Hoyos of Colombia, who said of Leonardo Boff, "Boff will have to ask God to forgive him, and when God answers, then the pope and I will know whether to forgive him or not." Cardinal Bernard Law of Boston, a conservative and Vatican favorite, was also at the Lima meeting.

On March 11, 1985, the Congregation for the Doctrine of the Faith issued a formal notice on Boff's *Church: Charism and Power.* The book endangers the faith, the congregation said, in its concept of dogma, its understanding of sacred power, and its overemphasis on the prophetic role of the church. On April 26, Ratzinger ordered a formal silencing of Leonardo Boff; it was announced on May 9. He was not to publish, teach, or speak publicly until further notice. Boff accepted the decision and, for a time, declined even to take phone calls from colleagues. "I prefer to walk with the church rather than to walk alone with my theology," he said. In a puzzling footnote, Balthasar told the *Frankfurter Allgemeine* on October 25, 1985, that the decision to silence Boff did not come from Ratzinger, and that Ratzinger had no choice but to sign it. Former Ratzinger student Hermann Häring publicly asked for a clarification of this statement in a 1986 essay, but none has ever been issued.[13]

Boff's was the second silencing since Vatican II; the first affected the French Dominican Jacques Pohier for his views on the resurrection. In the summer of 1985, a Catholic publishing house in Brazil planned to issue a volume containing all the back-and-forth correspondence between Boff and Ratzinger, as well as the transcript of the September 7 colloquy in Rome, but Ratzinger intervened to stop publication.

In August of 1985, Gutiérrez got into new trouble with Ratzinger by traveling to Nicaragua to express solidarity with Miguel D'Escoto, the Sandinista foreign minister and defrocked priest. D'Escoto had launched a hunger strike to protest violence against Nicaragua fomented by the United States. Gutiérrez said he agreed that "the big threat to Nicaragua" comes from the United States. He called the Sandinista revolution a "liberation process," despite the existence of some "historical ambiguities." Of D'Escoto, he said, "He's not a friend, he's a brother to me."

At the 1985 Synod of Bishops, called to evaluate the legacy of Vatican II, Brazilian bishop Ivo Lorscheiter delivered an intervention (the Vatican word for a speech) in which he said that liberation theology "does not justify Marxist ideology or break with the Catholic theological tradition." The point did not make it into the official Vatican summary of the synod's findings.

1986

For a brief time in 1986, it seemed as if liberation theology might stage a comeback. In January, acclaimed Catholic author Graham Greene endorsed liberation theology. Travelling in Nicaragua, he also said he felt religious and political freedom was respected under the Sandinistas. In the same month, several Brazilian bishops took their *ad limina* visit to Rome, a trip to Rome to see the pope that all bishops are obliged to make every five years. In his address, the pope warned against "grave deviations" that liberation theology can introduce into the faith and insisted that the church cannot be reduced to its sociopolitical role. The only real liberation, he said, is individual liberation from sin. Yet by March 13, when another entourage of Brazilians arrived in Rome, the pope struck a much more upbeat note. He urged the bishops to continue their work for social justice. "Purified of elements which can water it down," he said, "liberation theology is not only orthodox, but necessary."

The best was yet to come. On April 12, 1986, African cardinal Bernadin Gantin, then head of the Congregation for Bishops, spoke at a retreat for the members of the Brazilian bishops' conference. He brought a letter from the pope, which said of liberation theology that it is "not only opportune, but useful and necessary." Participants in the retreat said that as Gantin read these words, "alleluias" began to ring out among the bishops. Some got tears in their eyes. One bishop later said, "The pope has given liberation theology back to the bishops."

The positive currents continued in mid-1986, as several installments in a projected fifty-volume series on *Theology and Liberation* began to roll off the press. Drawing on the work of all the best-known theologians in the movement, including Boff, the series came with the official endorsement of 119 Catholic bishops, 79 from Brazil alone. Five were from the United States: Robert Sanchez of Santa Fe, New Mexico; auxiliary Thomas Gumbleton of Detroit, Michigan; Raymond Hunthausen of Seattle, Washington; Raymond Lucker in New Ulm, Minnesota; and auxiliary Peter Rosazza of Hartford, Connecticut.

In April, the long-awaited second Vatican document on liberation theology was issued. Entitled *Instruction on Christian freedom and liberation,* the text seemed to offer a more positive vision. "The quest for freedom and the aspiration to liberation, which are among the principal signs of the times in the modern world, have their first source in the Christian heritage, . . ." it read. "Those who are oppressed by poverty are the object of a love of preference on the part of the church, which since her origin and in spite of the failings of many of her members has not ceased to work for their relief, defense and liberation. She has done this through numberless works of charity which remain always and everywhere indispensable. In addition, through her social doctrine which she strives to apply, she has sought to promote structural changes in society so as to secure conditions of life worthy of the human person." The text accepted armed struggle as a last-ditch response to "prolonged tyranny," and it even applauded the base communities as a "source of great hope for the church."

Boff welcomed the document. He wrote Ratzinger a letter (addressed to "Dear Brother Ratzinger"), calling the new instruction a "decisive and historic" text that protects liberation theology. "Now there can no longer be any doubt: Rome is at the side of the oppressed and all those fighting against injustice," Boff wrote. The letter was also signed by his brother Clodovis.

A more sober reading of the April 5, 1986, document shows that it is far more ambiguous. In its opening lines, the statement notes: "On both the theoretical and practical levels, these aspirations [for liberation] sometimes assume expressions which are not always in conformity with the truth concerning man as it is manifested in the light of his creation and redemption. For this reason the Congregation for the Doctrine of the Faith has considered it necessary to draw attention to 'deviations, or risks of deviation, damaging to the Faith and to Christian living.' Far from being outmoded, these warnings appear ever more timely and relevant." It goes on to argue that in its philosophical underpinnings, liberation theology has embraced an understanding of truth, and of freedom, that enslaves rather than redeems. In a widely noticed twist, the "preferential option for the poor" became a "preferential *love* for the poor," a nuance that many people took as an implied repudiation of class struggle.

Boff's silence was lifted just before Easter. He referred to the decision as "a coherent attitude by Rome" in keeping with the spirit of the new instruction. Linking the decision to the Easter celebration, his friends proclaimed that "Brother Leonardo has been resurrected!" The euphoria of the time was such that some liberation theology supporters even called the act a "surrender" on the part of the Vatican. In fact, however, this was simply the eye of the storm. Over the next six years, Boff was repeatedly asked to clarify and/or modify his views until, in 1992, following the imposition of a ban on teaching, Boff opted to leave the Catholic priesthood.

Speculation has always surrounded the question of how Leonardo Boff came to be "Public Enemy Number One" in Ratzinger's anti-liberation theology campaign. Gutiérrez was better known internationally, and both Sobrino and Segundo had greater intellectual range. Yet Boff was the only liberation theologian who experienced an inquistorial process in Rome, the one silenced, the one whose writings were repeatedly condemned, the one whose movements were tracked in Rome with relentless precision. In a 1999 interview with *Newsweek,* Boff described Ratzinger's intelligence network during the period of his silencing in 1985. "Once I went to a remote Amazon village to participate in a religious retreat," he said. "Three days later, word had reached the Vatican."

Why Boff? There are four likely factors. The first, and probably most important, is that Boff applied the conceptual tools of liberation theology to the church. Boff argued that a "clerical aristocracy" had expropriated from the people of God the means of religious production, and hence had misappropriated their right to decisionmaking. In 1984, he publicly warned that if a "schism comes from the base" in Latin America, the "Vatican will bear the responsibility."

Ratzinger confirmed this analysis in February 2000, in a speech at a closed-door conference in Rome to review the implementation of Vatican II. Ratzinger said, in remarks reported by the *Catholic News Service,* that Boff had been the first public test of how the council's potentially ambiguous language about the church would be interpreted. *Lumen gentium,* Vatican II's document on the church, said that the "sole church of Christ . . . *subsists in* the Catholic church." Ratzinger said that Boff and others took that to mean that the one church of Christ can also subsist outside Catholicism, that the historical Jesus had in fact not intended to found an institutional church at all. This thesis, Ratzinger said, could be called "ecclesiological relativism." Thus Ratzinger himself attests that the Boff case was not primarily about liberation theology, but also about how one understands the church.

Second, Boff was a Brazilian. American Father Charles Curran, himself a Ratzinger target in the 1980s, put the point this way in 1999 interview with me: "This was a political decision. Brazil was a big, influential church, and Ratzinger wanted to send a message. Uruguay [Segundo's home] is certainly not the place to do that." In addition, the Brazilian hierarchy was, in the mid-1980s, solidly committed to the liberationist vision. If Ratzinger was going to succeed, Brazil was where that battle had to be fought.

Third, Boff did not have a sympathetic local bishop with enough power to run interference with Rome in the same way that Gutiérrez did during the early stages of his troubles. Though the majority of the Brazilian hierarchy may have been behind Boff, his own bishop, Cardinal Eugênio Sales, had been demanding action against Boff throughout the early 1980s.

Finally, there is a personal dimension. Ratzinger knew Boff, had worked with him as a student. Boff is a big, flamboyant personality, in a way that Gutiérrez, Sobrino, and Segundo were not. Boff, though far less deliberately confrontational than Hans Küng, shared something of the Swiss theologian's flair for making a splash in the press. In the late 1980s, for example, he called for the dissolution of the Vatican's national sovereignty and the recall of all papal nuncios. In a sense, Boff practically invited Ratzinger to pursue him.

In 1986, however, this future was not clear. Taking the three events of the year in combination—the seemingly more positive character of the new instruction, the lifting of Boff's silence, and the papal endorsement that liberation theology is "not only opportune, but useful and necessary"— Gutiérrez actually said at the end of 1986, "The debate is over." What he meant is that liberation theology had won. If so, it was to be a Pyrrhic victory.

1987

In 1987, John Paul II issued his encyclical *Sollicitudo rei socialis*, a document which integrated so many concerns held by Boff and the other Latin Americans that one commentator remarked, "it could have been written by the liberation theologians." John Paul wrote, "the aspiration to freedom is something noble and legitimate. This is the purpose of development." He even invoked several of the liberationists' favorite biblical passages, such as Matthew 25:31–46, and used them as the liberation theologians themselves do, as a call to social reform. His critical approach to both capitalism and communism led some Western critics to charge the pope with "moral relativism" because he did not condemn the Soviets.

Gutiérrez returned John Paul's overture, saying in an October interview with Vatican radio that the magisterium has a "duty and a right" to express criticisms about liberation theology. He called the two instructions "useful" and said they helped liberation theologians to correct some terms which were not quite accurate. "We ought to pay attention to them," he said.

Yet two events in 1987 suggested that dangerous days were ahead. Ratzinger blocked publication of a new book by Boff, suggesting a renewal of Rome's confrontational stance. More ominously, in November a group called the "Conference of American Armies," made up of representatives of the armies of fifteen Western hemisphere nations, including the United States and El Salvador, met to discuss a report on liberation theology. It condemned the movement and named certain of its leading exponents as hardcore Marxists who back "the objectives of the Communist revolution." The list included Jesuit Ignacio Ellacuría, who would later be one of six Jesuits murdered at the University of Central America. Other liberation theologians whose names were on the list were Pablo Richard, José Comblin, and Hugo Assmann. One human rights group would later refer to the report, entitled "Strategy of the International Communist Movement in Latin America through Various Modes of Action," as "almost a kiss of death."

1988

Three events in 1988 confirmed that Gustavo Gutiérrez's assessment in 1986—"the debate is over"—was premature. First, the Vatican confirmed a move that had been rumored for some time. Four new dioceses were being carved out of Cardinal Arns's archdiocese of São Paolo: Osasco, Itapecerica da Serra, Santo Amaro, and São Miguel Paulista. Although population changes in the archdiocese justified the move, Arns and his supporters felt it was meant chiefly to reduce his influence. Most of the poorest areas of the archdiocese, and therefore the strongest pockets of support for liberation theology, were assigned to the four new sees. They were given bishops who were not strong liberationists. Arns was left with the rich central city. The move was a signal that supporters of liberation theology, even at the highest level, were not immune from Vatican pressure. Any doubt of what was at stake was removed by Kloppenburg, who said the Vatican had to take action against those "who refuse to follow the pope's guidelines and who adopt positions that are irreconcilable with the official doctrine." He said it was "evident" and "obvious" that the move in São Paolo was done with this in mind.

In September, Ratzinger took the unusual step of silencing a bishop: Bishop Pedro Casaldaliga of the diocese of São Felix. Casaldaliga was ordered not to speak publicly, write, or leave his diocese without explicit permission. The decision followed an interrogation of Casaldaliga by Ratzinger and Gantin. They cited as causes for the action: (1) Casaldaliga's failure to come to Rome on his required *ad limina* visits; (2) his favorable writings on liberation theology; (3) his travel to Nicaragua to support Miguel D'Escoto's hunger strike (as mentioned earlier, this also got Gutiérrez into trouble); (4) his published "revisions" of the Mass for Indians and Blacks; (5) his reference to Oscar Romero as a "martyr" ahead of a formal declaration by the church. The Spanish-born Claretian had been asked by Ratzinger and Gantin to sign a statement promising not to engage in the offending behaviors. His refusal triggered the silencing three months later.

Ratzinger in 1988 published a commentary on the 1986 Vatican instruction, offering readers a sense of how he interpreted that document. He referred to "Marxist-inspired forms of the practice of liberation rejected by the church's teaching authority." He charged that most readers of the 1986 document had ignored its passages on truth and freedom, preferring to skip directly to what it said about the struggle for liberation. In doing so, he suggests, they missed how deeply at odds liberation theology is with core convictions of the Christian faith. Its promised "liberation" ends in anarchy, and eventually in tyranny, Ratzinger argues. "Anyone who thinks that what is really involved here are tiny casuistical distinctions which should not weigh in the balance in the great fight against tyranny fails to recognize the abyss that gapes between the two fundamental visions of freedom and human dignity that guide the different forms of practice." Though Ratzinger does not spell it out, the conclusion is obvious: these "two visions" are orthodox Catholicism on the one hand and liberation theology on the other.

1989 to 1990

Two events made the years 1989 to 1990 seem like the close of the liberation theology era in Latin American history. One was the fall of the Berlin Wall. With it, the old socialist dream seemed discredited and democratic capitalism vindicated. In 1990, the second act of this drama unfolded in Latin America, as the Sandinistas were voted out of power in Nicaragua. Their socialist utopia lasted barely a decade and was rejected by the people whose aspirations it had claimed to fulfill.

The epicenter of Nicaragua's revolutionary Catholic church during the 1970s and 1980s had been the Santa Maria de los Angeles parish in Managua under Franciscan Uriel Molina. The sanctuary featured a mural of a guerilla in olive-green fatigues carrying a cross and the Sandinista flag, while a greedy-looking Yankee attempts to despoil the Nicaraguan forest. In 1990, however, this too came to an end, as the Vatican ordered Molina out of the parish. In 1996, Molina was expelled from the Franciscan order.[14]

Some dynamics remained the same, such as the willingness of Latin American militaries to use force to muzzle dissent. On November 16, 1989, six Jesuits at the University of Central America in San Salvador—Ignacio Ellacuría, Ignacio Martin-Baro, Segundo Montes Mozo, Amando López Quintana, Juan Ramon Moreno, and Joaquin López y López—were shot to death, along with their cook, Julia Elba Ramos, and her fifteen-year-old daughter, Celina Ramos. The six Jesuits were murdered because they, and the university itself, were widely seen as opponents of the government. Ellacuría especially had a reputation in liberation theology circles as an acute mind.

Also in 1989, López Trujillo's Andes group held another session in Lima. They proposed something called "reconciliation theology" as an alternative to liberation theology. In addition to Trujillo, Cardinal Miguel Obando y Bravo of Managua and Bishop Oscar Rodriguez of Honduras, then serving as secretary-general of CELAM, attended the meeting. After the meeting, Trujillo told reporters, "Liberation theology has a materialistic, not a human, viewpoint. There's no Christian approach in this theological current." Around the same time, Lima's new archbishop, Augusto Vargas, said in a September 17 press release that he wanted to help Gustavo Gutiérrez "fully overcome any doctrinal difficulties." To that end, he said that he had ordered Gutiérrez to submit all his theological writings before publication.

In Haiti, another experiment with liberation theology in practice was also on life support. Jean-Bertrand Aristide, a priest and social reformer, had been expelled from the Salesian order in 1988 for "inciting violence, social hatred, and class struggle." The movement that had formed under his leadership was powerful enough to topple the Haitian dictator "Baby Doc" Duvalier and subsequently elect Aristide president, but not strong enough to prevent him from being chased out of the country in a military coup shortly thereafter.

In a move that still bewilders and shocks many Haitians, the Vatican was the only nation in the world to recognize the military regime after it assumed power in the 1991 coup. Supporters of Aristide responded by attacking and burning the papal nuncio's residence, seriously injuring a Zairian priest who was stationed there. The military was charged with causing more than 3,000 political murders until a U.S. intervention in 1994 restored Aristide to power. For many Haitians, Ratzinger's warnings about liberation theology leading to terror seemed especially hollow, as the Vatican appeared to be endorsing terror of a much more ruthless and systematic kind. Aristide went on to resign his priesthood and marry his American legal advisor, and the two now have children. He left the presidency in the mid-1990s, but as of early 2000 appeared to be considering a comeback.

1991 to 1992

In 1991, Ratzinger again struck at Boff, this time demanding that he step down as head of *Vozes,* the Franciscan journal he ran in Petrópolis. Boff accepted the verdict, but it was clear to friends that he was running out of patience. In 1992, Ratzinger banned Boff from teaching and imposed preventive censorship on all his writings, insisting that Boff had still not cleansed his ecclesiology of the elements of dissent and internal class struggle that had been at issue in 1984. It was too much. On May 26, 1992, Boff announced that he was leaving the Catholic priesthood. His exit line was memorable: "Ecclesiastical power is cruel and merciless. It forgets nothing. It forgives nothing. It demands everything."

Ironically, Boff said in 1999 that he has never received any paperwork from the Vatican formalizing his departure, so from a canonical point of view he continues to be a priest and friar. Boff said in that 1999 interview with *Newsweek* that he thinks of himself as a member of the church, though "more Franciscan than Roman Catholic." He still writes and lectures widely.

In October 1992, the fourth CELAM assembly was held in Santo Domingo. This time the liberationists could not avoid the assault they had feared at Puebla. The Vatican insisted that its own appointees, Secretary of State Angelo Sodano and Chilean cardinal Jorge Medina Estévez, chair the session. Medina was a liberation theology foe who had long been on friendly terms with Chile's General Agosto Pinochet. In 1999, when Pinochet was detained in London for possible trial on human rights abuse charges, Medina convinced the secretariat of state to intercede on his behalf with the English government. Under the guidance of Sodano and Medina, the final document in Santo Domingo struck some very familiar Ratzinger notes in its treatment of liberation theology.[15] The bishops formally denounced any identity of the kingdom of God with sociopolitical arrangements, "as some modern theologies have claimed." They asserted the kingdom can be glimpsed only in a "mysterious connection" of Christians with Jesus, not in any visible social order.

To the liberationists, Santo Domingo marks a sort of Waterloo for the movement launched at Medellín and tepidly supported at Puebla. The progressive consensus that once dominated Latin American Catholicism was a thing of the past, and the "official" spirituality of the church once again saw redemption largely in terms of individual experience, not in the collective aspirations of the poor for justice.

The final blow of 1992 came when the diocesan seminaries created by Dom Helder Cámara, the legendary bishop of Olinda-Recife in Brazil, were closed by new bishop José Cardoso Sobrinho. Camara's approach, which actually predated the liberation theology movement, was designed as a grassroots program of priestly formation for an agrarian population. Seminarians lived in small communities and engaged in pastoral work while they studied, similar to the approach in São Paolo under Arns. Most did some kind of agricultural work in order to stand alongside their people. Cámara called it the "theology of the hoe." These seminaries also trained lay leaders to assume pastoral responsibility in the base communities and parishes. Much of the theological underpinning for the seminaries was worked out by José Comblin.

In 1987, John Paul II installed the conservative Lucas Moreira Neves as bishop of São Salvador, which made him Olinda-Recife's metropolitan, in part so he could keep Cámara in check. The closing of the seminaries was painful for Cámara, hanging like a repudiation over the end of his career, but he never protested publicly. He died in 1999.[16]

1993 to 1999

After 1992, the battle over liberation theology was largely a mopping-up operation. Conservatives were named where progressive bishops had once sheltered liberation theologians: Fernando Saenz Lacalle, a priest of Opus Dei, in San Salvador, for example, and José Freire Falcão in Brasilia. In 1996, John Paul visited El Salvador and offered what sounded like a postmortem: "Liberation theology was somewhat a Marxist ideology. . . . Today, following the fall of communism, liberation theology has fallen a little, too." He proclaimed that the "era of liberation theology is over."

Disciplinary measures still flowed out of the doctrinal congregation. In 1995, Ivone Gebara, a theologian and member of the Sisters of Notre Dame, was ordered to refrain from speaking, teaching, and writing for two years. Gebara, who attempted to blend liberation thinking with ecology and feminism, was also required by Ratzinger to go to France to study "traditional theology." As with Boff, the flashpoint with Gebara was her critique of the church. Christianity adopted a patriarchal framework, she wrote, and the poor became the greatest consumers of patriarchy "because of the consolation it provides." "Our understanding of God must change," Gebara said. "We can no longer speak of a being-unto-himself, omnipotent, above all. We can no longer obey 'somebody up there.' That is the God built by patriarchy. Holistic ecofeminism questions theologies that see God as above all things."

John Paul continued his ambivalence with respect to liberation theology. In January 1999, he visited Mexico to present a document formally concluding the "Synod for America" that had taken place in late 1997 in Rome. In it the pope referred to "social sins" and bitterly criticized neoliberalism. He demanded justice for poor and indigenous people. Yet in the Air Italia jet on the way over, when John Paul was asked about Bishop Ruiz and the uprising in Chiapas, he returned to the old liberation-as-Marxism refrain: "There is consideration of substituting liberation theology with indigenous theology, which would be the translation, the inspiration of Marxism, and the church obviously does not agree and proposes another path, which is that of solidarity and dialogue."

Other echoes of the old controversies could still be heard in the late 1990s. Mexican bishop Arturo Lona Reyes of Tehuantepec refused to resign in 1998, for example, claiming that church authorities wanted him out because of his support for liberation theology. "I am with the poorest of the poor and they accuse me of dividing the church. . . . I have never supported neoliberalism and I prefer the poor, those excluded from the system," he told reporters. He said he would only step down if the pope asked him to do so in the presence of two witnesses. Yet when the emeritus bishop of Oaxaca called on all the bishops of Mexico to support Lona Reyes, the silence was deafening. The days when a Latin American bishops' conference would stand up to Rome, as the Brazilians did over Boff or the Peruvians over Gutiérrez, were long gone.

Taking Stock

Ratzinger came into office convinced that liberation theology was a menace to the faith. Over time, he called it a "heresy," "atheistic," and "un-Christian." He said that an "abyss that gapes" separates it from orthodoxy. During his first decade in power, roughly 1981 to 1991, Ratzinger's campaign to dismantle liberation theology was largely successful. As Comblin described the situation in 1998, "One may speak of liberation theology in Europe or the United States, but one may not speak of it in Latin America without immediately being marginalized. . . . We are returning to a rigid polarization in Latin America: clerical integralism versus charismatic pietism—with almost nothing in between. The alternative of Christian humanism, so present at Vatican II, has been reduced to silence."

This diagnosis may be overly pessimistic: base communities still meet, books about liberation theology are written, its ideals linger on in a thousand different forms. As Gutiérrez said in 1997, "As long as the poor suffer oppression, liberation theology will not die." When, for example, sixteen Catholic bishops from debtor and creditor nations flew to a G-7 meeting in Bonn, Germany, in 1999 to demand debt relief for the world's poorest nations, one glimpsed the legacy of liberation theology. Concern for social justice has become part of the job description for Catholic leaders.

Yet the progressive consensus that made liberation theology the dominant theology in Latin America, and that seemed poised to transform the region's social reality, is today a thing of the past. The question is, what does this crusade tell us about Ratzinger? What did it mean for the church and the world?

Lessons about Ratzinger

Three things seem clear. The first is that Ratzinger is capable of being petty when his full emotional energies are engaged in a fight. When he rebuked Gutiérrez for expressing solidarity with Tissa Balasuriya a matter of days before the congregation lifted Balasuriya's excommunication, when he reprimanded Gutiérrez and Casaldaliga for supporting their friend Miguel D'Escoto's hunger strike, when he reproached Casaldaliga for calling Romero a "martyr," and when he refused to allow Leonardo Boff's Franciscan brothers to so much as ride in the car with him to the doctrinal congregation's offices, Ratzinger exposed a mean streak that is at odds with his reputation for courtesy and fair play.

The second point is that in the Catholic church it pays to be Joseph Ratzinger's friend. His Latin American allies in the liberation theology fight have gone on to high church offices. Four now run curial offices themselves: Trujillo heads the Pontifical Council on the Family, Castrillón the Congregation for Clergy, Neves the all-powerful Congregation for Bishops, and Medina Estévez the Congregation for Divine Worship and the Discipline of the Sacraments. All four are today mentioned as *papabile,* or potential candidates for the papacy. Freire Falcão is a cardinal in Brasilia. Kloppenburg got his own diocese in Novo Hamburgo.

Meanwhile, opponents have been driven to the margins: Miguel D'Escoto, Ernesto Cardenal, Jean-Bertrand Aristide, and Leonardo Boff are out of the priesthood. Uriel Molina runs a Nicaraguan preschool, and Fernando Cardenal does Jesuit retreat work. The godfather of the movement, Gustavo Gutiérrez, keeps a low profile in Lima in order to avoid clashes with his Opus Dei bishop. The contrast is obvious to any Catholic with eyes.

The comprehensive scope of Ratzinger's demolition of liberation theology also proves that although he is closely aligned with John Paul, the two men have their differences. The pope did not instigate Ratzinger's campaign. John Paul had little patience for disobedient priests, but he also embraced some of the key themes of liberation theology in his own speeches and encyclicals. He called liberation theology "useful and necessary," and he instigated the drafting of what was intended to be a more positive statement about liberation theology following Ratzinger's condemnation of the movement in 1986. Some of John Paul's friends and advisors, such as Austrian cardinal Franz König, argued with the pope that the liberationists were a Latin American version of the Solidarity movement in Poland. Yet

Ratzinger persisted, and in the end it was his vision that determined the outcome. Ratzinger is not Rasputin. On other matters where he has differed with John Paul—on the advisability of making so many saints, or the doctrinal implications of holding prayer sessions with leaders of other religions—the pope has kept his own counsel. But on liberation theology, the depth of Ratzinger's passion and the steadiness of his resolve, combined with John Paul's ambivalence, sealed its fate. Ratzinger is thus capable of making things happen without the initiative or even the full support of the pope.

Ratzinger's protégé Joseph Fessio told me in a 1999 interview that the cardinal's disciplinary measures are "detached, not personal. It's a documentary issue. He deals with what lands on his desk." The story of the liberation theology campaign illustrates that Fessio is precisely right; Ratzinger's analysis of a writer or movement begins and ends at the study desk, where the theoretical implications of an idea can be followed to their logical ends. The question is not whether those who hold the idea are *in reality* revolutionaries, or Marxists, or atheists, or anarchists. The question is whether, from the perspective of the continental philosophy and theology in which Ratzinger is trained, their ideas lead to those outcomes. Ratzinger seems to believe that the humanity of theologians, who they actually are and what they really do and say, is not of much relevance to a judgment of their ideas.

For the Church and for the World

Segundo wrote in 1985 that what was at stake with liberation theology was not Marxism or class struggle. The crux was Vatican II's ecclesiology. For the council that issued *Gaudium et spes*, incarnational theology meant that God works through the universal human yearning for justice. The church must "take on flesh" by joining with social movements seeking to build an order that reflects human dignity. As Aquinas had done in the thirteenth century, the authors of *Gaudium et spes* wanted to do for the late twentieth: to restore the third term of theology, "nature," in between the poles of "sin" and "grace." In his closing address to the council on December 7, 1965, Paul VI asked rhetorically whether this Copernican shift toward the world as the center of Christian life was a betrayal of earlier church thinking. "Has all this and everything else that we could say about the human value of the council perhaps turned the mind of the church away toward the anthropocentric direction of modern culture? Turned away, no; turned, yes," the pope said.

Church authorities have always been wary of incarnational theology. In the years before Vatican II, Pius XII ordered a crackdown on French Catholicism because of its worker-priest movement and its use of modern, abstract art in church buildings. The reason is clear: church authorities derive their power from control over the means of salvation. If salvation is to be found "out there," in the world, as much as "in here," in the church, that power is diluted.

As for the impact of Ratzinger's campaign on the political development of Latin America, there is no way to determine what might have been if Ratzinger had spent as much energy supporting the liberationists as he did undercutting them. But there is a term of comparison: Poland. Here the full weight of Vatican support, both moral and logistical, was thrown behind a movement that involved the church in a common struggle with other groups to effect change. A seemingly intractable social order was felled by this combination of energy and daring. Poland is free today in large part because the Vatican, the episcopacy, and the laity were engaged in a common project of social transformation. Would such a combination have worked in Latin America? Perhaps not. But for those who believe that fidelity, not success, must be the measure, questioning the "practicality" of the liberationist vision puts the accent in the wrong place. As Comblin wrote, "That may be a sign that they previously confused the evangelical option for the poor with the option for victory."

After a decade of alleged neoliberal success in the 1990s, poverty is still endemic in Latin America. In general, the continent has merely held the line. According to a report from a regional monitoring agency, thirty-six percent of Latin American households lived below the poverty line in 1999, statistically identical to the thirty-five percent who did so in 1980. This means that 200 million people in the region are "poor," with 90 million classified as indigent. The fact that Latin America has put no statistical dent in poverty in a decade of surging economic growth testifies to its expanding inequality. The 1990s lifted many people, especially university graduates, closer than ever to the U.S. and European lifestyles they have always sought to emulate. But the losers of the new game, the uneducated and unskilled, were pushed into greater hardship.

Almost half of the world's one billion Catholics are Latin Americans. The world's two largest Catholic countries, Brazil and Mexico, are in the region. Where the Catholic church is such a dominant force, one is entitled to expect a social order that better reflects gospel values. Bringing the gospel into contact with society ought to be like dropping a live electrical cord into a pond; every corner of it should feel the jolt. That Latin American Catholicism has not had such an effect in the 1990s is, to a large extent, Joseph Ratzinger's responsibility.

When the 1984 instruction on liberation theology came out, the distinguished Belgian Dominican theologian Edward Schillebeeckx said, "The dictators of Latin America will receive [it] with joy because it will serve their

174

purposes. Whether it was intended to or not, this instruction is, in fact, being turned into a political instrument in the hands of the powerful in Latin America who, in turn, are being supported by the great foreign powers in order to consolidate the system that keeps the poor submissive in favor of some of the rich. Is this the good news we might have expected from Rome?" Today Latin America is run not by dictators but by presidents and CEOs, and the great powers are international financial institutions and corporations; but in its fundamentals, Schillebeeckx's analysis remains valid.

Theologically, siding with an unjust status quo cannot help but seem a distortion of the Christian message. As one theologian put it in 1962, writing on the subject of free expression in the church, "The meaning of prophecy is not so much in predicting the future as in the prophetic protest against the self-righteousness of the institutions. . . . God, throughout history, has not been on the side of the institutions but on that of the suffering and persecuted."[17]

That theologian was Joseph Ratzinger.

5

Cultural Warrior

Just before 8:00 A.M. on January 13, 1998, a thirty-nine-year-old Sicilian named Alfredo Ormando slipped into St. Peter's Square in Rome. It was a bright winter's morning, off-season for tourists, so the square was empty. Ormando took off his jacket, removed a can of gasoline, doused himself, then lit himself on fire. He began walking in the direction of St. Peter's Basilica "like a giant torch," as one witness put it. A woman cleaning one of the square's fountains ran to find two police officers, who intercepted Ormando just as he was reaching the steps of the great church. They wrestled him to the ground and extinguished the flames, which by then had covered nine-tenths of his body with burns. Still alive, Ormando muttered, "I couldn't even manage to kill myself." He was taken to a nearby hospital where he lingered for ten days before dying.

Ormando, it emerged, was gay. He had been born into a poor village in central Sicily, where homosexuality is still deeply stigmatized. Depressed and frustrated by his family's refusal to accept him, Ormando moved to Palermo where he aspired to be a writer, "an intellectual in a family of laborers," as his landlord recalled. He had little success, with only one book put out by a small local publisher. He enrolled in the university in Palermo seeking a degree in literature, which he had not yet completed on the morning he set himself ablaze. In the hospital, no member of Ormando's family came to visit him, a final rejection of the sort that had surrounded his entire life.

Roman police said they found letters in Ormando's jacket explaining his action in terms of his family's and society's refusal to accept gays. A rumor that in another letter he had placed blame on the Vatican turned out to be false. Homosexual activists and sympathizers from all over Italy, however, said that even in the absence of such a letter Ormando's choice of St.

Peter's Square could hardly be an accident: he was, in the end, bringing his problems back to their source. "It was to be expected that, sooner or later, someone would do something desperate to condemn the homophobia of the church," said a leader of the Italian gay rights group Arcigay. "In Italy, the antihomosexual positions of the church are the source of suffering."

Ormando's death dramatically illustrates the centrality of Roman Catholicism, and the social attitudes it helps to shape, to one of the two most deeply controversial civil rights struggles of the late twentieth century, the gay liberation movement. The women's movement is the other. Since the 1970s, feminism and the push for legal and social acceptance of homosexuality have formed the front lines of the "culture wars" in the developed world. The positions Ratzinger has articulated in response to these movements have pushed Catholicism closest to what is customarily known as the religious right.

Catholic leaders have denounced the cultural impact of feminism, linked as it often is to battles over birth control and abortion rights. The church has also said it cannot ordain women as priests. This refusal has been interpreted by some women as a form of gender discrimination. With respect to homosexuals, the church has strongly condemned antigay violence, but has branded homosexual conduct as immoral and has even endorsed some forms of legal discrimination.

Under John Paul II's papacy, the ban on women priests has been elevated to the status of a de facto infallible teaching, and further conversation about women's ordination has been ordered to a halt. Millions of Catholic women do not accept the Vatican's rhetoric about "complementarity," the idea that the two genders have equally important but different roles, as a basis for their exclusion from the priesthood. Medicine and law, the military, political office—these professions too once had doctrines to justify the exclusion of women. Under close scrutiny, such policies usually proved to be post-hoc exercises to justify prejudice.

Ratzinger has made resisting the inroads of feminism a top priority. His friend, Lutheran theologian Wolfhart Pannenberg, said after a 1997 session with the cardinal that he "left with the impression that women's ordination is the big obstacle to any ecumenical progress anywhere." This is especially true because Ratzinger sees the push for women priests as driven by "spokeswomen for radical feminists, especially for lesbians."[1]

The relationship between homosexuals and the church under Ratzinger has been even more hostile. Officially, the church teaches that homosexual acts are "intrinsically evil," but that homosexual persons must be treated with compassion. Most homosexuals, however, find that distinction untenable, because it condemns them to either living sexually unfulfilled lives or sinning in the eyes of the church. Many Catholic homosexuals construe the church's position as a form of tolerance for prejudice.

Catholic women and Catholic homosexuals for the most part do not wish to choose between their church and their conscience. They want Catholicism to reflect the same principles of equality they demand within civil society. Because Joseph Ratzinger has been the prime intellectual theorist behind the church's closure to the aspirations of these two groups, in the eyes of many Catholic women and Catholic homosexuals, he symbolizes all that angers them about the church.

In a letter defending John Paul II's 1994 ban on further discussion about women priests, Ratzinger asserted that an individual who pushes the issue is "perhaps allowing oneself to be conditioned too much by the ways and spirit of the age." This is the cornerstone of Ratzinger's thinking in this arena: the church must not allow itself to be bullied by the world. Feminism and the gay rights movement are expressions of a culture that has lost its capacity to accept limits imposed by authority and grounded in revelation. How can the church simply align itself with the "signs of the times," Ratzinger asks, in a fallen world?

Ratzinger and Women

On a beautiful northern California evening, Saturday, February 13, 1999, Ratzinger was delivering a lecture at St. Patrick's Seminary in Menlo Park, California, following three days of meetings with representatives of the doctrinal commissions of bishops' conferences in the United States, Canada, Australia, New Zealand, and the Pacific Islands. The assembled prelates included heavyweights such as Cardinal Aloysius Ambrozic of Toronto, Archbishop Daniel Pilarczyk of Cincinnati, and their host Archbishop William J. Levada of San Francisco. During their sessions, the twenty-plus men—they were *only* men—had some surprisingly positive things to say about women. At a press conference on the day before Ratzinger's lecture, Ambrozic called the relationship between the church and feminist thought "mutually enriching." The positive tone seemed to mark progress for Ratzinger, who has reserved some of his most sweeping criticism for "radical feminism." Ambrozic's comments received good play in American and Canadian newspapers on February 12, and to some Catholic women it seemed the church was holding out an olive branch.

The next evening Ratzinger gave his lecture on John Paul's encyclical *Fides et ratio*. Although he did not talk about feminism or women's issues, graciousness still seemed to be in the air. Looking out at a crowd that included an Anglican archbishop and a Buddhist monk, Ratzinger praised other faiths for fostering attitudes such as reverence, hope, and love of neighbor. Later at a reception he posed for a photo with a Buddhist monk, the Reverend Heng Sure of San Francisco, and the two made an interesting pair: one clad in black cassock with red trim and a scarlet cape, the other in flowing robes of pink and ivory.

The conviviality, however, did not extend much further than the doors of the reception hall. Just as Ratzinger mounted the podium, a small band of Catholic women was being told to "get off our property" of St. Patrick's by grim-faced clerics whispering into walkie-talkies. The five women had shown up for what was billed as a public lecture, only to learn that it was by invitation only. Security was airtight. Every entrance to the facility was staffed with young men wearing Roman collars, and tickets had to be produced before one could enter. Abandoning the idea of going in for a face-to-face with Ratzinger, the women unfurled a banner and began passing out postcards to invite people to an "inclusive liturgy" they were planning a week later in Oakland.

The women were ordered to leave. Victoria Rue, one of the organizers, responded that as Mass-going Catholics in the archdiocese they had helped to pay for the seminary and hence felt entitled to be present, but the clerical gendarmes were unmoved. The five women were pushed back to the street in front of the main entrance, where they continued to hand out postcards while the clerics waved people past. Whether a car stopped or not became something of a referendum on the driver's attitude toward women in the church; for the record, many cars did pull over, despite the fact that the guest list had been carefully screened.

Rue claims that one car driven by an unnamed cleric actually swerved toward her in a menacing fashion; whether she read the driver's intentions accurately or not, her perception is a telling indication of what the protestors were feeling that evening. She called their reception at the hands of seminary authorities "very jarring, very chilling." Pressed to explain why these five harmless women could not occupy a corner of the seminary's vast grounds rather than standing on a busy street, a spokesperson for the archdiocese said, "You could take that logic to an extreme, and it means that anybody could seize the pulpit."[2]

Thus less than twenty-four hours after a group of Catholic prelates seemed to offer hope of dialogue with women, five of those women were hustled off the seminary grounds by clergy. One could scarcely imagine a more visually poignant example of why many Catholic women feel alienated. On that night, with Ratzinger behind the seminary walls, there was literally no room for these women in the Catholic church.

Ordination

The point of departure for modern Catholic discussion of women's ordination is *Inter insigniores* (presented in English as "On Admission of Women to the Priesthood"), issued by Ratzinger's predecessor, Croatian cardinal Franjo Seper, on October 15, 1976, the feast day of St. Theresa of Avila. The document, issued in the wake of the decision by U.S. Episcopalians to ordain women, begins with an introduction on the role of women in modern society and in the church and is then divided into six parts. Its most important line sums up the argument: "The Catholic church has never felt that priestly or episcopal ordination can be validly conferred on women." Both Scripture and the church fathers, the document asserts, are unanimous that the sacrament of ordination is reserved to men.

Before we proceed to Ratzinger's attitudes on the question, it is worthwhile to consider why this teaching is difficult for many Catholics to accept. As Karl Rahner noted in an essay on women's ordination from the late 1970s, there are two types of tradition in the church: one that is binding because it stems from divine revelation, the other from human custom that simply goes unquestioned for a long time. The latter is always in principle open to change. Rahner suggested it is far from clear that the ban on women's ordination is not of the second type.

Other critics believe the "unbroken tradition" of excluding women from holy orders invoked by the Vatican is a product more of ideology than of careful historical study. For example, in Romans 16, St. Paul refers to a woman named Junia as "outstanding among the apostles." In many manuscripts and translations, her name was switched to Junias to make it masculine. It is illustrative, opponents of the Vatican position say, of the way women have been written out of the history of the church over two millennia.

Inter insigniores argues that because Jesus chose only male apostles, the church has no power to do otherwise. Yet Scripture scholars today are generally agreed that "the twelve" functioned for early Christians as a symbolic counterpart to "the twelve" patriarchs of ancient Israel who fathered the twelve tribes. As the founding fathers of the new chosen people, the twelve apostles have no successors. As ministers and servants of the community, however—the only capacity in which "apostolic succession" makes sense—the twelve were joined by both men and women. This understanding survived far longer in church history than is customarily understood. English theologian John Wijngaards, for example, has documented numerous cases of women ordained as deacons over several centuries.[3]

Nor does one have to reach into the far-distant past for examples of Catholic women performing priestly ministry. In the Czech Republic during the period of Communist oppression, a bishop named Felix Davidek ordained a handful of women as priests and deacons. The approximate numbers are six of each. The best known of Davidek's female priests is Ludmilla Javorova, who lives in the southern Czech city of Brno where today she works as a catechist at an elementary school. Javorova, whose father was a close friend of Davidek's, served after her ordination as the bishop's vicar until his death in 1988. Javorova and Davidek were very close; it has been reported in various places that they lived together as man and wife, though Javorova says this was a rumor planted on Voice of America radio by the Communists. In the small, tightly knit world of the Czech "church of silence," Javorova and the other women acted and were largely accepted as priests.

After the collapse of Communism, when the situation of the Czech church was normalized, the women were instructed by church authorities to stop functioning as priests. Some obeyed, but some continue to dispense the Sacraments quietly among friends and supporters. Papal spokesperson Joaquin Navarro Valls, asked about the ordinations in 1995, said they may have occurred but if so they were invalid. Most of the women ordained by Davidek, afraid of reprisals from either the church or people in their communities, have been unwilling to talk about their experiences. Even Javorova, who has toured the United States at the invitation of the Women's Ordination Conference, an activist group supporting the idea of female priests, will discuss her story in only the most oblique ways.

I learned this first hand when I visited Javorova at her apartment in Brno in late September 1999. The interview had been arranged through the Women's Ordination Conference, and Javorova had agreed through the organization's Czech-speaking intern to see me only if I promised not to write about our conversation. She later released me from part of this promise, agreeing that I could describe my visit in "general terms." Our encounter seemed to be star-crossed. I was to make the two-hour drive to Brno from Vienna, but I had gotten word a couple of days earlier that the translator I had been promised before I left the United States was backing out. I turned to a friend who works for the Austrian bishops' conference, but all he came up with was the name of someone hundreds of miles away in Slovakia, which he handed to me an hour before I was to leave. Thus I set out in my rental car with only a scrawled address and no concept of how I was going to find, let alone talk to, Javorova.

Fortunately, as I entered the heart of Brno I spotted a huge Best Western hotel and casino (I confess I had no idea Best Westerns run casinos in Eastern Europe). I parked and presented myself to the concierge, who had no reason to suspect I was not a guest. I explained my situation, and he quickly arranged for a translator from an English-language academy down the street. I hailed a cab, picked up my translator, and we made it to Javorova's apartment, located in a massive gray Soviet-era high rise in a crumbling part of town, with just a few moments to spare.

Javorova had coffee and crumb cake waiting, on a small coffee table beneath a large portrait of Davidek in her tiny living room. Slowly she began to tell her story. She explained that for Davidek, the decision to ordain women was not a feminist statement but rather a strategy for the pastoral care of women jailed by the Communists. Davidek had been imprisoned himself after spending six months in hiding, dressing as a woman during the day to avoid arrest. He was held in a place where the men stayed in one area and the women in another, coming into contact only in the exercise yard. A wall separated them. Davidek would say Mass while walking around the yard, jumping up and shouting the words of consecration over the wall so the women could hear. He realized this was inadequate and wanted to prepare a small number of women to administer the Sacraments in prison, on the assumption that some of them, since they were active in the underground church, would eventually be arrested. He felt authorized to do this because Pope Pius XII had given permission for Czech bishops to ordain priests in secret if they were unable to maintain contact with church authorities.

After her clandestine ordination, Javorova spent years waiting for the secret police to haul her away, all the time ministering in secret to a small band of underground believers. Understandably, she believes that her fidelity and courage were worthy of the priesthood. Though Javorova did not say so explicitly, I believe she harbors some hope of one day being recognized as a priest by the pope. (Her hope may have diminished: in February 2000, when a Vatican statement about underground priests in the Czech Republic said that "serious doubts" exist about the validity of some ordinations, "in particular those performed by Bishop Felix Maria Davidek," she gave me permission to relate this much of her story.)

Women's ordination advocates argue that from Junia to Javorova, there is a substantial, albeit largely suppressed, tradition of female priests in the Catholic church. Moreover, considerable evidence suggests that Catholics around the world may be ready to bring this tradition out into the light. In 1992, an assembly of Quebec bishops suggested it might be time to consider ordaining women, and in 1999 a synod in the Montreal diocese voted to carry that message to Rome. In Austria and Germany, a 1995 petition for reform in the church garnered almost three million signatures, with women's ordination among its five key demands. Polls of American Catholics show that today two-thirds favor admitting women to the priesthood, an increase of almost twenty percentage points over comparable poll results in the 1980s. Neither the arguments from tradition or the polling data, however, have convinced church leaders to revisit the issue. Ratzinger has aggressively enforced the teaching on women's ordination, with special attention to the United States, considered by most Vatican officials to be a nation whose political culture is uniquely in the thrall of feminism.

In 1981, shortly after Ratzinger took office, the doctrinal committee of the U.S. bishops' conference opened an investigation at his request of *Catholicism* by Father Richard McBrien. The book is enormous—1,184 pages in two volumes—and its ambition is to present a clear summation of the Catholic faith as well as a summary of current theological reflection on important topics. It has been phenomenally successful, with more than 100,000 copies sold and translations into several different languages. Jesuit Tom Reese, editor of the order's *America* magazine, says that the chief difference between a conservative seminary and a liberal one these days is that the conservatives use the universal Catechism and the liberals use McBrien. Among Ratzinger's chief complaints with *Catholicism* was that it gave the impression that church teaching on women's ordination and contraception might change.

McBrien, a theologian at the University of Notre Dame, was fortunate that the chair of the doctrinal committee at the time was San Francisco's moderate archbishop John Quinn, who is now retired. When the committee's report was issued in 1985, it cited some "potentially confusing" areas and called other sections "hypothetical," but also said the book had "many positive features" and ordered no disciplinary action. Nevertheless, the message seemed clear enough: theologians who question the teaching on women's ordination, or even defend the legitimacy of questioning it, do so at their own risk.

During the 1980s, the primary forum in the United States for debate over women in the church was the ill-fated attempt to draft a pastoral letter on women by the U.S. bishops' conference. The idea was first floated by Bishop Michael McAuliffe of Jefferson City, Missouri, in 1982. One year later, a six-bishop committee began work under the direction of Bishop Joseph Imesch of Joliet, Illinois. Imesch and his colleagues were determined that their document should reflect the experiences and perspectives of women, and to that end they spent much of 1985 and 1986 in consultations across the country. Something like 75,000 women participated.[4]

In April 1988, the committee issued a first draft, which included the "unfiltered" voices of women. Some voices were critical; some even broached the ordination issue. The committee went into a second stage of consultations to gather reactions to the first draft. Meanwhile, John Paul reacted to the document in a meeting with U.S. bishops in September 1988, urging the bishops to stress the theme of complementarity, that men and women have different but "complementary" roles, an argument often invoked by the Vatican to justify the ban on women's ordination. Many Catholic women find the notion of complementarity offensive, suggesting as it does an essential feminine nature that both shapes and limits the social and ecclesiastical roles open to women. A second draft was issued in March 1990. It added a strong reaffirmation of church teaching on birth control, dropped a clause that women's experience will contribute to church teaching on sexuality, and distinguished sharply between "Christian feminism" and "radical feminism."

These changes were not enough to allay Vatican fears. The U.S. bishops had planned to approve the document in November 1991, but curial officials asked for a delay so that a delegation from the conference could come to Rome for a consultation. Observers say Rome had watched how two previous pastoral letters of the U.S. bishops, *The challenge of peace* in 1983 and *Economic justice for all* in 1986, had been widely disseminated throughout the world and did not want this letter on women to exacerbate feminist pressures on Catholicism in other countries.

Ratzinger chaired this two-day session at the Vatican in the fall of 1991. Among the ecclesial heavy-hitters Ratzinger had assembled to confront the Americans were German bishop Walter Kasper, Australian archbishop Eric D'Arcy and Irish archbishop Desmond Connell. A U.S. bishop involved in the drafting told me of the meeting, speaking about it for the first time: "We were set up. I thought we were going to go in there and educate the hierarchies of other countries, share with them what our women were telling us. Instead I was battered around. There was no way we were going to get an open hearing." Ratzinger was blunt: the U.S. bishops must not go ahead with their letter as it stood.

The American bishop, who did not want to be identified in this book for fear of further harassment from Ratzinger's office, said he had described in this meeting the anger he had heard from educated and self-aware Catholic women. When he finished, an Italian prelate told him flatly, "We do not have this problem in Italy." In a flash of poetic justice, days later Italian women staged a demonstration in Rome to protest discrimination in the church.

The American bishop said Ratzinger expressed two main reservations about the document: first, that it was not clear enough about the ban on women's ordination; second, that it went too far toward inclusive language, avoiding gender-specific words where possible in liturgy and the Bible, for instance preferring "person" instead of "man." Attempting to respond to these criticisms without sacrificing too much of the input gathered from Catholic women, the committee returned to work. In March 1992, a third draft went out for consideration. It blended tougher language on the Vatican sticking points with a condemnation of the "sin of sexism" and suggested that a seminarian's inability to work with women ought to be considered a "negative indicator" for ordination.

Even this was too much for some voices within the conference. At their June 1992 meeting, the bishops decided to generate yet another draft. This time Archbishop William Levada of San Francisco, a conservative who had worked under Ratzinger in the Congregation for the Doctrine of the Faith in the early 1980s, was deputized to do the writing. By the time Levada's version came up for a vote in November of 1992, the document had moved so far to the right—condemning the sexual revolution, forms of feminism, and laws that treat men and women alike—that many women hoped the bishops would drop the entire project. On the floor, the draft failed to get the two-thirds vote it needed to pass.

After ten years, for the first time in the history of the conference, a pastoral letter had been rejected in an open vote. Though there were a number of other factors involved, it is probably fair to say that Joseph Ratzinger's intervention is the single most important reason the American bishops did not issue a pastoral letter on women. The case is important not only for the issue of women in the church but for the future of the U.S. bishops' conference itself. The era of large-scale pastoral letters, reflecting wide consultation and addressing socially critical topics, effectively ended in November 1992. In 1983 on nuclear weapons, and again in 1986 on economics, the U.S. bishops had made enormous contributions to a moral analysis of public policy issues in American culture. Thanks in large measure to Ratzinger, they would not have such impact again.

This is not to say that the church under John Paul II and Ratzinger has been silent on women. The pope actually prides himself on his understanding of women, and has devoted two encyclicals, *Redemptoris mater* (1987) and *Mulieres dignitatem* (1988) to them. Yet the document for which he will likely be remembered by most Catholic women is the thunderclap that rang out from Rome on May 22, 1994, in the form of *Ordinatio sacerdotalis*, rendered in English as "On the Reserving of Priestly Ordination to Men Alone." The document was just a few paragraphs long, suggesting that John Paul wanted his point to be crisp and clear. "Priestly ordination, which hands on the office entrusted by Christ to his apostles of teaching, sanctifying, and governing the faithful, has in the Catholic church from the beginning always been reserved to men alone. This tradition has also been faithfully maintained by the Oriental churches." Referring to the fact that the Blessed Virgin Mary was not chosen as an apostle, the pope says this proves "the nonadmission of women to priestly ordination cannot mean that women are of lesser dignity, nor can it be construed as discrimination against them."

Then he moved to the bottom line: "Wherefore, in order that all doubt may be removed regarding a matter of great importance, a matter which pertains to the church's divine constitution itself, in virtue of my ministry of confirming the brethren I declare that the church has no authority whatsoever to confer priestly ordination on women, and that this judgment is to be definitively held by all the church's faithful." *Ordinatio sacerdotalis* was interpreted to mean that not only is women's ordination off the table, advocating it is also forbidden. That gag order claimed its first victim in May 1995, when St. Meinrad's Seminary in Indiana fired Mercy sister Carmel McEnroy, one of 1,000 Catholics nationwide who signed an appeal to John Paul to reopen debate on the issue. Her dismissal, which led to an unsuccessful lawsuit against the seminary, stood as the church's answer.[5]

On October 28, 1995, Ratzinger issued a brief document, technically styled as a reponse to a *dubium,* or question, about the doctrinal force of *Ordinatio sacerdotalis.* The question was, is this teaching infallible? Ratzinger's answer was affirmative: "This teaching requires definitive assent, since, founded on the written Word of God, and from the beginning constantly preserved and applied in the Tradition of the church, it has been set forth infallibly by the ordinary and universal Magisterium. . . . Thus, in the present circumstances, the Roman Pontiff, exercising his proper office of confirming the brethren, has handed on this same teaching by a formal declaration, explicitly stating what is to be held always, everywhere, and by all, as belonging to the deposit of the faith." The statement was approved by the pope.

In an accompanying letter issued the same day, Ratzinger laid out his reasoning. First, he asserted that *Ordinatio sacerdotalis* had reassured many as to where the church stood. "Many consciences which in good faith had been disturbed, more by doubt than by uncertainty, found serenity once again thanks to the teaching of the Holy Father." Yet, Ratzinger said, debate persists. "Some perplexity continued, not only among those who, distant from the Catholic faith, do not accept the existence of a doctrinal authority within the church—that is, a Magisterium sacramentally invested with the authority of Christ—but also among some of the faithful to whom it continued to seem that the exclusion of women from the priestly ministry represents a form of injustice or discrimination against them."

Ratzinger said the church holds both the dignity of women and the impossibility of ordaining them. "If however, perhaps by allowing oneself to be conditioned too much by the ways and spirit of the age, one should assert that a contradiction exists between these two truths, the way of progress in the intelligence of the faith would be lost." The debate over ordination, he said, is often based on an inaccurate concept of ministry.

To understand that this teaching implies no injustice or discrimination against women, one has to consider the nature of the ministerial priesthood itself, which is a service and not a position of privilege or human power over others. Whoever, man or woman, conceives of the priesthood in terms of personal affirmation, as a goal or point of departure in a career of human success, is profoundly mistaken, for the true meaning of Christian priesthood, whether it be the common priesthood of the faithful or, in a most special way, the ministerial priesthood, can only be found in the sacrifice of one's own being in union with Christ, in service of the brethren.

On the precise question of infallibility, Ratzinger argues that *Ordinatio sacerdotalis* was not itself an exercise of infallibility; rather it testified to the preexisting infallibility of a teaching held always, everywhere, and by everyone. "In this case, an act of the ordinary Papal Magisterium, in itself not infallible, witnesses to the infallibility of the teaching of a doctrine already possessed by the church," he wrote. This analysis of infallibility has generated wide theological controversy. John Coleman, a Jesuit theologian and sociologist, called the approach "papal fundamentalism"—treating papal statements as ipso facto infallible. Some coined the term "creeping infallibilism."

Others defended Ratzinger on just this point, speculating that by proclaiming the ban on women priests to be de facto infallible he may have spared the church a full-blown formal declaration of infallibility. They pointed to an article by conservative German cardinal Joachim Meisner in the Catholic weekly *Reinischer Merkur* at the same time Ratzinger's *dubium* appeared. Meisner argued that *Ordinatio sacerdotalis* was an infallible papal statement that confirmed the unanimous teaching of the episcopal college. To some, the article suggested that Catholic conservatives had wanted a formal *ex cathedra* statement from the pope. German theologian Leo Scheffczyk, known to be close to John Paul, published an article in June 1995 in which he lamented that the pope had failed to pronounce the teaching as infallible *ex cathedra*.

It is impossible to verify this scenario; papal biographer George Weigel, who enjoyed unprecedented access to the pope, denies it. Only John Paul knows what his real intentions were. There is nothing in the record to suggest, however, that Ratzinger does not fully identity himself with the ban on women priests and the claim that this is a constant and unchangeable teaching.

The Catholic Theologial Society of America, the leading professional society for Catholic theologians in North America, adopted a statement in June 1997 disputing Ratzinger's conclusion. By a vote of 216 to 22, with 10 abstentions, the group endorsed a 5,000-word, tightly argued study that had been submitted to the society's 1,300 members months earlier and extensively revised since. "There are serious doubts," it read, about the grounds for maintaining that the teaching on ordination was infallible and part of the "deposit of faith," something to which all Catholics must assent. The document called for "further study, discussion, and prayer regarding this question." The Canon Law Society of England likewise concluded in 1996 that the pope's teaching on women priests was not infallible.

In January 1997, the Congregation for the Doctrine of the Faith published a collection of documents along with essays by theologians and historians supporting its reasoning on women's ordination. In a press conference to present the collection, Ratzinger addressed the question of whether Catholics who believe that women should be priests are heretics. Technically, he said, the term *heresy* refers to denial of a revealed truth such as the Incarnation or the Resurrection. The ban on women priests is instead a doctrinal conclusion derived from revelation, and as such those who deny it are not literally heretics. They do, however, "support erroneous doctrine that is incompatible with the faith" and exclude themselves from communion with the church. Such Catholics are, in other words, de facto excommunicated.

In July of 1998, John Paul issued a letter, *Ad tuendam fidem*, inserting into canon law penalties for dissent from his new category of "definitive teachings." Ratzinger issued a five-page commentary accompanying *Ad tuendam*, in which he enumerated examples of doctrines that would be included in this set of "definitive infallible" teaching: the ban on women priests, the ban on euthanasia, the immorality of prostitution and fornication, the legitimacy of a particular pope or ecumenical council, the canonization of saints, and the invalidity of the ordinations of Anglican priests. Ratzinger even suggested that the all-male priesthood might be on its way to becoming a formally defined infallible teaching. Many observers, such as McBrien, pointed out that Ratzinger's claim that these doctrines are infallible is not itself an infallible statement, and hence is open to debate.

The campaign to close discussion continued. In the fall of 1998, Ratzinger pressured Bishop John Kinney of St. Cloud, Minnesota, to order Liturgical Press in his diocese to withdraw the book *Women at the Altar* by the English nun Lavinia Byrne. In her book Byrne advances arguments for the ordination of women. She calls female priests a "profoundly Catholic notion," based on the idea that "the Word of God was conceived in a woman's body and brought forth to save us all." Initial news reports suggested that the 1,300 copies were to be actually burned, but the publisher of Liturgical Press later said Ratzinger's instructions were merely that the books were not to go into circulation. They continued to be available in England, where they were published by a secular press. Byrne herself, a well-known figure in British broadcasting, eventually left religious life.[6]

188

Reproductive Rights

As with the women's ordination question, a rumor has long circulated that Ratzinger prevented John Paul II from formally declaring the teaching of *Humanae vitae* infallible. One version of the rumor holds that John Paul had actually declared the ban infallible in an early draft of his 1993 encyclical *Veritatis splendor* but backed off under Ratzinger's influence. This hypothesis is based almost entirely on an interview Ratzinger gave to *Die Welt* in 1992, shortly before *Veritatis splendor* appeared. Asked about birth control, Ratzinger said then, "There will have to be a development in our thinking to get to the kernel of the problem." He also said the distinction between artificial and natural birth control was confusing and has obscured the "real problems." He said the church's teaching had not come up with anything very helpful on the subject of global overpopulation. He did not elucidate any of these remarks, but they were just enough for some to decide that Ratzinger had doubts about *Humanae vitae*. When *Veritatis splendor* came out without an infallible statement, some drew the conclusion that Ratzinger was responsible.

Once again it is impossible to judge the truth of the claim. It is worthwhile to note, however, that the leading proponent of the hypothesis that Ratzinger blocked an infallible statement is Hans Küng. Why does Küng believe Ratzinger did this? Because, Küng says, Ratzinger has been strongly influenced by Küng's critique of infallibility. "Who if not he will remember the enquiry which his then-colleague at Tübingen launched under the title *Infallible?* in 1970 and which has not yet been completed—and the furor that followed?" Küng may be correct, but it is difficult not to see the argument as self-serving, along the lines of "In his heart, Ratzinger knows I'm right."

In any event, Ratzinger clearly supports the heart of the teaching on birth control, even if he has problems with the way it has been formulated. One of Ratzinger's core ideas is that Western culture is too obsessed with its own power, too unwilling to accept "givens," whether from revelation or from biology. In *Salt of the Earth,* he said, "It is, I think—independently now of contraception—one of our great perils that we want to master the human condition with technology, that we have forgotten that there are primordial human problems that are not susceptible of technological solutions but that demand a certain lifestyle and certain life decisions." Ratzinger's argument is that culture, not technology, is the only reliable solution to most problems in the social sphere. Yet he also hesitates to condemn couples using contraception. "I would say that those are questions that ought to be discussed with one's spiritual director, with one's priest, because they can't be projected in the abstract."

Ratzinger's most systematic treatment of reproductive issues came in a 1987 document of the doctrinal congregation called *Donum vitae* (The gift of life). Although it repeated the bans on contraception and abortion, the document chiefly addressed the ethical dilemmas posed by new reproductive technologies such as in-vitro fertilization, artificial insemination, and surrogate motherhood, as well as related issues such as cloning and embryo experimentation. Ratzinger is proud of the document; he listed it along with the instructions on liberation theology and the Catechism in 1996's *Salt of the Earth* as the peak accomplishments of his term.

"One cannot derive criteria for guidance from mere technical efficiency, from research's possible usefulness to some at the expense of others, or worse still, from prevailing ideologies," Ratzinger writes. In a characteristic turn of phrase, he warns: "Science without conscience can only lead to man's ruin." The document condemns the use of prenatal diagnosis for procuring an abortion, experimentation on embryos unless for strictly therapeutic purposes, and the practice of keeping embryos alive for experimental or commercial purposes. On the question of physician-assisted fertilization, Ratzinger says the fundamental moral norm is this: "The gift of human life must be actualized in marriage through the specific and exclusive acts of husband and wife, in accordance with the laws inscribed in their persons and in their union." The conjugal act of husband and wife ties together the unitive and procreative purposes of sexuality; any other mode of reproduction splits them apart.

On the basis of these considerations, in-vitro fertilization in all forms must be rejected. For one thing, most forms of in-vitro involve the destruction of "surplus" embryos. "The abortion mentality which has made this procedure possible thus leads, whether one wants it or not, to man's domination over the life and death of his fellow human beings and can lead to a system of radical eugenics." The ban on in-vitro fertilization would remain, however, even where this abuse is avoided, because the procedure is "contrary to the unity of marriage, to the dignity of the spouses, to the vocation proper to parents, and to the child's right to be conceived and brought into the world in marriage and from marriage." Artificial insemination is likewise rejected unless it "helps the conjugal act to reach its natural objectives," a caveat that makes some kinds of fertility drugs licit. Under this codicil, the Vatican approved the use of the erection-inducing drug Viagra. But if artificial insemination "were to replace the conjugal act," it cannot be approved. For example, if sperm is obtained through masturbation, the procedure is immoral. Ratzinger argues that the civil law must prohibit the donation of gametes between unmarried persons, embryo banks, and surrogate motherhood.

Ratzinger acknowledges some of these conclusions will fall upon infertile Catholic couples as a burden. He reminds them, "Marriage does not confer upon the spouses the right to have a child," and advises struggling couples to find in their difficulties "an opportunity for sharing in a particular way in the Lord's Cross." In a remark that goes to the heart of Ratzinger's theology, he says the church through these prohibitions is "defending man against the excesses of his own power."

Donum vitae reflects careful reasoning. Ratzinger overcomes the quasi-fundamentalism of some Catholic moral theology by stating reproductive interventions "are not to be rejected on the grounds that they are artificial. As such, they bear witness to the possibilities of the art of medicine." Nevertheless, his blanket rejection of in-vitro fertilization, even when the reproductive materials come from two spouses in the context of a loving marriage, is difficult for many Catholics, especially women, to reconcile with the church's pro-life stance and its praise of motherhood.

On the abortion issue, Ratzinger's most direct involvement has come via Germany and a controversy that engulfed the Catholic church there for much of the late 1990s. Reunification left the country with two policies: liberal access to abortion in the East, restrictive standards in the West. No cultural issue was more divisive than the question of how to harmonize the two approaches, with the conservative Christian Democrats under former Chancellor Helmut Kohl, a Catholic, pushing for the more restrictive West German law. Eventually the country settled in 1995 on making abortion legal within the first twelve weeks of pregnancy. Many women, especially in the former West Germany, were embittered by what they perceived as a power grab by the Catholic church.

Women are obligated under the new law to prove they have received counseling before they may legally obtain an abortion. There are hundreds of counseling centers across the country licensed to issue certificates; approximately 260 of them are run by the Catholic church (most by the social services agency Caritas) with subsidies from Germany's sixteen states, or *Bundesländer*. Many Catholics believe the counseling system allows the church to show a pastoral face to women in need. Supporters also argue that the system works. Of the 20,000 women who receive counseling from the church's centers each year, roughly 5,000 of them decide to carry their pregnancies to term. Many pro-life advocates believe those are 5,000 abortions each year the church helped to avoid. Opponents such as Ratzinger, however, saw 15,000 abortions a year the church helped make possible.

In December 1997, John Paul II wrote to the German bishops and instructed them to disentangle the church from the counseling system. The letter triggered a two-year process of debate and negotiation between the Vatican and the German bishops, in which Ratzinger occupied center stage. It was an unusual position for a doctrinal czar. Because the counseling system was a political question concerning the proper relationship between church and state, it really belonged under the jurisdiction of Secretary of State Cardinal Angelo Sodano. Many Germans believe Sodano offered a moderate counterpoint within the Vatican to Ratzinger. Nevertheless, Ratzinger was the official conducting the correspondence and holding the meetings, and it was clear that he was the figure upon whose judgment the pope most relied. Over the years, Ratzinger has involved himself in the affairs of German-speaking churches in ways that go far beyond his role as an arbiter of doctrinal orthodoxy. The *Frankfurter Allgemeine* reported in August 1998 that in the eyes of many Germans, Ratzinger had become the pope's "special commissioner for Germany" and a sort of "deputy pope for German-speaking Catholics."

Impatient with what appeared to be foot-dragging by the bishops, Ratzinger sent a letter to the conference president, Bishop Karl Lehmann, on May 20, 1998, demanding that the bishops submit a model solution to the Vatican for review by the fall of 1998. Meanwhile the country's well-organized Catholic lay groups demanded that their bishops defend a system that seemed to work. Reaction to Ratzinger's letter was almost universally negative. The usually cautious Central Commitee of German Catholics (the highest-ranking lay organization in the country) sent a letter to Lehmann asking him to ask the pope to keep Ratzinger out of the debate. Such a request was justified, they said, because Ratzinger was upsetting "the communal consensus of the church in Germany."

In February 1999, Lehmann flew to Rome to hold talks with Ratzinger and other Vatican officials. German newspapers reported that Lehmann hoped to find grounds for some compromise. During their February meeting, the bishops were unable to agree upon a common solution and instead decided to propose four models to the pope and see which one he selected. The proposals ranged from allowing church counseling centers to continuing to issue certificates accompanied by a list of services for women who keep their babies, to forcing the centers to stop issuing certificates and allowing women to inform doctors themselves that they have received counseling. This plan would have required a modification of German law.

After this February session, the wait was on for a reaction from the Holy See. Behind-the-scenes lobbying was intense. Leaders of the German Christian Democratic Union political party, the main center-right party whose leadership is closely tied to the church, traveled to the Vatican to support the counseling system. A member of that delegation, Hermann Küs, later told the *Tageszeitung* that the group had met both with Ratzinger and with Sodano, and that Sodano seemed supportive, telling the group that he believed the current counseling system adequately protected unborn life. Küs also said that Ratzinger had asked the pope not to involve him in evaluating the four models proposed by the bishops. "I hope this is not just a tactic," Küs said. The *Tageszeitung* reported that Ratzinger had told associates in private that he didn't need to be involved in the review because he had already ensured that the pope would decide in favor of his position.

On June 3, a papal decision came down. If the certificates were to be issued by Catholic counseling centers at all, they must carry wording such as: "This certificate cannot be used to obtain legal abortions." The letter was not released to the public until June 22, one day after the bishops began their meeting in Würzburg, where the bishops voted to keep the counseling centers in the state-run system but also to print the pope's disclaimer on all certificates. The vote in favor was unanimous. Many German observers took this as a defeat for Ratzinger, but it was short-lived.

Shortly after the Würzburg session, conservative Cardinal Joachim Meisner of Cologne expressed reservations to the pope, reportedly echoed by Archbishop Johannes Dyba of Fulda, who never allowed the church to offer certificates in his diocese. As a result, a special German delegation, consisting of Meisner, Lehmann, and cardinals Freidrich Wetter of Munich and Georg Sterzinsky of Berlin, traveled to Castelgandolfo on September 16. They met with the pope, along with Sodano and Ratzinger. The result was yet another letter to the bishops' conference, this one cosigned by Sodano and Ratzinger stating that the new compromise was unacceptable.

Once more the bishops asked for time. In a show of resolve, they reelected Lehmann chairman by a two-thirds majority at their fall meeting. A statement said they would remain in the counseling system "for the time being" pending further appeal. In April 2000, however, the inevitable happened: the bishops announced that they would withdraw from the state system. They said they would somehow attempt to keep the counseling centers alive, though exactly how they would attract women without offering certificates remains unclear. In the German press, the outcome was treated as a decisive victory for Ratzinger over a majority in the country's bishops' conference.[7]

The debate over the counseling system posed a classic ethical dilemma: is it better to risk facilitating evil for the chance to do good, or to bypass an opportunity for good in order to ensure that evil is not promoted? The controversy also offered a test case for working out the implications of *Gaudium et spes*. Should the church enter into partnership with secular society, accepting that it cannot dictate the terms of that partnership, in order to promote the values of the kingdom of God; or should the church withdraw from such partnerships if they risk doctrinal or moral ambiguity? At both levels, Ratzinger's strong preference was for disengagement.

Inclusive Language

In Spike Lee's film *Malcolm X*, there is a powerful scene in which the young Malcolm Little, just beginning to fall under the spell of a member of the Nation of Islam, is in the jailhouse library. His new mentor puts a standard English dictionary in front of him and asks him to look up the word "white." As he reads, he finds it includes meanings such as "pure," "undefiled," "good." Then he turns to "black" and finds it connotes "menacing," "threatening," and "evil." It is an awakening experience for Malcolm: the first time he realizes that the very language he speaks has been used to rob him of full humanity.

As feminist thinkers in the 1960s and 1970s reflected on the roots of social and cultural bias, it became clear to them that women had been victimized by language in similar ways. Overt forms of discrimination such as unequal pay and glass ceilings were only the most visible expressions of a deeper problem, which they came to call "patriarchy": a social and intellectual system in which men dominate women, and a few men dominate everyone. As is any social structure, feminists pointed out, patriarchy is reinforced by a set of customs and assumptions including the use of language. When English speakers use "man" to refer to all people, for example, this presents masculinity as the human ideal. Some feminists also hear masculine language about God as an example of patriarchal thinking: Why does God have to be a man? Why can't God be "she" as well as "he"?

At the same time feminists were advancing this critique, biblical scholars and linguists were pointing out that just because the grammar of ancient languages required nouns to have gender, that does not mean the scope of the words in ancient languages was in fact restricted to one or the other sex. The Latin word *homines* is masculine, for example, but it usually means "people" in the sense of both men and women. To translate that word as "men" for modern English speakers therefore is inaccurate.

The confluence of these two streams of thought—one alert to the political uses of language, the other to linguistic accuracy—produced the inclusive language movement in biblical and liturgical scholarship. The push for inclusive language is hardly restricted to the Catholic, or even religious arenas; from academic and journalistic writing to the recasting of job titles, efforts at non-gender-specific terminology have long been underway. In 1997, for example, the Canadian Medical Association devoted an issue of its journal to a debate over whether residents should be trained in the use of gender-neutral language. Yet the issue took on a special force within Catholicism because it arose at roughly the same time the church decided to translate its liturgy into the vernacular languages. This meant that a host of liturgical texts had to be produced in English and other vernacular languages in the 1970s and regularly reviewed thereafter. The council decided to leave each bishops' conference free to determine the process it would follow to arrive at translations, on the principle that the native speakers and the local pastors were in the best position to determine how the Bible or the

Mass should sound in English, or in Russian, or in Japanese. Rome required only that the resulting translations come before the appropriate curial office—usually the Congregation for Divine Worship—for a *recognitio,* or formal recognition, without spelling out whether the *recognitio* was simply a way of giving the new text official legal status or whether it involved some kind of review in Rome.

A cohort of English-speaking bishops decided under the bleachers at Vatican II to create an agency, composed of the best linguists, Scripture scholars, and liturgists, to help them produce translations. The International Commission on English in the Liturgy resulted from that conversation. Based in Washington, D.C., the commission today represents twenty-one bishops' conferences in which English is a primary language.

During the first two decades after the council, an informal consensus emerged in liturgical translation circles, including those who worked with the international commission, that some kind of inclusive language was a necessary adaptation. A distinction arose between "horizontal" inclusive language, referring to language about humanity ("people" rather than "man") and "vertical" language about God ("the Lord's" instead of "his"). Most Catholic liturgists and Bible scholars felt that horizontal inclusive language ought to be used in most cases, and vertical inclusive language was appropriate in moderation. In neither case was accuracy to be sacrificed, but this was rarely a temptation. In most instances the more inclusive translation also turned out to be the most accurate. This consensus was formally expressed in 1990 when the U.S. bishops published their *Criteria for the evaluation of inclusive language.* It was intended to help bishops evaluate scriptural translations proposed for liturgical usage. The document states that there are two general principles for evaluating translations for liturgical use: "the principle of fidelity to the Word of God and the principle of respect for the nature of the liturgical assembly."

Even as the bishops were sending their statement to the printer, however, Ratzinger was preparing a counteroffensive. Inclusive language struck him as another instance of a sociological view of church that ignores the "givens" of the faith—in this case, actually rewriting the content of revelation—to make it more acceptable to "the world." In addition, Ratzinger had specific reasons for wanting to retain certain kinds of masculine vocabulary. He felt the use of masculine pronouns in the Old Testament psalms was important, for example, so the church could continue to read them as anticipations of Jesus; he said the term *man* in the New Testament is critical to "Christian anthropology," or the church's doctrine about the human person. *Man* is both a singular and a plural, working both as "*this* man" and in phrases like "the rise of man," so it integrates the shared history and common nature of all human beings as well as the singularity of each individual. To critics who argued that the sense of "man" had shifted in contemporary English usage to a gender-specific term, Ratzinger insisted that no other word expresses the biblical mind as well.

Based on these concerns, the doctrinal congregation developed its own set of norms for judging the appropriateness of inclusive language translations in the early 1990s, but to the great frustration of many liturgists, translators, and Bible scholars, these norms were not published until 1997, when a leaked copy appeared in the National Catholic Reporter. In general the norms took a much more stringent view of when inclusivity was appropriate.[8]

In the United States, the conservative liturgical watchdog group Adoremus was especially energetic in championing more "traditional" language. Adoremus has a three-member board of directors, one of whom is Jesuit Joseph Fessio, Ratzinger's old graduate student from Regensburg. Many groups on the Catholic right saw inclusive language as the beachhead of a broader feminist effort to reshape Catholicism; some feminist groups saw it in exactly the same way, arguing that language helps to shape attitudes and hence more inclusive speech during worship might help create a church more inclusive of women generally. Always in the background of the debate loomed the larger question of women's ordination, though this frustrated many translators and liturgists who wanted the language issue to be judged on its own merits and not as part of a theoretical "slippery slope" leading to female priests.

The tension over inclusive language surfaced in the English translation of the new Catechism for the Catholic Church, which was held up for two years while the Vatican insisted on removing inclusive language in hundreds of instances. This, however, was but a prelude to the fight over a new U.S. translation of the lectionary, or the collection of Bible readings arranged for use at the Mass. In November 1991, the U.S. bishops approved a new lectionary that included three basic texts: the 1986 New American Bible version of the New Testament, the 1970 New American Bible version of the Old Testament, and the 1991 revised New American Bible Psalter, or collection of psalms. Each was considered "moderately" inclusive, with the Psalter going the farthest toward gender-neutral language. In May 1992, the Congregation for Divine Worship confirmed the new lectionary. In June 1994, however, the U.S. bishops were notified that the confirmation had been revoked at the urging of the Congregation for the Doctrine of the Faith, which had suggested there were serious difficulties.

A series of letters, meetings, and consultations ensued, culminating in a move unique in the history of the U.S. Catholic church: the seven U.S. cardinals active at that time went to Rome in December 1996 seeking to resolve the dispute. They were Bernard Law of Boston, John O'Connor of

New York, James Hickey of Washington, D.C., Roger Mahony of Los Angeles, Anthony Bevilacqua of Philadelphia, William Keeler of Baltimore, and Adam Maida of Detroit. At the meeting, Ratzinger said it was time to tighten up the process. In a speech that was later distributed to members of the U.S. bishops' conference, Ratzinger told the cardinals that with the first generation of liturgical texts in the vernacular, "these translations were perhaps not as adequate as they might have been, but there was a real pastoral need to produce them quickly." With "second generation" texts, however, such as the new American lectionary, Ratzinger said more care must be taken. "They will shape the biblical vocabulary, and hence the doctrinal foundation of future generations of believers," he said. The message was clear: There will be no rubber-stamping this time around. Ratzinger also laid the issue on the line for the U.S. prelates. "I think we all recognize, from the perspective of doctrine, that the principal question is the use of inclusive language," he said.

In the wake of that session, a special eleven-man working group was created to put the American lectionary in final form. The working group met from February 24 to March 8, 1997, in the offices of the Congregation for Divine Worship. It consisted of four archbishops, five advisers, and two note-takers. Three members represented the United States: Levada, Archbishop Justin Rigali of St. Louis, and Bishop Jerome Hanus from Dubuque, Iowa. The group was chaired by Cardinal Francis Stafford, formerly of Denver and now head of the Pontifical Council for the Laity. Ratzinger convened the group and delivered an opening address, but did not take part in its deliberations. The other members were Marist Anthony Ward, Jesuit Mario Lessi-Ariosto, Father Thomas Fucinaro, Father Charles Brown, and Michael Waldstein. Ward, Lessi-Ariosto, and Fucinaro work for the Congregation for Divine Worship and the Discipline of the Sacraments, whereas Brown is an American from the New York archdiocese who works for the Congregation for the Doctrine of the Faith. Waldstein, an Austrian layman who was teaching at the University of Notre Dame at the time, was the lone outside expert. The group was rounded out by two note-takers: Father James Moroney, head of the U.S. bishops' Secretariat for Liturgy, and Father Joseph Hauer, Hanus's chancellor in Dubuque.

In November 1998, I published a story in the *National Catholic Reporter* that contained the names and backgrounds of the working group members. It found:

- only one of the eleven men held a graduate degree in Scripture studies;
- two members of the group were not native English-speakers, and another was from the United Kingdom without significant time in the United States—critical, some say, to an appreciation of idiomatic American English;

- at least one of the advisers was a graduate student at the time of the meeting;
- several members of the group had a history of objecting to inclusive-language translations, including two of the American archbishops and the lone Scripture scholar.

According to Benedictine Joseph Jensen, executive secretary of the Catholic Biblical Association, almost 100 Bible scholars in the United States had been involved in preparing the texts that formed the basis for the lectionary: twenty-one for the New Testament, forty for the Old Testament, and thirty-six for the Psalter. Now the fate of the project was in the hands of this group, handpicked by Ratzinger and frankly, according to many U.S. experts, not qualified to grasp the subtleties involved.

During its two-week session, the group decided to dump the more inclusive 1991 Psalter in favor of a 1950s-era translation with some alterations. With the rest of the Old Testament and the New Testament, the working group made hundreds of changes, some more inclusive and some less so. For example, in Romans 5:12, the group opted to change "through one person sin entered the world" back to "through one man" to better reflect that it was not just a single person who fell, but all of humanity. More generally, the group accepted the Vatican position that it is not permissible to change pronouns from singular ("his") to plural ("their") for the sake of inclusivity. The group also decided, however, to permit the Greek New Testament term *adelphoi* to be translated "brothers and sisters" in many cases rather than the more exclusive "brothers."

Rome approved their results, as did the U.S. bishops in June 1997, with a provision that they would review the matter after five years. It was the decision on the Psalter that most infuriated many inclusive-language advocates. A July newsletter from the U.S. bishops' liturgy committee, summarizing the results of the working group, said that the Hebrew psalms have few masculine pronouns for God; but the 1991 translation, which cut down on masculine pronouns, was rejected anyway. Benedictine Ruth Marlene Fox, who had followed the debate closely during the 1990s and written about it for several publications, said the working group "preferred to translate the Bible inaccurately rather than appear to concede to demands for more inclusive word choices."

At the June 1997 U.S. bishops' meeting, Bishop Donald Trautman of Erie, Pennsylvania, charged that the new lectionary was less inclusive even than recent translations for biblical fundamentalists. "If even fundamentalist traditions can use inclusive language and we cannot, what does that say about our biblical scholarship?" he asked. The lectionary had been "substantially and radically altered," Trautman said at the time, "rendering it no longer an inclusive-language text."

That a scholar such as Joseph Ratzinger was willing to stack the deck so thoroughly on this question, to call upon people he knew were not entirely right for the job in order to get the outcome he wanted, suggests that there was something very deep at stake here. One might conclude that for Ratzinger, feminism is a form of liberation theology for the developed Western world—an "interest group" ecclesiology willing to sacrifice truth for political gain.

As a postscript, the International Commission on English in the Liturgy (ICEL) continues to be a political hot potato. Although ICEL had little to do with the lectionary project, the commission has become the symbol for the fierce debate over inclusive language. In December 1999, the Congregation for Divine Worship and the Discipline of the Sacraments issued a sweeping demand for changes in the structure of the group, bringing it under much tighter Roman control. As of this writing, it is unclear how the bishops who govern the commission will respond. Nevertheless, Rome has accomplished at least one of its primary objectives: inclusive language in today's church is an invitation to trouble.[9]

Homosexuality

Joseph Ratzinger's apartment in Rome sits just above a stop of the number 64 bus, a short walk away from St. Peter's Square. Perhaps he was even looking out his window on the day in 1990 when a twenty-eight-year-old German sociologist named Thomas Migge was on board the 64. Migge was in Rome as a tourist and happened to be riding the bus when he felt a prodding in his lower back. At first he thought it was someone's umbrella, but the sensation did not go away and eventually he turned around to see what it was. His eyes fell upon an older priest in his Roman collar "smiling lustily," as Migge later described the scene, stroking the younger man's back.

Migge, from a Catholic household in Westphalia, was astonished that a priest would be so brazen in plain view of St. Peter's. He decided to make a research project out of the experience, and over the next year and a half he set out to see how many homosexual contacts he could make in the precincts of the Vatican. His plan was to cruise Roman sites where gays congregated (Piazza Navona, the Monte Caprino Park, and the beach at Castelfusano) and to place ads in gay periodicals ("young German priest alone in Rome seeks contact"). He also mixed with students from the Gregorian University. Migge would flirt until he was propositioned, and then attempt to engage the cleric in conversation, promising to respect his anonymity. Over eighteen months he made sixty-four such contacts, which he described in the German magazine *Der Spiegel* and again in his 1993 book *Kann denn Liebe Sünde sein? Gespräche mit homosexuellen Geistlichen* (Can love be sin? Conversations with homosexual clergy).[10]

Migge identified three types of contacts among the sixty-four. The first group, numbering sixteen in all, was the "fast ones," clerics who wanted to have sex quickly and without much conversation, and then return to the daily life of a man of the church. These priests seemed to be in denial of the conflict between their behavior and their status. Typical of this category was an American priest who led Migge into a dark side chapel of a Roman church. When he figured out that Migge only wanted to converse, he buttoned his pants and walked out: "I didn't come here to talk, you stupid kid," he said. The next group of thirty-seven Migge called the "sensualists," clerics who freely admit they live in conflict with church teaching. They live on a purely sensual, aesthetic level. Roberto, a German Franciscan, told Migge that he had become a monk because it was an easy life in which he did not have to work much and could be sexually fulfilled. The final group of eleven was composed of clerics who realize the contradiction between their conduct and church teaching, and who privately dissent from that teaching. "They have decided to live by God's will, not that of the office-holders in the church," Migge said. A Dominican named Klaus who was part of a circle of homosexual priests in Germany told Migge, "We have lots of ideas of changes we'd like to make, but we have even more fear of being discovered. In a way we're like the first Christians in the catacombs. We dare not fight publicly."[11]

The irony of this going on under Ratzinger's window is striking, and it is symbolic of the way the issue of homosexuality has pressed upon the Catholic church during his tenure in Rome. No doctrinal chief has ever written and spoken about homosexuality as extensively as Ratzinger has, largely because homosexuals have never had the freedom to organize and demand recognition they enjoy today. The American Psychiatric Association, for example, did not remove homosexuality from its list of mental illnesses until 1973. Moreover, scientific understanding of homosexuality has evolved considerably in the last three decades. Though debate continues, the medical community today tends to see homosexuality as a genetically determined trait. That change in understanding has placed tremendous strain on the Catholic approach to homosexuality, which focuses on physical acts rather than inner psychosexual orientation.

For these reasons, Ratzinger and the Catholic church have been forced for the first time to deal with homosexuality as a civil rights issue. To meet this new challenge, Ratzinger has employed an old concept: the objective immorality of homosexual acts regardless of context or intention.

Ratzinger's campaign to hold the line on homosexuality dates back to 1983, when the doctrinal congregation tried to block publication of *A Challenge to Love: Gay and Lesbian Catholics in the Church,* an anthology edited by Robert Nugent. The Salvatorian priest's pastoral work with gay and lesbian Catholics, often conducted in tandem with Sister Jeannine Gramick, was already attracting criticism. It would remain controversial for the better part of two decades until Ratzinger imposed lifetime bans on the pastoral work of both Nugent and Gramick in 1999. Ratzinger was unable to stop publication of *A Challenge to Love,* but he did succeed in forcing Bishop Walter Sullivan of the Richmond, Virginia, diocese to remove his name from it. Sullivan had written an introduction for the book.

In May 1984, Ratzinger asked Archbishop Peter Gerety of Newark, New Jersey, to withdraw his imprimatur from *Sexual Morality* by Philip S. Keane. Paulist Press, located in Gerety's archdiocese, had sold more than 28,000 copies of the book since it first appeared in 1977. The decision came at the same time that Ratzinger instructed Gerety to revoke his imprimatur from *Christ among Us,* a progressive post-Vatican II catechism that had sold more than 1.6 million copies. In that case, Paulist Press announced it would stop publishing the book, which was swiftly picked up by Harper San Francisco.

In the preface to *Sexual Morality,* Keane had written that although Catholic tradition has "a very worthwhile viewpoint on human sexuality," the tradition is also "impoverished because of certain historical distortions." It must be seen as "ever open to better expressions." Keane suggested that some practices, such as masturbation, homosexuality, premarital intercourse, contraception, and abortion are not absolutely immoral but rather "ontic evils" that become immoral "only if the act is placed without a proportionate reason." Ratzinger's action served notice that such an understanding was not welcome in the public discourse of the church.

Three events in 1986 combined to make it a "year of living dangerously" for Catholic homosexuals. In September, Archbishop Raymond Hunthausen of Seattle announced that in accordance with Vatican instructions he had transferred final authority in the diocese to his new auxiliary bishop, Donald Wuerl, in five areas: marriage annulments, liturgy, sterilizations at Catholic hospitals, clergy education, and ministry to homosexuals. It was clear the action was punitive, as it followed two separate Vatican-requested investigations of Hunthausen: one by then-Archbishop (now Cardinal) James Hickey of Washington, D.C., and another by a three-member commission composed of Cardinal Joseph Bernardin of Chicago, Archbishop John Quinn of San Francisco, and Cardinal John O'Connor of New York.

Because Hunthausen had a reputation as a peace activist, many American Catholics assumed that his problems concerned his politics. Hunthausan once called a nearby nuclear weapons facility "the Auschwitz of Puget Sound" and withheld half of his income taxes to protest military spending. Though these activities no doubt played a role, the origin of Ratzinger's interest in Hunthausen had to do with homosexuality.

Hunthausen first learned he was under review in the fall of 1983, while attending the National Conference of Catholic Bishops meeting in Chicago. Archbishop Pio Laghi, the pope's representative to the United States, told him his ministry was about to be reviewed. Just a few months earlier, Hunthausen had allowed an association of Catholic homosexuals called Dignity to hold a mass in the Seattle cathedral. That mass was celebrated by Jesuit John McNeill, who would later be forced out of the order for his advocacy of changes in church teaching on homosexuality. Dignity, founded in 1969, had become controversial among conservative Catholics because, although the group did not openly reject church teaching, it downplayed the bans on sexual acts and stressed a theology of creation in which the homosexual orientation is understood as positive. "They're Catholics too," Hunthausen said at the time. "They need a place to pray."

Hunthausen's authority was restored a year later. In May 1987, after nearly four months of private interviews and negotiation with the three-bishop commission, Wuerl was reassigned, and Bishop Thomas J. Murphy was appointed Hunthausen's new assistant, with the title coadjutor archbishop. Though the outcome was received as a victory for Hunthausen, he had been clearly chastened. Moreover, bishops had been put on notice that pastoral ministry to homosexuals, unless it is based on clear condemnation of homosexual conduct, invites serious trouble with Rome.

The second blow of 1986 came October 1, when Ratzinger released *Homosexualitatis problema* (Letter to the bishops of the Catholic church on the pastoral care of homosexual persons). Addressed to the universal church, it was released in the Vatican press office in English rather than Italian, suggesting it was aimed especially at the United States. Most observers believed the letter had been prompted by the Hunthausen affair, the emergence of groups such as Dignity, and the growing popularity of Nugent and Gramick's ministry.

Ratzinger's aim in the letter was to remove any ambiguity created by a 1975 declaration on sexual ethics issued by the doctrinal congregation. That document had distinguished between a "transitory" homosexual orientation and a "definitive" orientation, suggesting to some that the church might be moving toward tolerance of the latter. Ratzinger rejected any such speculation: "In the discussion which followed the publication of the declaration, however, an overly benign interpretation was given to the homosexual condition itself, some going so far as to call it neutral, or even good. Although the particular inclination of the homosexual person is not a sin, it is a more or less strong tendency ordered toward an intrinsic moral evil; and thus the inclination itself must be seen as an objective disorder." To the argument made by Dignity and others that homosexuality cannot be evil if it is a given in nature, Ratzinger in effect responded: You have radically underestimated the impact of sin.

In defense of treating homosexuality as an objective disorder, Ratzinger advances three arguments. The first is from Scripture. Ratzinger finds "clear consistency" in the Bible in condemning homosexual acts; he says "Paul is at a loss to find a clearer example of . . . disharmony than homosexual relations." Ratzinger next asserts that church tradition supports this position. Finally he draws on systematic theology, arguing that homosexuality upsets God's plan for male-female complementarity. The conclusion is blunt: "It is only in the marital relationship that the use of the sexual facility can be morally good. A person engaging in homosexual behavior therefore acts immorally."

Ratzinger warns bishops to be on guard against homosexual pressure groups seeking to undo this doctrine. "Those within the church who argue in this fashion often have close ties with those with similar views outside it. . . . They reflect, even if not entirely consciously, a materialistic ideology which denies the transcendent nature of the human person as well as the supernatural vocation of every individual." Such dissenters "either ignore the teaching of the church or seek somehow to undermine it." He stressed that church teaching "cannot be revised by pressure from civil legislation or trends of the moment."

Ratzinger's rhetoric heats up over the course of the document. "Even when the practice of homosexuality may seriously threaten the lives and well-being of a large number of people, its advocates remain undeterred and refuse to consider the magnitude of the risks involved," he writes. Andrew Sullivan, a gay Catholic and editor at the *New Republic,* would later observe that this comment, coming at the peak of the AIDS crisis, was "extraordinary for its lack of compassion." Ratzinger, however, says the church is concerned about those "who may have been tempted to believe" the "deceitful propaganda" of advocates of homosexuality. He asserts that homosexuality "has a direct impact on society's understanding of the nature and rights of the family and puts them in jeopardy." He warns that social tolerance of homosexuality unleashes other demons: "other distorted notions and practices gain ground, and irrational and violent reactions increase." This harsh language, which seemed to validate some of the most crude mythology about gays (AIDS as a gay disease, homosexuality as a kind of psychological problem), shocked many readers. "Some of its clauses read chillingly like comparable church documents produced in Europe in the 1930s," Sullivan wrote.

Ratzinger alerts bishops to be on guard against pastoral programs for homosexuals that might function as the leading edge of a campaign to change church teaching. "This congregation wishes to ask the bishops to be especially cautious of any programs which may seek to pressure the church to change her teaching, even while not claiming to do so," he wrote, in a comment some took as a reference to Nugent and Gramick. He warned of a "studied ambiguity" in statements and public presentations. "No authentic pastoral program will include organizations in which homosexual persons associate with each other without clearly stating that homosexual activity is immoral."

Both Ratzinger and Catholics involved in pastoral ministry with homosexuals stress compassion. For Ratzinger, however, compassion means telling homosexuals the full truth about church teaching, rather than encouraging what he sees as a flight from reality. For most pastoral workers, it means not stressing the church's condemnation of homosexuality at the expense of its positive statements on love and acceptance for homosexual persons. The truth is that many Catholics do believe church teaching should change on homosexuality (polls show about a fifty-fifty split in the American church), and those Catholics who choose to minister to homosexuals probably do, as Ratzinger charges, take refuge behind various forms of "studied ambiguity." There is no doubt that has been the case with Nugent and Gramick, who always carefully avoided making statements about their personal opinions on church teaching. But Ratzinger is disingenuous to accuse them of subterfuge, when his office makes it impossible for them to work openly. To insist that dedicated Catholics leave the church in order to conduct their ministry seems a bit like destroying the village in order to save it.

Ratzinger ends his letter by asking for a crackdown. "All support should be withdrawn from any organizations which seek to undermine the teaching of the church," he wrote. "Special attention should be given to the practice of scheduling religious services and to the use of church buildings by these groups, including the facilities of Catholic schools and colleges. To some, such permission to use church property may seem only just and charitable; but in reality it is contradictory to the purpose for which these institutions were founded, it is misleading and often scandalous." Immediately bishops in Atlanta, Buffalo, Brooklyn, Pensacola, and Vancouver announced that Dignity was no longer welcome. Within a few months, the organization was unwelcome on church property anywhere.

In reaction to the Ratzinger document, McNeill broke a public silence that had been imposed on him under pressure from Ratzinger's predecessor.

McNeill, a priest and psychotherapist, had published *The Church and the Homosexual* in 1976. In it he argued for change in church teaching, drawing on evidence from Scripture, church history, psychology, sociology, and moral theology. He argued that homosexual relationships should be judged by the same standards as heterosexual relationships. McNeill's book appeared with the permission of the Jesuits, but a year later the Vatican ordered the society to rescind that permission. McNeill was also ordered not to discuss these issues in public.

"Since most gay people experience their homosexual orientation as part of creation, if they accept this church teaching, they must see God as sadistically creating them with an intrinsic orientation to evil," McNeill said in a statement in response to the Ratzinger document. "In my more than twenty years experience of pastoral care with thousands of gay Catholics and other Christians, the gay men most likely to act out their sexual needs in an unsafe, compulsive way and therefore to expose themselves to the HIV virus, are precisely those persons who have internalized the self-hatred that their religions impose on them."

On October 19, the head of the Jesuit order, Father Hans-Peter Kolvenbach, notified McNeill that he either had to give up his public ministry with gay people or be dismissed from the Jesuits. McNeill said he could not give up, and hence was expelled from his community and effectively from the priesthood. Because McNeill, one of the cofounders of Dignity, was the living symbol of the hopes of most Catholic gays for change within the church, his expulsion was something of a watershed. For those gay Catholics who remained, it was time to head for the catacombs.[12]

Before 1986 ended, however, there was one more defeat in store. In December, Bishop Matthew Clark of Rochester, New York, received a letter from Ratzinger instructing him to withdraw his imprimatur from a book intended to help parents talk to their children. Entitled *Parents Talk Love: The Catholic Family Handbook about Sexuality*, the book was written by Father Matthew A. Kawiak and Susan K. Sullivan, a Catholic high school teacher. Ratzinger's letter cited the book's treatment of three topics: homosexuality, masturbation, and contraception. Clark announced that he had no choice in pulling the imprimatur, though his action did not stop stores from selling copies of the two-year-old title.

The AIDS crisis posed a new set of problems for church authorities. In December 1987, the administrative board of the U.S. bishops' conference released a document called *The many faces of AIDS: A gospel response*. The bishops suggested that in some circumstances condoms might be justified to fight the spread of the HIV virus. The document set off a fight within the conference; a group of approximately forty conservatives criticized the text for appearing to sanction a form of contraception. On May 29, 1988, Ratzinger sent a letter to Pio Laghi, the papal nuncio in the United States, for him to relay to the bishops. Ratzinger warned the bishops to consult with Rome before issuing documents: "In the first place, and on a more general level, one must keep in mind the problem posed by the worldwide reaction which accompanies certain documents issued by various episcopal conferences. . . . At least in some cases, when the subjects under discussion are of interest to the universal church, it would seem advisable to consult in advance with the Holy See."

Ratzinger then quoted from a *L'Osservatore Romano* article on AIDS widely believed to have originated with him: "To see a solution to the problem of infection by promoting the use of prophylactics would be to embark on a way not only insufficiently reliable from the technical point of view, but also and above all, unacceptable from the moral aspect. Such a proposal for 'safe' or at least 'safer' sex—as they say—ignores the real cause of the problem, namely, the permissiveness which, in the area of sex, as in that related to other causes, corrodes the moral fiber of the people." Ratzinger says that "in full fidelity to the doctrine of the church," Catholic institutions may not "give the impression of trying to condone practices which are immoral, for example, technical instructions in the use of prophylactic devices." It is critical to note, he says, that "the only medically safe means of preventing AIDS are those very types of behavior which conform to God's law and to the truth about man which the church has always taught and today is still called courageously to teach." The letter effectively killed the administrative board's statement, and left the church with a position on condoms that denies their use even to married couples, even if one spouse is HIV-positive and the goal is to prevent the spread of the disease.

One of the few times when Ratzinger has been publicly confronted by a constituency he has angered took place on January 28, 1988, when he appeared in New York to deliver a lecture on biblical scholarship. His talk, which was open to the public, was interrupted for about ten minutes by an outburst from pro-gay protesters scattered in the audience. They shouted "He's no man of God," "Inquisitor," and "Nazi." New York's cardinal John O'Connor sat somberly during the disruption. Police and plainclothesmen moved through the audience at the Lutheran St. Peter's Church, hustling demonstrators outside. Six were eventually arrested.

Meanwhile the campaign to hold the line continued. Father Andre Guindon, a theologian at St. Paul University in Ottawa, Canada, received a thirteen-page critique of his book *The Sexual Creators* from Ratzinger in February 1992. The book had been under investigation since 1988. Ratzinger asked Guindon to clarify his views in three areas: premarital sex, birth control, and homosexuality. In an unusually public move, the criticisms of Guindon were published in *L'Osservatore Romano,* suggesting there was not much room for compromise. In a 1986 interview with a Canadian newspaper, Guindon had argued forcefully that the church's doctrine on sexuality was in need of reform. "You could kill your neighbor and that was a sin, but real sin was sexual," he said of the traditional Catholic view. "As soon as someone touched his wee-wee, God almighty would fall right down." In *The Sexual Creators,* Guindon wrote that David and Jonathan were among the biblical characters who were homosexual lovers, and says few accounts of heterosexual love match the sensuous affection of their relationship. He concluded: "The ethically relevant question about gay sex had little to do with the level of sexual activity or with its techniques. It should rather address the issue of the properly human quality and significance of this sensuous celebration." Many members of the theological community expected Guindon to be silenced, but he died before the inquiry was completed.

In the early 1990s, as the AIDS crisis seemed to ebb slightly, the new social debate surrounding homosexuality concerned the legal rights of gays in areas such as housing, employment, and adoption. The right to marry and to raise children seemed in sight to many homosexuals. In July 1992, Ratzinger wrote to the bishops again, this time to make sure they were enlisted against any such social evolution. Ratzinger reminded the bishops of the teaching from his 1986 letter on the "intrinsic moral evil" of homosexuality. He notes that some are tempted to sympathy for gays in response to various hate crimes directed against them. Again quoting the 1986 document: "But the proper reaction to crimes committed against homosexual persons should not be to claim that the homosexual condition is not disordered," he said. "When such a claim is made and when homosexual activity is consequently condoned, or when civil legislation is introduced to protect behavior to which no one has any conceivable right, other distorted notions and practices gain ground."

Ratzinger advised the bishops: "There are areas in which it is not unjust discrimination to take sexual orientation into account, for example, in the consignment of children to adoption or foster care, in employment of teachers or coaches, and in military recruitment." He asserts that the rights of homosexuals "can be legitimately limited for objectively disordered conduct." He argues that any protection of the rights of homosexuals must be based on general human rights and not on a nonexistent "right to homosexuality. . . . The passage from the recognition of homosexuality as a factor on which basis it is illegal to discriminate can easily lead, if not automatically, to the legislative protection of homosexuality." Ratzinger demands that church leaders oppose measures such as domestic partnership laws or adoption rights for gays, even if church institutions are exempted. "The church has the responsibility to promote the public morality of the entire civil society on the basis of fundamental moral laws, not simply to protect herself from the application of harmful laws."[13]

Ratzinger then made what can only seem an astonishing suggestion: that sexual orientation is not analogous to race or gender as a basis for legal protection, because it is only pushy gays who are causing the problem. "Homosexual persons who assert their homosexuality tend to be precisely those who judge homosexual behavior or lifestyle to be either completely harmless, if not an entirely good thing, and hence worthy of public approval. It is from this quarter that one is more likely to find those who seek to manipulate the church by gaining the often well-intentioned support of her pastors with a view to changing civil statutes and laws."

Joseph Ratzinger is a well-read man, far more savvy about social currents than disgruntled Western Catholics often believe. He is not "out of touch" in the sense his critics usually mean. Yet one cannot escape the impression that on homosexuality, Ratzinger has not bothered to master the issues. His two major documents are littered with remarkably raw prejudice: AIDS as a gay disease, gays as destroyers of families, homosexuality as a cause of violence and disorder, the "deceitful propaganda" of the homosexual movement, and the idea that the demand for civil rights comes only from "asssertive" gays. It is his language on homosexuality, in fact, that brings Ratzinger closest to the kind of cultural warfare articulated by the American religious right, and it is no surprise that the documents were warmly received by both Pat Robertson and Pat Buchanan. New Ways Ministry in the United States, founded by Nugent and Gramick to meet the needs of Catholic homosexuals, referred to the 1992 Ratzinger letter as "unadulterated homophobia." At the same time, a Gallup poll showed that seventy-eight percent of U.S. Catholics favored employment protection for homosexuals.

The secretary of the Congregation for the Doctrine of the Faith, Archbishop Tarcisio Bertone, published an article in *L'Osservatore Romano* in December 1996 in which he asserted that certain papal teachings should be considered infallible, even in the absence of a formal ex cathedra statement. Bertone mentions three papal documents: *Veritatis splendor, Ordinatio sacerdotalis,* and *Evangelium vitae.* Because *Veritatis splendor* specifically proclaims the intrinsic evil of the homosexual condition, Bertone's argument marks the first time that a church official, albeit indirectly, claimed that this teaching is infallible.

Most of Ratzinger's attention to homosexuality has been directed to the United States, because this is where much of the energy for the gay rights movement originated. It is a movement with worldwide import, however, and even in the backyard of the Vatican there is disagreement. This point was confirmed in February 1997, when the Vatican imposed a new leader on the Pauline religious order, a community based in Milan that runs a host of popular Italian publications including one of the country's highest-circulation magazines, *Famiglia Cristiana*. Bishop Antonio Buoncristiani, a former Vatican diplomat and sociology professor, was assigned by the pope to take charge of the community and restore a more conservative editorial policy. The Vatican was especially aggrieved by a story in *Famiglia Cristiana* that advised parents not to force their views on an adult son if he chose to be gay, even if they disagreed with the choice. The papal move followed a 1991 letter from Ratzinger to the Paulines warning them to pay "greater attention" to what they publish on moral issues.

Some elements in the U.S. bishops' conference still believed it was possible to steer a more pastoral course on homosexuality: not to challenge the "intrinsic evil" of it but to stress acceptance and tolerance. The fruit of this effort was an October 1, 1997, document from the Marriage and Family Life committee called *Always our children*. Parents and activists welcomed its appeal to place support of gay and lesbian children above moral condemnation. Behind the scenes, Nugent and Gramick had played important roles in drafting the document.

The letter counsels compassion even as it underscores traditional teaching on the sinfulness of "homogenital behavior." Amid the strong emotions parents often experience when gay and lesbian children "come out," parents should avoid distancing themselves from their children, the committee urged, noting that rejection can increase the risk of suicide and substance abuse. Parents often feel anger, fear, guilt, loneliness, and shame. "Your love can be tested by this reality, but it can also grow stronger through your struggle to respond lovingly," the committee wrote. It urged parents to regard gay and lesbian children as "gifted and called for a purpose in God's design" and to seek "appropriate guidance."

The letter cautiously departed from seeing homosexuality as an intrinsic moral evil. "There seems to be no single cause of homosexual orientation. A common opinion of experts is that there are multiple factors—genetic, hormonal, psychological—that may give rise to it. Generally, homosexual orientation is experienced as a given, not as something freely chosen. By itself, therefore, a homosexual orientation cannot be considered sinful, for morality presumes the freedom to choose." It also seemed to offer hope that gay Catholics might be welcomed onto church property. "All homosexual persons have a right to be welcomed into the community, to hear the word of God and to receive pastoral care. Homosexual persons who are living chaste lives should have opportunities to lead and serve the community. However, the church has the right to deny public roles of service and leadership to persons, whether homosexual or heterosexual, whose public behavior openly violates its teachings."

Barely was the ink dry, however, before the counteroffensive began. Nugent pointed out that just as the letter was issued, Bishop Edward Egan of Bridgeport, Connecticut, refused to allow a retreat for Catholic parents of homosexuals on diocesan property. Ironically, *Always our children* recommends "participating in a retreat designed for Catholic parents of homosexual children." Egan later was named archbishop of New York, succeeding O'Connor.

By July of 1998, the Committee on Marriage and Family Life was in the embarrassing position of being forced to revise the letter under pressure from Ratzinger. The change that drew the most attention from pastoral ministers concerned a single word; the revised text shifted from describing sexual orientation as "a fundamental dimension of one's personality" to "a deep-seated dimension," which seemed to soften the idea of homosexuality as a "given."

A second passage had referred to adolescents "experimenting with some homosexual behaviors as part of the process of coming to terms with sexual identity." It said that "isolated acts do not make someone homosexual" and suggested that during such adolescent confusion, "sometimes the best approach may be a 'wait-and-see' attitude, while you try to maintain a trusting relationship and provide various kinds of support, information, and encouragement." The revised version refers to an adolescent "displaying traits which cause you anxiety, such as what the child is choosing to read or view in the media, intense friendships and other such observable characteristics and tendencies." It says: "What is called for on the part of parents is an approach which does not presume that your child has developed a homosexual orientation and which will help you maintain a loving relationship, while you provide support, information, encouragement, and moral guidance. Parents must always be vigilant about their children's behavior and exercise responsible interventions when necessary."

A third modification was the addition of a footnote to a passage that says that a homosexual orientation in itself "cannot be considered sinful." The footnote quotes from the *Catechism of the Catholic Church:* "This inclination, which is objectively disordered, constitutes for most a trial." A fourth modification was the deletion from the text of a quote from the catechism: "Everyone . . . should acknowledge and accept his sexual identity."

Following a passage about the call to chastity for all people, whatever their state in life, and the need to struggle against sin and draw strength from the sacraments of penance and Eucharist, the revised version adds a paragraph: "Furthermore, as homosexual persons 'dedicate their lives to understanding the nature of God's personal call to them, they will be able to celebrate the sacrament of penance more faithfully and receive the Lord's grace so freely offered there in order to convert their lives more fully to his way.' " The quotation in the paragraph is from Ratzinger's 1986 letter. A sixth revision deals with the document's statement, "Nothing in the Bible or in Catholic teaching can be used to justify prejudicial or discriminatory attitudes and behaviors" toward those with a homosexual orientation. The revision adds a footnote: "In matters where sexual orientation has a clear relevance, the common good does justify its being taken into account," as noted by the 1992 Ratzinger letter.

The final revision shortens an original passage that advised those in church ministry: "Use the words *homosexual, gay, lesbian* in honest and accurate ways, especially from the pulpit. In various and subtle ways you can give people permission to talk about homosexual issues among themselves and let them know that you're also willing to talk with them." The revised passage reads simply: "When speaking publicly, use the words *homosexual, gay* and *lesbian* in honest and accurate ways."

While the bishops and supporters of Catholic homosexuals tried to put the best face possible on the situation, it was clear that *Always our children* was a dead letter as far as the pastoral priorities of the U.S. bishops were concerned. Moreover, many analysts believe the controversy over the letter helped lead to the 1998 Vatican document *Apostolos suos*, which effectively forbade bishops' conferences from teaching in the name of the church unless their documents enjoy unanimous support from members of the conference or are approved in advance by Rome.

The impression that the handwriting was on the wall for pastoral outreach to gay Catholics was confirmed on May 31, 1999, when Ratzinger imposed a lifetime ban on pastoral ministry to homosexuals upon Nugent and Gramick. He also barred them from holding any leadership positions in their religious communities. It was strikingly similar to the ban placed on McNeill in the late 1970s. The decision capped two decades of investigation.[14]

At the request of the Congregation for Religious and Secular Institutes in the Vatican, Nugent and Gramick's religious communities had investigated their work three times, once in 1977 and twice more before 1985. Each time their pastoral work and publications were judged to be orthodox. Both had been ordered by Cardinal James Hickey of Washington, D.C., to disassociate themselves from New Ways Ministry in 1984. A formal Vatican investigation began in 1988, then lay dormant until 1994 when Cardinal Adam Maida of Detroit was charged with conducting a more aggressive review. After a series of hearings, Maida's report went to Rome.

Because the case was judged to have "doctrinal aspects," it went to Ratzinger's office. Negotiations led to an ultimatum from Rome: either sign a profession of faith or face disciplinary measures. The key language in the profession read:

I also firmly accept and hold that homosexual acts are always objectively evil. On the solid foundation of a constant biblical testimony, which presents homosexual acts as acts of grave depravity. . . . Tradition has always declared that homosexual acts are intrinsically disordered. . . . I adhere with religious submission of will and intellect to the teaching that the homosexual inclination, though not in itself a sin, constitutes a tendency towards behavior that is intrinsically evil, and therefore must be considered objectively disordered.

Gramick refused outright, whereas Nugent tried to reword the profession. His efforts were rejected, leading to the May 31 action.

Ratzinger's notice summarized the grounds for the action:

From the beginning, in presenting the church's teaching on homosexuality, Father Nugent and Sister Gramick have continually called central elements of that teaching into question. . . . Because of their statements and activities, the Congregation for the Doctrine of the Faith and the Congregation for Institutes of Consecrated Life and for Societies of Apostolic Life received numerous complaints and urgent requests for clarification from Bishops and others in the United States of America. It was clear that the activities of Sister Gramick and Father Nugent were causing difficulties in not a few dioceses and that they were continuing to present the teaching of the church as one possible option among others and as open to fundamental change. . . . The promotion of errors and ambiguities is not consistent with a Christian attitude of true respect and compassion: persons who are struggling with homosexuality no less than any others have the right to receive the authentic teaching of the church from those who minister to them.

Nugent claimed that the focus of the Vatican investigation had shifted over the years, from an examination of his public statements and ministries to a demand that he declare his conscience on the subject of homosexuality. "I believe that at the conclusion of the ten-year process no compelling evidence has been forthcoming to substantiate any charge of public, persistent dissent from any level of church teaching on homosexuality which would merit such a severe punishment," he said in a statement. "Having found no serious objections in my public presentations which were not clarified or corrected in my response to the *contestatio,* the primary object of the exercise had now become an attempt, through a uniquely crafted Profession of Faith, to elicit my internal adherence to a second-level definitive doctrine considered infallible by a non-defining act of the ordinary and universal magisterium."

Setting aside the technical church language, Nugent was arguing that Ratzinger could not find any basis in his writings to punish him, so Ratzinger went after him for what he would *not* say. Despite his obvious conviction that the process had been unfair, Nugent accepted the result. "As a son of the church, a presbyter, and a member of a religious congregation with a vow of obedience I accepted the decision of the CDF and expressed my intention to implement it accordingly," he said.

Gramick shared Nugent's criticism of the process.

What began as an inquiry about my public statements and writings on homosexuality became, in the end, an interrogation about my inner personal beliefs on the subject. My personal beliefs had earlier been avoided in the Vatican Commission hearings when Cardinal Adam Maida, the commission chair, inquired about them but then quickly acknowledged, "Maybe that's not a fair question." . . . I stand ready to proclaim my assent to all the core beliefs of our faith. Beyond this, my status as a vowed religious and as a public pastoral minister should not deprive me of the right which every believer has to maintain the privacy of her internal conscience in matters which are not central to our faith. To intrude, uninvited, into the sanctuary of another's conscience is both disrespectful and wrong.

She used stronger language than Nugent about the injustice she perceived. "I strongly believe in the need for authority and I respect those entrusted with exercising it. At the same time, my experience in this investigation was that justice was not served because of a lack of fair and open procedures. The People of God deserve impartial hearings and trials for any accused. There is a conflict of interest when any agency fulfills the roles of prosecutor, jury, and judge in the same case, as happened with the Vatican investigation of my ministry." In the end, Gramick opted to accept the ban and work for its reversal.

Just one year later, in May 2000, Nugent and Gramick were again summoned to Rome. They were informed by their religious superiors that they were now prohibited from:

- speaking or writing about the ban or the ecclesiastical processes that led up to it;
- speaking or writing on matters related to homosexuality;
- protesting against the ban or encouraging the faithful to publicly express dissent from the church's magisterium;
- criticizing the magisterium in any public form whatsoever concerning homosexuality or related issues.

It was an obvious expansion of the previous ban on ministry, probably triggered by the fact that both Nugent and Gramick had given talks in the United States critical of the actions against them. Nugent assented to the new orders, whereas Gramick refused, putting her on the road to possible expulsion from her community (the School Sisters of Notre Dame).

Most of the existing support groups for Catholic gays and lesbians such as New Ways Ministry and Dignity vowed to soldier on, and some leaders even asserted confidently that Ratzinger was struggling in vain to hold back the tide, but quietly most admitted that the censure of the two founding figures of the movement was deeply disheartening. The almost inevitable result, they admitted, is that many homosexual Catholics will seek more welcoming places to worship. Others will stay in the church but remain closeted, unable to share their deepest selves with their faith community. Still others will lose faith entirely, angry with God and the church, and will internalize that anger in the form of behavior destructive of themselves or others.

The Cost

How many homosexuals have been driven out of the church because of Catholic doctrine that their condition is "intrisically evil"? How many gay and lesbian couples have been unable to raise children because men like Ratzinger held that it is unacceptable? The number cannot be calculated. But one can approach these questions from the other end and speculate what the world might be like if the church were to embrace and support homosexuals in their desire to be judged, morally and legally, by the same standards as heterosexuals.

In Brazil, an overwhelmingly Catholic nation (75 percent of 162 million people, giving Brazil more Catholics than any other nation on earth), roving youth gangs regularly target homosexuals for beatings. Hit squads with names such as the "Black Horsemen" and "Al Koran" assassinate gay prostitutes. Police often fail to prevent such violence and decline to investigate, in part because many officers share the same antihomosexual prejudices as the perpetrators. Victims claim that the police sometimes even join in the beatings. According to one gay rights group in the country, 1,600 gay men have been murdered in Brazil since 1980, despite the fact that urban areas such as Rio de Janeiro tolerate open expressions of homosexuality even more readily than most American cities. Since 1995, several Brazilian homosexuals have received political asylum in the United States by convincing immigration judges they had well-grounded fears of persecution in their home country. Brazilian homosexuals have also won asylum in Canada, the

United Kingdom, and Australia. The hostile climate in Brazil owes a great deal to the attitudes of Catholic leaders. The nation's most popular television priest told his audience in 1998, "A lot of ideas will change the day homosexuality is proven to be an illness."[15]

Similar conditions exist in Italy. Roman police records show that eighteen gay men have been killed in murky circumstances since 1990, and ten of those cases remain unsolved. Given the extremely strong social prejudice against homosexuality in Italy, local gay rights groups believe these eighteen cases are merely the tip of the iceberg; one such group, Arcigay, believes that as many as 200 murders go unreported each year, and another 200 teenagers commit suicide annually because they find it impossible to cope with their homosexuality.[16]

Homosexuals are victimized by violence all over the world; in America, the tragic case of Matthew Shepherd is proof of the point. But Brazil and Italy seem to have special relevance, because Catholicism exercises such a deep impact on the culture in both places. Imagine the cultural revolution that would follow if the Catholic church were to declare unambiguously that homosexuality is moral and acceptable. Imagine the social import of church weddings for gay couples, in keeping with Leo XIII's statement in *Rerum novarum* (1891): "No human law can take away in any form at all the natural and primordial right of every human being to marry." Imagine the equally powerful symbolism of baptisms for the adopted children of gay parents. Such gestures could not help but have a transformative impact on cultural attitudes.

How many women have suffered violence because of patriarchal values for which Catholicism has acted as a carrier? How many women have seen their life options unnecessarily narrowed or spirituality diminished from watching the men take over at the altar? Again, one can only speculate how the world might be different if the church were different. Eugene Kennedy addressed the question imaginatively in the May 28, 1999, *National Catholic Reporter*. He asked: What would be the impact of ordaining women on the debate over abortion? "At the level at which things really happen—the one beneath our conversations and rationalizations of our attitudes and behavior—this change would strike the chains off the dynamic of control of women by men that lies, seldom if ever talked about in Catholicism, close to the bone of the abortion debate," he wrote. "Many women feel that the institutional church . . . is pitted against them, that the men have so long dominated women in matters of doctrine and discipline that this masculine overseeing of their innermost lives seems natural, indeed, supernatural—the way, in other words, God meant things to be. This subterranean struggle against being overwhelmed by males motivates many women who advocate the pro-choice position. Perhaps more women than we know are not as much for abortion as they are against what they have experienced as a historical oppression of them by men."

The implications of Kennedy's argument transcend the abortion issue. If the Catholic church were to reverse itself and open the door to women in all positions of leadership—if Catholicism had female priests, female bishops, female cardinals, even someday a female pope—the impact on women's self-understanding, and on social attitudes toward women, would be revolutionary. Women's ordination in the Catholic church would perhaps not eradicate the oppression of women, but it would surely lower the number of oppressed women. Whether that point has theological significance is open for debate. Ratzinger himself, in fairness, might well grant that greater approbation from the church would influence social attitudes about homosexuals or women. He would say, however, that one cannot pursue a good end with a faulty means, and ignoring church teaching would be just that. What no party to the debate can deny, however, is that as far as the church's attitude toward women and homosexuals is concerned, Joseph Ratzinger *matters*.

6

——·—·——

Holy Wars

Assisi, Italy, the home of St. Francis, has become a crossroads of the human spirit over the seven centuries since the birth of its most famous son. Mystic and peacemaker and lover of the earth, Francis is easily the most accessible Catholic saint, and all manner of seekers—from New Agers to ecoactivists to charismatics to pacifists, conservative and liberal, Catholic or not—have felt the tug of a pilgrimage to his birthplace. Even in light of that history, however, the group that assembled in Assisi in October 1986 was unique. It included rabbis wearing yarmulkes and Sikhs in turbans, Muslims praying on thick carpets and a Zoroastrian kindling a sacred fire. Robert Runcie, the Anglican archbishop of Canterbury, exchanged pleasantries with the Dalai Lama. Orthodox bishops chatted with Alan Boesak, the South African antiapartheid activist and president of the World Alliance of Reformed Churches.

This gathering of more than 200 religious leaders had come to Assisi at the invitation of John Paul II, not to "pray together"—according to the pope's advisors that would be theologically problematic, as prayer presupposes doctrinal agreement—but "to be together and pray" on behalf of peace. Despite strong pressure to abandon the idea, John Paul saw this gathering as an expression of his mission of promoting unity.

At one point during the day, each of the different faiths was assigned one of the dozens of churches scattered throughout Assisi to hold services. Buddhists chanted and beat drums, while Shintoists played haunting melodies on thin bamboo reed instruments. Afterward they all assembled with the pope and formed a circle to offer their own prayers for peace. Two animists from Africa prayed, "Almighty God, the Great Thumb we cannot avoid in tying any knot, the Roaring Thunder that splits mighty trees, the

All-Seeing Lord up on high who sees even the footprints of an antelope on a rock here on earth . . . you are the cornerstone of peace." John Pretty-on-Top, a Crow medicine man from Montana in full headgear and smoking a peace-pipe, offered, "O Great Spirit, I raise my pipe to you, to your messengers the four winds, and to mother earth, who provides for your children. . . . I pray that you bring peace to all my brothers and sisters of this world." After the prayers were finished the spiritual leaders gathered at a Franciscan monastery for a meal of bread, pizza, vegetables, Coke, and water. In a rare concession for Italians, no wine was served, so as not to offend believers for whom alcohol is forbidden.

This 1986 Interreligious Assembly was a breathtaking gesture from the Roman Catholic church, given that earlier in the century the church had branded many of these faiths as "pagan" or "heretic." John Paul's decision to pray at the same time, if not in the same voice, with this mixed crowd was equally dizzying, considering that Catholics were not permitted to as much as say the Lord's Prayer with other Christians until after Vatican II. It was hard to believe that this was the same church that had declared in 1217 at the Fourth Lateran Council: "There is indeed one universal church of the faithful, outside which no one at all is saved."

The event was a dream for the media, full of controversy and great pictures. Some secular left-wingers, who saw the gathering as empty symbolism, carried placards reading, "You Don't Pray for Peace, You Have to Fight For It." Other progressive religious leaders complained that John Paul's outreach would do little to heal divisions as long as Catholicism insists upon the superiority of its own approach to truth. By far, however, the most vocal criticism of the Assisi gathering came from the right. Followers of schismatic Catholic bishop Marcel Lefebvre, who rejected liturgical and doctrinal innovations since Vatican II, distributed flyers denouncing the pontiff as an apostate. Two years later, when Lefebvre formally went into schism by ordaining his own bishops, he said he was acting to protect Catholicism from the "spirit of Vatican II and the spirit of Assisi." Fundamentalist U.S. Protestant Carl McIntire echoed Lefebvre by calling the Assisi gathering the "greatest single abomination in church history." Conservative critics had a field day when news leaked that some Buddhists had accidentally placed their religious articles on top of a tabernacle in the Assisi church to which they had been assigned. (The tabernacle stores consecrated hosts—pieces of bread that Catholics believe embody the real presence of Christ—and is considered one of the most sacred objects in a church.)

Some members of the Roman curia, the closest advisers to the pope, voiced reservations. Ratzinger himself later told a German newspaper, "This cannot be the model!" In a 1987 press conference, Ratzinger said the common interpretation of what had happened in Assisi, that participants recognized each had a valid set of beliefs based on different historical experiences, was false. "That is the definitive rejection of truth," he said. "The debate on religions has to be begun all over. The category of truth and the dynamism of truth are put aside. The attitude that says that we all have values and nobody possesses the truth expresses a static position and is opposed to true progress. To accept that historical identity is to imprison oneself in historicism."[1]

Curial nervousness was clear again when the Vatican staged a similar gathering in Assisi in late October 1999; on that day, reporters were discouraged from even making the trip, there were no non-Catholic services in churches, and there was no joint prayer. Religious leaders were invited to pause before the tomb of St. Francis for a moment of silence together, conveniently out of range of television cameras and tape recorders.[2]

Given such resistance, it is little surprise that in the years since the first gathering at Assisi the hope for interreligious harmony it generated ran up against hard doctrinal realities. On the twin fronts of ecumenism, or relations among the different branches of Christianity, and interreligious dialogue, meaning conversations among the world's different religions, Ratzinger became increasingly alarmed during the 1990s that the push for unity was running ahead of doctrinal clarity. By 1996, Ratzinger was warning that the theology of religious pluralism—the attempt to find a theological basis for affirming humanity's religious diversity—had replaced liberation theology as the era's most grave danger to the faith. Over the several years since that 1996 speech, at least six different Catholic thinkers have been investigated, censured, or excommunicated for their work in religious pluralism.

Ratzinger does not question whether members of other religions can be saved. He said in *Salt of the Earth,* "It is definitely possible for someone to receive from his religion directives that help him become a pure person, which also, if we want to use the word, help him to please God and to reach salvation. . . . This undoubtedly happens on a large scale." The real debate, as the Jesuit theologian Jacques DuPuis phrased it in his 1997 book *Toward a Christian Theology of Religious Pluralism,* is whether religious pluralism exists de jure as well as de facto: whether the different religions are part of God's saving plan. Put in its simplest terms, the question is whether members of other religions are saved in spite of, or in and through, their non-Christian faith.

Given that religious differences are often lethal, a point written in blood from Kosovo to Kashmir, Ratzinger's broad reservations about the "spirit of Assisi" cannot help but have important real-world consequences.

Vatican II and Religious Pluralism

The theological questions raised by divisions among Christians and by the world's religious pluralism surfaced at Vatican II in four documents: *Nostra aetate,* the declaration on non-Christian religions; *Ad gentes divinitus,* the decree on missionary activity; *Dignitatis humanae,* the declaration on religious liberty; and *Unitatis redintegratio,* the declaration on ecumenism. The question also surfaced in debate over article 8 of *Lumen gentium,* the document on the church. That passage says the church of Christ "subsists in" the Roman Catholic church. It says that many elements of sanctification and truth can be found outside the visible structures of the Catholic church, though these elements properly belong to the church of Christ and hence "possess an inner dynamism towards Catholic unity." Taken together, these texts left the church with an unresolved tension. The council affirmed that truth is found in other religions and recognized the right of religious freedom; yet it also called for renewed missionary efforts because only the Catholic church possesses the fullness of the means of salvation. Whether these positions are fully consistent with one another, and which should dominate the church's thinking, frame the heart of the debate over religious pluralism that has unfolded ever since.

Ratzinger's attitude during the council can be gleaned in part through the public statements of Cardinal Frings. During debate over *Lumen gentium* in the second session, Frings applauded the "ecumenical spirit" of the document and its irenic approach to non-Christians. He praised Paul VI's statement of sorrow for the role of the Catholic church in creating divisions among Christians, and urged that similar language be worked into the text. Frings later spoke on behalf of ecumenism when he argued that the church should acknowledge mixed marriages contracted in the presence of a non-Catholic minister, and remove all ecclesiastical penalties for such a marriage.

Yet it is clear that Frings and Ratzinger were not prepared to abandon Christianity's claim to being "true" in a sense superior to other faiths nor to lessen evangelizing efforts. During the debate over the schema on missionary activity in the third session, Frings demanded a larger document. He insisted that "mission" should not be used to refer to the reevangelization of lapsed Catholics but must remain first and foremost the proclamation of the gospel to those outside the church. He proposed a yearly contribution from older dioceses to support missionary efforts, as it was unjust for missionary bishops to have to spend so much of their time begging for financial support.

Frings's speech sealed the fate of the existing draft on missionary activity, and the council decided to commission a completely new document. Ratzinger, as Frings's *peritus,* was assigned to work on the new text, along with Yves Congar and a number of other theologians. *Ad gentes divinitus* eventually made two points both Ratzinger and Frings considered essential: first, that evangelization, meaning the proclamation of the gospel with the aim of making converts, must remain the heart of missionary work, as opposed to social work and other "preevangelizing" activities; and, second, that support for the missions is a collegial responsibility binding on all bishops.

The document on religious liberty amounted to a near-total reversal of church teaching on the subject. Though Vatican observers had been present when the United Nations adopted its Universal Declaration of Human Rights in 1948, which included a guarantee of religious liberty, the concept was still officially heretical for Catholics going into the council. The standard teaching had been expressed in 1832 by Pope Gregory XVI, who described as "false and absurd or rather mad" the principle "that we must secure and guarantee to each one liberty of conscience; this is one of the most contagious of errors. . . . To this is attached liberty of the press, the most dangerous liberty, an execrable liberty, which can never inspire sufficient horror." As late as Pius X and the antimodernist campaign of the early twentieth century, these anathemas were vigorously enforced. They were part of Catholicism's reaction against the Enlightenment.

Thus Vatican IIs declaration that "the human person has a right to religious freedom" was hailed around the world as a startling and dramatic departure. Ratzinger played no direct role in the drafting of the document, but Frings delivered an intervention on September 15, 1965, during the initial round of discussion. He approved the document in broad strokes, but voiced reservations that Ratzinger would later develop. First, Frings said that the council should not argue for religious freedom on the basis of natural law, such questions were for philosophers to debate—but the council's business was to unfold the implications of revelation. Second, Frings emphasized that freedom from state coercion and freedom from the moral obligation of following Christ must not be treated as the same idea. Finally, Frings argued against including in the document a review of church history on the doctrine and practice of religious liberty. Taken together, the remarks suggest that for Frings, and by extension, for Ratzinger, religious liberty was to be understood as a political, not a theological, concept. The state should not coerce religious belief, but the church must not surrender its claim to being the unique path to salvation.

The Halbfas Affair

During Ratzinger's Tübingen years a controversy arose that underlined the distance between his understanding of religious pluralism and where many Catholics believed the church was heading. The dispute centered on Hubertus Halbfas, a popular theologian and religious educator who taught at the nearby *Hochschule* in Reutlingen (a *Hochschule* is the equivalent of a regional college; this one was located approximately 15 miles away from Tübingen). Halbfas is today retired and lives in the German city of Drolshagen.[3]

Halbfas's career path was in some ways similar to Ratzinger's. Born in 1932 into a family of farmers and laborers, he earned a doctorate in Catholic theology from the University of Munich, finishing his degree in 1957. He was ordained and served as a vicar in Brakel from 1957 to 1960. In 1960, he was appointed as a docent, or lecturer, in theology at the *Hochschule* in Paderborn in northern Germany between Essen and Hannover. In the summer of 1967, he moved to Reutlingen, where he spent only a year before being offered a similar position in Bonn.

Halbfas, however, was engulfed in controversy before he could take the job. In February 1968, his book *Fundamentalketechtik: Sprache und Erfahrung in Religionsunterricht* (Fundamentals of catechetics: Speech and experience in religious instruction) caused a sensation in German-speaking theological circles. In it, Halbfas aimed to show the consequences of the "exegetical sciences," especially modern biblical criticism, on Catholic dogma. In part, the book touched off what Halbfas calls a *Lehrstreit*, or doctrinal controversy, because of its approach to articles of faith such as the Resurrection, which Halbfas treated not as a historic fact but as an understanding that developed over time in the early church. The most explosive element of the book, however, was the way Halbfas defined the purpose of Christian missionary activity. It should not aim to make converts, he said, but to help "the Hindu to become a better Hindu, the Buddhist a better Buddhist, and the Moslem a better Moslem." Halbfas wrote in a 1999 E-mail exchange with me that his argument was especially controversial because he was working in religious education. The question became, what understanding should the church be passing on to the next generation?

Fundamentalketechtik was published without an imprimatur, but soon after its release Cardinal Frings and Bishop Josef Höffner, who would later succeed Frings, denounced it. In July 1968, the German bishops' conference issued a formal condemnation of the book, citing its position on missionary

222

activity. Bonn, where Halbfas had been offered a teaching job, is a suffragan see of Cologne, and thus it came as no surprise to church insiders when the vicar general there vetoed Halbfas's appointment to the *Hochschule*. Halbfas told me that to the best of his knowledge, Ratzinger played no role in either of these decisions.

Widespread Catholic outrage followed the news that Halbfas had been, in effect, censured by the bishops. In both Bonn and Reutlingen, students marched in the streets to support Halbfas. Fifty theology students at the University of Munich wrote an open letter to Cardinal Julius Döpfner of Munich, then head of the German bishops' conference, demanding that Halbfas be allowed to take the appointment in Bonn. The bishops did not budge. In fact, they asked that he recall his book and remove the offending portions. Support for Halbfas was not universal in the theological community, even among progressives: Karl Rahner, for example, said that the book "denied the essential ecclesial character of the theologian's vocation." Nevertheless, mainstream public sentiment in the church was solidly on Halbfas's side, and when his *missio canonica* as a Catholic theologian was revoked in November 1969, another round of protests was unleashed across the country.

The reaction can be explained in terms of three forces. First, Vatican II led many Catholics to expect that the era of lifting imprimaturs from books and revoking theological licenses was over. The Halbfas case was the first sign inside Germany that Catholics had misread these intentions. Second, many Catholics had assumed the church was moving toward an embrace of religious pluralism, and the Halbfas case confounded that expectation. Finally, the general revolutionary tenor of the late 1960s accelerated the tendency to revolt against any exercise of authority. Thus when Halbfas accused the German bishops in a December 1968 article in *Christ und Welt* of measuring contemporary expressions of the faith by criteria that were centuries old, his argument met with wide agreement in the German Catholic community.

There was strong pressure on the Catholic and Protestant theology faculties at Tübingen to support their colleague down the road in Reutlingen. Students put up handbills at the beginning of the winter semester in 1968 asking what the faculty planned to do about "the Halbfas affair." Many Tübingen faculty agreed they needed to take action. "We wanted to defend this man," Küng recalled. "We were very concerned about what was happening to him." Küng said the desire to take the side of Halbfas was nearly universal within the Catholic faculty, with the lone exception of Ratzinger, who happened to be serving as dean that year.

Halbfas told me that Ratzinger invited him to meet with the members of the Catholic theology faculty at Ratzinger's home in Tübingen for a private discussion. During the meeting, Halbfas said, Ratzinger told him that one certainly has the right to take the positions he did in his book, but then one should not do so as a Catholic theologian. Halbfas said Ratzinger was polite about it, and the exchange "did not have any recognizable consequences" for the relationship between the two men. The position Ratzinger took in the exchange was perhaps not surprising to Halbfas: despite the progressive tone of Ratzinger's commentaries on Vatican II, he had written in his 1966 monograph on the fourth session, "The prevailing optimism, which understands the world religions as in some way salvific agencies, is simply irreconcilable with the biblical assessment of these religions."

Küng said the faculty met later for over an hour to discuss the case, with Ratzinger implacably opposed to any expression of support for Halbfas or any intervention on his behalf with Bishop Karl-Josef Leiprecht of Rottenburg, whose diocese encompassed both Tübingen and Reutlingen. Küng remembers being startled by Ratzinger's strong stance: "It was the first time I experienced how Ratzinger is capable of defending a position with whatever arguments come to hand, even when they are mutually contradictory," he said. "He used every possible argument."[4]

Former Ratzinger graduate student Charles MacDonald, now a professor in Nova Scotia, remembers the Halbfas controversy as a defining moment for Ratzinger. As protests supporting Halbfas mounted, Ratzinger sensed he needed to make a public declaration of the reasons for his stand, MacDonald said, and so he scheduled a special public lecture on the Halbfas matter. More than 700 people showed up to hear Ratzinger present Halbfas's positions and his own. In what was then a surprising gesture, Ratzinger fielded questions from the floor when he was finished. MacDonald said most of the questions were hostile, but respectful of Ratzinger for being willing to take the heat. The key moment came, MacDonald said, when Ratzinger said with respect to a question about the way Halbfas understood a doctrine: "If I believed that, I could no longer honestly say the creed." It was then, MacDonald said, he realized how "deeply existential" the issue was for Ratzinger. MacDonald said that during Hans Küng's 1972 seminar on infallibility, when Ratzinger appeared as a guest speaker, he used the same language with respect to a position of Küng's view on the origins of the church: "If I believed that, I couldn't say the creed."

In 1970, Halbfas left the priesthood to marry. He continued to teach at Reutlingen, where he became a professor of religious education rather than of theology. At around the same time, Halbfas said, Ratzinger attacked his views on missionary work in a way Halbfas felt distorted what he had written. Halbfas did not respond, perhaps owing to the sensitivities of having just resigned the priesthood. However, the progressive German Catholic magazine *Publik-Forum* carried a long series of letters from readers discussing Ratzinger's criticism of Halbfas; most sided with Halbfas.

The controversy over Halbfas gradually receded. He went on to author several theological works, including the well-received *Das Dritte Auge* in 1982, developing his ideas on both catechesis and religious pluralism. "The Halbfas affair" offers an important window into Ratzinger's attitude on the issue of religious pluralism and, equally important, on the right and duty of church authorities to take disciplinary measures when theologians go too far. For Ratzinger, as early as 1968 the question of missionary work represented such a line in the sand. Evangelization, as Ratzinger sees it, means making more Christians, not better Hindus.

Ratzinger and Ecumenism

John Paul II envisions the third millennium as a period of reunification of the separated branches of Christianity, starting with the fifteen Orthodox churches, so that Christianity can again "breathe with both lungs," East and West. His pontificate has so far produced few concrete breakthroughs—biographer George Weigel believes the failure to achieve significant progress with the Orthodox branch is probably the pope's greatest disappointment—but the effort nevertheless has been a hallmark of John Paul's reign.

There is little evidence Ratzinger shares this commitment to reunion. He regards ecumenism as desirable, but he is much more skeptical about its prospects and much more guarded about compromises. In many cases, Ratzinger has acted as the brake on John Paul's ecumenical engine. The lone, though still ambiguous, exception is the Catholic dialogue with the Lutherans, where Ratzinger himself feels a deep personal stake in the conversation.

Ratzinger treated ecumenism most extensively in a collection of essays published in 1988 as *Church, Ecumenism and Politics*. In an essay on Europe after communism, he warns that capitalism is little better than nationalism or communism, in that all three propose false idols (prosperity, the *Volk*, and the state, respectively). Ratzinger argues that for Europe to build a humane civilization, it must rediscover two elements of its past: its classical Greek heritage and its common Christian identity. From the classical era, Europe should rediscover objective and eternal values that stand above politics, placing limits on power. Ratzinger uses the Greek term *eunomia* to describe this concept of the good; in that sense, one could say that Ratzinger is proposing a eunomic, rather than economic, model of European integration.

Christian anthropology, Ratzinger argues, should provide the values for this new eunomic European civilization. It is in the effort to build such a new Europe that Ratzinger holds out the most hope for ecumenical cooperation. Catholics, Orthodox, Anglicans, Lutherans, and the other branches of Christianity could work together to spread eunomic ideals. Ratzinger therefore puts the accent on outward-directed collaboration, not on inner doctrinal agreement.

In his essay "Ecumenical Problems," which comprises Part II of *Church, Ecumenism and Politics,* Ratzinger defines the goal of Catholic work on ecumenism: To transform the presently separated churches into "particular" churches in communion with Rome. Ratzinger says that Vatican II rightly encouraged work toward this aim, but perhaps created unrealistic expectations. Christian divisions, he believes, will not melt anytime soon, and it would be futile to pursue desperate solutions in an attempt to accelerate reunion. He predicts full communion is not likely to happen within the lifetime of the present generation.

Ratzinger rejects three such solutions he sees floated in ecumenical discussion. The first is a solution "from below." The idea is that believers in the various Christian traditions, impatient with theological foot-dragging, would simply begin gathering for common worship. In this scenario, hierarchies would be forced to accommodate the new reality on the ground. Ratzinger says there are two problems with this approach. It violates the notion of church as communion by positing a division between the hierarchy and the faithful drawn from secular political theory. Additionally, the sort of "world church" it envisions would be too fluid and unstable to create lasting unity.

The second possibility is reunion from above. This model, proposed in different forms by Catholic theologians such as Heinrich Fries and Karl Rahner, calls on church leaders to suspend the normal preconditions for entry into the Catholic communion on the premise that once new members were integrated into the life of the church, their doctrinal objections to Catholicism would dissipate. They would "grow into" being Catholic.

Interestingly, Ratzinger rejects this proposal as resting upon an exaggerated notion of papal authority. The pope is bound by the faith; he cannot simply dream something up ("illuminism") and put it into practice ("voluntarism"). The point is reminiscent of the discussion at Vatican II when Paul VI proposed inserting a line into *Lumen gentium* saying that the pope was limited by nothing in the exercise of his ecclesial powers. The council's theological commission rejected the proposal, noting that the pope is in fact bound by many things: by revelation, by the definitions of ecumenical councils, by infallible statements of previous popes, by the truth. He cannot decree that two plus two is five. At a Vatican symposium on the papacy in the 1990s, American Jesuit theologian Michael Buckley quoted a summary of this discussion from Ratzinger's commentary on *Lumen gentium*; Ratzinger had actually forgotten the reference, but agreed that the theology was correct.[5]

Finally, Ratzinger rejects the notion of reunion "from the side" in which the different branches of Christianity would be considered equally valid traditions while setting aside the question of which is "most true." Ratzinger argues that this approach is actually a recipe for stalemate, not progress. If there is no objective standard by which differing doctrines and policies may be judged, what is there to talk about? In this sense, Ratzinger argues that bland tolerance actually leaves Christians "imprisoned in historicity": we are stuck with our differences because there are no criteria by which change might be justified.

In place of these three alternatives, Ratzinger says true ecumenism must move from below, from above, and from the side all at once. It is from the interpenetration and slow maturity of insights from each of these three vantage points that real reunion will gradually emerge. It is a slow, deliberate process, with no guarantee of success. In the meantime Christians may collaborate on social work and in offering a common moral witness.

Ratzinger's impact on ecumenism can be gathered from examining his dealings with three different Christian churches: Orthodoxy, Anglicanism, and Lutheranism.

Orthodoxy

Ratzinger knows Orthodoxy well. He credited Russian Orthodox theologians with influencing Vatican II's recovery of eucharistic ecclesiology and has compared modern assaults on "clericalism" inside Catholicism with the *raskolniki* (or "Old Believers") schism in sixteenth-century Russia. At Vatican II, Ratzinger criticized the overly "Western" feel of the church under neoscholasticism, and hoped for a greater balance through restoration of Eastern insights and practices. He felt one of the crowning moments in the council's liturgies came when the Gospel was proclaimed in Greek. Ratzinger has on several occasions suggested that Rome's single condition for intercommunion with the Orthodox should be that they accept the teachings of the first millennium on the primacy of the pope.

In a May 28, 1992, letter to the bishops of the world on *Some aspects of the church understood as communion*, Ratzinger says that "in every valid celebration of the Eucharist the one, holy, catholic, and apostolic church becomes truly present." The vestigial communion with all Christian churches that survived the various ruptures of history exists "especially with the Orthodox."

Over the course of John Paul II's pontificate, there have been relatively minor breakthroughs with the Orthodox: the Catholic church and the Armenian Apostolic church signed a common christological definition in 1996, and in 1999 John Paul II became the first pope to visit predominantly Orthodox nations when he traveled to Romania and, at year's end, to the former Soviet state of Georgia. Yet there has been little progress toward unity, with the conversation stuck above all on what the "primacy" of the successor of Peter means. In *Ut unum sint,* John Paul suggested that this was the *only* issue still separating Rome and the Orthodox churches, a position that most Orthodox leaders have not endorsed; in 1997, Ecumenical Patriarch Bartholomew said that "the manner in which we exist has become ontologically different," which seems to point to deeper divisions.

Ratzinger has sponsored two Vatican symposia on papal primacy: one in 1989 on historical evidence concerning the exercise of the papal primacy in the first millennium, and another in 1996 on the theological dimensions of that history. The fruit of the two symposia was a November 1998 document entitled *The primacy of Peter in the mystery of the church.* Though the document is not specifically addressed to the Orthodox churches, it was greeted with intense interest by Orthodox leaders. In it, Ratzinger asserts that a strong papacy is not only the will of Christ, it also protects bishops and local churches against political interference from the state. Fear of such interference, in fact, helped give birth in France and Germany to the nineteenth-century push for the declaration of papal infallibility.

Ratzinger argues that episcopal collegiality, such as that exercised by the patriarchs in the Orthodox churches, "does not stand in opposition to the personal exercise of the primacy nor should it relativize it." Ratzinger argues that God's providence from the beginning included a link between the historic patriarchal sees, such as Antioch and Alexandria, and Rome. The primacy of the pope cannot be reduced to a "primacy of honor," nor can it be understood as "a political monarchy" capable of being merely symbolic. The pope must have full and supreme power over the church in order to protect it against arbitrariness and conformity. The pope must protect legitimate diversity and listen to the universal church in the exercise of his power, but in the end decisions are his to make alone.

Ratzinger asserts that every valid celebration of the Eucharist, by which he means primarily the Orthodox liturgy, "objectively calls for" full union with Rome because the primacy of the pope is part of the "interiority" of the eucharistic communion. Ratzinger grants that this primacy has been exercised in different ways over the centuries, and he leaves open the prospect of finding new forms today. Yet he cautions that this cannot be done by "looking for the least number of functions exercised historically."

Ratzinger says that recalling these essential points will allow the ecumenical dialogue to avoid traps already rejected in church history. He mentions Febronianism (a movement in eighteenth-century Germany calling for a German Catholic church independent of Rome), Gallicanism (a similar movement in France, though with overtones of state control), Ultramontanism (by which Ratzinger presumably means an exaggerated stress on papal primacy), and Conciliarism (the view that an ecumenical council rather than the pope holds supreme authority).

Alongside primacy, there are two other sticking points in the Catholic-Orthodox dialogue. The first is the so-called Uniate churches, communities with Eastern liturgies and traditions that acknowledge the primacy of the pope under the terms of the Union of Brest in 1596. Under the Soviets, the Uniate churches were especially oppressed because they were seen as a beachhead for the West. Much of their property was confiscated and handed over to the Orthodox. After the collapse of communism, the Uniate churches demanded the return of their parishes, icons, and other items. Rome has walked a tightrope on the issue, wishing neither to betray the Uniates nor to alienate the Orthodox.

By far the most difficult point separating Roman Catholicism and Orthodoxy today is missionary efforts. Orthodox leaders want a Vatican promise to foreswear making converts in their territory. Such an agreement was in fact produced in 1990 by the Joint Commission for Theological Dialogue between Local Orthodox Churches and the Roman Catholic Church, which met in Freising, Germany, the ancient seat of Ratzinger's Munich archdiocese. The commission issued a statement saying, "We reject uniatism as a way of seeking unity, because it is at odds with the common tradition of our churches." It adds, "Any attempt to convert the believers of one church to another—which is known as proselytism—should be ruled out as a distortion of pastoral activity."[6]

Though hailed as a breakthrough, the statement drew criticism on all sides. Many in the Uniate churches saw it as a betrayal, whereas most Orthodox leaders continued to suspect Rome of fostering missionary activity because conversions to Catholicism, either outright or through the Uniate churches, grew in Eastern Europe throughout the 1990s. Conservatives in the Vatican felt the agreement was a sell-out, arguing that the church should never surrender its right to preach the gospel. In practice, the agreement has made little difference either on the ground or in relations between Catholic and Orthodox leaders.

Anglicanism

In *Church, Ecumenism and Politics*, Ratzinger outlined his views on Catholic dialogue with the Anglican Communion. At a commonsense level, he wrote, it would seem that Anglicanism, because it is structured episcopally, offers hope of quick progress in talks with Rome. In reality, Ratzinger says, Anglicanism practices "dispersed authority" whereby no one can actually speak for Anglicans at large. Moreover, the Anglican understanding of core doctrinal matters has mutated. Anglican leaders, for example, acknowledge the inerrancy of ecumenical councils only so far as they agree with Scripture. Ratzinger responds that if someone outside a council can better determine the sense of Scripture, then one hardly needs the council in the first place. For Anglicans, "tradition" means the creeds and other documents from the church's past; Ratzinger says that for Catholics, it also means the living voice of the magisterium today. Thus the divisions between Rome and Canterbury, according to Ratzinger, go deeper than most people think.

In the middle of the 1976 decision of the Episcopal Church in the United States to ordain women, Ratzinger said: "A new situation has been brought about by two circumstances: the extending of the majority principle to questions of doctrine and the entrusting of doctrinal decisions to national churches," he said. "Both of these are in themselves nonsensical, because doctrine is either true or not true." In the end, Ratzinger says that what Anglicanism offers is merely a "strong Catholic potency,"not the readiness for full communion found in Orthodoxy.

Since Vatican II a formal dialogue has existed with Anglicanism under the name of ARCIC (the Anglican-Roman Catholic International Commission). In March 1982, just four months after taking over at the doctrinal congregation, Ratzinger rejected an ARCIC report that had been twelve years in the making. It dealt with a broad range of issues, such as eucharistic doctrine, ministry and ordination, and authority in the church. The document said that although Anglicans might be willing to accept the pope as the spiritual leader of a reunified church, they were not prepared to accept infallibility. The text did not address questions such as divorce or women's ordination. In a letter to the Catholic cochair of ARCIC, Ratzinger said the document was "an important ecumenical event" but "it is not yet possible to say that an agreement which is truly 'substantial' has been reached on the totality of the questions studied by the commission." Referring to "that clarity so indispensable for genuine dialogue," Ratzinger said "there are several points, held as dogmas by the Catholic church, which are not able to be accepted as such, or are able to be accepted only in part, by our Anglican brethren." Many Anglicans, angered that a twelve-year project could be summarily dismissed by someone new to the process, were offended by Ratzinger's language.

After the Episcopal Church in the United States voted to ordain women, the Vatican allowed whole Episcopal parishes to enter the Roman Catholic church while retaining much of their Anglican liturgy and tradition, in effect, launching a form of Anglican Uniatism. After the Church of England approved ordination of women by a scant two votes in November 1992, several English Anglicans petitioned Rome for a similar option. In the wake of the 1990 statement between Catholics and Orthodox leaders rejecting Uniatism, however, this was impossible. Other senior Anglican conservatives floated the idea of creating a personal prelature for breakaways, which would give them the same status as Opus Dei. A commission made up of Ratzinger, Australian cardinal Edward Cassidy, who heads the Vatican office on ecumenism, and English cardinal Basil Hume rejected that idea. Instead they decided to accept individual Anglican priests into the church. The priests were given instruction in Catholic doctrine and, most controversially, were reordained, a requirement suggesting their original Anglican ordinations were not valid. Those who were married were allowed to remain married.[7]

Many felt this was a pastorally sensitive approach. Any sense that Ratzinger was moving toward a more benign view of Anglicanism, however, was dashed in July 1998. In that month John Paul II issued *Ad tuendam fidem*, an apostolic letter adding penalties to canon law for dissent from infallible magisterial teaching not formally defined. Because it restated assertions already made under the new terms of the Code of Canon Law as well as documents such as *Ordinatio sacerdotalis*, the letter itself generated relatively little attention. More explosive was a commentary by Ratzinger in which he offered a series of doctrines as examples of this category of infallible teaching, including the teaching of Leo XIII's *Apostolicae curae* that declared Anglican ordinations to be "absolutely null and utterly void." In effect, Ratzinger was claiming that the illegitimacy of the Anglican priesthood is an infallible teaching of the Catholic church.

The response was immediate and angry. The Anglican archbishop of York, David Hope, said he was surprised by such a "stark statement." Archbishop Michael Peers said, "It's the only ecumenical reference in Cardinal Ratzinger's statement. It's only about us and it's entirely negative. So it's disappointing. . . . When Cardinal Ratzinger says this is definitive, it's as if nothing has happened in the last 102 years, whereas a lot has happened," Peers said. "But it does indicate that local agreements in the Roman Catholic tradition of course can come up against obstacles in Rome itself." Richard McBrien described the Ratzinger commentary as "astonishingly insensitive and provocative." In his 1999 biography of John Paul II, Weigel voiced doubt about the wisdom of Ratzinger's decision. "It remained unclear whether the examples used in the commentary had been as carefully thought out as the commentary's description of . . . authoritative teaching." In a footnote, Weigel indicated that he developed this impression on the basis of an October 1998 interview with Cassidy, suggesting tension between

Cassidy and Ratzinger on the point. Cassidy is Australian, and hence knows Anglicans well.

In this context, a May 1999 report from ARCIC entitled "The Gift of Authority" struck many observers as nearly miraculous. Despite the hardening of the Vatican position implied in Ratzinger's statement, the document declared that Anglicans might be prepared to recognize a "universal primacy" for the pope. Most astonishingly, commission members said they could envision Anglicans accepting such a primacy "even before our churches are in full communion." It was a remarkable gesture from the Anglican side, though one unlikely to result in swift progress. ARCIC can only propose agreements to their respective churches; it has no power to impose its plans.

Lutheranism

The Lutherans are to Ratzinger what the Orthodox are to John Paul: the separated brethren he knows the best, and for whom he has the greatest natural affinity. Of the approximately sixty-one million Lutherans in the world, half are German, and Ratzinger knows the tradition almost as well as he knows Catholicism. Luther looms large in Ratzinger's thought; after Augustine, there is probably no premodern Christian writer who has exercised more influence on Ratzinger's theological views. One of Ratzinger's closest friends is Lutheran theologian Wolfhart Pannenberg.

None of this means, however, that Ratzinger seeks hasty détente with the Lutherans. As with the Anglicans, Ratzinger laments the lack of a central doctrinal authority in the Lutheran tradition. When his American Jesuit protégé and friend Joseph Fessio once asked him about the prospects for unity with the Lutheran church, Ratzinger shot back: "As soon as there is *a* Lutheran church, we can discuss it." Moreover, his admiration of Luther is not unalloyed. In *Church, Ecumenism and Politics*, Ratzinger says there are two Luthers. There is the Luther of the catechisms, the great writer of hymns and promoter of liturgical reform. This Luther, Ratzinger says, anticipated much of the *ressourcement* that later surfaced in pre-Vatican II Catholicism. There is also, however, Luther the polemicist, whose radical view of individual salvation leaves the church entirely out of view.

In 1996 a rumor floated through Germany that John Paul wanted to rescind Luther's excommunication on the 450th anniversary of his death, but that this plan was quashed by Ratzinger and three German bishops. The rumor, published in the news magazine *Focus,* seems unlikely to be true, if only on logical grounds. Excommunication is a penalty against the living; after death, God's own judgment takes its place. If, however, Ratzinger did block some sort of gesture, it would be consistent with his statement in

1998 that the anathemas leveled at Lutherans by the Council of Trent are still in force.

The joint Catholic-Lutheran dialogue since Vatican II has a reputation as the most theologically substantive of the various ecumenical conversations. Yet Ratzinger wrote in 1988 that he held little hope for progress from interchurch statements, which usually attempt the impossible of trying to reconcile logically opposed positions of the past. Unity will not be found that way, Ratzinger wrote. It can only be found by taking "new steps" together, though he was vague on exactly what those new steps might be.

That passage seems prophetic in light of Ratzinger's role a decade later with respect to a 1998 agreement between the Holy See and the Lutheran World Federation. The agreement was announced to much fanfare in June 1998, then seemingly unraveled due to pressure from Ratzinger, and then rolled out again in June 1999.

On June 25, 1998, Cassidy held a news conference to present the *Joint Declaration on the Doctrine of Justification,* the fruit of decades of work by Lutheran and Catholic scholars. "It must be considered without doubt an outstanding achievement of the ecumenical movement and a milestone on the way to restoration of full, visible unity among the disciples of the one Lord and Savior Jesus Christ," he said. The document contained "forty-four common declarations," summarizing areas of agreement. Each side was able to offer its own explanation of the reasoning that allowed it to make the declaration. Cassidy said the "high level of consensus" reached in the document allowed both sides to state "the condemnations leveled at one another in the sixteenth century no longer apply to the respective partner today."

The heart of the agreement was this key sentence: "By grace alone, in faith in Christ's saving work and not because of any merit on our part, we are accepted by God and receive the Holy Spirit, who renews our hearts while equipping us and calling us to good works." The declaration "virtually resolves a long-disputed question at the close of the twentieth century," Cassidy declared.

Cassidy's positive spin was undercut, however, by the fact that the Vatican also issued a "response" to the declaration. The puzzling logic of issuing a "response" to one's own document suggested a behind-the-scenes struggle between Cassidy, ready to declare agreement with the Lutherans, and Ratzinger, who continued to see doctrinal differences. Most observers believe that if the response was not written personally by Ratzinger, it was significantly informed by his concerns.

The response asserted that the Lutheran understanding of justification, in which the human person remains *simul iustus et peccator*—simultaneouly justified and a sinner—was inconsistent with Catholic belief that baptism transforms the person and removes the stain of sin. The response also argued that Catholics believe in *both* salvation through faith *and* judgment on the basis of works. It was not clear, the response said, that the Lutheran understanding could be reconciled with the Catholic understanding of the sacrament of penance. The Lutheran insistence that justification is the cornerstone of the entire Christian faith was overblown; the doctrine of justification has to be incorporated into the organic whole of revelation. Echoing Ratzinger's comment to Fessio, the response voiced doubts as to whether the Lutheran signatories could speak for their church. "There remains, however, the question of the real authority of such a synodal consensus, today and also tomorrow, in the life and doctrine of the Lutheran community."

"The level of agreement is high," the response said, "but it does not yet allow us to affirm that all the differences separating Catholics and Lutherans in the doctrine concerning justification are simply a question of emphasis or language. . . . The divergencies must, on the contrary, be overcome before we can affirm, as is done generically, that these points no longer incur the condemnations of the Council of Trent." The response seemed to be a case of the left hand not knowing what the right hand was doing. Did the Catholic church stand behind the *Joint Declaration* or not? Were the anathemas of Trent reversed or not? No one quite knew. Many Lutherans were furious; one claimed that the Holy See had betrayed both the Lutheran and the Roman Catholic theologians who worked on the document and that it would take decades to reestablish trust.

That prediction proved overly gloomy. In the summer of 1999, Cassidy held a second press conference to again announce that an agreement had been reached. This time it came in the form of three documents: the *Joint Declaration* itself, an "official common statement" indicating how the two parties understand the *Joint Declaration*, and an "annex" which addressed the points raised in the response and additional concerns from the Lutheran side. The statement repeated Cassidy's 1998 claims that "consensus in basic truths of the doctrine of justification exists between Lutherans and Catholics." Cassidy said this did not mean the church had lifted the excommunication of Luther: "One cannot now do anything for Martin Luther because Martin Luther, wherever he is, is not worried about these condemnations." But on the doctrinal issue at stake, "We have put away the condemnations."

The annex amounted to a point-by-point refutation of the issues raised in the 1998 response. Baptism really does free humans from the power of sin, "yet we would be wrong to say that we are without sin"; "the working of God's grace does not exclude human action"; "in the final judgment, the justified will be judged also on their works"; "the doctrine of justification is the measure or touchstone for the Christian faith. No teaching may contradict this criterion"; and, most pointedly, "the response of the Catholic church does not intend to put in question the authority of Lutheran synods or of the Lutheran World Federation."

Despite his earlier reservations, it was Ratzinger who apparently made the agreement possible. "It was Ratzinger who untied the knots," said Bishop George Anderson, head of the Evangelical Lutheran Church of America, said to me at the time. "Without him we might not have an agreement."[8]

On July 14, 1998, Ratzinger published a letter in the German newspaper *Frankfurter Allgemeine* calling reports that he had torpedoed the original agreement a "smooth lie." He said that to scuttle the dialogue would be to "deny myself." On November 3, 1998, a special ad hoc working group met at the home of Ratzinger's brother Georg in Regensburg, Bavaria, to get the agreement back on track. Lutheran bishop Johannes Hanselmann convened the group, which consisted of Hanselmann, Ratzinger, Catholic theologian Heinz Schuette, and Lutheran theologian Joachim Track.

"He was very positive, very helpful," Track said when he spoke to me by telephone. Track said Ratzinger made three concessions that salvaged the agreement. First, he agreed that the goal of the ecumenical process is unity in diversity, not structural reintegration. "This was important to many Lutherans in Germany, who worried that the final aim of all this was coming back to Rome," Track said. Second, Ratzinger fully acknowledged the authority of the Lutheran World Federation to reach agreement with the Vatican. Finally, Ratzinger agreed that while Christians are obliged to do good works, justification and final judgment remain God's gracious acts.

Anderson said that although Lutherans are grateful for Ratzinger's help, the two churches still have much ground to cover before reaching full communion. "Since the Reformation, we've had separate histories. The declaration of papal infallibility on the Catholic side, and the ordination of women on ours, are two obvious examples," Anderson said.

Other Ecumenical Statements

Two other statements by Ratzinger with ecumenical implications should be noted. On November 26, 1983, the Congregation for the Doctrine of the Faith reiterated its ban on Catholic membership in Masonic associations. Catholics who become Masons "are involved in serious sin and may not approach Holy Communion," the statement said. Local bishops and priests do not have the authority to waive this declaration. For the estimated six million Masons worldwide, for whom the organization's anti-Catholic polemics are a thing of the past, the statement could not help but seem insensitive.

Even more provocative was Ratzinger's June 9, 1997, accusation that the World Council of Churches (WCC) had supported Marxist revolutionaries in Latin America.[9] Based in Geneva, Switzerland, the WCC claims more than 330 member churches, including the world's mainline Protestant, Anglican, and Orthodox bodies. Ratzinger's comment came at a Rome news conference announcing the publication of a book by Nicola Bux, a priest from southern Italy. Bux alleged that the WCC had supported "certain campaigns promoting revolution in Latin America" during the 1980s but did nothing to help "Christians and the 'churches of silence' in Eastern Europe." Ratzinger agreed. "Many Latin American bishops and I have deplored the fact that the WCC has given strong support to subversive movements. Perhaps this support was given in good faith, but it was highly damaging to the life of the gospel." WCC officials denied that the organization's money had supported armed revolution. The WCC had funded liberation theologians and church-related human rights groups, many considered enemies of the state by the military dictatorships then in power. In South Africa, WCC money did support the humanitarian activities of the African National Congress, which was also engaged in armed resistance to apartheid, but WCC officials insisted that was an isolated case.

Asked about the World Council of Church's call for an "ecumenical council of the entire church of Jesus Christ, in the sense of the ancient, undivided church," Ratzinger said the concept of Christian unity would remain "a romantic, unrealistic dream" without the "Petrine principle."

Ratzinger and Religious Pluralism

No theologian has been censured by Ratzinger for deviations pertaining to ecumenical dialogue. When Catholic theologians treat non-Christian religions, however, Ratzinger's doctrinal reservations become far more profound, and he has not hesitated to deploy the full powers of his office.

Ratzinger has compared the theology of religious pluralism to liberation theology, and the comparison is apt. Both movements reflect what theologians have called the "irruption" of the Third World into Catholic consciousness. Liberation theology calls attention to poverty in the Third World; pluralism begins with the observation that outside Latin America, most of the Third World is non-Christian. Both movements reflect the postconciliar turn in Catholic theology toward the "joys and hopes, the griefs and anxieties" of the wider world. Liberation theology seeks signs of God's purpose in the struggle for social and political emancipation; pluralism seeks elements of truth and grace in other religions. Both assume a more positive appraisal of "the world" than had been the norm before Vatican II.

Ratzinger also believes that liberation theology and many versions of religious pluralism share a defective understanding of truth. For both, Ratzinger believes, truth is defined as whatever is useful for progress: orthopraxis rather than orthodoxy. Liberation theologians reshape or ignore doctrines not conducive to their social and political goals; pluralists recast doctrines that stand in the way of interreligious harmony. Ratzinger believes this relativism is a special danger when Christianity encounters Eastern religions. There is a tendency, he says, for Western philosophical relativism to blend with Eastern emphasis on the ineffability of God. Relativism is thereby "baptized."

Ratzinger's most succinct treatment of interreligious dialogue came in an address he gave in Paris, later published in *Communio* in 1997.[10] Ratzinger says the world's religions can be broadly divided into mystical and theistic types. The former, by which he presumably means the religions of Asia though he does not name them, regard positive statements about God as impossible, preferring to be silent before ineffability. The latter believe in a God that can be named and who acts in history. Ratzinger says that three options seem available for relations among religions: the mystic type could subsume the theistic, the theistic could subsume the mystic, or all religions could set aside their differences for the sake of practical efforts on behalf of peace and justice.

The last option amounts to "orthopraxis," and as we have seen with respect to liberation theology, Ratzinger believes it is to surrender the truth. How do we know the right thing to do without some criteria of truth to point it out to us? Removing thorny doctrinal problems, as the mystical path seemingly does, may appear to provide a better basis for environmental and social collaboration, but Ratzinger argues that it does precisely the opposite. If God is entirely in the realm of spirit, the material world has no transcendent value; if God is unconcerned with history, all that matters is the inner life of the individual. Social ethics becomes something we construct, not the result of a divine mandate. This leaves only the theistic option as a basis for interreligious cooperation, and Ratzinger says it cannot be exercised by abandoning doctrine or setting aside missionary efforts. Religions can learn from each other, and can even learn to be critical of themselves, but the aim of dialogue cannot be a "unity" in which doctrinal differences melt away.

He concludes: "Anyone who expects the dialogue between religions to result in their unification is bound for disappointment. This is hardly possible within our historical time, and perhaps it is not even desirable."

The War against Pluralist Theology: Theory

Ratzinger's key speeches on religious pluralism both came before bishops who head doctrinal comimssions, and both took place in the Third World.

These facts are significant: Ratzinger is signaling that this is a theological threat, it originates in the Third World, and it must be met by energetic episcopal oversight.

In March 1993, Ratzinger spoke to the presidents of the Asian bishops' conferences and the heads of the doctrinal committees in Hong Kong on "Christ, Faith and the Challenge of Cultures." He wanted to critically examine the claim that the only way to evangelize Asia is to adapt Christian teaching and practice so that conversion to Christianity is not experienced as desertion of one's culture. "My intention is to consider the right and capacity of Christian faith to communicate itself to other cultures, to assimilate them and to impart itself to them," he said.[11]

Ratzinger began with a definition of culture: "The historically developed common form of expression of the insights and values which characterize the life of a community." If a culture is to be healthy, Ratzinger argues, it must be "open"; that is, ready to be transformed. The agent of transformation is the truth, because at the deepest level every human being, and thus every human culture, is oriented toward the truth. In this sense, Ratzinger says, Christians refer to the "adventistic dynamic" of non-Christian cultures, in that they prepare people to recognize and respond to the truth Christianity reveals. "Man's real poverty is darkness to truth," Ratzinger says. "Each culture is finally the expectation of truth."

Ratzinger says that the oft-repeated buzzword of "inculturation" is actually a misnomer, because it implies that a religion shorn of culture (Christianity) meets a culture independent of faith (for instance, Asia). This is not how things work. Asian cultures have deep spiritual ideals, whereas Christianity itself is a culture with historically mediated forms of expression, values, and ideals. Ratzinger proposes instead "interculturality" to capture the actual process of "reciprocal refinement and combination" that should occur when Christianity meets another culture. To regard cultures as closed off from one another, so that one cultural form cannot speak to another, would be "Manichaean." The conviction that Christianity is itself a culture leads Ratzinger to be wary of demands to "adapt" it: "God bound himself to a history which is now also his and one which we cannot cast off," Ratzinger says. "We cannot repeat the event of the incarnation to suit ourselves in the sense of taking away Christ's flesh and offering him another."

Ratzinger calls cultural relativism "the gravest problem of our time," because it cuts cultures off from the truth. This is why today "praxis has replaced truth and thereby shifted the axis of religions. We do not know what is true, but we do know what we must do, namely, usher in a better society, the 'kingdom' as it is frequently said, taking a word from the Bible and applying it in a profane, utopian sense." Ratzinger says this emphasis on unity at the level of action rather than belief drains Christianity of its content. "Church-centeredness, Christ-centeredness, God-centeredness, all of these seem to give way to kingdom-centeredness, the centering of the kingdom as the common task of all religions, under which point of view and standard they are supposed to meet." In this connection, Ratzinger alludes to the work of Jesuit Jacques DuPuis in a footnote—the first sign of trouble for DuPuis, who five years later would find himself under investigation by Ratzinger's office.

Ratzinger also blames the "dogma of relativism" for undercutting missionary work in its traditional sense, that is, making converts. "Mission becomes the arrogant presumption of a culture which thinks itself superior to the others and so would deprive them of what is good and proper to them." For Ratzinger this desire to close off cultures is futile: "The convergence of mankind toward a single community with a common life and destiny is unstoppable because such an inclination is grounded in man's essence." Anyway, technology makes cultural withdrawal impossible. "You cannot enclose men and cultures in a kind of spiritual nature reserve," Ratzinger says.

Ratzinger warns against the fusion of Western philosophical relativism with Eastern spirituality, which eschews definitive statements about God's nature. This combination, Ratzinger says, lends a spiritual dignity to relativism, as if it were more "enlightened" to renounce objective truth. As an example from the Hindu side, Ratzinger points to the twentieth-century thinker Radhakrishnan; from the Catholic side, he mentions Father Raimon Panikkar. Of Panikkar's argument that christological formulas are not reversible—for example, that Jesus is Christ, but Christ is not only Jesus—Ratzinger says this must be rejected. One cannot argue that "Christ" is also found in Buddhism, Hinduism, and so on, because to do so is to posit a disincarnate Christ.

Ratzinger sees the situation today as comparable to the late fourth century, after Christianity had become the official religion of the empire but before paganism had ceased to be a living religious option. Having failed to crush Christianity by force, Ratzinger says the pagans such as Symmachus and Julian the Apostate attempted to eviscerate it through tolerance, by convincing Christians to see their creed as only one of many paths to God. "One cannot succeed to so great a mystery by only one road," Symmachus said in imploring the Senate to reinstate its statue of the goddess Victory. The church fathers rejected this option, Ratzinger says, because to do otherwise would be to reject the universal claims of Christ. "What remains after its abandonment would be select elements of biblical tradition, but not the faith of the Bible itself. . . . Without this fundamental decision, there is no Christianity." The Fathers showed the proper sense of inculturation when they took over temples and converted them to churches, or used pagan images as the basis for saints' iconography. "It was not a relativistic philosophy of religion which gave them continued existence; in fact, it was this that had made them ineffective in the first place."

Ratzinger's second major speech on religious pluralism came in 1996, in Mexico, before a group of doctrinal commission heads from the Latin American bishops' conferences. He repeats many themes from Hong Kong but sharpens the rhetoric and adds some new ideas.[12]

Ratzinger begins with an explicit parallel to liberation theology: "In the eighties, the theology of liberation in its radical forms seemed to be the most urgent challenge for the faith of the church." The fall of European Marxism "turned out to be a kind of twilight of the gods for that theology of redeeming political praxis," he says. In the wake of the collapse of the Marxist dream, disillusionment seemed to justify nihilism or a surrender on absolute answers. This despair about the absolute attacks religion, too. "Relativism has thus become the central problem for the faith at the present time, Ratzinger says. "It is presented as a position defined positively by the concepts of tolerance and knowledge through dialogue and freedom, concepts which would be limited if the existence of one valid truth for all were affirmed."

Ratzinger says the "so-called pluralist theology of religion has been developing progressively since the fifties" but "only now has it come to the center of the Christian conscience." It is, he says, the fight of the decade for the church: "In some ways this conquest occupies today—with regard to the force of its problematic aspect and its presence in the different areas of culture—the place occupied by the theology of liberation in the preceding decade."

Echoing his warning in Hong Kong, Ratzinger says relativism is especially dangerous when it connects with Eastern religious thinking. "On the one hand, relativism is a typical offshoot of the Western world and its forms of philosophical thought, while on the other it is connected with the philosophical and religious intuitions of Asia especially, and surprisingly, with those of the Indian subcontinent." Later in the speech, Ratzinger says that among pluralists "there is a strange closeness between Europe's post-metaphysical philosophy and Asia's negative theology. . . . They seem to mutually confirm one another in their metaphysical and religious relativism. The religious and pragmatic relativism of Europe and America can get a kind of religious consecration from India which seems to give its renunciation of dogma the dignity of a greater respect before the mystery of God and of man."

Ratzinger names two examples: English theologian John Hick and American Paul Knitter. Of Hick, Ratzinger says that in his thinking "concepts such as church, dogma and sacraments must lose their unconditional character. . . . The notion of dialogue becomes the quintessence of the relativist creed and the antithesis of conversion and mission. . . . The relativist dissolution of christology, and even more of ecclesiology, thus becomes a central commandment of religion." For those who think like Hick, Ratzinger says, anyone who resists this vision of dialogue is an enemy of democracy and a stumbling block to the encounter of cultures, "which is well known to be the imperative of the present moment." Those who want "to stay with the faith of the Bible and the church" are pushed into a kind of cultural exile.

Ratzinger sees Knitter as the primary exponent of the pluralist view that praxis is more important than dogma. Interreligious dialogue should focus on building the kingdom, not on points of doctrine. Thus for Knitter, according to Ratzinger, interreligious dialogue reduces to an ethical or political program. This, Ratzinger says, is a self-contradictory stance, because if one abandons objective truth, then who is to say any particular ethics or politics is correct? "The relativist theories all flow into a state of not being obligatory and thus become superfluous, or else they presume to have an absolute standard which is not found in the praxis, by elevating it to an absolutism that has really no place."

Ratzinger's argument here represents a challenge that any theologian seeking to affirm religious pluralism must take up. Yet this 1996 speech is also one of the few times that Ratzinger has been publicly caught out as a theologian. To begin with, Ratzinger called Hick "an American Presbyterian," though in fact he is English (he lives in Birmingham). More seriously, Ratzinger acknowledged that his assessment of both Hick and Knitter was based on a 1995 book by the German theologian K. H. Menke, a young professor of dogmatics at the University of Bonn. Menke's book has a reputation in German theological circles as tendentious and error-prone, down to small details such as citing the wrong page numbers in footnoted references to other works.

Hick published an article in 1997 responding to Ratzinger.[13] In it he pointed out that Ratzinger had incorrectly identified one of Hick's books, *Evil and the God of Love,* as being about religious pluralism, when in fact it is on a different topic altogether (theodicy). Moreover, Ratzinger incorrectly asserted that Hick is both a religious pluralist and a moral relativist, but in reality he accepts the former while rejecting the latter. Hick said that Ratzinger accused him of denying transcendence, which is not accurate. Hick sees the great religions as different ways of conceiving the "intimate reality we call God," but he certainly does not deny God's transcendence. Hick concludes that much of Ratzinger's analysis is "misleading and evidently not based on proper study of the texts." Ratzinger never responded, in keeping with his general policy; a French journalist once reported that Ratzinger told a friend after the Paris newspapers had been especially hard on a speech he gave, "I'm like the cellist Rostropovich—I never read the critics."

The War against Pluralist Theology: Practice

Given the vast amount of theological literature produced each year, Ratzinger's congregation cannot possibly evaluate the work of every theologian or even master every theological current within Catholicism. It must prioritize, deciding where the greatest threats lie. (For details of how information flows into and out of Ratzinger's office, see chapter 7, "The Congregation in Action.") His identification of the theology of religious pluralism as the number one enemy of the faith has led to truncated careers and a climate of apprehension among Catholic theologians.

Tissa Balasuriya

On January 2, 1997, Sri Lankan oblate Tissa Balasuriya was excommunicated under the terms of canon 1364, a church law that applies to apostates and heretics, for his views on original sin, Mary, and the role of Christ in salvation. Balasuriya, who was 72 at the time, was a fairly obscure theologian in predominantly Buddhist Sri Lanka, where Christians make up only eight percent of the total population. The Sri Lankan bishops had been investigating him since 1994. The excommunication was triggered by Balasuriya's refusal to sign a profession of faith given to him by the doctrinal congregation, which included the prohibition on women's ordination. Balasuriya, who believes that the Blessed Virgin was the first female priest, instead proposed signing a profession of faith issued by Paul VI, but with a caveat that he agreed with the tenets "in the context of theological development and church practice since Vatican II and the freedom and responsibility of Christians and theological searchers under canon law." That was unacceptable to Ratzinger, and excommunication followed.

Around the world the dominant reaction was that the action seemed disproportionate. Balasuriya's book, *Mary and Human Liberation,* had been printed by his own small theological center and had sold only a few hundred copies before the Vatican action. Afterward it sold thousands, and Balasuriya became a cause célèbre. Many felt Ratzinger had erred by giving Balasuriya a platform he would never have achieved on his own, but Ratzinger clearly felt something deep was at stake.

The core issue, from Ratzinger's point of view, was Balasuriya's insistence that Asian religions are valid and true in their own right. The 1,800-word notice of excommunication signed by Ratzinger accused Balasuriya three times of "relativizing" or "relativism" in relation to the faith. Specifically, Ratzinger wrote that Balasuriya "does not recognize the supernatural, unique, and irrepeatable character of the revelation of Jesus Christ, by placing its presuppositions on the same level as those of other religions. In particular, he maintains that certain 'presuppositions' connected to myths were uncritically assumed to be revealed historical facts and, interpreted ideologically by clerical 'power holders' in the church, eventually became the teaching of the magisterium."

Balasuriya took the pronouncement largely in stride. "I am much more in the community of disciples of Jesus than ever before," he said. "There is also a mystical, spiritual communion. Maybe legally I am cut off but spiritually I am more in communion than ever before. The doctrinal congregation has put me in communion with people all over the world. This is a beautiful experience in life, so I think there is something providential in this."

In the end, his optimism proved justified. On January 15, 1998, his excommunication was lifted. Balasuriya said the outcome was the result of a "decent and honorable" agreement. Ratzinger rescinded his previous demand that Balasuriya sign a customized profession of faith. Instead, at a "reconciliation ceremony" he read a profession of faith composed by Pope Paul VI, minus the caveat that Ratzinger found objectionable. Balasuriya acknowledged "perceptions of error" and agreed to submit all future writings to his bishops for imprimatur. In a statement signed by him and published in the national Catholic newspaper of Sri Lanka on January 22, he said that "serious ambiguities and doctrinal errors were perceived" in his writings. He said he regretted "the harm" such perceptions had caused.

Church historians will debate who won this exchange, but the message from Rome was clear: Any Catholic theologian who goes too far toward embracing the independent validity of other religions, who seeks to "adapt" Catholic dogma for intercultural dialogue, faces draconian consequences. Few theologians are likely to look at the Balasuriya case, even with its apparent happy ending, as an incentive to pursue religious pluralism.

Perry Schmidt-Leukel

One of the points often made in Ratzinger's defense is that the actual number of theologians disciplined by the doctrinal congregation on his watch is fairly small. No one knows the true number because most of the cases remain secret, but the total of high-profile figures publicly censured is perhaps a dozen. Yet the impact of a Vatican censure transcends its immediate object. When Ratzinger denounces a theologian, he also implicitly rejects his or her theology, and thus anyone sympathetic to that person's views is put on notice. So too are church authorities at lower levels, and often disciplinary proceedings with no ostensible connection to Ratzinger are initiated because of the doctrinal priorities he has set out. The total number of theologians capsized in Ratzinger's wake thus far exceeds those few publicly swamped by him.

A case in point is German theologian Perry Schmidt-Leukel, a specialist in interreligious dialogue whose 1997 monograph *Theologie der Religionen: Probleme, Optionen, Argumente* (Theology of religions: Problems, options, arguments) is considered to be among the definitive works on the subject. Ratzinger's first footnote in his 1996 speech in Mexico attacking the theology of religious pluralism mentioned a literature review by Schmidt-Leukel; it suggests, among other things, that when Catholic theologians see their name in Ratzinger's footnotes, they might want to consult a good canon lawyer.

A married lay theologian with two adopted children, Schmidt-Leukel did his graduate work at the University of Munich, earning his doctorate on the Christian understanding of Buddhist concepts of salvation. In 1996, while working as an adjunct professor at Munich, he completed his *Habilitationschrift*. Schmidt-Leukel has described three general Christian approaches to religious pluralism: exclusivism (salvation is through Christ alone and non-Christians are excluded from it); inclusivism (salvation is through Christ but non-Christians may be included in it); and pluralism (salvation can occur through a variety of religious traditions). He leans toward the pluralist position, claiming that pluralism in this sense should at least be kept open as a legitimate hypothesis within Catholic theology.

After completing his *Habilitation,* Schmidt-Leukel applied for a full professor's position at the University of Munich. Under the terms of the Bavarian concordat with the Holy See, a candidate for a theology professor's job at a state university must be certified by the Bavarian minister of culture, who in turn must receive a *nihil obstat* from the archbishop of Munich certifying that the candidate is acceptable. Schmidt-Leukel was advised that Cardinal Friedrich Wetter had concerns about his writings and was invited in December 1996 for what was billed as an informal chat. In fact, he said, it was an inquisitorial procedure with witnesses. Wetter accused Schmidt-Leukel of treating Christianity as no more than a hypothesis, a position Schmidt-Leukel denied holding. He said later that it was obvious neither Wetter nor his advisors had actually read his work. He was called back for a second meeting three months later and had the impression that Wetter was coming around. "I thought that I succeeded in explaining some basic issues. He seemed to develop some kind of understanding for the problems," Schmidt-Leukel said. The meeting ended with the promise of a third session.

The third meeting never occurred. In March 1998, Schmidt-Leukel was notified that Wetter was denying him the *nihil obstat* and hence he was barred from the professor's chair. A letter from the Bavarian minister of culture, dated March 4, 1998, was blunt: "The Archbishop of Munich and Freising has in his letter of February 12, 1998, in view of article 3 paragraph 2 of the Bavarian Concordat raised an objection to granting the requested powers of instruction to Dr. Perry Schmidt-Leukel, on the basis that Dr. Schmidt-Leukel represents the pluralistic theology of religion which stands in contradiction to the central truth of the faith about redemption through Jesus Christ and to the understanding of Christian revelation. The state minister therefore lacks . . . the legal grounds to grant the requested power of instruction."[14]

In theory, Wetter's act barred Schmidt-Leukel only from a theology professorship in Munich. Its actual reach, however, was far greater. Church authorities pressured the University of Munich to get rid of Schmidt-Leukel as an adjunct professor, even though this position did not require a *nihil obstat*. Schmidt-Leukel found himself persona non grata in German-speaking Catholic theology departments everywhere, because no bishop wished to appear to contradict Wetter's decision. The next semester, Schmidt-Leukel was invited by the University of Salzburg in Austria to accept an interim lecturer's position while the university searched for a full-time faculty member. Archbishop Georg Eder of Salzburg forced the university to withdraw the invitation, then approved it on the condition that the university hold events where Schmidt-Leukel's position would be criticized. Eder withdrew even this permission twenty-four hours later when he found out Schmidt-Leukel had applied for the full-time position at Salzburg. Only when Schmidt-Leukel agreed to withdraw from this search did Eder allow his series of lectures to proceed.

Schmidt-Leukel and his family have since moved to Glasgow, Scotland, where he has accepted a professor's chair at the nondenominational University of Glasgow. "It came as a kind of salvation to me," Schmidt-Leukel said. "Otherwise I was looking at being forty-five, with two small adopted children and twenty years of education, out of work." Schmidt-Leukel said he considers it "likely" that Wetter consulted Ratzinger prior to denying him the *nihil obstat*, but he has no proof. The result of such censures, he said, is that "young students don't dare to say or write what they really think, especially the postgraduate students. They have too much to fear." Yet Schmidt-Leukel remains optimistic that Roman Catholicism will eventually embrace the pluralist ideal. "The church is not such a monolithic block as the people in Rome sometimes want it to be," he said.

Anthony de Mello

"Nobody can be said to have attained the pinnacle of Truth," Indian Jesuit Anthony de Mello once wrote, "until a thousand sincere people have denounced him for blasphemy." By that standard, August 23, 1998, brought de Mello a bit closer to the peak, as the Congregation for the Doctrine of the Faith condemned de Mello, known for his best-selling books that bridge Eastern and Western spirituality, for "relativizing" the faith and promoting "religious indifferentism." The doctrinal congregation accused de Mello, who died of a heart condition in 1987, of teaching that "to think the God of one's own religion is the only one is simply fanaticism."

In a July 23, 1998, letter, Ratzinger alerted the presidents of the world's bishops' conferences to the impending declaration. He asked the bishops to try to withdraw de Mello's books from circulation, or to ensure that they are printed with this notice:

> His works, which almost always take the form of brief stories, contain some valid elements of Oriental wisdom. These can be helpful in achieving self-mastery, in breaking the bonds and feelings that keep us from being free, and in approaching with serenity the various vicissitudes of life. . . . But already in certain passages in these early works and to a greater degree in his later publications, one notices a progressive distancing from the essential contents of the Christian faith. In place of the revelation which has come in the person of Jesus Christ, he substitutes an intuition of God without form or image, to the point of speaking of God as a pure void.

The congregation's notice goes on to warn that de Mello's thinking "leads even to a denial that the Bible contains valid statements about God." He believes Jesus is not the son of God, but one master alongside others; the question of life after death is irrelevant; there are no objective rules of morality; and the church is an impediment in the search for truth. Thus "this congregation declares that the above-mentioned positions are incompatible with the Catholic faith and can cause grave harm."[15]

Colleagues who knew de Mello largely rejected the claim that he undercut church teaching. "It's extremely hard for me to believe that anyone would find anything de Mello says to be anything other than orthodox," said Jesuit Francis Stroud. "He was a very devout churchman." Stroud, who collaborated with de Mello, now runs a "De Mello Spirituality Center" at Fordham University in New York. "De Mello did emphasize that God is a mystery," Stroud said. "But he would quote Thomas Aquinas saying the very same thing. . . . He never denied anything like a personal concept of God. When anybody would joke with him, say he was going to get into trouble, he would respond, 'Not this wily Jesuit.' Somebody's feeding him [Ratzinger] this stuff, stringing him along," Stroud said. "It's hard for me to believe that he would be taken in by that."

The Vatican action had been rumored for some time in India. In 1996, the then-Jesuit provincial for South Asia, Father Varkey Perekkatt, told the

UCA News service that he had requested assistance from colleagues around the world to defend de Mello against attacks by "Western right-wing Catholic papers." Perekkatt said much of the criticism focused on works published after de Mello's death. Perekkatt also said that tapes of de Mello's lectures and retreats were being published contrary to the late Jesuit's explicit instructions. That concern was echoed August 25, 1998, by the current South Asia Jesuit provincial, Father Lisbert D'Souza, who said some of these posthumously published works led to de Mello being "grossly misunderstood." The Indian Jesuits, he said, regard only nine books as authentic.

The timing of the declaration, coming more than ten years after de Mello's death, confused many. "It seems rather strange to condemn someone who has no right of reply," said Eric Major, director of the religious books program at Doubleday, which, through its Image imprint, is the largest publisher of de Mello's works in the United States. "Why do it now?" Doubleday has eight de Mello titles in print, with sales running into "the millions" collectively, according to Major. He said that withdrawing the works "can hardly be asked of a secular publishing house." Doubleday "would like to hear the objections, title by title," but Major said the company would "reserve the right as publisher, having published his work for twenty years without a hint of complaint, to continue to serve the Catholic church in its widest spheres." The edict did have at least one effect. In a Catholic bookshop in London, a notice posted above de Mello's works read: "Be informed that the Vatican has declared that Father Anthony de Mello's books are doctrinally inaccurate. You may read them at your own risk."

The Jesuit provincials of Asia came to de Mello's defense. "Anthony de Mello pioneered the integration of Asian and Christian spirituality and methods of prayer," they said. "He has helped thousands of people in South Asia and across the world in gaining freedom and in deepening their life of prayer, of which we have abundant testimonies and our own personal experiences." The provincials called for a "legitimate pluralism in theology within the unity of faith" and for "subsidiarity in decisionmaking in a church that is also a communion of local churches."

"There is a lack of appreciation of difference and of proper procedures, when decisions are taken unilaterally without a dialogue with the Asian churches," they said. "We are afraid that such interventions are eventually detrimental to the life of the church, to the cause of the Gospel and to the task of interpreting the Word to those who do not belong to the Western cultural tradition."

Jacques DuPuis

In November 1998, Belgian Jesuit Jacques DuPuis confirmed media rumors that he was taking a leave of absence from the Pontifical Gregorian University so he could respond to a doctrinal probe into his book *Toward a Christian Theology of Religious Pluralism* (Orbis, 1997). In the book, DuPuis—who spent thirty-six years teaching theology in India before going to Rome, where he taught and served as an advisor to the Pontifical Council for Interreligious Dialogue—tried to harmonize an affirmative view of non-Christian religions with traditional church teaching. He based his argument on a close reading of all the relevant magisterial documents on the subject. He took what most scholars in the area saw as a moderate position, ending up with a version of "inclusivism": the belief that salvation is offered in the most complete way through Jesus (his redemption is "constitutive" of humanity's salvation) but allows room for other saving acts in other traditions.

DuPuis draws on the Gospel of John to argue that because the Logos is eternal it existed prior to the incarnation in Jesus and was active in other cultures. It is a point made explicit in the Book of Hebrews, which says, "in times past God spoke in fragmentary and varied ways to our fathers; in this, the final ages, he has spoken to us through his son." By the same logic, the Logos can still be active in other religions, inspiring the saving insights each achieves, while Jesus remains the unique "sacrament" of God. DuPuis draws on God's covenants with Adam and Noah, which preceded the call of Abraham, and hence represent covenants with all humanity. If the church believes the covenant with Abraham is still in force, why not these other two? DuPuis argues that Christian missionary efforts should have broader aims than just making converts. Their goal should be building up the kingdom of God, what he described as a "regnocentric" view.

DuPuis's "regnocentric" approach has been influential; it was at the heart of the position the Federation of Asian Bishops took in their 1987 *Theses on interreligious dialogue*. The bishops said, "The focus of the church's mission of evangelization is building up the kingdom of God and building up the church to be at the service of the kingdom. The kingdom is, therefore, wider than the church."

DuPuis's book drew generally positive reviews. Among other honors, it received the second-place award in the category of books on theology from the U.S. Catholic Press Association; judges cited its "clarity and respect." The hardcover edition carried a blurb from Bishop Michael L. Fitzgerald, secretary of the Pontifical Council for Interreligious Dialogue. "A masterful presentation of the history of Christian attitudes towards other religions," Fitzgerald wrote. "Dupuis has provided a general theology of religions at the same time sure and stimulating." (The blurb was dropped from the subsequent paperback edition.) Lawrence S. Cunningham, former chair of the theology department at the University of Notre Dame, echoed the sentiment, writing in *Commonweal* in June 1998 that Dupuis's book "should become a standard study on this most pressing question in theology." Even the *Thomist,* a theological journal edited by Dominican Augustine Di Noia, the U.S. bishops' chief theologian, gave Dupuis's book cautious praise. A review said the book was "a major achievement" that "will be an essential point of reference on the topic for a long time to come."

The seventy-four-year-old Dupuis spoke to me from Rome in November 1998 about the interrogative survey from the doctrinal congregation. "The contents of the survey are strictly reserved," I quoted him as saying in the *National Catholic Reporter.* "I cannot enter into the details without making the case worse. I cannot discuss the matter even with my colleagues or my students. The only thing I am able to acknowledge publicly is the simple fact of my being questioned." Dupuis said the accompanying letter from the doctrinal congregation instructed him, while the investigation is pending, "not to spread the ideas for which I am being questioned in my teaching, writing, or public lectures."

Gregorian University issued a statement saying that Dupuis would be relieved of his teaching responsibilities for the next three months. Jesuit General Hans-Peter Kolvenbach, also vice chancellor of the Gregorian, said the action was intended to free Dupuis so he could prepare his response. Dupuis said the decision should not be understood as a "suspension," and that it was made with his consent. "It is the only thing to do," he said. "How can you teach if you can't say what you think?"

Some sources believed Ratzinger had been influenced by personal considerations. In the late 1980s, DuPuis served as one of the chief drafters of a document called *Dialogue and proclamation,* originally slated for release by the Pontifical Council for Interreligious Dialogue. Ratzinger, however, felt the early drafts of the document were too weak on missionary efforts, and instructed the Congregation for the Evangelization of Peoples to collaborate in revising the text. The result was a tug-of-war between the two congregations, with every positive statement about dialogue offered by the former balanced with a battle cry for new conversions by the latter. As frustration levels increased, DuPuis resigned. In later analyses of the document, DuPuis referred to the internal tensions of *Dialogue and proclamation* and suggested that it muddles the position of the magisterium. "I think this might be one of the reasons they came down on him," said a Catholic theologian familiar with both DuPuis and the doctrinal congregation. "He revealed how incoherent that document was."

The DuPuis case led to the highly unusual spectacle of two cardinals jousting in public when retired cardinal Franz König of Vienna, Austria, came to DuPuis's defense in an article in the London-based Catholic journal the *Tablet.* König called on Ratzinger's office to be less defensive when examining new thinking on interreligious issues. König warned the doctrinal agency that the Western background of its analysts makes understanding Eastern theological currents especially difficult. König, now ninety-three, served as the primate of the Austrian church during most of the cold war era and has long taken an interest in interreligious dialogue. König said: "I cannot keep silent, for my heart bleeds when I see such obvious harm being done to the common good of God's church." He suggested that the doctrinal congregation should be able to "find better ways of doing its job to serve the church effectively." König said that most of the doctrinal congregation members are "very much afraid that interreligious dialogue will reduce all religions to equal rank. . . . But that is the wrong approach for dialogue with the Eastern religions. It is reminiscent of colonialism and smacks of arrogance." König said that with Vatican II and the *Redemptoris missio,* the church revised its "apologetic and defensive attitude" toward non-Christian religions.[16]

Ratzinger fired off a response to the *Tablet,* arguing that his agency is only doing its job when it protects the faith and the faithful from concepts that would place all religions on the same level. Ratzinger expressed "astonishment" at König's criticisms. He said the request for clarification from Dupuis was an "attempt at dialogue" undertaken with discretion. "Is dialogue with authors to be forbidden to us? Is the attempt to reach confidential clarification on difficult questions something evil?" Ratzinger wrote. The congregation did not make the case public, he said. Whoever did may have wanted to "mobilize public opinion against our dicastery." Ratzinger said two crucial questions must be faced: "Can a Christian engaged in dialogue relinquish his faith conviction that Christ is the true son of God and that there is something unique in Christianity?" and "Is he being honest with himself and with others if he sets this conviction aside?" Ratzinger noted parenthetically that he did not think Dupuis had done this. Ratzinger said he was upset König had cited papal and Vatican II teaching against the congregation. "I cannot imagine that you seriously believe that the congregation's thinking is in contradiction with the Second Vatican Council and with the pope's fundamental encyclical letter on missionary activity," he said. If that were so, then the pope would not have personally approved the congregation's dialogue with Dupuis, "as in fact he did." Ratzinger asked König to reread the pope's encyclical.

König was not DuPuis's only defender. Archbishop Henry D'Souza of Calcutta, president of the Catholic Conference of Bishops of India, wrote DuPuis—who had served as a theological advisor for the Federation of Asian bishops' conferences—a letter of support. "I do not think you will have much difficulty in explaining your position," wrote D'Souza. "However, I am worried over the fallout. No theologian will be wanting to write his thoughts, if this is the approach." The archbishop said that Dupuis has been known for his "orthodoxy and steady pursuit of theological reflection in conformity with the church's teaching."

Balasuriya, who goes considerably farther than DuPuis on many questions, also rallied to his side. "He was with us for a long time, having spent twenty to thirty years in Asia, and he has learned something from here," Balasuriya said in an August 1999 interview. "Having learned from India, he wants to relate it in Rome. We have to defend our missionaries to the West. We appreciate him and believe that he has become a return missionary."

In late 1999 DuPuis learned that the lengthy clarification he submitted to the congregation was unsatisfactory. As of this writing, the outcome of his case is still uncertain.

Ratzinger and the Religions

Given the premise that Christianity alone offers the full truth about human existence, it follows that other religious traditions fall short of that truth. Thus it is unsurprising that Ratzinger has had some critical things to say about other religions. In most cases it is not a matter of Ratzinger being deliberately offensive; rather the question is whether his theological stance is inevitably divisive, and if so, what that means in the quest for peace among the religions.

Judaism

Ratzinger, echoing both *Nostra aetate* and John Paul II's outreach to Judaism, has rejected the Christian stereotype of Jews as the villains in the death of Jesus. In a 1994 address in Jerusalem, he quoted the new *Catechism of the Catholic Church:* "All sinners were the authors of Christ's passion." In that Jerusalem address, delivered at a first-ever International Jewish-Christian Conference on Modern Social and Scientific Challenges, Ratzinger urged understanding between Jews and Christians: "After Auschwitz, the mission of reconciliation and acceptance permits no deferral." He closed with a childhood insight. "I could not understand how some people wanted to derive a condemnation of Jews from the death of Jesus because the following thought had penetrated my soul as something profoundly consoling: Jesus' blood raises no calls for retaliation but calls all to reconciliation." Because Ratzinger's childhood unfolded in Nazi Germany, it was a dramatic remark.

Ratzinger stressed the close theological bond between the two faiths, picking up on St. Luke's account of the magi as a parable of how Jesus will lead all the nations into the people of God formed first with Abraham. Yet Ratzinger did not back away from the claim that Christianity "fulfills" Judaism. He quoted Augustine: "The New Testament lies hidden in the Old;

the Old is made explicit in the New." Ratzinger also said nothing about one of the most contested issues in Jewish-Christian relations: whether or not Christians should aim to convert Jews.

Ratzinger had suggested in a 1987 interview with the Italian newspaper *Il Sabato* that Jews could be fully true to their heritage only by becoming Christian. "The pope has offered respect, but also a theological line. This always implies our union with the faith of Abraham, but also the reality of Jesus Christ, in which the faith of Abraham finds its fulfillment," he said. Ratzinger referred to Edith Stein, a Jew who converted to Catholicism, became a Carmelite nun, and was murdered by the Nazis. "Finding faith in Christ, she entered into the full inheritance of Abraham," Ratzinger said, according to an Associated Press report on the Italian article. "She turned in her Jewish heritage to have a new and diverse heritage. But in entering into unity with Christ, she entered into the very heart of Judaism."

Many Jewish leaders were angered by the comments. A summit between Jewish and Catholic officials set for December 14–16, 1987, in Washington, D.C., was cancelled in protest. Ratzinger said his words had been taken out of context and mistranslated. The Vatican released a statement summarizing "the intention of Cardinal Ratzinger," along with the transcript of the interview in German. Some Jewish leaders remained unsatisfied. "German is my native language," said Rabbi Wolfe Kelman of New York, executive vice president of the Rabbinical Assembly of Conservative Judaism. In his view, the German text "does not modify [Ratzinger's] position; if anything it deepens it. . . . What Ratzinger is saying is that the ideal for Jews is to become Christian."

At a press conference in New York shortly after the article appeared, Ratzinger was asked whether Catholics can enter into dialogue believing that the Old Testament has its own integrity or if they have to say the Old Testament is incomplete without the New Testament. His answer was two-fold: "I think that good Christian theology must study profoundly the Old Testament and must also hear the Jewish interpretation, because they are the owners of the Old Testament. . . . New Testament is also Scripture in the sense that it gives Christians the key to the Old Testament, and without the Old Testament the New Testament could have nothing to give us."

Secondly, he said, the special point of the dialogue must be that Christians regard the New Testament as a "partial" fulfillment of the Old Testament, yet not the complete fulfillment because the Christian Scriptures speak of the kingdom of God still to come. "Jews would say this is not the case, and we must respect their position." Ratzinger added that he was sure that Jews also respect the Catholic position, "so about this point I think they can have a good dialogue." Told of Ratzinger's statement, Rabbi Henry

D. Michelman, executive director of the Synagogue Council of America, which represents the three major branches of Judaism, said, "I don't see any clarification. I don't see any particular step forward."

There is little question about Ratzinger's personal respect for Jews or opposition to anti-Semitism. He recalled seeing a slogan painted on Cardinal Faulhaber's residence in Munich in November 1938: "After the Jew, the Jew-lover." Faulhaber had resisted the efforts of Alfred Rosenberg and others to purge Christianity of its Jewish elements. For Ratzinger, that phrase on the cardinal's wall summed up where the church stood. In another context, Ratzinger was once asked by a Jewish leader if the existence of the state of Israel had any theological significance for Catholics as it does for Jews. His response: "If it has significance for you, it must have significance for us." Yet the theological position Ratzinger holds on Judaism—that for Christians, Jewish history and Scripture reach fulfillment only in Christ—is deeply offensive to some Jews, and has been branded a form of "theological anti-Semitism" by some scholars.

Islam

As the third great Western monotheistic religion, Islam too claims a special place in Christian thinking about religious pluralism. John Paul II has done more than most of his predecessors to reach out to Muslims. On August 19, 1985, he became the first pope to visit an Islamic nation when he spoke to 80,000 young people in Casabalanca, Morocco, at the invitation of King Hassan II. The pope said, "Your God and ours is the same, and we are brothers and sisters in the faith of Abraham." DuPuis argued that the pope's statement was "an implicit admission that Muslims are saved in their own way as heirs of the faith of Abraham."

Ratzinger has not offered any similarly dramatic gestures to Muslims. He did, however, in 1997 express regret over the Inquisition, which targeted both Jews and Muslims, especially in Spain (the Spanish Inquisition was distinct from the Holy Inquisition in Rome and has no direct ties to Ratzinger's office). "I don't know if I'm the right person to ask forgiveness, but I am convinced that we always need to be aware of the temptation for the church, as an institution, to transform itself into a state that persecutes its enemies," Ratzinger said in an interview in Bologna, Italy. At a personal level, Ratzinger has also had fruitful contacts with representatives of Islam. When the Iranian ayatollah Kashani, a member of the powerful Council of Guardians in Tehran, decided to write a book comparing Islamic and Christian eschatological themes, Ratzinger met with him in the Vatican and swapped views.

Yet as Islam has become the fastest-growing religion in Europe, especially in Germany (at three million, Muslims are now five percent of the total German population), Ratzinger has also expressed worries about its impact. Ratzinger has warned that Muslims see Western Christianity as bankrupt and weak. That should worry Westerners, Ratzinger said, because Islam is at its core nondemocratic. "One has to have a clear understanding that it is not simply a denomination that can be included in the free realm of a pluralistic society," he said. Islam also does not tolerate cultural differences. "Nor must we forget that Islam was at the head of the slave traffic and by no means displayed any great regard for the blacks. And above all Islam doesn't make any sort of concession to inculturation." Ratzinger accuses Islam of fomenting a kind of liberation theology vis-à-vis Israel, that liberation from Israel will be accomplished through divinely approved armed resistance.

Given these premises, it is unsurprising that Ratzinger has devoted little attention to dialogue with Islam. He appears to see a long struggle ahead.

Buddhism and Hinduism

In a 1997 interview, Ratzinger warned against the allure of Buddhism. "If Buddhism is attractive, it's only because it suggests that by belonging to it you can touch the infinite, and you can have joy without concrete religious obligations," Ratzinger said. "It's an auto-erotic spirituality. . . . In the 1950s someone said that the undoing of the Catholic church in the twentieth century wouldn't come from Marxism but from Buddhism," Ratzinger said. "They were right." Ratzinger warned against the "seductions" of the Eastern faith.[17]

The statement was widely seen as offensive. Mariangela Fala, head of Italy's small Buddhist community, noted that the religion "was founded on tolerance and mutual respect toward others, something that does not seem evident in Ratzinger's remarks." She called Ratzinger's comments "uninformed and provincial" and said that it cast a pall over Catholic-Buddhist dialogue. In the United States, a bishop took the rare step of actually apologizing for Ratzinger. Bishop Alexander J. Brunett of Helena, Montana, chairman of the U.S. bishops' Committee on Ecumenical and Interreligious Affairs, issued the apology in a statement of greeting in advance of the Buddhist holiday of Vesakh, celebrating the life of Gautama Buddha.

In other contexts, Ratzinger has written appreciatively of Buddhism. In his 1977 work on eschatology, for example, he explained the delay between individual death and universal judgment by arguing that individuals cannot be fully happy until everyone's fate is resolved. "And here we can point once again to Buddhism, with its idea of the Bodhisattva, who refuses to enter Nirvana so long as one human being remains in hell," he wrote. Yet he reminds the reader that only Christianity satisfies the longing expressed here: "Behind this impressive notion of Asian religiosity, the Christian sees the true Bodhisattva, Christ, in whom Asia's dream became true."

Ratzinger has called the doctrine of reincarnation "morally cruel" and a "coarsened" version of the Christian insight that an individual cannot be fulfilled as long as others suffer on his account. As stated above, he worries that Hindu "negative theology" lends support to relativism. In his 1991 book *The Nature and Mission of Theology*, Ratzinger approvingly quotes theologian Albert Görres about the "Hinduization" of Catholicism, in which doctrinal propositions no longer matter because the important thing is contact with a spiritual atmosphere that leads beyond everything that can be said.

Ratzinger seems to take for granted his reading of Hinduism as a relativist tradition. Yet as Jesuit scholar and expert on Hinduism Francis Clooney has pointed out, this is not a safe assumption:

> This traditional characterization—"traditional" because for centuries Europeans have had the habit of finding in India whatever they happen to be seeking—portrays Indians and Hindus as denying the reality of the world and being ambiguous about religious truth and tolerant of all religious viewpoints. Contrary to the cardinal's characterization, a century of Indological scholarship shows that the Hindu traditions are often exceedingly precise and developed in their doctrines and truth claims, and that, for the most part, they are quite willing to speak positively about the world, our responsibilities, and divine involvement in human affairs. . . . India is not a natural or obvious ally of relativism. Indeed, until they are studied closely and carefully, the Hindu traditions are best presumed to be nonaligned in Christian theological debates.[18]

Ratzinger's concern with Eastern contamination of Christianity was expressed in a December 14, 1989, document of the doctrinal congregation on *Some aspects of Christian meditation.* Its purpose was to establish guidelines for the use of prayer and meditation methods "inspired by Hinduism and Buddhism, such as Zen, transcendental meditation, or yoga." It says that authentic Christian prayer "flees from impersonal techniques or from concentrating on oneself, which can create a kind of rut, imprisoning the person praying in a spiritual privatism which is incapable of a free openness to the transcendental God." When a Christian prays, it is always in light of the "definitive self-revelation of God"; "there exists a strict relationship between revelation and prayer."

Even in private prayer, the Christian prays "within the authentic spirit of the church" and hence is connected to the communion of saints. Prayer is an exercise in *sentire cum ecclesia*, thinking with the church. In a vintage

Ratzinger touch, the document offers two examples of misguided notions of prayer from the ancient church: pseudognosticism, which held that the human person can achieve private illumination and pass beyond dogma; and Messalianism, which identified spiritual accomplishment with sensory experience. The document sees both tendencies in the New Age and charismatic movements, respectively.

> Some Christians do not hesitate to place that absolute without image or concepts, which is proper to Buddhist theory, on the same level as the majesty of God revealed in Christ, which towers above finite reality. To this end, they make use of a "negative theology" which transcends every affirmation seeking to express what God is and denies that the things of this world can offer traces of the infinity of God. They propose abandoning not only meditation on the salvific works accomplished in history by the God of the old and new covenant, but also the very idea of the one and triune God, who is love, in favor of an immersion "in the indeterminate abyss of the divinity."

The document says such methods must be "subjected to a thoroughgoing examination so as to avoid the danger of falling into syncretism."

"All the aspirations which the prayer of other religions expresses are fulfilled in the reality of Christianity beyond all measure," the document claimed. A Christian never *needs* to turn to other traditions, though it is acceptable "so long as the Christian conception of prayer, its logic and requirements are never obscured." It is important to avoid the "exaggerations and partiality" of Eastern spiritual traditions, which are too often recommended to people "who are not sufficiently prepared." The use of bodily postures (presumably a reference above all to yoga) is also dangerous: "It can degenerate into a cult of the body and can lead surreptitiously to considering all bodily sensations as spiritual experiences." Feelings of quiet and relaxation are desirable, but they must not be confused with the consolations of the Holy Spirit, especially if the moral life is out of alignment with the spiritual experience. "Giving [feelings] a symbolic significance typical of the mystical experience, when the moral condition of the person concerned does not correspond to such an experience, would represent a kind of mental schizophrenia which could also lead to psychic disturbance and, at times, to moral deviations."[19]

What Is at Stake

In the post-cold war world, religion is part of the volatile social cocktail that creates violence. Mixed with language, ethnicity, culture, and geography, religious differences are frequently lethal. In the Sudan, for example, where a long-running civil war pits Muslims in the north against Christians in the south, almost two million people have died since 1983, and another four million have been displaced. In Kashmir, a disputed province on the border between India and Pakistan, violence flares between Hindus and Muslims. In the 1990s, 24,000 people died by the Indian government's official count; others say 40,000, still others, 70,000. In Northern Ireland, violence between Catholic and Protestants over several decades has resulted in thousands of deaths. Around 500 regular British soldiers have been killed, most of them victims of the IRA. In the same period, British and provincial troops have killed about 300 people, some of whom were IRA members. By August 14, 1990, on the twenty-first anniversary of troop deployment in the province, 2,810 civilian lives had also been claimed. In the Balkans, where Orthodox Serbs battled the Western Christian nations of NATO as well as Muslim Kosovar Albanians, the Serbs took 5,000 military casualties and 2,000 civilian deaths. The Kosovars lost an estimed 10,000 lives, and more than 800,000 people at one time or another found themselves refugees. NATO estimates that mass murders took place in at least sixty-five villages.

A phrase from Hans Küng captures the sense of urgency many people feel about addressing these conflicts: "No peace in the world without peace among the religions." Like Ratzinger's crusades against liberation theology, feminism, and gay rights, the pall he has cast over ecumenism and interreligious dialogue has had consequences beyond the borders of academic theology. It has contributed to making the world a more fractured, and therefore a more dangerous, place. Perhaps it cannot be otherwise if institutional Catholicism is to endure. Many Catholics cannot help feeling, however, that exacerbating division is a curious way to keep faith with the Prince of Peace.

7

The Enforcer

*F*ather Charles Curran, the American moral theologian who became famous for his dissent from *Humanae vitae,* Paul VI's 1968 encyclical reiterating the ban on birth control, says he remembers how he first got wind that the Congregation for the Doctrine of the Faith was gunning for him. During the late 1970s, when he was teaching at the Catholic University of America, Curran got a cryptic letter from his colleague and mentor, the legendary Jesuit moral theologian Joseph Fuchs. He had written: "On the basis of certain facts, I have the impression that someone here might be interested in you." Curran eventually learned what those "certain facts" were. Fuchs had received a phone call from the librarian at Rome's Gregorian University, who asked him to return some books by Curran he had checked out. The Holy Office, the librarian said, was looking for them. By the way, the librarian asked, did Fuchs have anything else by Curran? The Holy Office would probably want those, too.

It was not a good sign.

Curran had been fired from Catholic University in 1967 for questioning the church's absolute condemnation of practices such as birth control and masturbation, only to be reinstated after a wildcat student strike. Not long after receiving the veiled warning from Fuchs, Curran noticed that his work was appearing in the footnotes of articles written by a well-known consultor for the doctrinal congregation. What would become one of the highest profile cases of Ratzinger's term had begun. (Curran's case was opened by Ratzinger's predecessor, Croatian cardinal Franjo Seper).

As the case against Curran unfolded, the question of access to his books would come up again when Curran complained that the congregation had never cited the work he felt was most directly relevant, *Dissent in and for the Church.*[1] In it Curran defended a group of theologians who had publicly proclaimed that Catholics could choose not to follow the pope's ban on birth control and still remain good Catholics. To do so, he developed a set of principles for legitimate theological dissent from the church's magisterium. Curran later found out, again from Fuchs, that the reason the congregation never cited the book was that the Gregorian University library did not have a copy! Curran actually sent a copy to the congregation at one point; they wrote back that after careful review it had not altered their judgment.

Well before Rome notified him that he was a target, Curran had picked up clues that trouble was brewing. In 1979, he was invited to speak in Louisiana. The bishop of Baton Rouge, Joseph V. Sullivan, refused to allow the use of diocesan facilities for the talk. On April 29, 1979, Archbishop Jerome Hamer, then the secretary of the Congregation for the Doctrine of the Faith, had written to Sullivan congratulating him for his stance and "for providing public clarification of some of the ambiguous and erroneous teachings of Father Curran." Curran was thus not shocked when Cardinal William Baum, then the archbishop of Washington, D.C., and the chancellor of Catholic University, formally told Curran on August 2, 1979, that he was under investigation in Rome. Curran learned from the Hamer letter that his protocol number in Rome is 48/66—meaning that the file on him at the Vatican had been opened in 1966, just after he came to Catholic University from St. Bernard's Seminary in Rochester, New York.

Curran eventually lost his license to teach Catholic theology after an exchange of correspondence with the doctrinal congregation and an "informal" meeting with Ratzinger in Rome on March 8, 1986. After Ratzinger concluded that Curran's views were unacceptable, he was fired from his position at Catholic University in January 1987. The university is still under censure from the American Association of University Professors for its handling of the case. Curran filed suit, but the judge in the case declined to overrule the university. Today, Curran teaches at Southern Methodist University in Dallas, where he is a widely respected ethicist. He is regarded by all sides as one of the nicest men in the academy. Whatever one makes of his theological views, virtually no one who knows him could construe Charlie Curran as an enemy of the faith. To this day, he remains well connected at Catholic University, even among faculty generally viewed as conservative.

During the 1980s, the Curran affair became the highest-profile test of the relationship between the doctrinal congregation under Ratzinger and the Catholic theological community. Curran's case resonated with many Catholics because he seemed to be advocating plain common sense; not *every* instance of birth control or masturbation can possibly be evil. In addition, Curran staked his defense on what he saw as a right to dissent from noninfallible magisterial teaching. Thus Curran put the core issues into stark relief: How many doctrinal propositions do theologians need to assent to in order to call themselves "Catholic"? Who gets to decide? The split between "magisterial" theologians, a minority reflexively loyal to Rome, and the majority of professional Catholic theologians, who value creative tension between themselves and church authority, came into sharpest focus during the Curran case.

Jesuit Thomas Reese, an astute observer of the contemporary church, recently summed up Ratzinger's impact on Catholic theology this way: "The relationship between the magisterium and theologians is worse today than at any time since the Reformation." His argument is that cases such as Curran's have left Catholic theologians frustrated and angry, with the result that a breach has opened up between the hierarchy and theologians. Reese likens it to the senior management of a large corporation and its research and development department not being on speaking terms; in his words, a "recipe for disaster."[2]

Fueled by this tension, rumblings of schism during the Ratzinger years have grown persistent. In a few limited cases, divisions in the church have erupted into open and formal revolts, as in Rochester, New York, in 1998, where the pastoral team and two-thirds of the progressive Corpus Christi parish pulled up stakes *en masse* and formed their own faith community, now called Spiritus Christi. Significantly, the pastor whose removal triggered the uprising in Rochester, Father James Callan, insisted that Ratzinger had ordered the crackdown, despite Bishop Matthew Clark's declaration that he acted on his own initiative. More often, however, contemporary Catholic schism is quiet and individual. People simply walk away.

Both kinds of defections—spectacular but isolated eruption and unheralded but steady erosion—have been realities for two millennia. Church leaders know that taking *any* stand, enforcing *any* discipline, will inevitably alienate someone. In a church of one billion people, even if a policy angers a scant one-tenth of one percent of the total, that amounts to one million critics, whose voices, in the age of the Internet and around-the-clock cable news channels, are instantly, and sometimes disproportionately amplified. Journalists instinctively seek "all sides" of a discussion, even if that means giving roughly equal treatment to spokespersons who speak for hundreds of millions of Catholics, and others who perhaps represent a few dozen. Conflict in the church under these conditions is constant and inevitable.

Given that reality, the question is, how should church leaders respond? Do they, as John XXIII once said, attempt to govern both for those with their foot on the accelerator and those with their foot on the brake? Or do they "take sides," casting their lot with one party in the church's ongoing debates, accepting the deeper and more profound divisions such a strategy will create? The central charge against Ratzinger in the theological community is that he chose the latter course. He has functioned not as a neutral arbiter of "orthodoxy," they argue, but as an advocate of the reaction against the postconciliar period that took shape in journals such as *Communio*. The man who once complained that the Holy Office was insufficiently tolerant of different theological schools has shown too little tolerance himself, these critics say.

Ratzinger has consistently asserted that the church of the future may need to be smaller and less culturally significant in order to remain faithful. In that sense, his willingness to polarize, to draw lines in the sand, flows consistently from his ecclesiology. Whether he is right that a church without many of its leading thinkers and pastors—a church without Charles Curran, for example—would be more faithful, cuts to the heart of any debate over the future of Roman Catholicism.

Vatican II and the Holy Office

Ratzinger's defenders frequently contend that set against the long history of the Holy Office, his administration has been relatively open and restrained. To his critics, however, comparisons to inquisitors of earlier eras miss the point; the proper context for evaluating the office should be the reforms inspired by Vatican II and promulgated by Paul VI. On December 7, 1965, Paul issued a document entitled *Integrae servandae* (Preserving intact). It was actually published on the last day of Vatican II.

The reforms in the Holy Office laid out in *Integrae servandae* included the following:

- Changing the name of the office from the Supreme Sacred Congregation of the Holy Office to the Congregation for the Doctrine of the Faith
- Ending the secrecy of the congregation's operations, bringing its inner workings into the realm of public church law
- Establishing the right of appeal and of judicial representation for all those called into doctrinal suspicion by decisions of the congregation
- Ensuring that regional conferences of bishops are consulted when their subjects are under suspicion
- Ensuring that specialists and experts on the issues under consideration are consulted before a decision is made on a particular theologian's work
- Abolishing the Index of Forbidden Books.[3]

Integrae servandae also called for the creation of a body of consultors to assist the newly named congregation, putting them in touch with the best theological minds in the Catholic world. The resulting International Theological Commission first met in 1967. The document also called for close coordination between the doctrinal congregation and the Pontifical Biblical Commission.

Integrae servandae also stipulated that all matters of faith and morals would be the purview of the doctrinal congregation, even issues that had formerly been reserved to different Vatican departments. Ostensibly, the idea was to prevent other congregations from short-circuiting these reforms by claiming areas of the doctrinal office's authority. In fact, however, this provision has made the doctrinal agency a "supercongregation." It has a power of judicial review over the decisions of every other office, as virtually anything the Vatican does can be interpreted to have doctrinal significance.

The overall aim of *Integrae servandae* was to transform the doctrinal congregation from a defensive, watchdog agency into an apostle of Catholic teaching. Persuasion rather than censorship was to be the leading idea. "Since charity banishes fear," Paul VI wrote, "it seems more appropriate now to preserve the faith by means of an office for promoting doctrine. Although it will still correct errors and gently recall those in error to moral excellence, new emphasis is to be given to preaching the Gospel. . . . Besides, the progress of human civilization, in which the importance of religion cannot be overlooked, is affecting the faithful in such a way that they will follow the church's lead more fully and more lovingly if they are provided with full explanations for the church's definitions and laws. Regarding matters of faith and morals, this is evident by the very nature of things."

As the most recent papal charter for the doctrinal congregation, *Integrae servandae* sets the standard by which Ratzinger's relationship with the theological community has to be assessed.

Ratzinger and Catholic Theology

As a professional theologian, Ratzinger has worked out a core set of his own theological ideas, summarized in chapter 3, chief among them his understanding of eschatology as the only Christian antidote to utopianism and his stress on a communion ecclesiology. As prefect, Ratzinger has also developed attitudes *about* Catholic theology: what theology is for, what its premises should be, what its spirit should be, what its perennial temptations are. These core principles run through the documents issued by the doctrinal congregation since the early 1980s as well as in Ratzinger's own writing over the same period. They are worked out most fully, however, in his 1993 book *The Nature and Mission of Theology*. This volume brings together Ratzinger's most important essays and speeches on the subject, as well as a previously unpublished reaction to public criticism of the congregation's 1990 *Instruction on the ecclesial vocation of the theologian.*[4]

In order to appreciate the relationship between theologians and the doctrinal congregation under Ratzinger's stewardship, one first must grasp how Ratzinger understands the essence of Catholic theology.

"Faith Seeking Understanding"

Ratzinger's deepest conviction about Catholic theology is captured in this familiar phrase from St. Anselm. Ratzinger believes that theology starts with a set of "givens," by which he means data from revelation. Subsequent theorizing can be justified only to the extent it respects these givens. Theology can explore the content of revelation but may not avoid or reinterpret it to suit an agenda from some other source. Usually, in Ratzinger's mind, that source is the zeitgeist; one of the Scripture passages he cites most often is Romans 12:2, Paul's warning about not conforming oneself to the spirit of the age.

The Simple Believers

The first point Ratzinger makes to those who claim he has strained the relationship between the magisterium and the theological community is that keeping theologians happy is not his main concern. Above all, he must protect the right of "simple believers" to have the faith preserved in each generation. This concern extends as far back as 1966 to the closing page of Ratzinger's commentary on the fourth session of Vatican II: "In the final analysis the church lives, in sad as well as joyous times, from the faith of those who are simple at heart. . . . The faith of those who are simple of heart is the most precious treasure of the church." The perspective has stayed with him. In a 1988 interview with the Austrian daily *Die Presse,* he said his role was to defend those Catholics "who do not write books or learned articles." He has defined his primary task as the defense of those who "can't fight back," meaning Catholics who lack the tools of theological sophistication, against assaults on their faith. Ratzinger undoubtedly draws consolation in this stance from his great-uncle Georg, whose political career was devoted to defending the "simple ones" in rural Bavaria against assault by intellectual and commercial elites.

Historical Parallelism

Ratzinger believes that the church fathers have already encountered and responded to many of the pressures facing Catholicism today. Too often, he suggests, Catholics want to excogitate new solutions when the proper answer is lying in the tradition. Liberation theology, for example, recapitulated for Ratzinger many elements of the Spiritual Franciscan crisis of the thirteenth century. The push for tolerance of religious pluralism recalls the late antique period when pagan thinkers, having failed to crush Christianity by force, attempted to subvert it through relativism. Modernity by and large lacks originality; it offers new versions of perennial temptations, and orthodox Christianity must withstand those allurements now just as it has in the past.

The Truth

Orthodox theology for Ratzinger presumes epistemic realism: the human mind is ordered to the truth, it can ascertain truth in nature and recognize truth in revelation. These truths become the basis for universally valid conclusions in anthropology, ethics, and theology. Modern thinkers, as Ratzinger sees it, are too much under the spell of Kant and his distinction between the noumenal and the phenomenal. We never meet objective truth as such except as it is filtered through human consciousness. In the absence of objectivity, the only standard for judging propositions is their practical value (does believing this help us build a better world?). Thus modern theology stresses an instrumental view of the truth: truth is something humanity makes, not something it finds. Ratzinger sees this view of the truth as both a false humility and a false pride. The human person is capable of knowing truth, Ratzinger insists, and in that sense the truth-as-doing model gives up on humanity too soon; on the other hand, if humanity can invent truth, then there are no limits on our behavior, and in that sense it is a dangerously arrogant idea.

The Nazi Experience

Ratzinger sees the experience of the German churches and theologians under Hitler as proof of the need for church-centered theology. "Theology either exists in the church and from the church, or it does not exist at all," he concluded. If theology severs its bond to the church, it will turn to the surrounding culture and end up absolutizing a particular social or political arrangement. Moreover, theology shorn of its connection to the teaching office of the church becomes merely another academic discipline, enjoying no more certainty than political science. Its hypotheses are merely probable, not enough to stake one's life on. The Nazi experience shows that one needs more than that.

Diachronic Nature of the Sensus Fidelium

Progressives, pointing to poll numbers that show a majority of Catholics support birth control, married priests, women priests, a right to dissent, and so on, often reproach Ratzinger and other church leaders for failing to heed the *sensus fidelium*. The phrase refers to an ancient Catholic doctrine, confirmed again at Vatican II, that one way to ascertain "the faith" on a given point is to see what is believed by the whole people of God, who by virtue of supernatural grace cannot fail to uphold the truth. Ratzinger accepts this doctrine, but he rejects an identification of the "sense of the faithful" with a statistical majority as determined by polling data. He insists that the whole "people of God" includes both the magisterium and the rank-and-file believers, so any attempt to distinguish a "faithful" that stands against magisterial teaching is misconceived. Moreover, the "people of God" exceeds those currently living: it includes all those generations who have gone before, and whose testimony to the faith is included in the creeds and conciliar declarations and papal teaching that is part of the Catholic patrimony. Thus the "sense of the faithful" properly understood is "diachronic," meaning that it cuts across time. To show that sixty percent of Catholics in the United States and Europe, for example, support the ordination of women is far from demonstrating the sense of the faithful on the issue. It is always possible, Ratzinger argues, at any given moment in history for a large number of believers to go astray. The ancient heresy of Arianism makes that point. It is the function of the magisterium to uphold the testimony of every generation of believers over against the tyranny of the present. It is in that sense, Ratzinger argues, that the magisterium reflects a genuinely democratic principle: it honors the witness to the faith of Catholics from every era of church history.

The Implied Contract

Ratzinger sees an all-too-frequent abuse of trust by theologians who use the platform afforded them in the church to promote what is actually their own private system. He has complained that dissenting theologians generally owe whatever following they enjoy to the fact that they teach in the name of the church. One's license as a Catholic theologian, however, creates a contractual relationship that obliges the theologian to present Catholic doctrine with accuracy and fidelity. Even where a license has not been issued, if a theologian is teaching at a Catholic university or in some other capacity that rests upon the reputation of the church, there is a moral obligation to speak for the church and not for oneself. At the most basic level, Ratzinger sees the failure to honor this contract as a matter of pride—too many theologians exalt themselves, celebrate their own originality, rather than handing on what has been received. After all, Ratzinger argues, when a student signs up for a course in Catholic theology, or a parishioner comes to Mass expecting to experience the Catholic liturgy, or a seeker opens a Catholic cate-chism, each has a right to hear the authentic voice of the church.

The Responsibility of Theologians for Ecclesial Decline

Ratzinger believes the empty churches of the West are at least in part the fault of progressive theologians who have reinterpreted Christianity to such an extent that it is virtually indistinguishable from the culture. "Theologians should ponder to what extent they are to blame for the fact that increasing numbers of people seek refuge in narrow or unhealthy forms of religion," Ratzinger said in *Salt of the Earth*. "When one no longer offers anything but questions and doesn't offer any positive way to faith, such flights are in-evitable." To nonbelievers, Christianity today often seems helplessly mired in internal debates with little positive energy to offer the overwhelming ma-jority of the world that is non-Christian. "The Church is, as it were, con-stantly preoccupied with herself on a couple of fixed points. In the midst of all this, there is too little attention to the fact that eighty percent of the peo-ple of this world are non-Christians who are waiting for the gospel, or for whom, at any rate, the gospel is also intended," he said in 1996. "We shouldn't constantly be agonizing over our own questions but should be pondering how we as Christians can express today in this world what we believe and thereby say something to those people."

Favorite Metaphor I: The Symphony

Ratzinger uses two metaphors to express how he understands the proper re-lationship between theologians and the hierarchy. The first is that of a sym-phony. Ratzinger is a music lover; he grew up in the shadow of Salzburg, Austria, and its rich musical heritage, and he is himself an accomplished amateur pianist. The concept of a Christian *symphonia* is found in the church fathers, who used the term to characterize the relationship between the Old and New Testaments, and later the relationship uniting all Chris-tians. The symphony is "the very form of the church," Ratzinger wrote in 1986, and hence is "the structural form upon which it is founded." What this metaphor means to him is that pluralism becomes chaos without core principles. Dozens of instruments playing at once can be cacophonous; uni-fied by a common melody and under the direction of a conductor, however, they produce astonishing beauty. Of course the metaphor is open to criti-cism. Surely the Catholic experience is broad enough to encompass more than a single piece, or even style, of music. But the *symphonia* image cap-tures something essential to understanding Ratzinger: his belief in the beauty of orthodoxy. Ratzinger's tenacity as a doctrinal enforcer comes not primarily from fear or defensiveness; it comes from the passion of someone profoundly in love with Catholicism.

Favorite Metaphor II: Medicine

Ratzinger's other favorite analogy for theologians is the medical profession. Doctors cannot be concerned with their own freedom, Ratzinger argues; they must first of all be concerned with the patient's health. In different ways, the same truth holds for theologians. Ratzinger made the point in a 1999 press conference in Menlo Park, California: "As you see with a medical faculty, you have complete academic freedom, but the discipline is such that the sense of medicine determines the exercise of this freedom. As a medical person you cannot do what you will, you are in service of the life. Service of the life determines the just application of academic freedom," he said. "So theology also has its inner exigencies. Catholic theology is not individual reflection on what could be God and what could be a religious community, but Catholic theology is thinking with the faith of the church." In his 1986 essay on pluralism, he had also used the image: "When a doctor errs and, instead of patiently accommodating himself to the laws of anatomy and life, risks a 'creative' idea, the consequences are readily apparent. Although the damage is not so immediately noticeable in the case of a theologian, in reality even here too much is at stake for him to trust himself simply to his momentary conviction, for he is dealing with a matter which affects man and his future and in which every failed intervention has its consequences." Again, one can argue with the image. The field of medicine progresses not by dogmatism but by constant self-criticism. Still, this metaphor too expresses something deep within Ratzinger's psyche, the conviction that theology is serious business. It is no intellectual parlor game, but a means of dealing with the deepest and most important questions facing the human person.

Legitimate Pluralism

Ratzinger stresses the unity that lies at the center of pluralism. Common agreement on core principles, in fact, is the only thing that makes genuine pluralism possible. If every theologian posits his or her own creed, the result is multiple hegemonies, not pluralism. Pluralism results from different perspectives on the same reality, different attempts to probe the same concept. Logically speaking, pluralism is impossible without underlying unity. Thus the differing Jesuit and Dominican understandings of grace offer an example of genuine pluralism; Hans Küng's reading of infallibility, however, does not, because Küng rejects the doctrine altogether rather than beginning his reflection by accepting it. Ratzinger would say that dissent and pluralism are not only different, they are logically opposed, in that one presumes rejection of church teaching and the other submission to it. In his essay on "Pluralism as a Problem for the Church," Ratzinger notes that the concept of pluralism arose in political theory as a way to place limits on state power. A person, according to pluralist theory, is not merely a citizen; he or she also belongs to many other social groups, such as the family, civic associations, a trade, and so forth, and the state must respect the autonomy of those other identities. Thus pluralism was envisioned as a way of preventing totalitarianism, and as such has value, Ratzinger says. The problem is that it is too easy to conceive of the church as merely one among many other social groups, and lose sight of its transcendent dimension. One cannot apply pluralism inside the church, forgetting it is not a state but a communion. Ratzinger argues that the church is already a model of genuine pluralism: no lobby or political party, he says, would tolerate the internal diversity that exists inside Catholicism.[5]

Dissent

In *Milestones,* Ratzinger offers what he considers to be the proper disposition for a theologian who genuinely practices *sentire cum ecclesia,* or "thinking with the church." He says that his professor and mentor in Munich, Gottlieb Söhngen, had grave reservations about using papal infallibility to proclaim the Assumption of Mary. Yet when Söhngen was asked if he would dissent if the pope did so, he said no: "If the dogma comes, then I will remember that the Church is wiser than I and that I must trust her more than my own erudition." Ratzinger sees open, public disagreement as a prideful "alternative magisterium" violating the charter of theology, which is to take the faith of the church as its point of departure. Ratzinger also charges those such as Curran and Küng and their supporters with attempting to use the tactics of political pressure—the mass media, petition drives, demonstrations—to force the church to change its teaching. He sees this as further evidence of the extent to which modern Western theology has capitulated to the zeitgeist, in which truth has been replaced by power, and utterly lost the proper sense of the church.

The Congregation in Action

To understand the nature of the relationship between Ratzinger and the Catholic theological community, one needs a sense of how the Congregation for the Doctrine of the Faith works. Despite the mystery and intrigue that surrounds the agency, much about its internal operation is reasonably well known. Staff members are listed in the *Annuario Pontifico,* an annual directory of Vatican offices and employees, and the congregation's procedures are published in a document called the *Ratio agendi* (System of action). Congregation staffers are for the most part willing, at least in an off-the-record capacity, to talk about their work.[6]

Technically, the word "congregation" in the name of Ratzinger's agency refers not to the staffers and assistants who work for him, but to the group of twenty cardinals, archbishops, and bishops from fourteen different nations who make up the supreme decisionmaking body, a sort of board of directors for the doctrinal agency. Each Vatican congregation is governed by a similar body of bishops and presided over by a cardinal prefect (pontifical councils are usually run by archbishops). The full body of bishops who govern the congregation, called the Plenaria, meets only once every year and a half, and then only to provide a general review of the office's work.

Day-to-day functions are in the hands of Ratzinger's staff, currently a total of thirty-eight decisionmakers, secretaries, and support staff. His top lieutenants are Archbishop Tarcisio Bertone, the congregation's secretary, and Father Gianfranco Girotti, the undersecretary. Both are from Italy. The congregation also draws on a body of consultors, mostly theologians who teach at various Roman universities. It is often assumed that these theologians are selected because they are safe; on the other hand, I dined in Rome during the 1999 European synod with a theologian who just that day had received a book from the doctrinal congregation for review. The theologian is mildly liberal and had no idea he was under consideration to serve as a consultor. He had no reason to believe the congregation would heed his opinion, but then he was surprised they had asked for it in the first place.

In terms of its internal organization, the congregation is divided into four sections: doctrinal, sacerdotal, matrimonial, and disciplinary. The first deals with theologians and writers; the second handles applications from priests who want to be released from their vows (that department is working itself out of business, as responsibility for these cases is being transferred to another congregation); the third prepares requests for a certain kind of annulment ("favor of the faith" cases that go straight to the pope and are prepared by the congregation); and the fourth is a catchall for cases that fall out of the mainstream, such as the veracity of purported visions. The doctrinal section is by far the most active and influential.

The front line of the staff is composed of junior priests on loan from various dioceses and religious orders. As a rule, these officials have to be younger than thirty-five when they begin their first Vatican assignment. There is no formal system of application; generally a departing staff member has a role in selecting his replacement. Other times the prefect or secretary will call on a trusted bishop or religious superior to recommend someone. Technically these junior staffers must know at least one language other than Italian, and generally a balance is maintained among native speakers in the major languages of the church: Italian, French, German, English, Portuguese, and Spanish. Often these lower-level staffers will be called on to translate a document into their native language. There is an informal rule that certain countries will be represented by at least one staffer. There is always at least one American, currently Father Charles Brown of the Archdiocese of New York. Holding that spot typically helps a clerical career: Archbishop William Levada of San Francisco, for example, was the American in the doctrinal congregation in the late 1970s and early 1980s.

Ratzinger has acknowledged that his office receives a great deal of mail from Catholics around the world, most "preoccupied with the notion that the church should remain the church"—in other words, conservatives. In the doctrinal section, there are approximately twelve junior staffers whose job it is to sort this mail, determine the seriousness of charges, and make an initial determination of how to proceed. If a particular case is determined to have enough significance, perhaps because of the gravity of the charge, perhaps because the referral comes from a bishop, perhaps because the staffer knows that the subject matter reflects a priority of the congregation's leadership, it will move up the chain of command. One critical variable is whether the theologian in question is a priest or member of a religious congregation. If it concerns a layperson teaching at a non-Catholic university, the congregation has no means to exercise control over that person and usually will refrain from launching an investigation.

If Ratzinger approves the decision to initiate a case file, it will go back down the chain through the secretary, the subsecretary, and the section head, eventually to be assigned to one of the junior staff members. That official studies the theologian's work, compiles relevant documents and makes an initial assessment. The information is then brought to a regular weekly meeting of the officials of the congregation, called the "particular congress."

The particular congress can take one of several actions. If the issues raised by the case have already been settled, either in a document of the congregation or a disciplinary action directed at someone else, the congregation might send a letter to the bishop or religious superior of the theologian in question. The letter will reference the earlier decision and invite the person in authority to initiate a review. That could include requiring the theologian to submit "clarifications" to the congregation. This step always implies the possibility that if the clarifications are unsatisfactory the congregation may decide to initiate its own action. Another option is to decide that the case really belongs with another Vatican office. If it concerns a liturgical abuse, for example, the particular congress might refer it to the Congregation for Divine Worship and the Discipline of the Sacraments.

If the decision is made to proceed with an investigation—in the language of the congregation, an "ordinary examination"—then the author's work will be assigned to one of the congregation's consultors, or perhaps two of them independently, to render opinions. The junior staffer will monitor the case, collecting materials and preparing an analysis for senior officials. The particular congress also appoints a *relatore pro auctore* on behalf of the theologian, roughly speaking, a defense attorney whose function is to bring out the positive aspects of his or her work. This is done without consulting the theologian, who at this stage is unaware, at least in theory, that any action is unfolding against him or her.

If, after studying the consultors' reports, the congress decides to pursue an investigation, the case will go before the Ordinary Session of the Congregation. This body meets on the fourth Wednesday of every month and consists of all the bishop members of the congregation, but in reality it is largely made up of those bishops who happen to be in Rome. It decides whether to submit a list of objections to the theologian, or whether sufficient grounds exist to proceed to emergency action. The decisions of the ordinary session go before the pope, who must approve them before they are issued. Ratzinger has a regular weekly meeting with the pope on Fridays in which cases are discussed.

If the decision is made to proceed, the next step will be to ask the theologian for clarifications, perhaps in response to a set of observations on the theologian's work. The documentation then goes to the bishop or religious superior of the theologian, and only then through him to the theologian. The theologian is given three canonical months to respond. He or she may appoint an advisor to assist in the preparation of the response with the approval of the bishop or religious superior.

Theoretically speaking, theologians under scrutiny are only informed of the process unfolding against them at this stage; that is, after the congress, the ordinary session, and the pope himself have decided that grave concerns exist about their work. In fact, many theologians with decent connections in Rome learn "through the grapevine" well in advance that the congregation is looking at their work. Nevertheless, most theologians feel that by the time their input is requested the die has already been cast. Only a public retraction, in most cases, will suffice to head off disciplinary action.

Because the congregation's process takes so long to unfold, often several years, Vatican officials routinely refer to it as "careful" and "deliberate," as if any disciplinary action is the last resort after every other alternative has been exhausted. But many theologians feel this is a façade. The process takes a long time because that is the nature of the Vatican, they say, but the eventual outcome is reduced to two options at the very outset: surrender or censure. Curran has called the congregation's methods a violation of the most basic notions of due process, including the right of the accused to be informed at every stage of the proceedings, the right to counsel of his or her own choosing, and the right to see one's own case file. Curran and Küng have both been asking for years to see their case files and both have been steadily refused.[7]

During the ordinary examination stage, the theologian under investigation may request a meeting with congregation officials with an advisor of his or her choice taking an active part. If such a meeting takes place, minutes are to be prepared with all parties signing them as to accuracy. These minutes, along with the theologian's formal response, go back to the congress and then to the ordinary session. If these bodies decide errors still exist, then "adequate measures are taken for the good of the faithful." These adequate measures can include the loss of one's license as a Catholic theologian or a formal silencing. The pope always approves these decisions before they are proclaimed, so there is no formal recourse or court of appeal.

This is the ordinary process as envisioned by the revised *Ratio agendi* issued on June 29, 1997. At the initial stage of examination, however, the rules allow the congress to decide the case is of sufficient gravity to warrant an "examination in cases of urgency." This would be true in cases when "the writing is clearly and certainly erroneous" and "its dissemination could cause or already had caused grave harm to the faithful." Under this expedited process, the congress can prepare a dossier to be forwarded to the ordinary session and then to the pope, which is then presented to the bishop or religious superior, and through them to the theologian, with a request for correction within two canonical months.

In the case of either examination, if the end result is a decision that the theologian is guilty of heresy, apostasy, or schism, then a penalty of excommunication may be declared (this is what happened in the Tissa Balasuriya case). If the doctrinal offenses are of a lesser nature, other penalties may be issued, such as a ban on publications, a penitential silence, or a loss of one's license to teach Catholic theology. If a member of a religious community refuses to submit, he or she may be expelled; a priest may be forcibly reduced to lay status. The pope gave his approval to this *Ratio agendi,* including the articles on disciplinary measures.

According to congregation staffers, most investigations occur at the request of either bishops or other Vatican offices. In general, the complaints that pour in from around the world do not lead to formal proceedings. "The machinery of the Vatican is not going to come to a halt because someone is unhappy with their second-grade religion teacher," as one former staffer told me. Another staffer said it is not true that congregation officials are influenced in their choice of targets by right-wing Catholic journals such as the *Wanderer*. "Ratzinger and Bertone don't know what that is, they don't read it," the official said. "That idea is a fantasy." Other staffers point out that sometimes the congregation acts as a firebreak against demands from a hot-tempered bishop or other church official for immediate action against someone. These cases, they say ruefully, never make it into the papers.

In deciding which theological movements warrant concern, the doctrinal congregation is theoretically supposed to call upon the International Theological Commission, the body created in the wake of Vatican II to give the congregation direct access to the best minds in Catholic theology. Paul VI's vision was that the commission would represent a cross-section of theological methods and opinions, hence ensuring balance in the congregation's approach. The first set of appointments on May 1, 1969, seemed to be consistent with this aim. They included Bernard Lonergan and Karl Rahner as well as Hans Urs von Balthasar, not to mention Joseph Ratzinger. Yet by 1974, Lonergan and Rahner were gone; Rahner announced that it was clear to him the commission existed simply to rubber-stamp the decisions of the congregation.

From that time forward, most Catholic theologians have come to regard the commission as an arm of the doctrinal congregation, useful as a way to glimpse its priorities but certainly not a representative body of Catholic theologians. American Jesuit Walter J. Burghardt, who runs his "Preaching the Just Word" project out of the Woodstock Theological Center in Washington, D.C., confirms this verdict in his recent theological memoirs, *Long Have I Loved You,* published by Orbis Books. Burghardt served on the International Theological Commission through much of the 1970s, and he recalled vividly the few weeks the commission gave itself to work on its document on liberation theology. During that time not a single liberationist was invited to participate or even speak to the group. Consulting with those whose views the commission decides to assess was not then, and is not now, part of its standard operating procedure. Mercy sister Margaret Farley of Yale, president of the Catholic Theological Society of America, 1999–2000, noted that there is not a single feminist scholar on the commission, despite the fact that feminism is an extremely important current in contemporary Catholic thought and is routinely criticized by Vatican officials.[8]

The Curran Affair

No case in Ratzinger's nearly two decades in Rome better encapsulates the divisions between him and the bulk of the Catholic theological community than that of Charles Curran. It pitted two well-regarded theologians against one another, both dedicated priests, and both convinced that their stand was critical for the long-term welfare of the church. Curran enjoyed the overwhelming support of his colleagues and all the mainstream organizations of Catholic theologians. He premised his defense not on the stands on sexual ethics that had originally gotten him into trouble, but on the right of theologians to dissent from magisterial teaching. In that sense, Ratzinger's handling of the Curran case was the most important case of his tenure because it established how the congregation would respond to any public expression of theological disagreement.[9]

Curran actually has a fair bit in common with Ratzinger. He was born just seven years later, in 1934. Both men come from middle-class families. Both were ordained at the age of twenty-four, Ratzinger in Munich and Curran in his home diocese of Rochester, New York. Both are mild-mannered in ways that belie their public images as, respectively, a reactionary and a firebrand. Curran is in fact widely recognized as one of the kindest, most accessible public figures in contemporary Catholicism. He has remained popular over the years even with colleagues who bitterly disagree with his theological positions, in much the same way that former students of Ratzinger who have evolved in different theological directions still speak with fondness about the graciousness of their professor.

Both had taken initial positions in their theological careers that they would later revise. Ratzinger had been among the progressive forces at Vatican II; Curran was steeped in the legalistic, by-the-book moral theology of the preconciliar years, but later became a leading exponent of the new approach to Catholic morality exemplified by his teacher and friend Bernard Häring. This approach was more careful about issuing absolute rules, tending to emphasize the context and intention of the moral act. What counted most from this new frame of reference was fidelity to Christ, not to a rule book, which meant leaving room for creativity and personal decisions of conscience. For ordinary Catholics, this shift in moral thinking was, after the changes in the liturgy, probably the aspect of the postconciliar era that reached into their lives most directly. This was especially the case in the wake of Paul VI's 1968 encyclical *Humanae vitae* reaffirming the ban on birth control. Millions of Catholics, reacting against that decision, embraced what the new breed of moral theologians were telling them—that for good reasons, they could dissent from official church teaching and remain Catholics.

By the time *Humanae vitae* was issued, Curran was already a controversial figure in American Catholicism. During the mid-1960s he had published articles, both in learned scholarly journals and in the popular media, arguing for a new Catholic approach to family planning and reproduction. A moral reevaluation of birth control was part of Curran's argument. He had also suggested that various issues in sexual ethics—masturbation, homosexuality, and the like—neither were as gravely sinful as once taught nor could be dealt with through blanket condemnations. This was enough to attract the attention of Catholic conservatives, some of whom began writing to church authorities to complain. In some cases invitations to speak were withdrawn, though for the most part Curran drew overwhelming support even from the leadership ranks of the church.

He was appointed in September 1965 to the faculty of the Catholic University of America, the country's flagship Catholic university. Because the theology department there is considered a pontifical faculty, professors need the *missio canonica* to teach. As Curran continued to spread his views, however, the atmosphere became increasingly tense, and on April 17, 1967, he was informed that the board of trustees of the university, which includes all the American cardinals and several other important bishops, had voted not to renew his contract. A *Washington Post* article later reported that Archbishop Egidio Vagnozzi, the papal ambassador at the time, claimed he was responsible for the decision. Observers believed that Rome wanted to make an example of a liberal American priest, and because Curran had achieved such prominence he was a perfect target. It was the curia's way of drawing a line in the sand to postconciliar revolution in the church.

Yet things did not quite work out that way. The theology faculty voted to strike unless Curran was reinstated. Within days, students and faculty from across the campus joined in the strike and the university was effectively shut down. The full faculty voted 400 to 18 in favor of the strike. Recognizing the inevitable, university authorities backed down. By April 21, they announced that the firing was rescinded and that Curran would be invited back at the rank of associate professor. A campus historian announced that this was the first successful university strike since the Middle Ages.

The strike and its aftermath received extensive coverage in the American press, so that by the time July 1968 rolled around, Charles Curran was already a well-known Catholic figure, and the media would have looked to him in any event for comment on the papal encyclical. Curran and his colleagues, however, decided to do more than comment. They seized the release of the encyclical as a teaching moment, a chance to say something to the broader Catholic world about dissent from noninfallible teaching. Curran and ten other theologians met on the day the encyclical was released, July 29, and prepared a statement. Its conclusion was clear: "As Roman Catholic theologians, conscious of our duty and our limitations, we conclude that spouses may responsibly decide according to their conscience that artificial contraception in some circumstances is permissible and indeed necessary to preserve and foster the values and sacredness of marriage." Eventually more than 600 theologians added their names.

Cardinal James Francis McIntyre of Los Angeles, widely known as an archconservative, immediately introduced a resolution at the Catholic University Board of Trustees calling Curran's action a breach of contract and calling for his termination along with the other signers. In view of the drama of 1967, however, McIntyre's resolution went nowhere. The board called for an inquiry to determine if the professors had violated their responsibilities. The inquiry unfolded over 1968 and 1969 but eventually ended with no firings and no disciplinary measures. Curran and his colleagues thought they had won, that they had established a right of dissent from noninfallible teaching.

It was easy enough for them to draw that conclusion, as the American bishops adopted a document that year called *Human life in our day,* also in response to *Humanae vitae,* in which they accepted the legitimacy of public theological dissent if it meets three conditions: if the reasons are serious and well-founded, if the manner of dissent does not impugn the teaching authority of the church, and if it does not give scandal. Throughout his long exchange of letters with Rome over the course of the next two decades, Curran would constantly refer to these norms established by the U.S. bishops to justify his stance. Ratzinger never accepted the argument. In effect, many observers believe, in the Curran case Ratzinger repealed a document of the U.S. bishops' conference without ever formally explaining his basis, or authority, for doing so.

Curran formally learned in August 1979 that he was under investigation by the doctrinal congregation in a letter from Cardinal Franjo Seper, Ratzinger's predecessor. The letter was dated July 13, but the process obviously had been going on for some time. On October 4, 1979, Curran responded to the set of "observations" on his work issued by the congregation with five questions that he felt had to be answered before any conversation about his specific theological positions could be meaningful. Those five questions were:

- Does the teaching of the ordinary noninfallible authoritative hierarchical magisterium constitute the only factor or always the decisive factor in the total magisterial activity of the church? In other words is the theologian ever justified in going against such a teaching?
- Does there exist the possibility and even the right of public dissent from authoritative noninfallible hierarchical teaching when a theologian is convinced there are serious reasons to overcome the presumption of truth in favor of the teaching and judges that such an expression of public dissent will be for the ultimate good of the church?
- Is *silentium obsequiosum* the only legitimate response for a theologian who is convinced that there are serious reasons which overturn the pre-

sumption in favor of the teaching of the authoritative noninfallible hierarchical magisterium?

■ Can the ordinary faithful prudently make a decision to act against the teaching of the ordinary authentic noninfallible hierarchical magisterium?

■ In the course of history have there been errors in the teaching of the ordinary noninfallible magisterium which have been subsequently corrected, often because of the dissent of theologians?

Through the course of the next eight years, leading up to his eventual termination at Catholic University in 1987, Curran strove to elicit a response from Rome to these questions. He never succeeded. The congregation's focus was on establishing the *fact* of Curran's dissent, a point he never disputed, though he insisted his dissent was always partial and should be understood in the context of a more basic assent. Curran acknowledged that in some areas his position differed from that of the magisterium. What he wanted to establish is that it is possible for a Catholic theologian to hold contrary views on noninfallible teachings and still remain Catholic.

Ratzinger did not dispute the legitimacy of honest disagreement in principle, but he saw Curran's view of infallibility as unacceptably attenuated. Curran could not pretend that only those doctrines that had been formally defined were binding on a Catholic theologian. The specific matters in question—contraception, homosexuality, divorce, and remarriage—fell into a category Ratzinger called "definitive teaching" that demanded firm assent. Disagreement on these issues, which had been taught by the church across time and cultures, meant that Curran had separated himself from the Catholic *communio*. Worse yet, he was promulgating his restricted view of infallibility, a position that Ratzinger believed derived essentially from the Protestant Reformation, from every lectern in the land. Curran's logic seemed to Ratzinger to lead to the conclusion that Catholics are obligated only to accept a few core dogmatic principles—the Trinity, for example, or the resurrection of the body—and all else is up for grabs.

Thus over their six-year exchange of letters, as well as in their 1986 meeting, Curran and Ratzinger were operating out of fundamentally different theoretical frameworks, and both felt the other never really understood what was at stake. Curran could never get Ratzinger to talk about the norms of dissent; Ratzinger could never get Curran to acknowledge the full scope of binding doctrine. Each felt the other man was being selective in his reading of the tradition, and each wondered how the other could hold the beliefs he did and imagine himself unassailably "Catholic."

Ratzinger took over the Curran file from Seper in late 1981, and in June 1982 Curran wrote to him for the first time, sending his second set of responses to the observations on his work first issued by the doctrinal congregation in July 1979. Curran reminded Ratzinger of his procedural objections, namely that the congregation had already condemned him, both through the highly critical "observations" and in Archbishop Hamer's letter to Bishop Sullivan mentioned in the opening of this chapter. It seemed unlikely to him that he could get a fair hearing. Further, Curran noted with frustration that the congregation had refused to spell out any norms governing public theological dissent.

Ratzinger responded in April 1983 in a document divided into three sections. First, he takes up the issue of dissent. In a few brief paragraphs, he makes two points: that the fact of personal dissent from church teaching does not justify a right to public dissent from the ordinary magisterium; and that Curran "effectively treats the position of the magisterium as he would the opinion of an ordinary theologian." Responding to Curran's argument that singling him out is unfair because many other theologians hold the same views, the document says: "It is not just Father Curran who cites other theologians in disagreement with the church, but they in turn also cite him. This circular method of contestation cannot enjoy immunity from criticism by the church, even though in singling out the tenets of a particular theologian, the church may at first risk being perceived as unjust."

The document then briefly summarizes the points upon which it considers Curran's dissent to be clear: artificial contraception, the indissolubility of marriage, abortion and euthanasia, masturbation, premarital intercourse, and homosexual acts. Finally, it sets out certain issues it considers still unclear. Chief among them is Curran's "theory of compromise," which holds that despite the human person's best efforts life will sometimes present situations in which moral choice means doing some evil. In a telling comment, the document warns that such a standard is likely to give people an excuse to settle for sinful behavior, because "the element of self-justification" inevitably enters in to moral decisionmaking. In other words, once the moral norm is no longer absolute, most people will not exert themselves to meet it but will justify immoral behavior on the basis of "compromise." Curran has often said that one of the basic differences between himself and Ratzinger is that he is more Thomistic and Ratzinger more Augustinian. Their differences on the "theory of compromise" appear to support that view. Curran assumes that most people, left to apply human reason to morally complex situations, will make the appropriate judgment; Ratzinger seems to assume that fallen humanity needs absolutes as a kind of insurance policy against moral weakness.

Ratzinger goes on to say that Curran's argument for the church to change its teaching on the indissolubility of marriage—namely, that many Catholics disregard it in practice—is "profoundly legalistic." The church teaches that Christian marriage is indissoluble because it is, Ratzinger says, not the other way around. It is an instance in which Ratzinger believes Curran willfully ignores one of the "givens" of revelation. The church does not canvas its members and then decide what to teach; the church begins with revelation and then helps its members, and the world at large, to understand its implications.

Curran responded in June of 1983, expressing impatience with the congregation's refusal to engage the issue of theological dissent. "True and fruitful dialogue requires that both parties be willing to express what the norms are that they are following and how these norms are to be applied," Curran wrote. "I do not think that true dialogue can continue unless the congregation will clearly state whether or not it accepts any possibility of legitimate public theological dissent in the church." Curran then moves on to the specifics of Ratzinger's April document. He grounds public dissent on the right of Catholics to know about diverse theological opinions, the duty of theologians to inform them, the right to free self-expression, and the duty to avoid scandal when the absence of dissent from magisterial teaching threatens to create it (as Curran believes was the case with *Humanae vitae*). Curran also objects to Ratzinger's statement that Curran treats the magisterium as simply one more theologian; he points out that his books and articles are filled with respectful presentation of magisterial teaching, even when he disagrees with it. "I have never given such an importance or prominence to the work of any one theologian," Curran says. He again makes the point that many other Catholic theologians around the world hold the same views he does.

In response to a letter from Archbishop James Hickey of Washington, D.C., Curran expressed exasperation at the unwillingness of the doctrinal congregation to discuss the norms governing dissent. "Why has the congregation been unwilling to answer that question?" he asked on February 28, 1984. "Why are they stalling?" This elicited a letter from Ratzinger dated April 13, in which he insists that the congregation has made itself clear.

"To dissent even privately requires personal certitude that the teaching of the church is incorrect," he writes, quoting the previous set of observations sent to Curran. "To further dissent publicly and to encourage dissent in others runs the risk of causing scandal to the faithful, and to assume a certain responsibility for the confusion caused by setting up one's own theological opinion in contradiction to the position taken by the church." Ratzinger then goes on to remind Curran that he is still obligated to respond to the specific observations about the moral issues on which he dissents: contraception, euthanasia, masturbation, and so on.

It was hardly a response that could satisfy Curran. Does the statement that private dissent requires "personal certitude that the teaching of the church is incorrect" mean that dissent is forbidden? Does saying that public dissent "runs the risk" of confusing the faithful mean that under certain conditions this risk can be avoided? These comments are obviously not the systematic treatment of the rules governing dissent for which Curran had been asking.

Curran sent a response, under protest, covering the theological specifics in August 1984. In September 1985, Ratzinger wrote back informing him that one who held such views cannot be considered a Catholic theologian. Curran was given one final chance to retract his views, and in the absence of such a retraction, he would be stripped of his *missio canonica*.

In January 1986, Curran wrote to Ratzinger requesting a face-to-face meeting in Rome in a last-ditch attempt to reach a compromise. Ratzinger assented, provided that Curran understood this would not be an official session because such a meeting was required under the *Ratio agendi* only if there was uncertainty about an author's views. In this case, it was quite clear that Curran dissented. Curran accepted and said he would bring Bernard Häring, his old mentor and friend, along as his advisor. Monsignor George Higgins of the University of Notre Dame, America's leading labor priest and a longtime friend of Curran, also accompanied him on the trip, as did the dean of the School of Religious Studies at the Catholic University of America, William Cenkner. Ratzinger and Curran had agreed on a press release before the meeting occurred, to be released after the session was over. The meeting was described as "cordial."

In the weeks leading up to the meeting, Curran, who is not only a gifted theologian but a tenacious political strategist, was attempting to work out a compromise. He suggested that he be prohibited from teaching sexual ethics at Catholic University, as he had not been teaching the course for several years and had no plans to resume doing so. Rome could issue a document pointing out the "errors" in his theology, and could impose a year away from teaching because he had planned to take a sabbatical in 1986 anyway. He approached Hickey and Cardinal Joseph Bernardin of Chicago, who by this time was also acting as an intermediary. They agreed to take the proposal to Rome. After doing so, they informed Curran that his plan would probably not be accepted.

On Saturday, March 8, Curran, Häring, Higgins, and Cenkner arrived at the Piazza del S. Uffizio, 11, at 11:00 A.M. and were met in an anteroom by Ratzinger. He escorted Curran and Häring into the meeting while Higgins and Cenkner waited outside. Present in the room were Curran, Häring, Ratzinger, the secretary of the congregation, Archbishop Alberto Bovone, and two note-takers: American staffer Father Thomas Herron and Father Edouard Hamel, a Jesuit who taught moral theology at the Gregorian University. The session lasted two hours. Häring asked for permission to begin, and did so by presenting a two-page paper entitled "The Frequent and

Long-Lasting Dissent of the Inquisition/Holy Office/CDF from and against the *Opinio (Sententia, Convictio) Communior* as a Major Ecclesiological, Ecumenical and Human Problem." A gauntlet had certainly been flung down! Häring pointed to a number of errors on the part of the Holy Office through history, including the temporal power of the church, the torture and burning of witches, usury, slavery, crackdowns on religious liberty, and the *nouvelle theologie*. Häring's argument was that in these cases the Holy Office had been the real dissenter, and perhaps this was true again in the Curran case.

Ratzinger granted to Curran one of the capital points in his argument, namely that he had never denied a teaching that commanded the assent of faith. Beyond that, however, little real movement occurred in the meeting. Curran asked about the proposed compromise, and Häring urged Ratzinger to accept it. Ratzinger deflected the question, saying the final decision rested with the cardinal members of the congregation. The most difficult moment came when Curran again stressed that his position was very much in the theological mainstream. Ratzinger asked Curran to name others who held his views, and Curran did so—pointedly, they were all German. Ratzinger then asked if Curran would like to accuse these thinkers, because if so the congregation would be happy to open an investigation. Curran said he wished to accuse no one. He was simply pointing out what Ratzinger, an accomplished and respected theologian, obviously knew to be true. This inquisitorial flourish—"Shall we then investigate your friends too?"—struck Curran as inconsistent with Ratzinger's general reputation for personal decency.

Two days after the meeting, Ratzinger wrote to Hickey requesting Curran's final written response to the charges against him, a firm signal that the proposed compromise had been rejected. Curran replied on April 1, 1986, indicating he could not retract the disputed opinions. On July 25, 1986, Ratzinger wrote Curran to inform him that he was being stripped of his right to teach as a Catholic theologian. Despite public declarations of support from most of his theological colleagues, including nine past presidents of the Catholic Theological Society of America, Curran was fired from the Catholic University of America in January 1987. He filed suit, but it was dismissed. As noted earlier, today Curran teaches at Southern Methodist University in Dallas, where he remains a respected and popular theologian.

To this day, Curran believes he was targeted not for the radical nature of his views, which by prevailing theological standards are not radical at all, but for political reasons. In part, it was payback for dissent from *Humanae vitae;* in part, it was a shot across the bow at Catholic moral theology in North America; and it part it was a warning to the entire American Catholic church not to drift too far from Rome's orbit. "They targeted me because the U.S. church is rich and powerful and they wanted to send a message,"

Curran said. "It's hard to avoid the conclusion that these were political calculations."

Curran says he wonders sometimes how personally engaged Ratzinger was with his case. When they met in March 1986, Ratzinger seemed surprised that Curran spoke Italian and in fact seemed not to know that he had studied in Rome (Curran actually holds the very first doctorate awarded by the Alphonsianum, Rome's premier institute of moral theology). Ratzinger also appeared ignorant of the proposed compromise that Hickey and Bernardin had carried to Rome. The American in the doctrinal congregation, Father Tom Herron, filled Ratzinger in quickly on the details during the meeting. In an April 1999 interview with me, Curran said that someone told him that Ratzinger had once said the Curran case was the most difficult he ever had to deal with, but in the end it was taken out of his hands. To Curran, the remark suggested that the decision on his case came from the pope. The comment is reminiscent of von Balthasar's remark that Ratzinger was forced into the silencing of Leonardo Boff. Wherever the final decision came from, it is clear that the arguments employed to justify it were vintage Ratzinger themes, and if he had serious reservations they were never voiced in public.

The most lasting effect of the Curran case was not on moral theology, though many observers believe the discipline has become less creative in its aftermath. Instead the case was a warning to all Catholic theologians about public dissent. Quiet disagreement with magisterial teaching risks a doctrinal review; public agitation for change invites it. The result, in the eyes of many theologians, is that only those few theologians with nothing to lose are likely to voice dissenting opinions, and the whole theological enterprise slows down, becomes more cautious, and produces less thinking and writing of lasting worth.

Curran puts the point this way. He said in April 1999 that if he and Ratzinger somehow ended up trapped on a deserted island together, the one thing he would want to talk to him about would be the need for the hierarchical magisterium to learn before it teaches. "Even in such a fundamental matter as the Trinity, they learned that before they taught it, it wasn't there from the beginning," Curran said. "So how is the learning happening today? And what's the role of the theologian in making it happen?"

The Theologian and the Church

In 1989 and again in 1990, Ratzinger's congregation moved to nail down the relationship between the theologian and the church, and to answer once and for all the question of dissent that had been at the heart of the Curran case.

On March 1, 1989, two new loyalty oaths required of certain office-holders in the church took effect. The first, formally titled a "Profession of Faith," was a revision of an oath that had been in effect since 1967; the second, called the "Oath of Fidelity," was an expanded version of an oath that had previously been required only of bishops. The Profession of Faith contains the Nicene-Constantinopolitan Creed, plus three additional paragraphs that require assent to other types of church teaching. The 1967 profession, adopted in the wake of Vatican II, restricted itself to the creed; the new profession returned the church to a situation similar to the period 1910 to 1967, when the profession had included an oath against modernism issued under Pius X.[10]

Most Catholic universities in the United States did not mandate either the new profession or the oath, though a few did so with much pomp and circumstance. The Franciscan University of Steubenville, Ohio, an aggressively orthodox institution under the leadership of Third Order Franciscan Michael Scanlon, made a point of being the first school in the country to require both from its faculty and administration. Vincentian David O'Connell, the new president of Catholic University, later made headlines in 1998 when he took the loyalty oath upon assuming his office. The vast majority of Catholic university presidents declined to follow suit.

Nineteen eighty-nine was also the year of the Cologne Declaration. Prompted by the appointment of conservative Joachim Mesiner to the archbishop's position in Cologne, Germany, against the wishes of the local church, the Cologne Declaration was issued on January 6, 1989, the Feast of the Epiphany. Signed by 163 theologians from Germany, Austria, Switzerland and the Netherlands, it argued that certain church policies were frustrating the task of carrying the gospel to the world. Those policies included:

- John Paul's appointment of bishops "without respecting the suggestions of the local churches and neglecting their established rights," which runs counter to the Catholic tradition that the selection of bishops "is not some private choice of the pope's";
- the Vatican's refusal to grant official license to theologians with whom it disagrees, part of its general campaign to silence dissent, representing "a dangerous intrusion into the freedom of research and teaching";
- the pope's "overstepping and enforcing in an inadmissible way" his proper doctrinal competence, insisting that every pronouncement of the magisterium be treated as infallible. The declaration called special attention to the ban on birth control.

Complaining that the collegiality called for by Vatican II was "being smothered by a new Roman centralism," the declaration predicted, "If the pope undertakes things that are not part of his role, then he cannot demand obedience in the name of Catholicism. He must expect dissent."[11]

Some of the finest names in Catholic theology signed, including Edward Schillebeeckx, Johann Baptist Metz, Hans Küng, Norbert Greinacher, and Ottmar Fuchs. Others, most prominently Bernard Häring, signed later. Eventually 130 theologians from France, 23 from Spain, 52 from Belgium, and 63 from Italy, including some from Rome itself, signed the statement. The uprising angered Ratzinger, especially because the declaration originated with his old colleagues in Germany. In a press conference after it was issued, Ratzinger suggested that perhaps the theological situation in Germany needed to be reexamined, with an eye toward eliminating some of the teaching positions that seemed redundant or unnecessary. It was an obvious instance of saber-rattling, warning his colleagues that if they continued to rock the boat, the Holy See might pressure the German government under the terms of its concordat to get rid of some of their jobs. In that context, the issuance of the new loyalty oaths struck many theologians as yet another sign from the Vatican that public discontent was not to be tolerated.

One year later, on May 24, 1990, the doctrinal congregation issued a document that came close to providing the systematic treatment of dissent for which Curran had been asking. The *Instruction on the ecclesial vocation of the theologian* amounts to a summary of Ratzinger's vision of the role and mission of the Catholic theologian. In presenting the document to the press, Ratzinger explained why he felt it was necessary.

After their success at Vatican II, many theologians developed a too-exalted view of their profession. "Theologians increasingly felt themselves to be the true teachers of the church and even of the bishops," Ratzinger said. "Moreover, since the council they had been discovered by the mass media and had captured their interest." In this circumstance, it has become necessary to reflect anew on the proper relationship between the theologian and the magisterium.

The bottom line for Ratzinger: "Theology is never simply the private idea of one theologian." The church is the "vital milieu" for the theologian; it is the church, in fact, that makes theological activity possible. Thus for the theologian, there are two traits that are both sine qua non: the first, a methodological rigor that is part and parcel of the business of scholarship; second, "inner participation in the organic structure of the church." Then comes Ratzinger's favorite image: "Only in this symphony does theology come into being." Ratzinger acknowledges there will be tensions between theologians and the magisterium, but sees these tensions as healthy as long as each side sees that its function is "intrinsically ordered to that of the other."

In the press conference, Ratzinger said the instruction "states—perhaps for the first time with such candor—that there are magisterial decisions which cannot be the final word on a given matter as such but, despite the permanent value of their principles, are chiefly also a signal for pastoral prudence, a sort of provisional policy." As examples, he mentions the pontifical statements of the nineteenth century on religious freedom and the antimodernist decisions at the beginning of the twentieth, especially those regarding biblical studies. "Their kernel remains valid, but the particulars determined by circumstances can stand in need of correction," he said.

In the tidal wave of criticism that followed the document, this comment was largely forgotten. Yet it is worth noting that the highest doctrinal authority of the Catholic church publicly acknowledged that on two issues that popes once insisted threatened the very survival of the faith, issues over which theologians were silenced and whole theologies anathematized, the church overreacted. That seems an important concession, and perhaps creates the possibility of further dialogue as to how one determines which papal statements are "definitive" and which are matters of "provisional policy." The document itself asserts that only time can offer this perspective, but even this argument would seem to provide some breathing room for critical theological perspectives. One could justify theological dissent, for example, as a service to future discernment.

The *Instruction on the ecclesial vocation of the theologian* opens with a meditation on the truth as "God's gift to his people." In this connection, the document refers to the "supernatural sense of the faithful." Contrary to some reform-minded Catholics who see the *sensus fidelium* as a pole of opposition to the hierarchy, the document quotes *Lumen gentium* to the effect that this supernatural sense runs "from the bishops to the last of the faithful" when they manifest a "universal consent in matters of faith and morals." Thus for the document, the *sensus fidelium* is not a call to reform so much as a call to conservation; it reminds the faithful of their own responsibility for preserving and passing on the deposit of faith. The document later asserts that Catholic public opinion is especially vulnerable to manipulation in this age of mass media.

The document then turns to the role of the theologian. Theological science is one way to respond to the invitation of faith to explore the truth God communicates to humanity. Its origin is in revealed truth, and in the love for God this truth inspires. In this sense, "the theologian is called to deepen his own life of faith and continuously unite his scientific research with prayer." This will insulate the theologian against a "critical spirit which is born of feeling or prejudice."

The heart of the document's argument about the proper role of the theologian follows. "The freedom proper to theological research is exercised within the church's faith. Thus while the theologian might often feel the urge to be daring in his work, this will not bear fruit or 'edify' unless it is accompanied by that patience which permits maturation to occur." Quoting John Paul II in an address delivered at the Marian shrine in Altötting, Bavaria, the document says, "New proposals advanced for understanding the faith 'are but an offering made to the whole church. Many corrections and broadening of perspectives within the context of fraternal dialogue may be needed before the moment comes when the whole Church can accept them.' "

Knowing that many Catholic theologians invoke academic freedom against oversight by the magisterium, the document argues this is a misunderstanding. "Freedom of research, which the academic community rightly holds most precious, means an openness to accepting the truth that emerges at the end of an investigation in which no element has intruded that is foreign to the methodology corresponding to the object under study. In theology this freedom of inquiry is the hallmark of a rational discipline whose object is given by revelation, handed on and interpreted in the church under the authority of the magisterium, and received by faith. These givens have the force of principles. To eliminate them would mean to cease doing theology."

The document then turns to the function of the magisterium. Most commentary on the instruction skipped this section, because in the wake of the Cologne Declaration and the new loyalty oaths reporters were most interested in what the document said about theologians. Yet the instruction actually has a twin purpose: to call theologians back to fidelity and to call bishops to greater vigilance. "As successors of the apostles, the bishops of the church 'receive from the Lord, to whom all power is given in heaven and on earth, the mission of teaching all peoples, and of preaching the Gospel to every creature, so that all men may attain to salvation. . . .' They have been entrusted then with the task of preserving, explaining, and spreading the Word of God of which they are servants."

The document asserts that the magisterium can make "definitive" pronouncements even in the absence of a formal declaration of infallibility. This argument would reach its logical conclusion in 1998 with the papal document *Ad tuendam fidem,* when penalties for dissent from this category of "definitive" teaching were written into canon law. "By its nature, the task of religiously guarding and loyally expounding the deposit of divine Revelation, implies that the Magisterium can make a pronouncement 'in a definitive way' on propositions which, even if not contained among the truths of faith, are nonetheless intimately connected with them, in such a way that the definitive character of such affirmations derives in the final analysis from revelation itself," the document says.

The document acknowledges that theologians might from time to time have good reasons for doubting a nonirreformable magisterial teaching. "In cases like these, the theologian should avoid turning to the 'mass media,' but have recourse to the responsible authority, for it is not by seeking to exert the pressure of public opinion that one contributes to the clarification of doctrinal issues and renders service to the truth." The document acknowledges that a theologian, faced with a sincere conviction that the church is in error, can be frustrated by the inability to express that conviction in the public forum. "For a loyal spirit, animated by love for the Church, such a situation can certainly prove a difficult trial. It can be a call to suffer for the truth, in silence and prayer, but with the certainty, that if the truth really is at stake, it will ultimately prevail," it says. Above all, turning to the mass media and organized pressure groups threatens the theologian with losing his or her bearings and "conforming to this age."

Critics often find a contradiction in the Vatican's support for religious liberty in the secular realm and its unwillingness to practice freedom of expression inside the church. The document sees this as a false comparison. "One cannot appeal to these rights of man in order to oppose the interventions of the magisterium. Such behavior fails to recognize the nature and mission of the church which has received from the Lord the task to proclaim the truth of salvation to all men. She fulfills this task by walking in Christ's footsteps, knowing that 'truth can impose itself on the mind only by virtue of its own truth, which wins over the mind with both gentleness and power.'" Further, one has to distinguish between oppression of a person and a judgment on certain ideas. "This judgment, however, does not concern the person of the theologian but the intellectual positions which he has publicly espoused. The fact that these procedures can be improved does not mean that they are contrary to justice and right. To speak in this instance of a violation of human rights is out of place for it indicates a failure to recognize the proper hierarchy of these rights as well as the nature of the ecclesial community and her common good."

Finally, the sanctuary of conscience also cannot support a right to dissent. "Setting up a supreme magisterium of conscience in opposition to the magisterium of the Church means adopting a principle of free examination incompatible with the economy of revelation and its transmission in the church and thus also with a correct understanding of theology and the role of the theologian. The propositions of faith are not the product of mere individual research and free criticism of the Word of God but constitute an ecclesial heritage. If a separation occurs from the Bishops who watch over and keep the apostolic tradition alive, it is the bond with Christ which is irreparably compromised."

Ratzinger recognized in a 1993 essay that the document had ignited a controversy "which in part has proceeded in a vehement tone." This is especially so, he ruefully observed, in German-speaking countries. In this essay, published in *Wesen und Auftrag der Theologie* (Nature and mission of theology), he offered a defense. He says the idea that the instruction sees the theologian as a mere delegate of magisterium is "simply false." On the matter of loyalty oaths, he notes that German professors also profess loyaly to the state. "To date it has seemingly not occurred to any German theologian that the oath of loyalty to the constitution which is required of those entering upon state professorships might represent an unreasonable restriction of scholarly freedom and that it might be incompatible with a conscience formed by the Sermon on the Mount."

Ratzinger wonders aloud if the developments of the twelfth century, when theology left the monastery and entered the university, were ultimately positive. Doing so "radically altered its spiritual and scientific complexion," he writes. In the end, this cynicism about the impact of the university seems the fundamental division between Ratzinger and the Catholic theological community.

The Matthew Fox Case

Another sign of the breach between Ratzinger and the Catholic theological community came in the case of the Dominican Matthew Fox, an energetic and endlessly creative theologian who invented what he called "creation spirituality" in order to express a more positive and more ecofriendly vision of Christianity. Fox, an intentionally provocative figure, flirted with New Age ideas, invited a member of Wicca to join his creation spirituality institute in Oakland, and wrote books with titles such as *On Becoming a Musical, Mystical Bear: Spirituality American Style*. In 1998 Fox bowed to Vatican demands that he cease teaching, lecturing, and preaching about creation spirituality.

Fox, then forty-seven, had been under investigation by the congregation since 1984. In a press conference just before beginning his silence, Fox called Ratzinger's objections to his work "unbelievably thin." He was faulted, he said, for referring to God as "Mother" in one of his books. "Yet the Scriptures, the medieval mystics, and even Pope John Paul I all used motherly images for God," Fox stated. "The inability of the Vatican to deal with God as Mother tells us more about the sin of patriarchy than it does about the Godhead." He also was criticized for being a "fervent feminist." "Jesus was a feminist," Fox said in his defense. "I do not understand how any follower of Jesus could be so deaf to the suffering of women in recent western history that she or he would not be a feminist."

Before beginning his "period of silence" on December 15, he issued a scathing evaluation of Ratzinger and the doctrinal congregation. In a sixteen-page open letter to Ratzinger, Fox charged top Vatican leaders with being addicted to power, unfaithful to the examples of Jesus, obsessed with sex, and inflicting a "creeping fascism" on the church.

"I . . . hear deep dissatisfaction from cardinals about your concessions to Marcel Lefebvre and Vatican support of Opus Dei," he wrote Ratzinger. "I hear bishops telling jokes about the Vatican and begging that the pope not come to their diocese lest it, too, be thrown into insurmountable debt; I hear leaders of religious orders telling me that your congregation has 'nothing but third-rate theologians in it.' . . . Yet no one tells you these things. Everyone refuses to confront the person who most needs to hear the truth," Fox wrote.

He likened the church today to "a dysfunctional family where the alcoholic father, for example, is always appeased and placated in hopes that he will not become violent yet another time." Noting that such appeasement only prolongs the illness, he said, "It is time that Catholic theologians, ministers, and laity speak out about the injustices occurring within the Catholic Church." Fox said that "the Vatican's obsession with sex is a worldwide scandal which demonstrates a serious psychic imbalance. . . . Obsession with sex is characteristic of the dysfunctional personality." He charged the Vatican with playing "control games . . . for example, appointing bishops whose only gift is their blind obedience to Vatican edicts."

Continuing the analogy, he said that an organization thus afflicted "refuses to engage in self-evaluation and self-criticism. In its arrogance it sees all its problems as coming from the outside—as if Protestants, liberation theologians, women, homosexual people, theologians of creation spirituality, and the press were the source of the church's problems." Fox suggested the Catholic Church is "reverting to fascism." Citing the popular saying that the church is not a democracy, he said, "Maybe it should be . . . because democracy is much closer to Jesus' understanding of authority, of the example of his servanthood." Surely, he continued, "Jesus did not intend a fascist institution, did he?"

Fox said he found signs of "creeping fascism" in "your [Ratzinger's] method of dealing with diverse opinions by attempting to silence persons and abort meaningful dialogue. In a healthy and inspired organization one would expect discussion and dialogue. . . . Your treatment of scholars is not unlike the burning of books by fascist regimes." A further symptom of fascist tendencies, he said, "is in choosing to reward authoritarian personalities. . . . It concerns me deeply that today's Catholic Church seems to reward authoritarian personalities who are clearly ill, violent, sexually obsessed, and unable to remember the past." He cited as an example the late Cardinal John Cody of Chicago, in whose archdiocese Fox lived and worked for thirteen years. Even before the financial scandal involving Cody that became public shortly before his death, Fox said, "I was asking myself, 'How is it possible that a man of this little morality and spirituality could make it to the top in the Catholic Church?' "

Fox suggested that Ratzinger take a sabbatical. "Why not take a year off and step down from your isolated and privileged life at the Vatican to do circle dances with women and men, some in their twenties, some in their seventies, who come from all over the world in search of an authentic spirituality?" He concluded the letter, "Wishing you compassion, I remain your brother."

In 1992, Fox was formally dismissed from the Dominicans for refusing to give up his work in Oakland to return to his home province of Chicago. "I regret this act of institutional violence done me, my person, and my thirty-four years of service in the Dominican Order," Fox said in a prepared statement. Eventually Fox left the Catholic church to accept ordination as an Episcopal priest. In the mainstream Catholic theological community, Fox was always perceived as something of a gadfly, and few theologians rushed to his defense as they had for Curran. Nevertheless, his letter to Ratzinger, even if the rhetoric was heated, touched a nerve. It put into the language of prophecy many of the complaints that had been rumbling within the theological community, and thus helped to bring into the open issues within the church that were obviously festering.[12]

Ad tuendam fidem

On June 30, 1998, the Vatican released the text of an apostolic letter from John Paul II that added certain provisions to canon law, along with a commentary on the changes authored by Ratzinger. The clear purpose of these changes was to establish definitive but not formally infallible doctrines as a principle of canon law, and to create the basis for punishing those who dissent from them. Because Ratzinger had long asserted the existence of this category of teaching—it was embodied in the 1989 profession of faith—some theologians thought the issuance of Ad tuendam was a nonevent. "In the circles in which I move, this is a nonissue," said Jesuit Joseph O'Hare, president of Fordham College in New York. "The actual content here is a pretty minor housekeeping action . . . it doesn't call for a rush to the barricades."[13]

Many critics said the Ratzinger commentary was actually more worrisome than the papal letter. In it he offered several examples of definitive teaching that had not been infallibly declared, including the bans on abortion, euthanasia, and women priests, and, as was discussed in chapter 6, the invalidity of Anglican ordinations.

Taken together, the understanding of church teaching expressed in *Ad tuendam* and the Ratzinger commentary may be schematized in the following way.

Divinely Revealed

This highest category of teaching includes doctrines contained in the Word of God, written or handed down, and defined with a solemn judgment of the church as divinely revealed truths by any of the following:

- The Pope speaking *ex cathedra*
- The College of Bishops gathered in council
- Infallibly proposed by the ordinary and universal Magisterium

Examples would include: the articles of faith of the creed; the various christological dogmas; the various Marian dogmas; the doctrine of the real and substantial presence of Christ in the Eucharist; the doctrine on the primacy and infallibility of the pope; the doctrine on the existence of original sin.

Definitively Proposed

Doctrines definitively proposed by the Church on faith and morals which are necessary for faithfully keeping and expounding the deposit of faith, even if they have not been proposed by the magisterium of the church as *formally* revealed. They can be:

- defined by the pope;
- defined by the College of Bishops gathered in council;
- taught infallibly by the ordinary and universal magisterium of the church.

Such doctrines are joined to revealed truths by a historical relationship or by a logical connection. Even though they are not proposed as formally revealed they could, by dogmatic development, one day be declared as revealed. Examples of doctrines connected by historical necessity include the legitimacy of the election of a given pope, the acts of an ecumenical council, the canonizations of saints, the declaration of Pope Leo XIII in the apostolic letter *Apostolicae curae* on the invalidity of Anglican ordinations. Examples of doctrines connected by logical necessity include the doctrine that priestly ordination is reserved only to men, the doctrine on the illicitness of euthanasia, the teaching on the illicitness of prostitution, the teaching on the illicitness of fornication.

Authentic Ordinary Magisterium

Teachings presented as true, or at least as sure, even if they have not been defined with a solemn judgment or proposed as definitive by the ordinary and universal magisterium, whether of the pope or of the College of Bishops. Examples would include comments made by the pope during his general audiences, the pastoral letters of bishops or the pope, the documents of the Roman curia when issued with the approval of the pope.

Although some theologians thought *Ad tuendam* simply codified what the pope and Ratzinger had been claiming all along, others saw the decision to amend canon law in this way as momentous. The French Jesuit theologian Bernard Sesboué, for example, wrote, "We are in the presence of a new domain of the exercise of infallibility of the church." For that reason, Sesboué said *Ad tuendam* is a development virtually as grave as the declaration of papal infallibility at Vatican I in 1870. This argument was echoed by Father Ladislas Örsy of Georgetown University in the United States.

Responding to Örsy in the Irish journal *Céide,* Ratzinger insisted that the new canonical language in *Ad tuendam* simply codified the "secondary object of infallibility" to which Vatican II had referred. He said it was not true that Vatican II had envisioned getting rid of sanctions and penalties for theological dissent. Moreover, he said many bishops in the world today wish canon law were even harsher in some respects, so they could deal more easily with priests guilty of pedophilia. In any event, Ratzinger says the purpose of the 1989 profession of faith and oath of fidelity, as well as *Ad tuendam,* is simply to clarify the three-fold division of teaching that has always been implicit in the tradition. He also says that his own commentary, where he listed several controversial examples of such teaching, is not itself a magisterial document. It was not "given a binding force"; it was simply "an aid for the understanding of the texts"; and "no one need feel an authoritarian imposition or restriction by these texts."[14]

The Cost

The actions of the doctrinal congregation under Ratzinger's stewardship have created deep divisions between the magisterium and the theological community. On this point even many of his supporters would agree. "It's a really unfortunate thing that a high level of irritation among many academic theologians has developed," said Michael Waldstein, an Austrian theologian who spent several years teaching at the University of Notre Dame. "I saw it when I was at Notre Dame. It would have helped a lot if Ratzinger had reached out more."

It is not that Ratzinger lacks defenders within the theological community. "I do not believe any credible case could be made for him as an authoritarian," said Dominican Augustine Di Noia, theological adviser for the U.S. bishops' conference, in an April 1999 interview. "Faith is not the suppression of intelligence, but its exaltation. The fundamental divide between dissenting or revisionist theologians and the mode of John Paul II and Ratzinger lies along this fault. Ratzinger is stating points which would have been totally noncontroversial even fifty years ago," Di Noia said.

Yet Di Noia, despite his official status and his reputation as an able and gracious theologian, represents a distinctly minority view within the professional Catholic theological community. The majority view seems closer to that expressed by Curran: "It's not a matter of authority versus conscience. Truth is the third term, and to that extent Ratzinger is right. The problem is that he has too readily identified the truth with what the magisterium has taught at a given moment. The Holy Office cannot have a copyright on what it means to be Catholic." Curran and others suggest that Ratzinger is responsible for what they call a "chill factor," a climate of fear in the theological community that discourages honesty in areas such as sexual ethics, religious pluralism, and political theology. Thinkers in these areas are conditioned, critics say, to fear censure, silencing, and excommunication should they go too far. "The type of theologians most subject to this pressure today are those who are priests, religious or employed in seminaries," Tom Reese said.

Some critics have compared this "chill factor" to the antimodernist drive of Pius X in the first decade of the twentieth century. In both cases, they argue, conservative popes set out to stem theological currents that had developed under their moderate predecessors. The pastoral and intellectual toll exacted by the antimodernist drive, by most accounts, was vast. "Everything went underground," said Jay Dolan, a church history expert at Notre Dame. "Good work was still being done, but it was done out of public view—in liturgy, in Scripture studies. Seminarians coming up through the system weren't learning anything creative. It wasn't exactly brain rot, but it was an unhealthy situation." Dolan says the more exact parallel to the Ratzinger campaign may be with what happened under Pius XII after the publication of *Humani generis* in 1950. That encyclical, condemning modernizing tendencies in theology, led to the silencing or intimidation of some of the leading theologians of the time, such as the American Jesuit John Courtney Murray, widely regarded as the driving force behind Vatican II's document on religious liberty. Many of the same thinkers would later emerge as key advisers at the council.

Theologians sympathetic to Ratzinger scoff at suggestions of a similar "chill factor" today. Waldstein said he did not see evidence of a repressive climate at Notre Dame. "Observing Richard McBrien and Dick McCormick reasonably closely, I don't think they were in the least crimped or limited by what was done to Charlie Curran, for example. McBrien proposed that Curran be hired at Notre Dame. In the new *Encyclopedia of Catholicism*, Curran wrote the article on contraception. In actual fact, taking these guys as examples, I don't see that their action has been limited by what was imposed," Waldstein said. Others, however, say that the good fortune of a few high-profile theologians in evading Vatican scrutiny is not a reliable bellwether for the true state of the discipline.

Reese argues that Ratzinger might have better luck if he just let theology alone. "The mistake the Vatican makes is to not realize that the theological community is a self-correcting community of scholars, like any other discipline," Reese said. "Often the worst thing the Vatican can do is to condemn a theologian, because no one will criticize that person for fear of looking like a toady of the Vatican." He mentioned Hans Küng's position on papal infallibility and certain elements in liberation theology as examples.

In the end, how can Ratzinger justify the high level of antagonism that even his supporters concede exists between theologians and his office? In the typical style of the Vatican, Ratzinger "thinks in centuries." He is not looking to win today's battle, his supporters say, but to shape the way the church thinks about a controversy 200 years from now. "I think he and John Paul are thinking very much in the long run," Waldstein said. "In the present, the fronts of discussion are often very hard. It isn't easy to sway people's minds. I've yet to meet a theologian who said before *Humanae vitae* that I was in favor of contraception, but then I changed my mind. That's not the kind of response they're looking for. In the long run, when some of the controversies of the present are forgotten, then you can expect an impact."

As a case in point, Waldstein looks to Jansenism, a theological movement premised on certain views of grace and freedom popular in seventeenth-century Europe. "At the time, papal condemnations did not have the effect of convincing the theologians in Paris to change their minds," Waldstein said. "But when people eventually had the wherewithal to oppose it, they had the papal documents in place. Today Jansenism is not a viable force."Reese argues that a sober perusal of church history does not warrant such confidence. "The record of the Vatican in this area is not very good, considering that many theologians condemned in the past now are recognized as great thinkers and loyal churchmen," Reese said, such as Congar and Murray. "There's a clear historical record of the Vatican condemning people and later having to say, 'Sorry, they're really fine theologians.' "

"Faithful Catholics do want to surrender to authority," said Yale's Margaret Farley, who said she admires Ratzinger as a theologian. "But it's so clear to most people that not all voices are heard. If there is to be a center to speak for the church, its credibility depends in part on whether it has listened to the faithful." In the eyes of many of his peers, and even some of his admirers in the Catholic theological community, Joseph Ratzinger's legacy will be a diminishment in the credibility of church authority. By insisting so strongly on the need for theologians to bind themselves to the church, many believe Ratzinger has eclipsed the even more fundamental need for both to bind themselves to the gospel—and to stand under its judgment.

8

Ratzinger and the Next Conclave

Various versions of an old joke still make the rounds on the Internet and in clerical circles. Hans Küng, Leonardo Boff, and Joseph Ratzinger die at the same time and appear together in a waiting room outside St. Peter's gates. Peter appears and points at Küng, saying: "Jesus will see you now." Küng disappears into an office, leaving the other two men waiting. After more than two hours, Küng emerges with an expression of wonder on his face: "How could I have been so mistaken?" he asks. Next, Peter gestures to Boff. The fiery Brazilian liberation theologian is gone for more than five hours. He, too, eventually stumbles out of the office, dumbfounded. "How could I have been so foolish?" he asks, dazed. Finally Peter gestures to Ratzinger. His Eminence rises, gathers his papers, and walks slowly into the office. The better part of a day goes by, and periodically sounds of shouting and then weeping fill the air. Eventually the door swings open . . . and Jesus Christ himself walks out, asking: "How could I have gotten everything so wrong?"

The joke serves as a summary of how many observers see Ratzinger: more Catholic than Jesus.

Joseph Ratzinger is, in terms of public opinion in the Catholic church, a chiaroscuro figure, all light and shadow, few hues in between. This polarized reaction is reflected in the habit of the European press of referring to Ratzinger as the "Panzer Kardinal," and the frequent plays on the cardinal's name in progressive Catholic circles ("Rat-zinger" being the most obvious). The scorn sometimes shades off into rage. One of the more lurid stories that broke in the Catholic world in late 1999, for example, concerned a Web site for gay priests and religious that had been hacked into by a right-wing group. The hackers collected E-mails and pictures from the site and made them available to the wider world. The images were graphic indeed, but the E-mails were remarkable less for their sexual content, which ranged from tender to sophomoric, than for the vitriol that sluiced through them about Ratzinger. The clergy and, in one case, a South African auxiliary bishop called Ratzinger a "Nazi in Rome" and "Der Fürher's Oberst Ratzinger." There were joking references to his need for sex, even to the possibility of killing him. It was obvious that Ratzinger had become the focus for the anger these men felt about the church.

On the other extreme are teary-eyed admirers of Ratzinger, often eager to place a halo on his head themselves. Lutheran convert Richard John Neuhaus in his journal *First Things,* recently wrote, "Many of his admirers think his appointment as prefect of the Congregation for the Doctrine of the Faith deprived the church of the enormous contribution he would have made through his writing and teaching. Others are immeasurably grateful that John Paul II called him to a universal classroom where, in a time of darkened confusion, he has encouraged students beyond number in rekindling lights of theological inquiry in service to Christ and his church, and therefore in service to the world." Neuhaus called Ratzinger "the greatest intellectual influence in shaping the direction of the Catholic Church over these past twenty years" next to the pope. Ratzinger's graduate student and U.S. publisher, Jesuit Joseph Fessio, makes no bones about it; he predicts the cardinal will be remembered as one of the great saints of this age.

Ratzinger is a polarizing figure in a way that John Paul II is not. Popes are evaluated based on their policies *ad extra,* in the outside world, as well as *ad intra,* or inside the church. With respect to John Paul, there is little serious debate over the course he has steered *ad extra:* he has spoken vigorously in favor of human rights and religious freedom to wide acclaim. Catholics are proud that their pope helped bring down communism, and they even admire him when he takes political stands against the death penalty or against abortion with which they do not fully agree. It is his policies *ad intra* that have proved bitterly divisive—the suppression of theologians, the rollback of Vatican II reforms, the steady recentralization of authority in Rome. On most of these matters, Joseph Ratzinger and not Karol Wojtyla has been the architect of the disputed policies.

There is a conservative element within Roman Catholicism that disagrees with John Paul's policies *ad intra* from a different vantage point. They objected to the 1986 Assisi gathering of world religious leaders on the grounds that it promoted syncretism and compromised the teaching that Roman Catholicism is the unique medium of salvation; they feel the pope's 1988 *indult* permitting use of the Latin Mass did not go nearly far enough and has been allowed to languish; they fear Wojtyla's fondness for philosophical personalism has facilitated the collapse of a distinctly Catholic approach to philosophy in universities and seminaries; and they watched the 2000 "Day of Pardon" liturgy in horror, fearing that the pope was handing an enormous victory to the enemies of the church by offering apologies for a litany of supposed offenses. For this faction, Ratzinger is often viewed as a standard-bearer because he is assumed to share their critique.

It is for these reasons that I believe the next papal conclave will be, in effect, a referendum on Ratzinger. Moderates to progressives within the College of Cardinals will be looking for someone unlike Ratzinger to steer a new course ad intra; conservatives will be looking for someone like Ratzinger to do exactly the same thing, but in a vastly different direction. In that rare moment of democracy in the Catholic church, when 120 or so members of the College of Cardinals vote in a series of secret ballots for the next supreme pontiff, it will be Ratzinger's legacy that hangs in the balance, more so than that of John Paul. The cardinals will be looking either for a candidate who shares Ratzinger's vision of the church or one who repudiates it.

That is not to say the cardinals will be voting for or against Ratzinger the man. The debate in the next conclave will not pivot on Joseph Ratzinger personally, but on his ecclesiology, his understanding of authority, and the ecclesial *ancien regime* he has spent the last twenty years of his enormously talented life defending.

Could Ratzinger Be Pope?

When the College of Cardinals next processes into the Sistine Chapel for a papal election, Joseph Ratzinger will almost certainly be among them. He is seventy-three, with seven more years before he becomes ineligible to take part. Twice before Ratzinger has filed into a conclave, both in 1978, and both times the international press feted him as *papabile,* a candidate to be pope. In the second conclave of 1978, Ratzinger is rumored to have been one of the kingmakers who engineered the election of Karol Wojtyla.

Today Ratzinger is by far the single most famous member of the College of Cardinals. The nearest competitor would be Carlo Maria Martini of Milan, the perennial liberal front-runner for the papacy. Ratzinger possesses well-recognized intellectual gifts and has obvious Vatican experience. He speaks all the right languages, and on a personal level he is charming. For most of Ratzinger's twenty years in Rome, the German press has assumed that he was next in line for the top job. As recently as two or three years ago, bookmakers across Europe still gave him good odds. Today, however, despite his undeniable attractions, it is widely assumed by Vaticanologists that Ratzinger is out of the running, a combination of both age and controversy. Poor health is also a consideration. In September 1991 Ratzinger had a cerebral hemorrhage that affected his left field of vision; in August 1992 he fell against a radiator and was knocked unconscious, bleeding profusely. Though he is now said to be fully recovered, the possibility of another John Paul I (who died after thirty days in office) worries electors.

Church-watchers say different things about Ratzinger's chances. Fessio thinks he could be elected. "If the present pope died suddenly, they might want an older person for interim continuity," he told me in 1999. "Ratzinger has many abilities the rest of the cardinals are aware of—his command of languages, his knowledge of cultures, his knowledge of the faith." Fellow Jesuit Tom Reese, however, editor of *America* magazine, says it won't happen. For one thing, Ratzinger would be almost seventy-five, and Reese doesn't think the cardinals will elect someone so close to the official retirement age. Anyway, Ratzinger has "become too controversial. They will look for someone who can heal divisions rather than exacerbate them," Reese said. He added, "I could be wrong."

So could we all; and Reese may indeed be wrong about the age factor. Although no one wants another John Paul I, they also are unlikely to want a repeat of John Paul II's twenty-year-plus papacy, already the sixth longest in history. It seems likely the cardinals will lean toward an older man. Moreover, Angelo Roncalli was nearly seventy-seven when he was elected as John XXIII in 1959. Ratzinger has at least one declared supporter within the college, the Italian Cardinal Silvio Oddi, who said in 1996 that Ratzinger was the only man he could support: "I like his way of doing things, his intelligence, his faith."[1] Unfortunately for Ratzinger's candidacy, Oddi is eighty-nine and hence well past the age limit of eighty to cast a ballot.

In the end, I see four reasons Ratzinger will probably not become Pius XIII (the name by which he might choose to be known, associating himself with the conservative papacies of Pius IX, X, and XII; or, given his fondness for the North African church fathers, he might select Clement XV after Clement of Alexandria; or he could recognize his Bavarian roots by becoming Ludwig I, in the same way Wojtyla briefly flirted with being called Stanislaus I as a nod to Poland).

1. Ratzinger will not be pope because he has little pastoral experience. The curial cardinals call the shots in Rome, but the diocesan cardinals are by far the numerical majority and hence have the votes to put one of their own in the top job. Because the pope must himself be a pastor, both to the Rome diocese and in a sense to the universal church, many cardinals consider it essential that he have a record as a good diocesan leader. Ratzinger was a pastor for a scant three years, as archbishop of Munich, and drew mixed reviews. Moreover, because many residential cardinals seem to feel that too much power has been concentrated in the curia

during the waning years of John Paul's pontificate, it seems even less likely they would elect the man who personifies that concentration of authority. This block of cardinals will want someone with the strength to stand up to the church's bureaucracy, but not someone who will govern the church like a member of the curia himself. This is the single greatest drawback to a Ratzinger candidacy.

2. Ratzinger will not be pope because he is a non-Italian European. As is well known, most popes have been Italians. There is a body of opinion that holds, all things being equal, the pope *should* be Italian. He is the bishop of Rome; moreover, there is something inescapably Italian in both the operational style and the mentality of the Vatican, and in some ways only an insider can fully understand its ways. Alongside this preference, however, there will be another block of opinion in the next conclave, shaped by awareness that they are electing the first pope of the third Christian millennium. That reality will call for a forward-looking choice, and given that by 2020 some eighty percent of the world's Christians will live in the southern hemisphere, this view would point to a pope from the Third World. That could mean an African, a Latin American, even an Asian. What it will not mean is another pope from the Old World, especially one so seemingly locked into classically European values and attitudes. Whether the pendulum swings to an Italian or a candidate from the Third World, therefore, Ratzinger's prospects are dim.

3. Ratzinger will not be pope because he is too identified with the policies of the current papacy. As many students of papal elections have noted, there is a *contrapasso* dynamic that often develops in a conclave, where cardinals look for a candidate to remedy whatever they perceive to be the failings of the pope who has just died. This explains why men almost entirely appointed by one pope can elect someone quite different to succeed him, as was the case when Pius XII gave way to John XXIII. Most observers believe that John Paul's pontificate has been a bruising, divisive one within the church. In that light, the cardinals will likely be seeking a unifier, someone who can heal wounds and bring people together. They will probably conclude Ratzinger is not that person. Oddi, Ratzinger's avowed supporter, acknowledged that the custom of following "a fat pope with a lean one," meaning someone completely different, would count against his man.

4. Ratzinger will not be pope because he cannot get the votes. Even in today's church, there remains a core of moderate-to-progressive cardinals large enough to prevent any candidate from obtaining a two-thirds vote in a conclave if they act in a united fashion. There is every reason to believe that a Ratzinger candidacy might unify them in an opposition role.

Of course, under new conclave rules promulgated by John Paul II in 1988, after thirty ballots spread over at least twelve days, only a majority is needed to elect a pope. But it seems far-fetched that a conservative pro-Ratzinger coalition could hold together that long simply for the sake of electing someone who would, from the very beginning, be perceived as a weakened pope because he could not be elected through the normal process.[2]

A Ratzinger Papacy

What if this analysis is wrong and Ratzinger is elected? In the main, his papacy would likely take shape along predictable lines. He would pursue an accelerated "reform of the reform" in liturgy, probably encouraging a limited return to Latin, experiments with the altar turned toward the East rather than the people, and placing the focus in worship more on the transcendent and less on the assembly; he would ensure that theological speculation is contained within fairly narrow limits, and that where theologians are required to have a mandate, they honor its terms; and he would continue the erosion of national bishops' conferences as counterweights to Roman authority. He would travel less, projecting a more ethereal style reminiscent of Pius XII.

One can, however, anticipate elements of a Ratzinger pontificate that would come as a surprise to the general Catholic public, and that would mark a departure from the policies of Wojtyla. Three points especially suggest themselves.

No Ex corde Fight

One of the longest and most public controversies in the United States during John Paul II's papacy came over the fate of Catholic colleges and universities. In 1990, the pope issued an apostolic constitution entitled *Ex corde ecclesiae,* calling on Catholic colleges to reemphasize their links with the church. In part, the document was motivated by fear that the 240-plus Catholic colleges in the United States would go the way of their Protestant counterparts, gradually becoming secularized. To Vatican officials, watching prestigious Catholic institutions such as Georgetown convulsed in debates about whether to display such minimum tokens of Catholicity as crucifixes in the classroom, this prospect seems all too real. The most controversial provision of the pope's document requires Catholic theologians to receive a *mandatum,* or license, from their local bishop. After years of controversy, the U.S. bishops finally approved a set of norms to implement *Ex corde* in 1999 that gave the Vatican most of what it wanted.

Under Ratzinger, the Vatican would be much less likely to expend its resources struggling to preserve institutions it perceives as already lost to secularism. In *Milestones,* Ratzinger reflected on the German church's desperate struggle to hold onto its schools under the Nazis, concluding that the wiser course would have been to let them go. "Already then it dawned on me that, with their insistence on preserving institutions, these letters [from the bishops] in part misread the reality. I mean that merely to guarantee institutions is useless if there are no people to support those institutions from inner conviction." Ratzinger said that the older generation of teachers in the Third Reich was largely anticlerical, whereas the younger was pro-Nazi. "So in both these cases it was inane to insist on an institutionally guaranteed Christianity," he concluded.

Applied to the current debate over Catholic colleges, Ratzinger's instinct in at least some cases would be to drop the pretense that these are still Catholic institutions. He would likely allow them to go their own way, in exchange for abandoning their claim to church affiliation. He said in *Salt of the Earth:* "Once the church has acquired some good or position, she inclines to defend it. The capacity for self-moderation and self-pruning is not adequately developed. . . it's precisely the fact that the church clings to the institutional structure when nothing really stands behind it any longer that brings the church into disrepute."

The point applies not just to colleges, but also to hospitals, social service centers, and other institutions operated by the church. In St. Louis, a bitter fight erupted in 1997 between the president of the Jesuit St. Louis University and the local bishop over the president's right to sell his school's teaching hospital. The archbishop, Justin Rigali, tried to block the sale. Eventually a compromise was struck, leaving the core issue largely unresolved: who owns the hospital, the bishop or the religious community? Here again, a Ratzinger papacy would be much more hesitant to throw resources at maintaining institutions that, at least in his eyes, appear Catholic in name only. Ratzinger's governing metaphor for the church of the future is the mustard seed: it will have to be smaller to be faithful, and that may mean casting off some of its institutions that have lost their spiritual elan vital.

Shrinking Church Government

Because Ratzinger is the prime theoretician of papal authority, it is often assumed that under a Ratzinger papacy the Vatican machinery would take on even more massive proportions. In fact, like most conservatives, Ratzinger feels an instinctive aversion to big government. He believes that bureaucracies become self-perpetuating and take on their own agendas, rarely reflecting the best interests of the people they are intended to serve. His experience of Germany, where the Catholic church has the most extensive ecclesial infrastructure anywhere in the world because of the country's church tax, has cemented that impression. Ratzinger's mistrust of church bureaucrats is a large part of his dislike of bishops' conferences.

"The power typical of political rule or technical management cannot be and must not be the style of the church's power," Ratzinger wrote in 1988's *A New Song for the Lord*. "In the past two decades an excessive amount of institutionalization has come about in the church, which is alarming. . . . Future reforms should therefore aim not at the creation of yet more institutions, but at their reduction."[3]

Ratzinger would not hesitate to make decisions in Rome that others believe should be the province of the local church; for instance, revoking imprimaturs, replacing translations, and dismissing theologians. However, he would not erect a large new Vatican apparatus for this purpose. Priority areas such as doctrine and liturgy might attract new resources, but many other offices would likely be combined or even eliminated. Hence the Pontifical Council for Interreligious Dialogue and the Pontifical Council for Promoting Christian Unity might be merged with a smaller staff and restricted mandate; the Synod of Bishops, a supposedly consultative body whose usefulness Ratzinger has always doubted, might well be eliminated. Further, Ratzinger would encourage bishops' conferences and dioceses to shed layers of bureaucracy where possible. The overall thrust would be for smaller size, less paperwork, and more focus on core concerns.

Better Bishops

Most Vatican watchers would agree that the greatest failing of the Wojtyla pontificate is the mediocre quality of many of his episcopal appointments. Some have been spectacularly bad, such as Wolfgang Haas in Switzerland, Hans Hermann Gröer and Kurt Krenn in Austria, Jan Gijsen in Holland, and Fabian Bruskewitz in Lincoln, Nebraska. These men, bellicose and divisive, have badly destabilized their respective dioceses, countries, and bishops' conferences.

Why does John Paul make such short-sighted appointments? Two reasons seem most plausible. First, the pope has made doctrinal reliability the sine qua non of higher office, and thus a given nominee's loyalty covers a multitude of other sins. Second, the pope appears to favor appointing extremists when he feels it is useful in balancing a bishops' conference that has swung too far to the left. He felt the Dutch had gotten out of control after Vatican II, which explains Gijsen as well as the extraordinary Dutch synod in 1980; similarly, he worried that Cardinal Franz König of Vienna had allowed things to drift in Austria, and he knew Krenn would push them sharply back to the right. These appointments have been a form of "shock therapy."

According to Austrian journalist Norbert Stanzel, when König retired in 1985, the pope's personal secretary Stanislaw Dziwisz, a friend of Krenn, told the Congregation for Bishops that the pope had Krenn in mind as König's successor. John Paul had earlier made Krenn an auxiliary in Vienna with special responsibility for cultural affairs; this appointment was widely ridiculed after Krenn admitted on national television that he could not name a single living Austrian artist, painter, poet, sculptor, novelist, musician, or scientist. Though it has never been conclusively established, it is widely believed in Austria that Ratzinger blocked Krenn's appointment to the cardinal's post. Stanzel reported the theory in his 1999 biography of Krenn, *Die Geisel Gottes* (The scourge of God). Krenn had studied under Ratzinger at Tübingen in 1965, and the two were colleagues on the theology faculty at Regensburg during the 1970s. Sources told Stanzel that Ratzinger had strong personal reservations about Krenn. Though Stanzel does not spell out what those reservations are, it is not hard to guess; beneath Krenn's absolute loyalty to the pope is a personality that craves the spotlight and cannot be happy outside a verbal boxing ring. Ratzinger knew that Krenn would be a disaster in a high-profile forum such as Vienna.[4]

Given his long years of observing and evaluating potential prelates (he serves on the Congregation for Bishops), Ratzinger would know the backgrounds of most of his appointees quite well and would be able to spot potential loose cannons. Moreover, Ratzinger is his own man; there has never been any suggestion that his secretary, Monsignor Josef Clemens, exercises over him anything like the influence Dziwisz has with John Paul. Hence backdoor channels would be less likely to generate surprise picks. Ratzinger's appointments would be solidly conservative, on occasion even reactionary, but they would also generally be men of intelligence and solid administrative skill. Especially as Ratzinger's deconstruction of bishops' conferences accelerated, he would feel the importance of appointing good diocesan bishops all the more acutely.

Listening to Ratzinger

Because Ratzinger is a polarizing figure, reaction to him is often uncritical, driven more by emotion and instinct than sober reflection. Progressives do not read his books, they disregard his public statements, and they assume every position he takes is based on power politics; conservatives revere most of what he says as holy writ, often spouting it mindlessly without penetrating to the principle or value he sees at stake. Neither response takes Ratzinger seriously. Any challenge to Ratzinger will seem incredible to all but the most ardent ideologues if it is not accompanied by a grasp of his legitimate insights. I offer four points that have stayed with me after spending more than a year of my life listening—listening *hard*—to Ratzinger.

First, Ratzinger makes an urgently important point about submission to the truth. As sons and daughters of consumer culture conditioned to seek gratification, we are too often tempted to repress or rationalize truths that get in our way. We recoil at limits on our freedom, failing to distinguish between those limits that imprison because they are arbitrary, and those that liberate because they are rooted in our nature. We break faith and abandon commitments, and rationalize doing so on the basis of "growth" or "change"; we choose the path of least resistance and then exalt "choice" into a moral principle. No one who listens to our political discourse, where content has been replaced by spin, can escape the sense that something toxic has been unleashed in this society. Ratzinger is right that a culture of lies reaches its apogee in Auschwitz, because when truth no longer puts limits to power, everyone is at risk. We need to recover faith in a standard beyond ourselves, in a truth that exists beyond the reach of our own subjectivity.

Of course, the modern revolt against objectivity was, in its origins, partly a rebellion against ecclesiastical authority that abused the concept of truth to secure its own power. One can argue that Ratzinger's concern for truth is not fully consistent unless he renounces the inquisitorial abuses that helped make skepticism seem plausible in the first place. But that caveat does not make Ratzinger's warning any less important, or his insight into the modern condition any less penetrating.

Second, Ratzinger is right when he talks about the diachronic nature of the sense of the faithful. I am reminded of G. K. Chesterton's argument that tradition is nothing more than democracy extended through time, that it is precisely a sense of tradition that protects the church against the tyranny of the present. Too often one hears activists on all sides of church debates cite poll numbers, petition drives or Mass attendance numbers as if, by themselves, they justify whatever cause they are advocating. From a Catholic point of view, such data is incomplete. We are linked in a sacramental bond with generations that have gone before, and their voices too must be heard. Thus Ratzinger is correct that a cavalier disregard of tradition, or movements that pay lip service to tradition but in truth care only about interest-group politics of the moment, are missing an essential element of Catholicity.

One can press the point farther. Just reading the magisterial documents of ages past, though important, is not enough to express the sense of the faithful; we also have to consider the hopes, dreams, and beliefs of past generations of Catholics as embodied in their songs and their devotions, in their literature and their art, in their cathedrals and their homes, in the faith life that pulses through virtually every aspect of Catholic culture in different eras and in different places. This means a deliberate, even conservative approach to change; it also means, however, an ecclesiology in which the voice of the whole people of God is essential.

Ratzinger is also right that belonging to a disparate, global family of faith means that we can't always shape the church in our image. In the inevitable tension between fidelity to one's own vision and preserving the community, being Catholic sometimes means picking the latter. Progressives must acknowledge that it is possible the Catholic world may not be ready to abandon calling God "father," or to celebrate homosexual marriages; conservatives need to see that we may not be prepared to go back to Latin or to communion on the tongue. If some believers choose to strive toward those goals, the Catholic instinct is to do so from within the *kononia,* the community. While one should not apply the point uncritically, there is a need for Catholics to practice a "religious submission" that trusts in the church, in its future if not always its present. Inculturation is not merely a one-way street, as if it is exclusively the church's task to adjust itself to me. I, too, must acculturate to the church. Although open defiance such as the breakaway Spiritus Christi faith community in Rochester, New York, or the Lefevrite Pius X movement, or more quiet schisms such as women's eucharistic communities may satisfy aggrieved parties on a short-term basis, in the end they can signal a loss of faith in the church.

Finally, Ratzinger sounds an important warning about the dangers of being mesmerized by the culture. We live in a world in which the average person is exposed to 1,600 commercial messages per day, in which massive corporate interests determine what news we hear and what drama we watch, in which a feel-good ideology encourages consumption and frivolity. Meanwhile, thousands of children die each day of hunger and preventable disease. In the United States we complain when gas prices rise above $1.25 a gallon, while more than 500,000 Iraqi children have died under the impact of sanctions whose stated purpose is to promote political and military stability in the Middle East, and whose obvious though unstated aim is to ensure a steady flow of oil to the world market. Closer to home, we live in a world in which it is possible to be beaten to death simply for being gay, or black, or homeless, or a woman, or simply for *being.* For all the good that stirs continually in human hearts, there is something infernal about our culture, and we Christians are, with a few courageous exceptions, far too comfortable inside it.

Ratzinger has said, rightly: "We ought to have the courage to rise up against what is regarded as 'normal' for a person at the end of the twentieth century and to rediscover faith in its simplicity." The point leads to some questions for church practice: Should parishes be scheduling five Masses every Sunday, sundering our sense of community for the sake of convenience? Should pastors offer general absolution because people today feel "more comfortable" with it? Should we strive to make liturgy more relevant, moral teachings more achievable, catechetics more fun? Or do we need, in at least some of these cases, to be less accommodating, to insist upon inconvenience and discomfort in order to reawaken our people to the "sign of contradiction" that Christian faith is supposed to be? Shouldn't we be fostering our ability to resist? These are judgments that cannot be made without an intimate knowledge of a particular community and its needs, but they are questions that I fear are too infrequently asked.

Perhaps it is ironic that this call to be countercultural should come from the Vatican, an institution that borrowed its form directly from the Roman Empire and one that continues to practice the hierarchical politics of a royal court. But in his insistence that Christian spirituality must not skip from Incarnation to Resurrection without passing through the Passion, that Christians must sometimes invite scorn and embrace sacrifice in order to be faithful, Ratzinger is striking exactly the note his church needs to hear.

Truth, tradition, communion, the cross—these are values Joseph Ratzinger has defended in an era when they are often ignored and, for just that reason, desperately needed. Catholicism, and the broader culture, should be grateful.

Five Questions for the Conclave

With these positive contributions in mind, the next conclave still shapes up as a referendum on Ratzinger; specifically, on his theological attitudes and policies that have dominated the church for two decades. This referendum can be analyzed in terms of five questions facing Catholicism as it enters its third millennium.

1. What Is the Relationship between the Universal and the Local Church?

Under Ratzinger's influence, a Platonic conception of church has dominated this pontificate. A 1992 document from the doctrinal congregation on *Some aspects of the church understood as communion* contains the key line, asserting that the universal church is "a reality ontologically and temporally prior to every individual particular church." Among other places where one can discern its influence, this idea formed the theological heart of John Paul II's May 1998 apostolic letter *Apostolos suos* denying bishops' conferences the authority to teach. Ratzinger has argued that the universal church is the prime reality, with local churches after-the-fact expressions in space and time of this metaphysical unity. Christ came to proclaim the universal church; the apostles then founded local communities to spread its message.

In practical terms, Ratzinger's stress on the universal church at the expense of the local translates into a strong emphasis on centralization in Rome and on loyalty to the papacy. Ratzinger has said that the local church is church *at all* only to the extent that it is in communion with the pope; without the "Petrine principle," a particular assembly is simply not the church.

Ratzinger's "ontologically prior" universal church seems to float above human concerns, existing in an ethereal realm of pure contemplation. The danger in this view has been expressed by Nathan Mitchell, a liturgist at the University of Notre Dame, in a simple question: "Who belongs to it?" His point is that an ontologically prior church is a disincarnate church, a docetic particle of eternity that appears in history but exists in its most real sense apart from it. Under Ratzinger, the model of an ontologically prior universal church has meant that the voice of human experience rising up from local communities has found little echo in Rome. First World churches have been frustrated in their attempts to open doors to the legitimate aspirations of emancipated women; Third World churches have been rebuffed in calls for inculturation and open-ended dialogue with other religious traditions. An ontologically prior church in practice tends to be a static church, a teaching rather than a learning church, a corporate headquarters with franchisees rather than a genuine communion. Almost by definition, it cannot learn from experience, because its form comes from a realm beyond experience.

How different all this is from the Ratzinger of 1962, who said, "The church cannot be considered as pure abstraction, independent of and divorced from these her human members. Rather this church lives in these men even though she transcends mankind by the divine grace which she transmits to them. . . . The idealization of a church divorced from the human element corresponds to no historical reality."[5] Or the Ratzinger of 1965, who said, "The church was first realized in the individual local church, which was not merely part of a larger administrative body, but which contained the total reality of the church within it. The local churches were not administrative branches of a large organization; they were the living cells, in each of which the *whole* mystery of the *one* body of the church was present, so that each was simply called *ecclesia,* church. I believe that this rediscovery of the local church is one of the most significant and pertinent statements of the doctrine of collegiality, for it again becomes clear that the one church comprises the plurality of churches, that unity and multiplicity are not contradictions in the church."[6]

This, then, is the first question for the conclave: granted that a sound Catholic ecclesiology acknowledges both universal and local dimensions to church, how do we keep the two in balance? Has that balance shifted under Ratzinger, toward a conception that is intellectually compelling but too distant from local realities? Has this meant too much emphasis on uniformity, too little on legitimate pluralism? Has it meant too much accumulation of power in Rome, too much micromanagement from the center?

Finally, perhaps the ultimate question: Did Jesus come to proclaim an "ontologically prior universal church?" Or did he come to look into the eyes of men and women, to heal their wounds and drive out their demons, and to say: "My kingdom lives and breathes in you"?

2. How Should Authority in the Church Be Distributed?

In some ways this second question depends upon an answer to the first; if the universal church is truly "ontologically prior" to the local, there are obvious consequences for the allocation of power. Ratzinger has devoted an extraordinary amount of intellectual capital to articulating the theological basis for Roman centralization. Church-watchers from all points of view agree that the tension between centralization and local authority will be one of the key issues on the minds of the cardinals as they ready to elect a successor to John Paul.

In chapter 2, we noted the evolution in Ratzinger's thinking on episcopal conferences. At the time of Vatican II, Ratzinger saw them as legitimate bearers of authority, analogous to the regional synods in the ancient church; today Ratzinger argues that conferences are purely administrative and bureaucratic realities with no mandate to teach or govern. Also as we saw, this shift is part of a broader revision of Ratzinger's views on collegiality. This is not mere theory. Ratzinger engineered the overhaul of the American lectionary in 1997, despite the fact that it had been approved by a two-thirds majority of the U.S. bishops over a period of several years, drawing on the best American linguists, liturgists, and Scripture scholars. He also took a lead role in overturning a series of resolutions to an abortion counseling controversy that had been exhaustively studied and debated by the German bishops.

From a historical point of view, it is beginning to become clear that the climax of the ultramontane movement of the nineteenth century was not in 1870, with the declaration of papal infallibility under Pius IX. The imperial papacy continued to build steam through 1917, when the new *Code of Canon Law,* edited by the future Pius XII, codified the pope's right to appoint virtually all the bishops of the world. This was an innovation; as late as 1829 the pope had appointed only twenty-four of the world's 666 bishops. Papal centralization has exploded under John Paul II, whose travels and aggressive intervention in the affairs of the local churches have made the papacy a direct and immediate force in the lives of average Catholics.

These popes built the structural and cultural foundations for the imperial papacy; Ratzinger has erected the theological scaffolding to support it. His communion ecclesiology, his theological assault on bishops' conferences, his assertion of ontological priority for the universal church (which in practice means Rome), all have the effect of legitimizing the concentration of power in the hands of the pope and his immediate advisors in the Roman curia.

This, too, must weigh on the minds of the cardinals who tap John Paul's successor. Is the imperial papacy a healthy thing in the life of the church? Does Ratzinger's theological defense of it serve the church well? Or is it time to finish what many Catholics, including the young Ratzinger, saw as the work of Vatican II: to balance the emphasis on the power of the pope with new attention to the rights and the dignity of bishops and the local churches they are supposed to represent?

3. What Does It Mean to Be Catholic?

In terms of his impact on Catholic theology, the most lasting, and certainly the most bitterly contested, aspect of Ratzinger's legacy will be his expansion of the boundaries of infallibility. In public discussion of encyclicals such as *Evangelium vitae* and *Muleris dignitatem,* in his response to a dubium on *Ordinatio sacerdotalis,* and in his commentary on *Ad tuendam fidem,* Ratzinger has consistently argued that Catholics are bound to accept as infallible a host of doctrines that have never formally been defined as such by a pope or a council.

Ratzinger believes that after Vatican I a form of what he calls "theological positivism" developed, in which Catholics were encouraged to draw sharp distinctions between infallible and noninfallible teachings, and to regard anything in the latter category as "up for grabs." He says the formal declaration of infallibility in 1870 encouraged this development by placing exaggerated stress on formal declarations of infallible teachings. In fact, Ratzinger argues, this positivism has distorted the traditional Catholic understanding that there is a wide range of doctrines or decisions which, without any formal declaration, are de facto certain and unchangeable. For example, declarations of sainthood, the acts of ecumenical councils, the elections of popes, and the declarations in papal encyclicals are all matters the church has traditionally considered "infallible."

Taken on its own, Ratzinger's critique of positivism makes an important point: being a Catholic should not be a "least common denominator" affair, where one strives to accept only minimum essentials. To be Catholic is to accept the church as an ongoing source of revelation. It means one trusts the church, gives it the benefit of the doubt, submits to it even in dubious cases, and accepts its authority. It means that one does not demand a certificate of authenticity before making a novena or reading the life of a saint; we trust that the church has reliably pointed out this practice and that person as worthy.

Many voices in the church today, however, believe this useful reminder has too often been converted by Ratzinger into a cudgel, used to drive out anyone whose assent is not quick enough, whose approach to a given doctrine is loyal but critical, whose level of personal certainty is not high enough on points with a remote connection to revelation. Thus, for example, Charles Curran was deprived of his license to teach as a Catholic theologian for saying that artificial birth control or masturbation may not always be morally evil. Curran's is a nuanced, respectful stance, and Ratzinger's insistence that there is no room for it within the *communio* simply does not convince many Catholics. Similarly, the exclusion of women from holy orders, whatever one makes of it theologically, cannot, in the minds of most Catholics, be an *articulus stantis et cadentis ecclesiae,* a matter upon which the church stands or falls. That this papacy under Ratzinger has treated it as such has diminished respect for the teaching office.

The next conclave will have to consider whether it makes sense to hope for a "springtime of evangelization," a new burst of missionary efforts, given that the Catholic church does not seem to want many of the members it now has. Pope Pius X, author of the antimodernist campaign, once famously said, "Kindness is for fools." John XXIII, by way of contrast, said that errors in the church tend to vanish like mists in the morning sun, and that hunters who shoot too early are likely to bag the wrong victims. Those approaches are, to some extent, mutually exclusive, and the next conclave will have to choose a man to lead the church forward who leans one way or the other.

4. How Should the Church Relate to the World?

Ratzinger's critics often portray him as a man driven by fear—of losing power, of women, of sex, of modernity. People who actually know Ratzinger, even those who disagree with his theological positions, say this is a myth; he is a refined man with a lively sense of humor, not someone working out his personal pathologies through the power of his office. In a 1997 interview with Bavarian television, Ratzinger's quick-witted response to a question about fear was: "I'm only afraid at the dentist."

The accusation nevertheless carries its element of truth, in that one of Ratzinger's deepest convictions is a profound skepticism about the world. We have seen how Ratzinger felt early on that *Gaudium et spes* was an unfortunate note upon which to end Vatican II, with its overoptimistic treatment of nature, humanity, and history. Ratzinger's accusation was that *Gaudium et spes* had forgotten the cross by minimizing the pervasive power of sin. A Christianity in solidarity with the world runs the risk of forgetting itself. This was precisely the issue at stake in the struggle over liberation theology, as it is in the current battles over religious pluralism. These earthly concerns are a distraction from, not a means toward, the Christian vocation.

Remember Ratzinger's mustard seed: the church as a small, seemingly insignificant presence, whose magnitude will unfold only in the eschatological fullness of time. Christianity is perennially faced with a choice between size and sincerity, between being a mass movement and a Mass movement. "The word 'subculture' should not frighten us," Ratzinger wrote in 1990. "In the face of the zeitgeist, it is imperative that the faithful take upon themselves the condition of being foreign." Ratzinger has consistently worked to reinsert the theological wedge between church and world that *Gaudium et spes* intended to remove. One sees the fruit of this campaign in a new breed of seminarians who don birettas and reject television as evil, in bishops more concerned with the placement of the tabernacle than with the impact of economic globalization, in Vatican offices determined to wrest control of liturgy and language away from local cultures because they cannot be trusted.

Again, all this is remote from the Ratzinger of an earlier era. He wrote in 1968's *Introduction to Christianity:* "Let us be plain, even at the risk of being misunderstood: the true Christian is not the denominational party-member but he who through being a Christian has become truly human; not he who slavishly observes a system of norms, thinking as he does so only of himself, but he who has become freed to simple human goodness." This sentiment is difficult to reconcile with deep skepticism about Christianity's place in the world, and certainly the next conclave will feel this tension. The church cannot declare that the "joy and hope, grief and anguish" of humanity forms its central concern and at the same time be governed by men who see the catacombs as the proper Christian dwelling.

5. What Would Jesus Do?

An old joke illustrates this point. A group of priests is having lunch with the bishop, swapping stories about the latest goings-on in their parishes. Peals of laughter bounce off the walls as the men share experiences. One young priest launches into an anecdote about a wedding Mass he had recently celebrated in his parish. The bonhomie continues as he relates how bad his homily was, how the choir director had laryngitis that day, and so on. Finally, he says that when it came time for communion, another problem flared up: he spotted a man and his wife whom he knew to be Protestants steadily moving up the line. He said he panicked, not sure what to do. Then, he said, it hit him: "I just asked myself, what would Jesus do?" The laughter suddenly died as the bishop, now deadly serious, turned to the young priest and said: "You didn't do *that,* did you?"

The joke never fails to get a chuckle from Catholics, because it rings true. Jesus is an enormously threatening figure to anyone charged with enforcing rules of religious observance. Of course, most Catholics are realistic enough to grant that *any* human institution needs structure. That concession, however, does not change the fact that many Catholics see in their church the same concentration of power, the same focus on rules at the expense of compassion, that the Jesus of the Gospels rejected in the religious authorities of his time.

This is a criticism with which Ratzinger is familiar. He addressed it in a 1994 Jerusalem lecture on the relationship between Christianity and Judaism. In the lecture, Ratzinger rejects the "common view" that Jesus acted as a prophet, offering a critique of an overly rigorous approach to the law. "In Jesus' exchange with the Jewish authorities of his time, we are not dealing with a confrontation between a liberal reformer and an ossified traditionalist hierarchy," Ratzinger said. This reading "fundamentally misunderstands the conflict of the New Testament and does justice neither to Jesus nor to Israel." What then? Ratzinger says that Jesus "opens up the law" to the nations conscious of his own authority as God's son. Thus the conflict between Jesus and the Israelite religious establishment is over his acting *ex auctoritate divina,* in other words, his claim to be God. Clearly Ratzinger perceives the notion of Jesus as a prophet attacking ecclesial power as facile; in a space of four short paragraphs in this essay he manages to impugn the phrase "liberal reformer" four times.[7]

As Harvard theologian Harvey Cox discovered with respect to the struggle over liberation theology, Ratzinger is, in striking ways, uncomfortable with the historical Jesus. It is not difficult to see why. Jesus did not associate himself with the religious establishment; Jesus preached the priority of human needs over cultic obligations; Jesus suggested that caring for others was as important as ritual performance; and Jesus warned against religious leaders who failed to heed the demands of justice. In that sense, the historical Jesus embodies a critique of religious institutions as relevant today as it was two millenia ago. Perhaps he was not a "liberal reformer," but neither was he a clerical conservative. Both moral relativism and ecclesial authoritarianism seem incompatible with the Jesus one meets in the Gospels.

Recent church history offers two examples of attempts to apply the gospel to the internal life of the church. Paul VI's 1965 reform of the Holy Office sought to transform it into a positive promoter of doctrine, on the basis that charity banishes error more successfully than fear. Yet under Ratzinger, the tools of discipline and control have returned to routine use, including investigations without consultation, silencings, excommunications, censures, revoked imprimaturs and banned books, the threat of job loss, and public accusation as an enemy of the faith. As they consider how best the church might bring the gospel to the world—how best to be faithful to Jesus—the 120-some cardinals in the next conclave face a basic choice between the spirit of the Pauline reform and the reality of Ratzinger's tenure.

"The whole New Testament was written under the sign of the cross, not the sign of wordly power," Ratzinger wrote in 1965, reflecting on how Jesus rejected any attempt to use external force to assert the gospel. "The New Testament testifies to God's weakness in that he chose to approach man not with legions of angels but solely with the gospel of his Word and the testimony of a love willing to die." It is a sobering reminder. In Vatican II's *Declaration on religious liberty*, Catholicism renounced the appeal to force *ad extra;* it is for the next conclave to decide whether the time has come to cross the same bridge *ad intra.*

Seeking Pardon

On March 12, 2000, John Paul II staged an unprecedented "Day of Pardon" liturgy in Rome. In order that the church might "purify its memory" as it enters the third millennium, the pope offered a sweeping apology to God for two millennia of sin by Christians. During the ceremony, Ratzinger was assigned the role of acknowledging "sins committed in the service of truth." He said before the world, "Let us pray that each one of us, looking to the Lord Jesus, meek and humble of heart, will recognize that even men of the church, in the name of faith and morals, have sometimes used methods not in keeping with the gospel in the solemn duty of defending the truth." The pope responded, "In certain periods of history Christians have at times given into intolerance and have not been faithful to the great commandment of love, sullying in this way the face of the church." It was a remarkable moment. Because it was Joseph Ratzinger in St. Peter's Square, this theological titan and passionate "coworker of the truth," the words carried a special resonance.

Sociologists caution that it is a mistake to personalize structural issues, and indeed, if it had not been Ratzinger expressing contrition for "methods not in keeping with the gospel," it would doubtless have been someone else, arguably someone much less knowledgeable of the issues and even more disposed to authoritarian solutions. Perhaps, however, that is precisely the point. Joseph Ratzinger is in most ways the best and brightest the Catholic church of his generation had to offer, a musician and man of culture, a genteel intellectual and polyglot, a deep true believer. Yet he has left behind a fractured church, one where many Catholics of good will and deep faith cannot feel at home. Perhaps, when the College of Cardinals next assembles to carry out its most sacred task, this is the question that should lie before them: is the theological system Joseph Ratzinger represents the right one to carry the church forward? Is it what Jesus would have wanted?

In 1963, in his commentary on the first session of Vatican II, Ratzinger expressed the fundamental option facing the council: "Was the intellectual position of 'anti-modernism'—the old policy of exclusiveness, condemnation and defense leading to an almost neurotic denial of all that was good—to be continued? Or would the church, after it had taken all the necessary precautions to protect the faith, turn over a new leaf and move on into a new and positive encounter with its own origins, with its brothers and with the world of today?" It is a crossroads that lies perenially before the church. Ratzinger's twenty years as prefect well illustrate the contemporary perils and possibilities of the first path; perhaps it is time to consider anew the second.

In the end, how will history judge Joseph Ratzinger? The French Catholic philosopher Jacques Maritain once said, "The important thing is not to be a success. The important thing is to be in history bearing the witness." Under that standard, Ratzinger may, in the fullness of time, be viewed favorably. He has stood fast for his vision, weathered the scorn of colleagues and confreres, sacrificed his own intellectual interests for the sake of serving the church. One can question his policies but not his fidelity.

Yet there are other yardsticks by which leaders must be measured. In his biography of Robert Kennedy, Arthur Schlesinger, Jr., described standing at Kennedy's funeral and watching Chicago mayor Richard Daley and Yippie activist Tom Hayden, such bitter enemies in that summer of 1968, quietly sobbing in different corners. Schlesinger wrote that a friend was reminded of a line from Pascal: "A man does not show his greatness by being at one extremity, but rather by touching both at once." If that is the test, then despite his intellect, his piety, his sense of purpose, all that makes him remarkable, Joseph Ratzinger has fallen short of greatness. How to bring together the extremes in Roman Catholicism that are now so thoroughly divided is the question facing the next conclave; it is the question facing the people of God.

Notes

Chapter 1: Growing Up in Hitler's Shadow

1. Basic biographical information can be found in *Bayerische Biographie: 1000 Persönlichkeiten aus 15 Jahrhunderten*, edited by Karl Bosl (Verlag Friedrich Pustet, 1985) as well as in the 1917 edition of *The Catholic Encyclopedia* in the article under "Ratzinger, Georg" by Friedrich Lauchert.
2. *Christians and Jews in Germany: Religion, Politics and Ideology in the Second Reich, 1870–1914*, by Uriel Tal (Cornell University Press, 1975).
3. Much of the information on Traunstein during the war in this section is drawn from three works: *Traunstein 1918–1945: Ein Beitrag zur Geschichte der Stadt und des Landkreis Traunstein*, by Gerd Evers (Drei Linden Verlag, 1991); *Verfolgung und Widerstand in der NS-Zeit im Landkreis Traunstein 1933–1945*, edited and published by the Kreisjugendring Traunstein (1994); and *Befreiung, Besatzung, Erneuerung: Kreis und Stadt Traunstein 1945–1949*, by Gerd Evers (Verlag Ising, 1996). The three works were generously provided to the author by Dr. Franz Haselbeck of the state archives in Traunstein.
4. This section reflects especially *Verfolgung und Widerstand in der NS-Zeit im Landkreis Traunstein 1933–1945*, cited above.
5. The quotation is found in *Bayern in der NS-Zeit: Soziale Lage und politisches Verhalten der Bevölkerung im Spiegel vertraulicher Berichte*, edited by Martin Broszat, Elke Fröhlich, and Falk Wiesemann (R. Oldenbourg Verlag, 1977). This multivolume set collects invaluable documentation for understanding Bavaria during the Nazi period.
6. The *Time* article by Richard Ostling appeared under the headline of "Keeper of the Straight and Narrow" in the December 6, 1993, issue.

7. This study of events in the west-central German hamlet of Oberschopfheim during the war may be found in *The Nazi Impact on a German Village,* by Walter Rinderle and Bernard Norling (University Press of Kentucky, 1993).

8. A good treatment of the Deutsche Christen movement can be bound in *Twisted Cross: The German Christian Movement in the Third Reich,* by Doris L. Bergen (University of North Carolina Press, 1996).

9. The lecture may be found in Ratzinger's *The Nature and Mission of Theology: Approaches to Understanding Its Role in the Light of Present Controversy* (Ignatius Press, 1995).

10. *Theologians under Hitler: Gerhard Kittel, Paul Althaus, and Emanuel Hirsch,* by Robert P. Ericksen (Yale University Press, 1985).

11. An excellent biography of Guardini is available in English: *Romano Guardini: A Precursor of Vatican II,* by Robert A. Krieg, C.S.C. (University of Notre Dame Press, 1997). Krieg discusses Ratzinger's appropriation of Guardini, noting the way in which both Ratzinger and von Balthasar downplay Guardini's struggles with ecclesiastical authorities.

12. An extremely helpful collection of von Balthasar's writings is available in *The Von Balthasar Reader,* edited by Medard Kehl and Werner Löser (Crossroad Publishing, 1985). It was translated into English by Robert J. Daly, S.J., and Fred Lawrence.

13. These details are drawn from two contemporary accounts of the event published in the local newspaper, provided to me by Dr. Franz Haselback of the Traunstein state archives.

Chapter 2: An Erstwhile Liberal

1. The line comes from Robert MacAfee Brown's *Observer in Rome: A Protestant Report on the Vatican Council* (Doubleday, 1964), p. 150. After saying that Frings had blown the dome off St. Peter's, Brown added, "and in just what form it will come down and be reassembled, nobody knows."

2. The book is *The Rhine Flows into the Tiber: A History of Vatican II,* by Ralph Wiltgen, S.V.D. It was originally published by Hawthorne Books, 1967. My copy is a 1985 reprint by Tan Books, a conservative Catholic publisher best known for reprinting the Baltimore Catechism. Though Wiltgen would never have intended it himself, his book has found new life among right-wing critics of Vatican II who harvest his account for support of their theory that the council was hijacked by a cabal of European liberals.

3. Küng made the remark in an interview with me for a story that appeared in the November 13, 1998, issue of the *National Catholic Reporter.* As an aside, Catholic writer Russell Shaw later pointed to this comment as an example of rhetoric that he felt to be inappropriate; in turn, Jesuit Joseph Fessio suggested such language was characteristic of *NCR,* as if the newspaper rather than Küng had made the remark.

4. Jesuit Tom Reese, in his superb study *Inside the Vatican: The Politics and Organization of the Catholic Church* (Harvard University Press, 1996), makes the point that under John Paul II the Congregation for the Doctrine of the Faith has become a "gatekeeper." Any Vatican document must pass doctrinal review be-

fore it can be issued. In this way, Ratzinger's office has amassed tremendous authority over other Vatican agencies. Ratzinger has encouraged the doctrinal commissions of national bishops' conferences to play a similar gatekeeper role with respect to the documents of that conference.

5. See Ratzinger's comments on attempts to arrive at an image of Jesus on purely historical grounds in *Behold the Pierced One* (Ignatius Press, 1986), p. 44. Even though Ratzinger has often accused Scripture scholars of setting themselves up as the sole judges of what is authentically Christian, he never lapsed into the sort of quasi-fundamentalism that some deeply conservative Catholics adopt. In a 1988 news conference in New York, for example, Ratzinger heaped praise upon Sulpician Raymond Brown, the leading Catholic biblical scholar of his generation and a man whose defense of historical-critical study of the Bible brought him much grief from conservative Catholic critics. "I wish we had many scholars like Father Brown," Ratzinger said, in a gesture of graciousness that many still remember.

6. After Frings returned to Cologne after the council, his instinctive conservatism reasserted itself. In 1968, Frings forbade a Catholic memorial service for Martin Luther King, Jr., because the Social Democrat minister-president of North-Rhine Westphalia, Heinz Kühn, was to be a participant. Kühn was a lapsed Catholic.

7. In German, these commentaries are: *Die erste Sitzunsperiode des Zweiten Vatikan Konzils: Ein Rückblick*, 1963; *Das Konzil auf dem Weg: Rückblick auf die zweite Sitzungsperiode*, 1964; *Ergebnisse und Probleme der dritten Konzilsperiode*, 1965; *Die letze Sitzungsperiode des Konzils*, 1966.

8. The book is *Im Sprung Gehemmt: Was mir nach dem Konzil noch alles fehlt* by Helmut Krätzl (Verlag St. Gabriel, 1998). Krätzl was the close friend and secretary of Cardinal Franz König.

9. The most exhaustive example of this argument can be found in *Volk Gottes—Leib Christ: Die Ekklesiologie Joseph Ratzingers und ihr Einfluss auf das Zweite Vatikanische Konzil*, a study by Thomas Weiler, then a seminarian in Mainz (published by Matthias-Grünewald Verlag, 1997). Ratzinger contributed a foreword essentially endorsing this reading of his stance. Among those who have given me a version of the *aggiornamento-ressourcement* distinction to argue for an essential continuity in Ratzinger's thought are Joseph Fessio, Charles Curran, and Augustine Di Noia.

10. The line appears on page 304 of Volume I of the *Commentary on the Documents of Vatican II*, edited by Herbert Vorgrimler (Crossroad Publishing, 1989).

11. "The pastoral implications of collegiality," *Concilium* (no. 1, 1965), p. 30.

12. The *National Catholic Reporter* carried a story on the Nijmegen statement in its January 1, 1969, issue, under the headline "Scholars plead for theological freedom." There the statement's full list of proposals for reforms can be found.

13. American Jesuit Walter Burghardt, who served on the International Theological Commission (ITC) from its first meeting in 1967, wrote in his recent memoirs *Long Have I Loved You* (Orbis Books, 1999) that during the few weeks the commission devoted to its 1976 document on liberation theology, not one rep-

resentative of that theological approach was invited to consult with the group. It reflects the "closed shop" that many believe the ITC has become.

14. Ratzinger's comments came in a mid-December 1998 interview with the Italian publication *Lo Stato*. He added that one must try to convince the bishops, since "even if some of them misuse their discretion and do not respect the rights of the faithful, they are not persons of bad will."

15. The retrospective is found in "Der Weltdienst der Kirche. Auswirkungen von *Gaudium et Spes* im letzten Jahrzehnt," in *Zehn Jahre Vaticanum II*, edited by M. Seybold (Regensburg, 1976), p. 36.

16. The story of Brazier's efforts, along with reproductions of some of the forms used by the group, can be found in the May 21, 1999, issue of the *National Catholic Reporter* under the headline "Ecclesial watchdogs snapping in Australia."

17. Wiltgen, *The Rhine Flows into the Tiber*, p. 285.

Chapter 3: All Roads Lead to Rome

1. See "Free Expression and Obedience in the Church" in *The Church: Readings in Theology*, edited by Hugo Rahner (P. J. Kenedy, 1963), p. 212. Written just as Vatican II opened, the essay is a remarkable window into Ratzinger's attitudes about theology and dissent at the time.

2. In this section I draw heavily on *The Theology of Joseph Ratzinger* by Aidan Nichols, O.P. (T&T Clark, 1988). It is an excellent study of Ratzinger's theology and, though written from the point of view of an admirer, quite even-handed.

3. The citation occurs in *Theologische Prinzipienlehre: Bausteine zur Fundamentaltheologie* (Wewel Verlag, 1982), p. 340; the book appeared in English as *Principles of Catholic Theology: Building Stones for a Fundamental Theology* (Ignatius Press, 1987).

4. *Der Weltkatechismus: Therapie oder Symptom einer kranken Kirche?* by Hansjürgen Verweyen (Patmos Verlag, 1994).

5. The talk may be located on the Web site of the German branch of the "We Are Church" movement at http://www.we-are-church.org/de. It is archived under "documents." The title is "Zur gegenwärtigen Lage in der römisch-katholischen Kirche."

6. Ratzinger has used this corporate analogy himself to characterize what he sees as the duplicity of Catholic theologians who offer their own theories under the guise of church teaching. In a 1992 foreword to a collection of his works on the nature of theology, he wrote: "Everyone is free—within the framework of the responsibility of conscience before the truth—to think whatever this responsibility permits him to think or to say. But not everyone is free to assert that what he says represents Catholic theology. Here there is a sort of 'trademark.'" See Ratzinger's *The Nature and Mission of Theology: Approaches to Understanding Its Role in the Light of Present Controversy* (Ignatius Press, 1995), p. 8.

7. The book is *Die Menschen, die Kirche, das Land: Christentum als Gesellschaftliche Herausforderung* (Molden Verlag, 1998). Ironically, in his foreword Schönborn acknowledges editorial assistance by Hubert Feichtlbauer, a dean of Austria's press corps, in putting the book together; Feichtlbauer shortly thereafter became the spokesperson for the Austrian "We Are Church" movement.

8. In the spring of 1999 Schönborn was rumored to be headed to Rome for a Vatican post; a *National Catholic Reporter* story, with biographical background on Schönborn, appeared in the May 28, 1999, issue.

9. For a treatment of the subject from the time period in question, see *Student Revolts: The New Left in West Germany* by F. C. Hunnis (War Resisters' International, 1968).

10. Despite Döpfner's statements in Essen, his advocacy of a change in the teaching on birth control produced an estrangement from Paul VI from which he never recovered. He was also badly hurt over the Matthias Defregger case, mentioned in chapter 1. It turned out that Döpfner had never informed the Vatican of his auxiliary bishop's background, which created the impression of a cover-up. As for Ranke-Heinemann, she studied with Ratzinger in Munich and was the first woman to qualify for a chair in Catholic theology at a German university. She made waves in the early 1990s when she told Italian reporters, apropos of Ratzinger's student days, that he was exceptionally bright but suffered from "an absence of any erotic." Ranke's description of Döpfner's reactions at the Katholikentag came in a 1999 telephone interview with me from her home in Essen. I had earlier interviewed Ranke-Heinemann when she ran for Germany's presidency in the spring of 1999 to protest the NATO bombing campaign in Serbia.

11. Ratzinger's involvement in the Gustav Siewerth Akademie was confirmed for me in a faxed letter from Dr. Alma von Stockhausen of July 28, 1999.

12. Szulc's account appears in his *Pope John Paul II: The Biography* (Scribner, 1995); Hebblethwaite's version can be found in several of his works on the early stages of the John Paul II papacy.

13. That John Paul II had initially offered Ratzinger the Congregation for Catholic Education was first revealed, to the best of my knowledge, by George Weigel in his massive biography of John Paul II, *Witness to Hope* (Cliff Street Books, 1999), p. 419. Weigel cites an interview with Ratzinger on September 12, 1996, as the source for the information.

14. See *The 1980 Synod of Bishops 'On the Role of the Family': An Exposition of the Event and an Analysis of Its Texts*, by Jan Grootaers and Joseph A. Selling (Leuven University Press, 1983), especially pages 77–78.

15. The episode is related in detail in an article in Munich's *Süddeutsche Zeitung* of May 21, 1981, under the headline "Ein ermutigendes Signal aus dem Vatikan."

16. Rahner's full protest is published in the November 14, 1979, issue of the *Süddeutsche Zeitung* under the headline "Ich protestiere!" Ratzinger answered Rahner in cursory fashion one month later in comments printed by the *Süddeutsche Zeitung* on December 18, 1979.

17. All the documentation is collected in *Küng in Conflict*, edited by Leonard Swidler (Image Books, 1981).

Chapter 4: Authentic Liberation

1. Comblin's *Called for Freedom: The Changing Context of Liberation Theology* (Orbis Books, 1998) is required reading for anyone who wishes to understand the changed historical situation facing liberation theology today.

2. These estimates were quoted to me by Philip Berryman, an author and translator in the area of liberation theology, during a telephone interview in the summer of 1999.

3. The booklet was published by Franciscan Herald Press in Chicago, Ill., in 1974. See also Kloppenburg's *The People's Church: A Defense of My Church,* also published by Franciscan Herald Press in 1977.

4. These remarks are quoted by Peter Hebblethwaite in an essay on liberation theology in the *National Catholic Reporter* on November 12, 1976.

5. Local observers, however, say the defections to Protestantism in Chiapas actually have more to do with the evangelicals' teetotaling stance on alcohol: alcoholism is a serious problem among indigenous peoples and the strict moral code of the evangelical Protestants seems to be the only "recovery program" to meet with wide success. Klaus Blume's coverage of the situation in Chiapas for the Deutsche Presse-Agentur has well illustrated this point. See "Bloody religious conflict rages in southern Mexico," July 20, 1999.

6. The text is available in *International Theological Commission: Texts and Documents 1969–1985,* edited by Michael Sharkey (Ignatius Press, 1989). Ratzinger contributed a preface to the collection.

7. Stories with extensive quotations from Ratzinger's remarks appeared in the *Süddeutsche Zeitung* on September 28, 1978, under the headline "Ratzinger: Amerika wird Schwerpunkt der Kirche" and on October 6, 1978, under the headline "Finanzielles Engagement genügt nicht."

8. The information concerning this meeting and the decision about Romero is drawn from Jonathan Kwitny's biography of John Paul II, *Man of the Century* (Henry Holt and Company, 1997), p. 353. Kwitny says in a footnote that Oddi volunteered the information approximately one hour into a personal interview. His memories, Kwitny says, were clear and precise. Seper and Baggio are both dead and hence could not confirm Oddi's comment.

9. See Lernoux, *People of God.* Nor was the Reagan administration's concern with liberation theology voiced only in confidential position papers. In a 1984 address to a group called "Christian Rescue Efforts for the Emancipation of Dissidents," Eliot Abrams, then the U.S. assistant secretary of state for human rights, said: "The Soviets are exploiting liberation theology as a means of subverting the churches of the west." The remark was reported in the *National Catholic Reporter,* December 7, 1984.

10. Rahner's letter is quoted by Juan Luis Segundo in *Theology and the Church: A Response to Cardinal Ratzinger and a Warning to the Whole Church* (Seabury, 1985), p. 17. Segundo notes that by asserting the liberation theology represented by Gutiérrez is "entirely orthodox," Rahner did not necessarily mean that it is true, simply that it does not pose a danger to the faith. It is, in other words, within the acceptable limits of Roman Catholic theological discussion.

11. See the report in the *National Catholic Reporter,* November 16, 1984. Ratzinger and Höffner had served together in the German bishops' conference.

12. The details of the meeting are drawn from *The Silencing of Leonardo Boff: The Vatican and the Future of World Christianity,* by Harvey Cox (Meyer-Stone

Books, 1988). Cox had the benefit of Boff's personal testimony in compiling his account.

13. Häring made the request in an endnote to his essay "Joseph Ratzinger's 'Nightmare Theology,'" in *The Church in Anguish: Has the Vatican Betrayed Vatican II?*, edited by Hans Küng and Leonard Swidler (Harper and Row, 1987).

14. Ratzinger's familiarity with Molina helped fuel his sense of a connection between liberation theology and revolutionary violence. In November 1985, Molina celebrated a commemorative Mass for members of Colombia's M-19 guerilla movement, draping an M-19 banner across the altar and calling the revolutionaries "martyrs." Six days before, forty-one guerillas had been killed in an assault on the Colombian Ministry of Justice, an attack in which ninety-five soldiers and civilians also lost their lives.

15. Medina Estévez went on to become the prefect of the Congregation for Divine Worship and the Discipline of the Sacraments, where since 1996 he has led an assault on the international agency created by English-speaking bishops' conferences to handle translations of liturgical texts, the International Commission on English in the Liturgy. His effort to bring liturgical translation back under Roman control parallels Ratzinger's own efforts to reverse many of the powers and prerogatives of bishops' conferences. It is worth noting that in *Milestones,* Ratzinger identified himself on page 142 with four other former Vatican II *periti* who became disillusioned after the council with the direction of the church; the others were Henri de Lubac, Philippe Delhaye, M. J. leGuillou, and Jorge Medina Estévez.

16. An interview with Bishop Antonio Fragoso, the retired bishop of Crateus in Brazil and a lifelong friend of Helder Camara, appeared in the June 20, 1999, issue of the *Catholic New Times* of Canada. Fragoso said that Helder Camara never protested the decision to close the seminaries because he was "profoundly loyal," but the decision had been the cause of "great suffering." Fragoso noted that José Comblin had influenced the development of the seminaries.

17. The citation is drawn from Ratzinger's 1962 essay "Free Expression and Obedience in the Church," in Wiegel, *The Church: Readings in Theology*. It is also cited in Lernoux, *People of God*, p. 81.

Chapter 5: Cultural Warrior

1. The comment was reported by Patricia Lefevere in the May 27, 1994, issue of the *National Catholic Reporter*. Lefevere interviewed Pannenberg during a speaking tour of the eastern United States.

2. I covered this visit by Ratzinger to Menlo Park. My story about the incident with the women appeared in the May 26, 1999, issue of the *National Catholic Reporter*. I didn't learn about it until after the fact; I was already inside the lecture hall by the time the protestors took up their positions.

3. Wijngaards is a former superior of the Mill Hill Fathers who resigned his priesthood in 1998 to protest *Ad tuendam fidem*, the papal document that established canonical penalties for dissent from "definitive" teachings, among which,

according to Ratzinger, is the ban on women priests. Wijngaards has collected an impressive set of evidence pointing to a tradition of women deacons in the church, which is available on his Web site at www.womenpriests.org.

4. For most of the narrative surrounding the women's pastoral I am following *Sexuality and Catholicism,* by Thomas C. Fox (George Braziller, 1995), pp. 232–44.

5. An initial lawsuit was rejected. In April 2000, McEnroy's appeal to the U.S. Supreme Court was rejected, apparently exhausting her legal options.

6. In January 2000 Byrne resigned from her community, the Institute of the Blessed Virgin Mary, which she had joined in 1964 at the age of 17. She reported that the Congregation for the Doctrine of the Faith had asked her to make a public proclamation of assent to the church's teachings on birth control and priestly ordination. Byrne, known in the United Kingdom for her religious broadcasts on the BBC, decided to abandon religious life instead. See the January 24, 2000, issue of *Newsweek* (Atlantic Edition), p. 64.

7. The running coverage of the abortion counseling controversy in *This Week in Germany,* a publication of the German Information Center, is probably the best available.

8. The norms appeared in the July 4, 1997, issue of the *National Catholic Reporter.*

9. The campaign against inclusive language continues to gather steam as of this writing. The Congregation for Divine Worship ordered the International Commission on English in the Liturgy on January 14, 2000, to pull its 1993 inclusive language collection of the Old Testament psalms out of use, despite any obstacles that might be posed by copyright laws. One of the things that ICEL personnel say consistently, though mostly off the record, is how astonished they are to find themselves branded left-wing extremists, as they have been working under the terms of a 1969 Vatican document on translation called *Comme le prévoit,* which said that each member of the liturgical assembly should be able to hear himself or herself named in the text. See "About face on liturgical language," the *National Catholic Reporter,* January 14, 2000.

10. The article appeared in *Der Spiegel* on April 17, 1992.

11. Migge's research has not been widely circulated either in Germany or in the English-speaking world. The issue of homosexuality within the Catholic clergy, however, broke into open discussion in the United States in 2000 with the publication of *The Changing Face of the Priesthood: A Reflection on the Priest's Crisis of Soul* by Father Donald B. Cozzens, rector of St. Mary's Seminary in Cleveland (Liturgical Press). Cozzens devotes a chapter to the question of a "gay culture" within the priesthood.

12. See McNeill's memoirs, published as *Both Feet Firmly Planted in Midair: My Spiritual Journey* (Westminster John Knox Press, 1998).

13. An example of the kind of situation Ratzinger may have had in mind arose in San Francisco in early 1997, when Archbishop William J. Levada threatened to sue the city after it passed a law requiring all agencies with city contracts to provide domestic partnership benefits. Catholic Charities in San Francisco, which received $5.6 million from the city, faced the prospect of losing that

funding. In the end, Levada brokered an agreement with the city whereby any member of an employee's household—a child, a sick relative, an elderly parent—could be designated to receive the equivalent of spousal benefits. Thus the church was satisfied it was not sanctioning homosexual marriage, and Catholic Charities could go on doing work in the city, and its employees received a new benefit. The agreement was widely hailed by Catholic and civic leaders.

14. Teresa Malcolm's superb reporting of the news of the ban appeared in the July 30, 1999, issue of the *National Catholic Reporter*.

15. See "Why Brazil's homosexuals find asylum in the U.S.," the *Christian Science Monitor*, December 7, 1998, and "Rio deadly haven for homosexual men; police sometimes participate in attacks, gay rights group alleges" in the *Houston Chronicle*, March 14, 1999. Both pieces were by Jack Epstein, a freelance reporter based in Rio de Janiero.

16. See "Following spate of murders, Italian gays declare state of emergency," carried by the Deutsche Presse-Agentur, March 4, 1998.

Chapter 6: Holy Wars

1. Ratzinger's comment that Assisi "cannot be the model" was reported in the Austrian daily *Die Presse* on April 4, 1998, in a review of his memoirs under the headline "Der römische Packesel." His statements at the 1987 press conference were reported in the Italian daily *Il Sabato;* see the *National Catholic Reporter* of November 6, 1987, under the headline "Ratzinger knocks Green party, dialogue with Jews."

2. I was present for the second Interreligious Assembly in Assisi in late October 1999. Before the event, Nigerian Cardinal Francis Arinze, who runs the Pontifical Council for Interreligious Dialogue, told reporters that the gathering was a "private" event but that "you don't need my permission to go to Assisi." As it happens, Assisi was swarming with reporters. Arinze went to great lengths to avoid any repeat of 1986, stressing that delegates were to "leave aside speculative discussion," that "listening" was the prime objective. Participants would not pray together, Arinze insisted, because "prayer depends on what you believe, and we do not believe the same things." My story on the event appeared in the November 12, 1999, issue of the *National Catholic Reporter*.

3. For a summary of the debate surrounding Halbfas in German Catholicism, see "Der Fall Halbfas" by Gunter Koch in *Das politische Engagement des Christen heute* (H. Bouvier Verlag, 1970). Our E-mail exchange took place in the summer of 1999.

4. This telephone interview with Küng took place on July 28, 1999.

5. Ratzinger's account of the papal intervention and the council's response may be found in volume I of the Vorgrimler *Commentary on the Documents of Vatican II*, pp. 297–305.

6. See "Pope has no intention of converting Eastern Orthodox to Catholicism," in *Current Digest of the Post-Soviet Press*, May 13, 1992.

7. See "Pope to accept married Anglican priests" in the *Independent* of London, December 6, 1993, p. 2.

8. My article, "Ratzinger credited with saving Lutheran pact," appeared in the September 10, 1999, issue of the *National Catholic Reporter.*
9. See "Ratzinger assails WCC" in the *Christian Century,* June 18, 1997, p. 582.
10. The essay appears as part of *Die Vielfalt der Religionen und der Eine Bund,* published in English as *Many Religions, One Covenant* (Ignatius Press, 1999).
11. The text of Ratzinger's address is available on-line at www.ewtn.com. Follow the link to the document library and then search under "Ratzinger."
12. The address was published in *Origins* under the headline "Relativism: The Central Problem for Faith Today," October 31, 1996 (vol. 26, no. 20).
13. See "Ratzinger absolutely wrong on relativism" by John Hick in the October 24, 1997, issue of the *National Catholic Reporter.*
14. Schmidt-Leukel provided me with copies of his correspondence with the Bavarian ministry for instruction, culture, science, and art. One amusing wrinkle to the story is that the original letter informing Schmidt-Leukel he would not be granted clearance, dated April 3, 1998, referred to his theories standing in contradiction to "ethical revelation." After he pointed out the error, the ministry sent him a new letter, dated June 5, 1998, clarifying that he had contradicted "Christian revelation."
15. See "De Mello censure reflects Vatican misgivings about Eastern thinking" in the *National Catholic Reporter*, September 4, 1998.
16. König's article appeared in the *Tablet,* January 16, 1999, and Ratzinger's reply was published in the March 13, 1999, issue. See also "König at 94 still carrying torch of renewal," in the October 8, 1999, *National Catholic Reporter*. König has a deep commitment to interreligious dialogue, rooted in his own academic background as well as his pastor's sensitivity to healing division.
17. The interview appeared in the March 21 issue of the French newsweekly *L'Express.*
18. Clooney's article appeared in the January 31, 1997, issue of *Commonweal.*
19. The document is available in *Origins,* December 28, 1989 (vol. 19, no. 30), under the headline "Some aspects of Christian meditation."

Chapter 7: The Enforcer

1. *Dissent in and for the Church: Theologians and Humanae Vitae,* by Charles Curran and Robert E. Hunt (Sheed and Ward, 1970). The book is substantially the first part of the testimony prepared by the professors subject to the inquiry at Catholic University following the protest against *Humanae vitae.* The second part of the written testimony by their counsel forms the nucleus of a companion volume: *The Responsibility of Dissent: The Church and Academic Freedom,* by John F. Hunt and Terrence R. Connelly (Sheed and Ward, 1970).
2. Reese's comments appear in my April 16, 1999, profile of Ratzinger in the *National Catholic Reporter,* which appeared under the headline "The Vatican's enforcer."
3. See "Positive thinking for Holy Office" in the *National Catholic Reporter,* December 15, 1965. The paper carried a National Catholic News Service article by Father John P. Donnelly on *Integrae servandae.*

4. The full title is *Wesen und Auftrag der Theologie: Versuche zu ihrer Ortsbestimmung im Disput der Gegenwart*. The book was published in English as *The Nature and Mission of Catholic Theology: Approaches to Understanding Its Role in the Light of Present Controversy* (Ignatius Press, 1995).

5. The essay originally appeared in *Forum katholische Theologie* 2 (1986), pp. 81–96. It is reproduced in English in *The Nature and Mission of Catholic Theology*, pp. 73–98.

6. See the article on the new *Ratio agendi* published in the *Catholic World Report* of October 1997 under the headline "Misdirection play?" pp. 26–28. The full text of the *Ratio agendi* may be found online at www.cin.org/. Follow the prompts to the documents of Vatican congregations.

7. Curran's case file is noted in the introduction to this chapter; Küng's is 399/57/i. Vatican correspondence typically notes the file to which the letter pertains in the upper left-hand corner, in a space for the "protocol number."

8. Farley's comments also appeared in my April 16 profile of Ratzinger in *NCR*.

9. The full text of Curran's correspondence with the Congregation for the Doctrine of the Faith, along with a narrative by Curran and his own reflections on the experience, appeared in his book *Faithful Dissent* (Sheed and Ward, 1986). The book was published before Curran's final dismissal from Catholic University in January 1987.

10. The March 1, 1989, Profession of Faith and Oath of Fidelity may be found online at www.ewtn.com. Follow the link to the documents library and search under "profession of faith."

11. See "Theologians in Europe challenge pope's conservative leadership," in the *New York Times*, July 14, 1989, p. 1.

12. See Fox's memoirs, *Confessions: The Making of a Postdenominational Priest* (HarperSanFrancisco, 1996).

13. See "Others see little change caused by dissent decree" in the *National Catholic Reporter*, July 31, 1998. A number of Catholic educators were quoted as saying that *Ad tuendam fidem* was "old news" and thus not of great concern to them.

14. Ratzinger's essay, along with a response from Örsy, was published in the May/June 1999 issue of *Céide: A Review from the Margins* (vol. 2, no. 5), pp. 28–34.

Chapter 8: Ratzinger and the Next Conclave

1. The quotation from Oddi appears in *The Next Pope: A Behind-the-Scenes Look at How the Successor to John Paul II Will Be Elected and Where He Will Lead the Catholic Church* (HarperSanFrancisco, 2000). This was Peter Hebblethwaite's last book, now reedited and updated by his widow, Margaret Hebblethwaite. Margaret, though she agrees Ratzinger is an unlikely choice, feels he would quickly be accepted by the Catholic public; his "Bavarian smile" would charm the world, she says.

2. Reese discusses the dramatic changes introduced by John Paul II to the rules for papal elections in *Inside the Vatican*, pp. 86–87.

3. *A New Song for the Lord: Faith in Christ and Liturgy Today* (Crossroad, 1997).

4. Norbert Stanzel, *Die Geisel Gottes: Bishof Kurt Krenn und die Kirchenkrise* (Molden Verlag, 1999).
5. The line is from "Free Expression and Obedience in the Church," pp. 204, 206.
6. See *Theological Highlights of Vatican II* (Paulist Deus Books, 1966), p. 121.
7. The lecture was published in *Many Religions, One Covenant: Israel, the Church, and the World* (Ignatius Press, 1999), pp. 38–40.

Works by Joseph Ratzinger

Essential English-language resources for readers seeking deeper familiarity with Ratzinger's thought are noted here.

Behold the Pierced One: An Approach to Spiritual Christology (Ignatius Press, 1986).

Called to Communion: Understanding the Church Today (Ignatius Press, 1996).

The Church, Ecumenism and Politics: New Essays on Ecclesiology (Crossroad Publishing Company, 1988).

Commentary on the Documents of Vatican II, Herbert Vorgrimler, ed. (Crossroad Publishing, 1989; originally published in German in 1966). See the articles by Ratzinger on the prefatory note to *Lumen gentium* in volume I; on *Dei verbum* in volume III; and on *Gaudium et spes* in volume V.

Eschatology: Death and Eternal Life, volume IX in the series *Dogmatic Theology*, edited by Johann Auer and Joseph Ratzinger (Catholic University of America Press, 1988).

"Free Expression and Obedience in the Church," in *The Church: Readings in Theology*, edited by Hugo Rahner (P. J. Kenedy & Sons, 1963).

Gospel, Catechesis, Catechism: Sidelights on the Catechism of the Catholic Church (Ignatius Press, 1997).

Introduction to Christianity (Seabury Press, 1979; originally published in German, 1968).

Many Religions—One Covenant: Israel, the Church, and the World (Ignatius Press, 1999).

The Meaning of Christian Brotherhood (Ignatius Press, 1993; originally published in German in 1960).

Milestones: Memoirs 1927–1977 (Ignatius Press, 1998).

The Nature and Mission of Theology: Essays to Orient Theology in Today's Debates (Ignatius Press, 1995).

A New Song for the Lord: Faith in Christ and Liturgy Today (Crossroad Publishing Company, 1997).

Principles of Catholic Theology: Building Stones for a Fundamental Theology (Ignatius Press, 1987).

The Ratzinger Report: An Exclusive Interview on the State of the Church (Ignatius Press, 1985).

Salt of the Earth: The Church at the End of the Millennium (Ignatius Press, 1997).

Theological Highlights of Vatican II (Paulist Deus Books, 1966). This book collects the four essays on the individual sessions of Vatican II Ratzinger published from 1963 to 1966.

Index

Protestantism, 83
  defections to, 145–146
  refutation of, 6
  during the Third Reich, 25
Prussia, 4
Prussian State Council, 29
Psalter, 197
Publik-Forum, 223–224
"Puebla Declaration," 150

Quadragesimo anno, 22
Quickborn, 38–39
Quinn, Archbishop John, 182, 200
Quintana, Amando López, 167

racism
  Nazi, 29–30
Radhakrishnan, 238
Rahner, Karl, 16, 39, 41, 48, 54, 67, 125,
    138, 155, 179, 272
Rahner-Ratzinger draft, 55–56
Ramos, Celina, 167
Ramos, Julia Elba, 167
Ranke-Heinemann, Uta, 117
Ratzinger, Cardinal Joseph Aloysius
  in the Annus Mirabilis of 1968,
    113–118
  birth, 1–2
  as cardinal, 120–130
  and Catholic theology, 261–267
  celebrity status, 45–47
  childhood, 2–3
  collegiality, 57–61
  dissent and, 267
  ecclesiological perspective of Catholic
    church, 48–49
  evolution of, 56–78
  faith and, 86–87
  friends of, 141–143
  future and, 295–314
  graduate studies in Munich, 34–43
  at the Gustav Siewerth Akademie,
    118–120
  historical perspective of Catholic
    church, 47–48
  and homosexuality, 198–215
  judgment of, 314
  liberalism, 45–88
  on liturgy, 71–74
  meditation, 95
  metaphors of, 265–266

military service, 21–23
ordination, 43–44
and other religions, 250–256
papacy, 300–303
political perspective of Catholic
  church, 48
power and, 87–88
on relativism, 236
study of Augustine, 35–36
study of Bonaventure, 36–38
study of Hans Urs von Balthasar,
  40–43
study of Romano Guardini, 38–40
symbolism to Christ, 2
as teacher, 103–113
as theologian, 92–103
tradition and, 69–71
on truth, 143–144
two careers of, 49–51
at Vatican II, 51–56
views on Anglicanism, 228–231
views on anthropology, 225
views on Buddhism, 253–255
views on ecumenism, 74–76, 224–235
views on Hinduism, 253–255
views on Islam, 252–253
views on Judaism, 250–252
views on Lutheranism, 231–234
views on obedience, 33
views on Orthodoxy, 226–228
views on pluralism, 235–241
views on Third Reich, 23–33
and women, 177–198
works by, 327–328
Ratzinger, Georg (brother), 2, 9, 234
Ratzinger, Georg (great-uncle), 2–3, 5–9
Ratzinger, Maria (mother), 9
Ratzinger, Maria (sister), 9
The Ratzinger Report, 31, 63, 78–79,
  120, 132, 146
Reagan, President Ronald, 152–153
reconciliation, viii
"red bishop," 146
Redemptoris mater, 184
"Red Guard," 4
Reese, Thomas, 112, 182, 259, 293,
  297
Regensburg, 91–92
Reichstag, 7, 27
Reinischer Merkur, 186
relativism, 236